"Sada Mire grew up in the Horn of Africa and senses a continuity in sacred landscapes that cuts across space and time and the boundaries of states and religions. Her book provides a brave and bold conception of the regional system based on an almost forensic analysis of the evidence. Mire shows how the inclusion of material culture as evidence is central to understanding how continuities are created over time, but also how history can be masked at the same time as it is revealed. The argument is engrossing; chapter by chapter she builds up a convincing and absorbing argument for a discursive regional trajectory centred on the beauty and power of place curated over time by different faiths. The book illustrates the importance of location for symbolic action, knowledge and cultural memory, and the centrality of place as an entry point to understanding the deep past through an ongoing present. Underlying the history of the region is a syncretic trajectory, a multi-temporality, that is often challenged by fundamentalist positions but with an underlying structure that is centred on kinship deeply connected to a sacred landscape. As she concludes: 'From out of the womb of ancient indigenous and regional religions there has arisen a set of ideas reflected in practices, features and objects, all of which seem to connect the north and the west of the Horn of Africa with the south and the east.' The book is an exceptional study of cultural memory in place; a rich encounter with the deep history of symbolic action, emotion and aesthetic affect."

—Howard Morphy FASSA. FAHA.
Emeritus Professor
Head of the Centre for Digital Humanities Research,
Research School of Humanities and the Arts
Author of, among other books, Ancestral Connections: Art and
an Aboriginal System of Knowledge

"This is a confident, masterly piece of work by somebody uniquely qualified to carry out the relevant research . . . a remarkable and vivid book, which probably only Sada Mire (with her combination of theoretical proficiency in several academic disciplines and local intimacy) could have achieved. This is scholarly work, with a much wider general appeal".

—Neal Ascherson,
Historian, journalist and writer,
Formerly, The Observer, former
editor of Public Archaeology
Author of, among other books,
The King Incorporated

Divine Fertility

This book uniquely explores the impact of indigenous ideology and thought on everyday life in Northeast Africa. Furthermore, in highlighting the diversity in pre-Christian, pre-Islamic regional beliefs and practices that extend beyond the simplistic political arguments of the current dominant narratives, the study shows that for millennia complex indigenous institutions have bound people together beyond the labels of Christianity and Islam; they have sustained peace through cultural exchange and tolerance (if not always complete acceptance).

Through recent archaeological and ethnographic research, the concepts, landscapes, materials and rituals believed to be associated with the indigenous and shared culture of the Sky-God belief are examined. The author makes sense, for the first time, of the relationship between the notion of sacred fertility and a number of regional archaeological features and on-going ancient practices including FGM, spirit possessions, and other physically invasive practices and the ritual hunt. The book explores one of the most important pilgrimage centres in Somaliland and Somalia, the sacred landscape of Saint Aw-Barkhadle, founded ca. 12–13th century AD. It is believed to be the burial place of the rulers of the first Muslim Ifat and Awdal dynasties in this region, and potentially the lost first capital of Awdal kingdom before Harar. This ritual centre is seen as a 'microcosm' of the ancient Horn of Africa with its exceptional multi-religious heritage, through which the author lays out a locally appropriate archaeological interpretational framework, the "Ritual Set," also applied here to the Ethiopian sites of Tiya, Sheikh Hussein Bale, Aksum and Lalibela, setting these places against a wider historical background of indigenous Sky-God belief.

This archaeological study of sacred landscapes, stelae traditions, ancient Christian and medieval Muslim centres of Northeast Africa is the first to put forward a theoretical and analytical framework for the interpretation of the shared regional heritage and the indigenous archaeology of the region. It will be invaluable to archaeologists, anthropologists, historians and policymakers interested in Africa and beyond.

Sada Mire is an award-winning Swedish-Somali archaeologist with a PhD from UCL's Institute of Archaeology. She is founder and executive director of Horn Heritage Organisation, an archaeology and heritage research institution with offices in the Horn of Africa and The Netherlands. Mire was the founding director of Somaliland's Department of Archaeology until 2012 and since then has held academic positions at a several European universities including Leiden University. She has received a number of honours for her work, including being selected for lists such as New Scientist's "Most Inspiring Women in Science of All Times" in 2016 and The Hay Festival of Literature and Arts' list of 30 Global Thinkers and Writers. Mire's popular contributions as well as commissioned features on her work appear regularly in the international media, such as the BBC, The Guardian, CNN and Channel Four, UK. At the moment, she is working on a book on Somali Heritage and Identity Conflicts.

UCL Institute of Archaeology Publications

General Editor: Ruth Whitehouse

Director of the Institute: Sue Hamilton
Founding Series Editor: Peter Ucko

The Institute of Archaeology of University College London is one of the oldest, largest and most prestigious archaeology research facilities in the world. Its extensive publications programme includes the best theory, research, pedagogy and reference materials in archaeology, cultural heritage and cognate disciplines, through publishing exemplary work of scholars worldwide. Through its publications, the Institute brings together key areas of theoretical and substantive knowledge, improves archaeological and heritage practice and brings archaeological findings to the general public, researchers and practitioners. It also publishes staff research projects, site and survey reports, ethnographic work and conference proceedings. The publications programme, formerly developed in-house or in conjunction firstly with UCL Press and then with Left Coast Press, is now produced in partnership with Routledge, a part of the Taylor & Francis group. Details of the Institute's 80-plus publications can be found at https://www.routledge.com/series?title=institute+of+archaeology.

The Institute's publications programme consists of two series: a General Series, reflecting the Institute's wide-ranging archaeological research; and a Critical Cultural Heritage Series, promoting research that differs radically from the existing canon of cultural heritage texts.

This volume is part of the Institute's General Series.

UCL Institute of Archaeology can be accessed on line at www.ucl.ac.uk/archaeology.

Divine Fertility

The Continuity in Transformation of
an Ideology of Sacred Kinship in
Northeast Africa

Sada Mire

Routledge
Taylor & Francis Group

LONDON AND NEW YORK

First published 2020 by Routledge

2 Park Square, Milton Park, Abingdon, Oxon OX14 4RN
605 Third Avenue, New York, NY 10017

Routledge is an imprint of the Taylor & Francis Group, an informa business

First issued in paperback 2021

Publisher's Note

The publisher has gone to great lengths to ensure the quality of this reprint
but points out that some imperfections in the original copies may be apparent.

British Library Cataloguing-in-Publication Data
A catalogue record for this book is available from the British Library

Library of Congress Cataloging-in-Publication Data
A catalog record for this book has been requested

ISBN: 978-1-138-36850-7 (hbk)
ISBN: 978-1-03-217485-3 (pbk)
DOI: 10.4324/9780429769252

Typeset in Sabon
by Apex CoVantage, LLC

This book is dedicated to children whose lives are stolen by injustice and wars and particularly to those my sister Sohur and I shared an orphanage school with in Mogadishu.

Contents

x   *Contents*

About this book

In pre-Christian and pre-Islamic times, the peoples of the Horn of Africa followed their own indigenous religions. How did these relate to other religious institutions in northeastern Africa? And what can they tell us about the history of statehood and the extension of kinship – and about religious syncretism – in the region? This book analyses and puts into context the fundamental practices that shaped, and to some extent still shape, the communities of northeastern Africa. It does so in the light of new anthropological and archaeological discoveries and through an innovative theoretical and multidisciplinary approach. What are the relationships between, say, the Sufi Saint Shrines, the olive forests, the (phallic) stelae traditions, ancient Christian ritual centres and the ruined towns of medieval Muslim kingdoms? Why do Somalis practice *zar* (spirit possessions)? What is the (original) purpose of a practice such as female circumcision? Or the *wagar* rituals, which involve burning the bellies of women? Or the nomadic tradition of fertility baths for brides and grooms? Or the butterfly bush (*tiire*) roots inserted into the vaginas of women?

The purpose of this book is to analyse both the present-day and the historical significance of the notion of fertility in religious practices in this region. One of the most important pilgrimage centres in the Horn of Africa is the shrine of Saint Aw-Barkhadle, founded *c.* twelfth century AD and one of the potential medieval capitals and a burial place of the rulers of the first Muslim Ifat and Awdal dynasties in this region. This shrine is seen as a 'microcosm' of the Horn of Africa and demonstrates the diversity in culture and beliefs amongst the Somali and reveals strong links with other non-Islamic peoples in the region. I present a holistic interpretation of ritual and ceremonial practices at this shrine. Given its multireligious archaeology and practices, this site provides a unique opportunity to assess Ethiopian sites such as the Sheikh Hussein Bale, as well as the Christian sites of Aksum and Lalibela. These sites can be placed within the wider historical background of indigenous 'Cushitic institutions' and spirit possession cults. The author argues that contemporary practices carried out in the Horn of Africa still contain elements of pre-existing religious traditions. These are exemplified both through abstract concepts, such as that of the Sky-God, and the cultural uses of shrines and features of the landscape such as shrines, sacred water sources, hills and trees. I pay particular attention to the relationship between kinship (genealogy) and human fertility rites as mediated through the use of particular sacred objects. In addition, I construct a 'Ritual Set', a set of investigative tools through which data on indigenous practices and the syncretism of religions can be recorded and analysed to provide a springboard for further research. I use the stelae cemetery site of Tiya in the Soddo-region of Ethiopia to show how this Ritual Set can be adapted and applied within a local interpretational framework.

In writing this book, I have drawn upon the ethnographic data I have collected. I interviewed over 150 people, mainly from the Horn of Africa (including Somalia, Somaliland, Ethiopia, Kenya and Djibouti), but also Sudan, South Sudan and Egypt. The majority of these interviews took place during fieldwork: some 30 with sheikhs and sheikhas from congregations and religious and ritual leaders, over 70 women with fertility issues who have visited the site of Aw-Barkhadle or other sacred landscapes or features for fertility purposes, at least 20 elderly women who have a knowledge of history and ritual expertise and over 30 different men with an expertise in history. I have also interviewed Oromo people both in Ethiopia and in Europe and conducted interviews whenever the opportunity arose during my fieldwork in 2005, 2006, 2007, 2010, 2011 and 2013–2017. Most of my interviews took place with small groups, depending on the topic. I have in addition participated in many of the rituals I describe in the following pages and, in some cases, have been subjected to them during my child-hood. I have taken part, for example, in the *Siti*, *roobdoon* and prayers at Aw-Barkhadle and at other sites dedicated to individual sheikhs and saints. I have made pilgrimages to sacred sites.

Divine Fertility makes an important contribution to the understanding of sacred and ritual landscapes, past and present; fertility (sustainability), peace and kinship ideology in Northeast Africa. As such it will be of great interest to academics, intellectuals, students and policy makers. *Divine Fertility* is the result of over 10 years of research by the author who has for most of her life lived and worked amongst different communities in the Horn of Africa.

Illustrations

Figures

Tables

Acknowledgments

The late pioneering Africanist and Oxford Professor Terrence Ranger in 2010 kindly read what was then my PhD thesis; he urged me to publish it as a book, adding the sobering comment 'an unpublished PhD is a still-born child.' This comment had a lasting effect on me as I went through the nearly decade-long process of adding essential further research and analysis. I would also like to acknowledge Professor Merrick Posnansky whose academic work and direct encouragement were critical to my academic confidence. The late professor Peter Ucko similarly encouraged me until his untimely passing, and he also recommended me to Professor David Wengrow who supported my bridging of anthropology and archaeology in the Horn of Africa. I thank the peer reviewers Professor David Phillipson and Neal Ascherson (who waived their anonymity) for their constructive comments. I would also like to thank the Editorial teams of Routledge and the UCL Institute of Archaeology Series: Professor Ruth Whitehouse, Series Editor, for her inspirational support for this book and Marion Cutting who kept letting me know that I remained a priority even when a full-time job and raising a family caused me to defer work on the manuscript. She edited this book with a beautiful combination of patience and encouragement.

I want to thank Muriid Guleed of Aw-Barkhadle, his wife and family, as well as Sheikh Abdirahman and other Aw-Barkhadle male and female religious leaders and elders. I am grateful to many interviewees, both men and women, who offered their perspectives and experiences. I am also indebted to conversations with the Beesha Mohamed Haniifa, including Suldan Ibrahim and other elders. In the broader context of this study, I would like to thank everyone who has supported me generally and this work in particular. I can only mention a few here: the leadership and staff in the Department of Archaeology and Tourism and in the various Somaliland ministries under which this department has functioned and the Horn Heritage Organisation which has been a vital implementation partner for my fieldwork since 2011. I would also like to thank the many sheikhs and sheikhas in Somaliland who support my work and offer their perspectives, including the late Sheikh Aw-Sa'iid of the Saahil region who provided useful information about Sufism in Somali society. Many university librarians across the globe have helped me find rare books, unpublished dissertations and other publications, and I would like to thank them all, especially the staff at the library of the School of Oriental and African Studies, London, and the library of the African Studies Centre, Leiden. I would also like to thank the Rijksmusuem van Oudheden, Bonham Auction House and Eric Lafforgue for permission to reproduce their images.

Family and friends provided a great support by reading parts of the text and/or by enabling me to carry out this huge endeavour. To mention but a few: Dr Francesca Cigna, Joanne Porch, Marilyn Downes, Riekie Geertzen, Wendy Coleman, Kirsty Norman, Sheila Ruiz, Professor Richard van Dyck – and my friends at the Workshop Café in Norwich where I sat and wrote the more recent parts of the work. On a more general level, I am forever indebted to the intellectual upbringing that my parents, Ugaso Kahin Bulhan and A. A. Mire, achieved with only modest resources at a difficult time in Somali society. In particular, I am grateful to the adventurous and openminded spirit with which my mother still accompanies me on some of my missions. I would also like to thank my many brothers whose presence in my early life prepared me for thriving in the male-dominated milieu, such as the archaeology field. I thank my sister, Layla, for bringing laughter into my life since day one – and without whose efforts to get us out of war-torn Somalia in 1991 I could simply never have become an archaeologist. I am forever grateful to my inspiring twin-sister, Sohur, for sharing not only our womb but everything else too, even the long and tough journey from the grim Orphanage College of Madina, Mogadishu, to London universities and professional futures.

A note on transliteration

The Somali letter **X** (in Arabic ﺡ) is written as an 'H' in some cases (f. ex. *Dhagax* becomes *dhagah*) but in other cases I have kept the Somali **X**. Similarly, the Somali letter **C** (in Arabic ﻉ) is written as an inverted comma ' in some cases (f. ex. Bu'ur Ba'ayr, instead of Bucur Bacayr), but in other cases I have kept the Somali **C**. The Somali **A** and **E** are interchangeable in some words as in *wayn* or *weyn* (lit. big) etc. Similarly, some Oromo words appear in slight variations in different books, for example *siqqee* is written *siqe* or *siqqoo* in different books. I have therefore retained these different spellings so readers of these original languages can understand it. Finally, sometimes **Z replaces S** where for example *saar* becomes *zar* or *zaar*. Also note that in some words differentiation occurs without changing the meaning when f. ex. short vowel (single **A**) becomes a long vowel (double **AA**) as in *waq* and *Waaq* or *zar* and *zaar*. Similarly, the Somali letter **DH** (as in *dhagah*) can become just **D** (as in *dagah/daga*) in some dialects of Somali or other Eastern Cushitic languages.

Preface

One single moment can trigger something in you that will influence your life for years to come. . . . One day, over 14 years ago, my grandmother passed away and left me the *wagar* she used to treasure. The *wagar* is passed on amongst the females in the family as a means of protecting its keeper from evil spirits. My grandmother had inherited hers from her grandmother, making the *wagar* about a hundred years old. I immediately wondered why Somalis believe that the *wagar* is sacred. I decided to do some research and write about my grandmother's *wagar* in a short essay for my undergraduate course on African Art at the School of Oriental and African Studies. I did not then know that not only would I write a short essay about this old friend of my grandmother's but that I would also write a whole book inspired by the many different directions in which its revelations would lead me.

However, things were not as easy and straightforward as this account implies. I also at about the same time decided to write my BA dissertation on Somali heritage. I was drawn to this heritage subject because almost all the refugees I met questioned why I wanted to become an archaeologist; they saw it as a waste of my hard-earned good grades. A Bangladeshi high school classmate whom I bumped into years later, upon hearing about my choice of method, sweetly teased me with 'I always knew you were odd (*konstig*)'. We had done the four-year Natural Science Program together in Sweden. It had been a gruelling programme – and not just because we were refugees; we had all set our hearts on becoming doctors or lawyers upon graduation.

Most Somalis thought my choice of subject was interesting; others thought it was weird and a few (a very few, but enough to annoy me) implied I was a 'white-wannabe' with statements such as 'Oh so you are studying archaeology and art history. . . . Isn't that what Prince William studied? Or was it Prince Harry? Anyway, it's only people who don't really need a degree who study subjects like archaeology.' Many European and aspiring archaeologists, too, have cast doubt on my ability to study the subject and have questioned my interest in doing so. Their scepticism arose partly because my country of origin is a war-zone in which it is almost impossible to carry out any archaeology and partly because of the current limitations of archaeology as a discipline in relation to both women and Africans.

If Somalia had been a peaceful country and I had been sent to Europe to study archaeology for the nation, then perhaps people's views would have been different but given that we were all immigrants in a world that was completely different to the one we had once known and that our country was in an on-going war, with terrorism, piracy, poverty, droughts and what have you, archaeology was the last thing on the Somali mind. But although the practice of archaeology had been almost unknown in our society, the Somali nationalist movement did after all aim to influence every branch of education. It was therefore upon the shoulders of previous generations and their demand for decolonisation that I had to justify my choice. And it is in this spirit that I later went to Somaliland. My first experience of archaeology was in Sweden, however, where I enrolled to study World and Scandinavian Archaeology at Lund University. By the time I arrived in the UK, I was taking archaeology for granted, like the Swede I had become.

Asking Somalis a simple question such as 'what is your heritage?' led to answers that were an eye-opening experience for me. I concluded that the Somalis' approach to heritage is inspired not by archaeology but by the oral culture and the transfer of skill and knowledge. Furthermore, when talking about their experiences, the Somalis would draw upon nomadic landscapes and the memories of the grandparents who had taught them about their culture. It is this knowledge and skill, rather than objects and monuments, that constitute a heritage that is preserved and passed on. I summarised these ideas in the notion of the 'Knowledge-Centred' Approach (Mire, 2007, 2011). The unintended consequence of the contradictory dialogue I had had with my Somali fellows inspired me enormously. Yes, we have a war, no, we are not thinking about archaeology and no, we know nothing about the subject, but we know about our culture and that knowledge is our life, our past and our future. I wanted to know more about the *wagar*. I had to see my mother back home in Sweden to talk to her about both it and the *tiire* (the butterfly bush). My mother was taken aback by my sudden and relentless inquisitiveness about issues that lay deep within the most veiled activities of the Somali women, the taboos of our society. She talked somewhat evasively about the subject. She told me that the *wagar* was used by women who were trying to conceive who would use its tip to burn their lower abdominal area.

I first explored a site called Tiya for my MA dissertation (Mire, 2006b) and could not help but observe that the *wagar* is not merely a stand-alone piece of 'art historical research'; the material that I was actually observing and studying at this cemetery site, along with other sites in Ethiopia, all involved similar themes and ideas. When the time came for me to study for my PhD, I decided to focus on a site that I had already heard much about. My mother had happened to mention a place called Aw-Barkhadle. This name rang a bell. I had heard of it before, a long time ago, in Somalia. Perhaps it had featured in one of my grandmother's stories. I therefore decided to explore the issue of Somali female fertility rituals and the centre of Aw-Barkhadle for my PhD. Thus I begun a journey that, after 16 years of exile, would take me back to the Somali peninsula.

I found myself exploring the same landscapes through which I had wandered absent-mindedly as a 14-year-old IDP (Internally Displaced Person), having only known the city of Mogadishu where I grew up. This time, I was not that lost and terrified child refugee, trying with my family to dodge militia, bandits, rapists and the landmines that littered these landscapes. Instead, I was now there as an explorer, eager to discover the importance of the land, past and present, for my ancestors and myself.

I have discovered that the hegemonic and orthodox historical narrative eliminates both the poor and the women; it robs them of their historical and current contributions to society and strips the latter of any significance beyond their reproductive role. The extent of the women's knowledge and their capability, at least in Somali society, had become clear to me both from my grandmother, who transferred so much of her knowledge to my mother, and from my mother, who became a nurse and a midwife through this apprenticeship. My parents seized whatever training was available to become part of the generation of professionals who helped to build Somalia into a nation. My father trained to become an expert in criminal law and, as a crime investigator at the Criminal Investigation Department, became the first Somali to use fingerprint technology. It is my parents' work in education, community service and in the pursuit of justice that has nurtured both myself and my siblings. They became fluent in the colonial languages as well as Arabic. However, a true democratisation of knowledge never fully took place despite the fact that our Somali governments and society in general embarked on an ambitious education project. My family experienced something very different. As the dictatorship unfolded, so families like mine faced clan discrimination to the point where their children, especially the top students, were expelled from schools. Both my sister Sohur and I experienced this first-hand as we were forced to leave our primary school and resort to the only place that would accept us, an orphanage college, in order to gain a primary school certificate.

In terms of the historical narrative, the (often elitist) historiographers spent their time during the colonial and postcolonial eras mainly amongst those sections of society that facilitated and reinforced their status. Commentaries mixed socialism, nationalism and Arabism, all of which were anti-colonial and intended to unite Somali society, yet these accounts at the same time created dominant ideas that served the elites. Prominent historians and anthropologists in the Horn of Africa, such as I. M. Lewis, focused on male history and 'noble clans', leading to the neglect of any evidence that might deviate and challenge the homogeneity. In this endeavour they were fuelled by ideologies that were either political or religious or a mixture of both. When I announced that 'I will study Somali history,' the Somali elite reacted with 'good, study the Ancient Egyptian heritage of the Somali' whilst the Westerners reacted with 'study long-distance trade routes.' Both these topics are of course of interest, but they each adhere much too closely to an elitist history that tells us too little about either the places that are geographically closer to us or the indigenous traditions within our society over, say, the past 2000 years. The same criticism can be made of archaeologists interested in megalithic monumentality in the Horn of Africa. Another issue, taken out of context and oversimplified, is the history of nation-building and statehood. In Ethiopia, for example, the fascinating history of northern statehood and churchdom (best exemplified by the works of Taddesse Tamrat, 1972 as well as Sergew Hable Sellassie, 1972) becomes the story against which are contrasted the seemingly less distinguishable entities in the south. It seems archaeologists have either followed the footsteps of historians or tried too hard to fill the gaps they have inevitably left.

Research methods have had an impact on local communities and how they are represented (Smith, 1999). The emergence of anticolonialist approaches in archaeology follows a movement in the humanities whereby anthropologists, historians and archaeologists have sought to shed light on the dominance of colonial beliefs by adopting a more nuanced image of 'the rest'. In this context, the 'rest', at least in African archaeology, feature mostly as 'interviewees' and, more recently, as 'collaborators'. However, even today, we are faced with the problem of defining our target audience. When this audience is mainly the 'West', a viewpoint justified by the fact that tax payers from the 'West' are paying for these studies, then research is funded, formulated and categorised by the 'West' and thus takes, as an example, 'long distance trade' as its focus. Such power relationships feed unavoidably into both the agenda and the outcome of the work. How can decolonisation take place in the presence of such relationships? What relevant knowledge can we call upon to appeal to those who fund our research whilst still attracting, as it should and must, its core audience in the societies we study?

It is through examining the politics of knowledge production in terms of gender, religion, class and global economic relations that this book will differ from many others. Through the topic I have chosen I have been able to make my main target audience the people I am studying. I hope they will be empowered, not passive, critics. Scientists need to expand their appeal to a wider audience so that their work can be critiqued by local communities. We as archaeologists will only continue to distance ourselves further from local communities if we continue to see archaeology as exclusively our 'thing' and limit the role of those communities to one of providing ethnographic evidence for us as we struggle to promote heritage awareness. In so doing, we may well consolidate our control and our sense of superiority, but we will not be advancing the science of archaeology. Developing that science involves thinking about topics, language, methodology and access to research results. Feedback (i.e. peer-review) needs to come not just from those who have the same or equivalent academic credentials but also from an audience of local practitioners and 'interviewees' and those whom we unintentionally and unimaginatively burden with our failures. I am not talking about charity here. I am talking about making the science more accurate, more scientific.

In the layers of social subalterns, the minorities in the Somali territories are socially, politically, economically and culturally oppressed. Yet the material studied in Somali archaeology reflects the whole of society, not just one segment. The Knowledge-Centred Approach allows me to move away from the dominant group to the sources of knowledge, wherever they may be. It helps me capture the deposits of knowledge that have been curated and held by the marginalised as well as the dominant. The role that marginalised peoples, in a global sense, have played in the formation of the 'modern' world is an issue that has been long debated (Hall, 1992). Some of the communities that I study, though living on the edge of their society (i.e. marginalised), nevertheless play a vital role in that society. When we look only at the dominant narrative, no matter what the context (whether it be a Eurocentric explanation of modernity or a Somali master narrative), we realise that external as well as internal factors have facilitated this dominance (cf. Hall, 1992).

So far, what has been written about these societies is in line with 'the West and the Rest' notions of 'noble and ignoble' savages, where communities (the Somali Bantu, the Gabooye, the Beesha Mohamed Haniifa/the Yibir etc.) are identified with the ignoble. The rights and heritage of these communities must be acknowledged both internationally and locally. For example, the Yibir, like many other Somali minority groups, suffer discrimination and racism akin to that seen by many indigenous peoples (see, for example, Wiessner, 2011). Long overdue in the Somali context are the kind of steps taken to help oppressed peoples elsewhere around the world (see, for example, Smith, 1999). One way to do this is to have an inclusive debate about what is essentially a shared heritage and about the rights of *all* peoples, especially in relation to communally sacred sites.

Similarly, the Somali 'noble' clans are often lifted out of the 'savages' category or embedded in the 'noble savage' discourse. This very act of creating narrative can result in exclusion, selection and omission. I have seen this in the revisionist movement within the newly independent African states or in the nationalist struggles against the hegemonic, colonial and imperialist ideologies that once subjugated them. However, this movement is seeking a partial (re)construction of history. I know from reading authors like Hall (1992) and Said (1978) that the bourgeoisie in Africa are also creating their own narrative within the political and economic structures of the colonial era. In my view, the omissions within this narrative have also led to people disowning part of their heritage, including part of their identity. In *Things Fall Apart*, Chinua Achebe talks about a society that is forced by outsiders to question its traditional religious ideologies and cultural values, sometimes to the point of the loss of social orientation (Achebe, 1958). The new ideologies become a sign of modernity and civilisation.

With religious change and the subsequent striving for a national dominant narrative in the Horn of Africa, I have observed what I see as a 'disowner-ship' of heritage. This disownership is both intentional and unintentional. In Somali society, it may well be the case that society has been so transfigured that whole groups of people appear to have been disowned: I can identify a continuing alienation and the subsequent loss of knowledge by using the Knowledge-Centred Approach as a method of analysis. For example, the groups concerned with traditional medicinal knowledge remain margin-alised and their subsistence under threat despite often finding themselves in situations where their knowledge is much needed. One such sphere of knowledge is to do with what I call fertility practices.

I was surprised to find out that no research had as yet been done into the link between the archaeology and the heritage of fertility in the Horn of Africa. In Somali society, there had been plenty of anthropological research into *Gudniin*/female genital mutilation (FGM). However, except for FGM, very little was known about women's experience of the cultural, social and physical shaping of their womanhood. The survivors of this appalling prac-tice, of whom I am one, do not have access to the academic domain. And even as I analyse female circumcision as part of a wider ideology, and not just as an isolated 'savage act', I am reminded how very few survivors of FGM like me have written academic works on the topic. I am reminded, too, of Spivak's critique of the hegemonic narrative and equitation in relation to the meanings of the *Sati*[1] in India (Spivak, 1988). Moreover, many practition-ers, who are themselves outcasts, take the view that any investigation into the history of this practice ought not to be limited to the fight against FGM but look at the wider historical picture. At some point in the not too distant past, the knowledge and practice of *gudniin*/(female) circumcision belonged within the practice of traditional medicine and surgery. It is still the case that the vast majority of Somalis in the Somali territories cannot afford or access modern medicine. FGM is only one of the many roles traditional practition-ers carry out. Despite this, the official view taken of traditional healers and their knowledge has been dismissive, with terms such as 'magic,' 'wicked' and 'ignorant' used to describe them. I cannot therefore separate FGM from the other practices that shape female bodies physically as well as culturally. The indigenous knowledge systems form an intrinsic part of my ideas about the materiality that arises from the practices that give meaning to the sacred, the legends, the myths, kinship, statehood ideologies and the landscapes. Writing this book has made me realise just how much this tangle of concepts and practices reassembles an interwoven mat/*kebed* of knowledge.

Beyond Aw-Barkhadle, my research into the *wagar* and Tiya continued to push me to northeast Africa, to Lalibela, Aksum and other important sites in the region. The ideas that I am going to explore in the book relate to what D. Levine has called the common traits of 'Greater Ethiopia'. I only learnt about Levine's chapter (2000) on the common foundations many years after finishing my research, but his work has nevertheless shown me that I had been on to something all along. I thus came to explore topics that archaeologists, anthropologists and historians have only been dimly aware of and have never really been able to explore – ideas, practices, spaces and materials that they conveniently, and for want of a better understanding, have lumped together under umbrella terms such as 'Old Cushitic'/or 'Cushitic Institutions' or even 'Greater Ethiopia' or 'northeast Africa'. Common indigenous traits, though sporadically noted in the general literature, had still, it seemed, been very little explored, and much less understood, materially, ritually and ideologically. I believe my background as a native of the region and as a woman has helped me to draw three conclusions. First, these traits have certain similarities in common. Second, these similarities are not random but systematic. And third, this systematic scheme, though not essentialising, is related to a core set of ideas that acts like glue to bind together these traits and common practices. Even those who have so far failed to study or understand these ideas will surely have no choice but to take note of them, even if only in passing.

Note

1 I mention the Sati, which is the now outlawed practice of burning the bride with her deceased husband, as a 'barbaric' ritual comparible to FGM, in my discussion of the hegemonic narrative that superficially isolates one ritual without looking at the whole philosophical context in Somali society in general and in the notion of the 'noble savage' in particular.

Bibliography

Achebe, C. 1958. *Things Fall Apart*. London: William Heinemann Ltd.
Hall, S. 1992. The West and the Rest: Discourse and Power. In S. Hall and B. Gieben (eds.) *Formations of Modernity*. Trowbridge: Redwood Books.
Levine, D. N. 2000. *Greater Ethiopia: The Evolution of a Multiethnic Society*. 2nd ed. Chicago and London: University of Chicago Press.
Mire, S. 2007. Preserving Knowledge, Not Objects: A Somali Perspective for Heritage Management and Archaeological Research. *African Archaeological Review*, 24: 49–71.
Mire, S. 2006b. *Sacred Materials and Associated Rituals of an Ideology of Fertility in Early Second Millennium AD Ethiopia: Contextualizing the Archaeology of the Horn of Africa*. Unpublished MA thesis, University College London.
Mire, S. 2011. The Knowledge-Centred Approach to the Somali Cultural Emergency and Heritage Development Assistance in Somaliland. In F. Sulas ed. Africa's Fragile Heritages. *Special Issue African Archaeological Review*, 29(1): 71–91.
Said, E. W. 1978. *Orientalism*. London: Routledge & Paul Kegan.
Sergew Hable Sellassie. 1972. *Ancient and Medieval Ethiopian History to 1270*. Addis Ababa: United Printers.
Smith, L.T. 1999. Decolonizing methodologies: Research and Indigenous Peoples. London: Zed Books.
Taddesse Tamrat 1972. *Church and State in Ethiopia 1270–1527*. Clarendon Press: Oxford.
Wiessner, S. 2011. The Cultural Rights of Indigenous Peoples: Achievements and Continuing Challenges. *The European Journal of International Law*, 22(1): 121–140.

1   Introduction

Aims, structure, concepts, terminology, the movement of peoples and ideas

Aims

I use both theoretical and methodological approaches to explore the material culture, rituals and sacred landscapes of the Horn of Africa. I ask many questions, for example, what religions were practised before the arrival of Christianity and Islam? What are fertility rituals and what can they tell us about the archaeology of medieval kingdoms, historical figures and religious practice in the Horn of Africa? What evidence is there for the existence of Christianity in the Somali region? How can the recent destruction of many high-profile Sufi Saint Shrines in Africa be explained? What can research reveal to us about the original purpose of *Gudniin*/female circumcision? These are but a few of the questions I explore in this book in an attempt to shed light on the complexity of the history and prehistory of the Horn of Africa and its relevant past and present.

I advance a new theoretical framework based on a multidisciplinary approach which includes oral history, religion, ethnographic methods, medical anthropology, historical-linguistics, archaeology, history and the history of art. My aim is to inspire scholars and students alike and to give the general reader ideas for further research topics and reading. As such, I hope that this book will benefit anthropologists, archaeologists and historians studying similar ritually complex sites and societies. I am also targeting policy makers dealing with medical anthropology (including FGM) and the protection and management of Sufi Saint Shrines and other politically threatened multireligious heritage sites as well as the aftermath of their destruction. Many of the topics – such as female genital mutilation and the destruction of World Heritage Sufi Saint Shrines Sites – have a strong contemporary relevance and I want to put these issues into context for the general reader. I also want to fill in a gap in current research with the use of anthropological and archaeological perspectives.

My purpose is to examine fundamental practices and ideas within the society and culture of the Horn of Africa. I therefore analyse both the contemporary and the historical significance of what I term 'divine fertility' in ritual practices. I hope that the book will represent an important contribution to the understanding of Islamic shrines and kinship ideology in northeast Africa and is of considerable relevance to the wider debate about indigenous institutions. I analyse the relationship between the spread of orthodox Christianity and aspects of the Islamic movement in many parts of the world, both of which involve notions of saint worship or veneration and both of which have been strongly influenced by the indigenous notion of ancestral worship or veneration. I also explore the multiple layers of rituals and meaning with which the living heritage of Aw-Barkhadle is associated (something I call 'sacred landscapes'). I also hope to offer an innovative approach to the study of the indigenous institutions of the Horn of Africa, a topic currently very little understood in either anthropology or archaeology. I use a multidisciplinary approach to give a holistic perspective on the material culture, rituals and the landscapes of these beliefs. Some of the discoveries I present in this book can directly benefit the practice of both archaeology and anthropology by providing a new methodology, that of the Ritual Set. Other findings have implications for scientific and medical research, for example that about the butterfly bush (*rotheca myricoides*).

I hope that this book will also promote peace and security in the Horn of Africa because by understanding our past and common shared heritage we can learn to better understand each other. In other words, if we can accept that our ancestors were different from us then we may also be able to accept that our present-day neighbours are different from us. Hence by exploring the history and cultures of the Horn of Africa and by identifying sacred fertility and the common ideas of peace (*nagi*), this work can help bring people together in a region that in the past four decades has been beset by so many nationalist and religious inspired wars. Also, by exploring the multireligious past of any society it becomes possible to discover ideological connections that existed in the past but which have now disappeared. In short, this book will hopefully be of great interest not just to academics, intellectuals, students, local communities and health professionals but to cultural diplomacy and policy as well.

African Archaeology appears, currently, to make little use of any anthropological research into the issue of rituals in the past and carries out even less of its own anthropological research into this topic in contemporary society. Often anthropologists do not speak the local languages, and this limits their understanding of how rituals are described and enacted. Archaeology in the Horn of Africa is no different, as there is presently no study that explores either the complicated relationship between the ritual systems and practices of Sufi Islam and local traditional religions or how these relate to, and impact, the local archaeological heritage. The Knowledge-Centred Approach looks at the transmission of the non-material part of knowledge and in this way can reveal that the material object is often not nearly as significant as the steps associated with the ritual and its performance. The relationship between fertility, ideology, kinship and the widespread belief in the Sky-God has much to say about the indigenous practices and ritual systems of religions. It is my hope that this work will assist others by acting as a springboard for further research.

Structure

This first chapter discusses the topics, concepts, terminology and historical and geographical scope of this book. It presents the theoretical problems raised by this study and introduces some of the arguments relevant to the cultural traditions out of which grew some of the prominent archaeological sites of the Horn of Africa and demonstrates how they may be potentially linked ideologically. It explores the perceptions, practices and problems inherent in the approaches so often adopted by those who study these topics. It emphasises the need to study the historical significance and the symbolism of pre-Islamic religious heritage, indigenous religious systems in this region and the relevance of a transdisciplinary approach which combines the archaeological data with case-specific oral history and ethnographic participant observation, history and historical linguistic material. It advances the need for a new theoretical framework within which to study pre-Islamic and pre-Christian ritual material culture in the Horn of Africa.

Chapter Two introduces notions of sacred landscapes and fertility rituals to the archaeology of the Somali region. It describes the site of Aw-Barkhadle with its complex political and historical characteristics. It sets out the site's challenges: narratives, contestations, kinship, outcasts, myths and gender issues. The chapter builds a theoretical framework within which the archaeology of the Horn of Africa in general, and the site of Aw-Barkhadle in particular, become central to the understanding of these challenges.

Chapter Three analyses the rituals, archaeological and landscape features, and ritual space, in relation to activities observed at the site of Aw-Barkhadle. The chapter discusses the authority of Saint Aw-Barkhadle (Sheikh Sharif Yusuf Al-Kawnayn) in Sufi Islam in Somali society, as well as the Somali myth of 'Origin'. It also introduces the legend of Bu'ur Ba'ayr and what are considered by some of the people I interviewed to be pre-Islamic practices at Aw-Barkhadle and at the sacred Bu'ur Ba'ayr Hill too. It analyses the significance of both the pre-Islamic religious figures and the practices credited to them in terms of the rituals taking place in the surrounding landscape. I focus on fertility rituals and ritually significant archaeological features such as tombs, megalithic burials, stones, shrines and hilltops. I introduce the phallic stones I discovered during my research and discuss their probable link to ideas of fertility and its symbolism. I introduce another discovery, a gravestone standing *in situ*, which remarkably carries a carving of a Coptic cross that is similar to the ones that appear on fourth–sixth century Aksumite coins and tombs. This stele lends further credence to the multireligious significance of the site. The chapter also explores the potential relationship between these features and non-/pre-Islamic and non-/pre-Christian religion at the site by investigating the historical legends of the alleged pre-Islamic figure, Bu'ur Ba'ayr, that are associated with this landscape. A knowledge of the female rituals, I argue, will enhance an understanding of the archaeological landscape at Aw-Barkhadle and of kinship ideology as a whole. Using these rituals as data importantly sheds light on the possible continuity of ritual use within this landscape. In addition, some stelae at this site might link with ancient astrology and the rain-making practices potentially associated with this site, an association that future excavations may elucidate.

Chapter 4 contextualises the female fertility practices noted at Aw-Barkhadle by placing them within the broader fertility practices in Somali society. A number of rituals are explored: infertility treatment or *baanashada dumarka*, the *Siti* ceremony, the *wagar* ritual, the fertility bath, *zar* (spirit possessions), the *istunka* (stick fight) and *gudniin* (female circumcision). Some of these practices have never been studied before while others have not been studied in depth or considered within the wider context of Somali female practices. New anthropological research into these rituals offers a fresh perspective by investigating these practices from the viewpoint of fertility. For example, I examine *zar* in terms of women's need for the treatment and how the *zar* itself is related to the *baanashada dumarka* (an infertility treatment which involves the use of medicinal plants). This leads into a discussion of *zar* as part of the pre-Islamic and pre-Christian ritual systems of Northeast Africa and how it may even in ancient times have signified the Sky-God. I also discuss ritual celebrations of womanhood through the *Siti* commemoration of Eve and Fatima and the female veneration of female religious ancestors. The text explores the relationship between ancestral worship and the notion of sacred fertility. It investigates both the women's use of the *wagar*, a wooden anthropomorphic sculpture used for fertility purposes, and its relationship with the site of Aw-Barkhadle and child protection. It suggests that the *wagar* may be a depiction of the Sky-God, worshiped in this region before Saint Aw-Barkhadle arrived. The Sky-God belief was one of the pre-Islamic beliefs of the Cushitic speaking peoples in this region and it is even today followed by many Eastern Cushitic speaking communities. The origin of the practice of *gudniin*/female circumcision (also known as Pharaonic circumcision) in the Horn of Africa, where many believe it originated, is discussed and a possible association is drawn between its ritual aspects, fertility rituals and what I call a 'divine[1] kinship'. I argue that its origin is not to be found in the relationship between men and women, as is so often suggested, but instead with practices originally intended as forms of sacrifice. I suggest that *gudniin*/female circumcision may have been a medium through which to gain sacred fertility via the sacrifice of the profane for the sacred, in other words, via a sacrificial transaction between the divine and the human, in extension of the righteous blood.

Chapter Five analyses the broader shared foundations of the Horn of Africa in general, and of the modern-day Cushitic speaking society in particular. It does so in the light of the possible continuity of the fertility rituals described in the preceding chapter. It explores the triadic relationship between the symbolism of materials, rituals and landscape as demonstrated through the cultural heritage of Aw-Barkhadle. In doing so, it sheds light on the potential non-/pre-Islamic and non-/pre-Christian religions and beliefs represented at the site. Without losing its critical cultural perspective, it focuses on the relationship between Sufism, the origin of the Somali people and the indigenous institutions of the Horn of Africa. It also compares relevant practices in parts of Southern Arabia (the Red Sea region). Within this context, it examines the idea of continuity of indigenous practices including those relating to the ritual hunt, ancestral worship, saint veneration and sacrifice for fertility. It reveals the amalgamation of Islamic Sufi rituals with pre-existing wider Horn of Africa practices such as the Sky-God belief as well as Christian rituals. The chapter explores, by way of example, different Eastern Cushitic groups and their practices involving fertility as it relates to sacred trees, water sources and stones (including phallic stones) and discovers that the Somali data are best understood when set against their Cushitic background. In maintaining this, I am not saying that any one trait on its own has any fixed correlation to ethnic identity. Instead, I use the term Cushitic in this context because these Eastern Cushitic speaking peoples share many of the characteristics I have identified from my own linguistic and field observations.

Chapter Six discusses what I call a fertility ideology and the notion of divine kinship within the societies of the Horn of Africa and explores the implications of its rituals and practices for the archaeological heritage of this area. It contextualises the case of Aw-Barkhadle within the archaeology of the region as a whole by using anthropological and ethno-historical records to analyse further the data from that site. To do this, I construct a locally contextualised framework which I call a Ritual Set (Chapter 6, Tables 6.1a-c). The Ritual Set is a model consisting of the materials I saw used in the rituals. Its aim is to serve as a springboard for further research into the study of religious symbolism and ritual material heritage in the Northeast Africa. This chapter also demonstrates the use of the Ritual Set by applying its methodology to the decorated cemetery site of Tiya in Ethiopia. I suggest that the Ritual Set be applied to the regional Horn of Africa archaeology of the last 2000 years. I interpret the Aksumite and Lalibela sites from the perspectives of the sacred landscapes and the regional continuities of a wider shared indigenous belief, perspectives that extend beyond Christianity.

In its concluding chapter, the book restates the importance of fertility rituals and their symbolism. Their study can illuminate archaeological and anthropological material culture. It is the underlying indigenous concepts and ideologies that sustain and bind together these societies across geography and religion.

Concepts, terminology and the movement of peoples and ideas

Some of the concepts and terms used in this book need to be explained and placed within the context of the movement of peoples, cultures and religions over time.

The Horn of Africa

The 'Horn of Africa' refers not only to the Somali peninsula but also to Ethiopia, Eritrea, Kenya and Djibouti. I will focus on Somali and Ethiopian sites (Figure 1.1 and Figure 1.2). However, the Horn of Africa also has historical links with neighboring present-day Sudan, Egypt and the adjacent regions of South Arabia and Hadramaut. These regions were at various points in prehistory and history ruled by local empires which expanded their powers in one direction or the other. I have learnt, however, that certain elements, such as the fertility rituals, are fundamental across the region which, despite certain variations, continue to bind the past to the present.

Christianity, Islam and the Cushitic institutions

The religious concepts identified in this book are Christianity, Islam and Indigenous Institutions, or 'Cushitic[2] Institutions', according to earlier ethnographers. My use of the latter term is based on my understanding of the Sky-God religion, which itself may be as syncretic as Christianity and Islam. I use the term to denote earlier regional religious beliefs that are linked with the notion of Sky-God/Heaven God in the Horn of Africa. I do not, however, use 'Cushitic' as a blanket term to cover all the 'indigenous' religious or ritual concepts. Nor do I use it to denote all the potentially indigenous practices and observations that I make in relation to the past and the present. I would not, for example, argue that a phallic symbol is a 'Cushite' symbol. Instead, I would argue that this symbol, though found across northeastern Africa and the African continent in the past, and even today, has a particular meaning for the Horn of Africa speaking peoples in general and, perhaps, for the Cushitic speaking peoples in particular in so far as it is an integral part of the cultural context. For many of the Cushitic speaking peoples, this symbol is associated in general with the notion of fertility rituals and in particular with the kinship ideology of sacred ancestors and, particularly, with the Sky-God religion. I have come to understand the Sky-God religion as an entity in itself, in much the same way as I understand Christianity or Islam. The Boorana religion is a good example of this. I am therefore interested in the practices of the Sky-God beliefs in the Horn of Africa, and in the variations within its ritual system. In short, the term 'Cushitic institutions' refers to those practices associated with a belief, in some form or other, in the Sky-God.

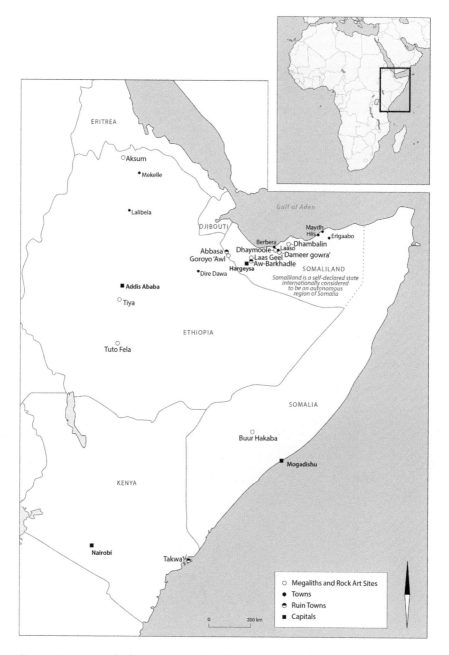

Figure 1.1 Horn of Africa and Somaliland sites mentioned in the book

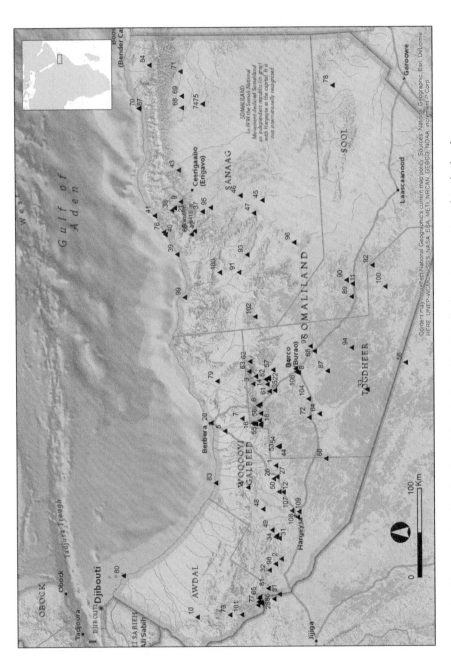

Figure 1.2 Map showing distribution of sites in Somaliland, including sites mentioned in the book

The 'Ritual Set'

I construct what I call a Ritual Set (Chapter 6, Tables 6.1a-c) by observing the persistent and consistent characteristics of the landscapes, their features, associated myths, rituals, material culture and architectural features. I am thereby able to categorise these scattered, yet common, aspects of religious heritage in the Horn of Africa. It is beyond the scope of this work to investigate whether these go back to the times of the Kingdoms of Kush or Aksum. However, were I to paint the Horn of Africa with the broad sweep of a shared heritage, that heritage would be dominated by its ritual system, by its particular and shared terminology and languages, and by the practices of its 'Old Cushitic' heritage, a heritage that goes back beyond both Christianity and Islam.

Great civilisations, ideologies and syncretism across the centuries

This is not to say that the Christian and Islamic religions have not been 'indigenised' in the Horn of Africa: indeed, both religions have early roots in this part of Africa and have been shaped by local ideas. As this book shows, it is not only in 'Ethiopia' that ancient Christianity has been preserved, just as it is not only in 'Somalia' that ancient Islam has survived. It appears that a major pre-Christian and pre-Islamic religion once existed in the Horn of Africa. This religion became fragmented and scattered after the introduction of Christianity and influences from areas bordering the Red Sea. This early regional belief system, it can be safely said, permeated and transformed its ideology and indigenised both Christianity and Islam, thus making these religions acceptable to the wider community and a part of the deep-seated ideologies of the Horn of Africa. In the heartland of Christian Ethiopia, for example, live the Agaw, a Cushitic speaking people whose traditions are, it is said, embedded deeply in the Christian heritage of places such as Aksum and Lalibela. Historical sources suggest that the Agaw were the original inhabitants of much of northern Ethiopia. They were first mentioned in the third and sixth centuries AD in Aksumite inscriptions recorded by Cosmas Indicopleustes in the sixth century (Ullendorff in Phillipson, 2007: 2; Conti Rossini, 1928). According to Phillipson:

> By early in the last millennium BC, the highlands of northern Ethiopia and southern Eritrea were inhabited by farming peoples, some of whom lived in rectangular stone-built houses; their crops, domestic animals, pottery and stone tools all showing signs of long local ancestry.
>
> (Phillipson, 2007: 2)

In his argument for a 'proto-Ethiopian' culture for Greater Ethiopia, the sociologist Donald N. Levine (2000: 46) describes 'pan-Ethiopian' themes with deep roots in the Horn of Africa and concludes:

> The fact is that the peoples of Greater Ethiopia are relatively homogenous in a number of respects. Some of the culture traits they share may

derive from a common aboriginal proto-Ethiopian culture, some may represent similar adaptive responses to similar situations, and others probably reflect a coalescence of traits deriving from prolonged interaction in the distant past.

Phillipson adds that significant changes only occurred in about the eighth and seventh centuries BC. These changes are usually grouped under the name 'Pre-Aksumite' period or D'MT (e.g. Finneran, 2007), a term which, Phillipson argues, implies 'a serious misinterpretation of the archaeological evidence' (ibid.) since the farming economy and the basic non-elite material culture 'shows strong similarities to those of earlier times' (Phillipson, 2007). He refers to 'colonists' from across the Red Sea who gradually assimilated with the 'indigenous Ethiopian communities'. The divergence of the language of the 'colonists' from their origin (Yemen) shows the strength of the indigenous culture over the 'colonists' and suggests that they were perhaps 'a small number of people . . . settled in scattered fertile places' (ibid.) in northern Ethiopia.

Archaeologists' labelling of ancient cultures is simultaneously both an act of exclusion and inclusion. The deep history of this region demands a much more multidisciplinary approach. The two main contributions of the 'colonists' are supposed to be 'writing and architecture'. Yet one could argue that not only do the stelae practices exist within an indigenous tradition (Fattovich, 1987): the language, too, seems equally locally grounded. However, from a purely linguistic point of view, the language of the stelae has a complex origin in both the Afro-asiatic language and the African (Semitic) language (*Ge'ez*). And it seems that archaeologists are even now discovering more scripts written in this language in the Horn than Arabia.

It has been established that the Agaw were the original inhabitants of the highlands (Conti Rossini, 1905; Ullendorff, 1955). The question remains as to how the Agaw relate to the speakers of Tigrinya and Amharic. Ullendorff (1960: 47–54, 116–124 in Phillipson, 2007: 2) argues that 'a form of Semitic speech was brought to the Ethiopian highlands at this time, soon largely replacing – while absorbing much vocabulary and other elements from – distantly related Cushitic languages previously spoken in that area' (ibid.). Furthermore, Phillipson and Sulas (2005) have argued for the continuity of indigenous stone tools, pottery and the farming economy throughout the so-called Pre-Aksumite and Aksumite periods.

The local cultural continuity is maintained during the Zagwe dynasty which, by AD 1000, if not earlier, appears to have filled the gap left by Aksum's decline from about AD 800 onwards. The Zagwe, Phillipson says, was a 'southward transfer of political authority to the more southerly Zagwe, and the strong desire of the latter to emphasize their Aksumite antecedents as a prop for their legitimacy' (2007: 11). Phillipson notes '[T]he Zagwe rulers descended from the old Cushitic speaking population of the highlands, although it is clear that they had adopted Christianity and, at least for most purposes, the Semitic speech of Aksum' (ibid.: 11). It is important to add here that the Aksumite empire extended farther to the east then is generally known. Furthermore, it could be argued that those early Muslims fighting the Solomonic dynasty also had an Aksumite heritage, whether or not they were aware of the fact. The remains of ancient Christian burials and of ancient Christian scripts written in what look like Ethiopian languages have been found in modern-day Somali territories (Mire, 2015). Furthermore, Phillipson has pointed out that lithic material associated with Aksumite culture is also recorded in eastern Somali territories. The key point here is that a possible Aksumite Christian heritage was not entirely destroyed by the Muslims, even in their own region, as can be demonstrated at Aw-Barkhadle where Christianity remained highly relevant materially, mythically and ritually. However, as I will demonstrate, the medieval Islamic rulers of Awdal and the Ifat kingdoms made use of the Islamic heritage of Saint Aw-Barkhadle and use his conversion of a Christian and traditional religious centre as an inspiration for their own ideological and religious expansionism.

This continuity between the Aksumite and Zagwe dynasties is also reflected in the Solomonic period when there is evidence for the continuity and spread of rock-hewn architectural features ranging from defences lacking any Christian connotations to Christian churches spreading as far south as beyond the Awash, as Phillipson notes. However, the erection of stelae and the megalithic[3] architecture is a tradition that is African in origin (Fattovich, 1987). Hence in any discussion of the architectural contribution made by the 'colonists', it is important to remember that the 'Semitic' stelae of the Near East differ from the indigenous African stelae tradition found in Ethiopia (ibid.). Whilst recognising the historical and linguistic links between Ethiopian and Semitic speaking people across the Red Sea, Fattovich points out the danger of attributing this tradition to the latter because, according to him, there is plenty of evidence to contradict this idea of diffusion. He distinguishes the cemetery and the sacrificial nature concomitant with the Ethiopian stelae (ibid.: 46). He points out that they were connected to an 'ancestral cult' rather than to an individual personage. Nevertheless, he accepts that the idea that the *nephesh* (Syrian-Palestinian mausoleums) might later have had some impact on Aksumite architecture, even though he remains adamant that: 'The Ethiopian monuments underwent some external influence rather than being a direct derivation from the Near East monuments' (ibid.: 47). Fattovich postulates that 'the use of the funerary monoliths seems to be more frequent in Africa than in the Near East and the Arabian Peninsula' (ibid.: 62). Summarising evidence from an east–west belt of Africa, he shows that:

> On the whole, the comparison between the Aksumite monoliths and the ones discovered in the other regions suggests that they belong to an ancient African tradition. In fact the use of monoliths to indicate the general cemetery area is documented at Aksum, Kassala, Aniba and

perhaps in some Saharan sites too. . . . To conclude the Aksumite stelae can be attributed to a regional cultural tradition of Eastern Sudan and Northern Ethiopia going back to the late 3rd millennium BC.

(ibid.: 63)

Both Fattovich and Phillipson agree about the African roots of the ancient Aksumite civilization. Furthermore, Joussaume (2007) also concludes that the twelfth–thirteenth century stelae of southern Ethiopia probably have their origin in the 1st millennium BC stelae of the Borana country in the south (ibid.). This would mean that stelae traditions would not necessarily have spread from northern Ethiopia; instead, both the north and the south might have shared an ancient regional tradition of stelae erection, a practice existing in much of the east–west belt of Africa.

The cultural continuity that Phillipson argues for within the indigenous heritage of the highlands of northern Ethiopia is critical to this book's argument. Furthermore, the tradition of stelae erection is an ancient African indigenous tradition going back to at least as early as the 1st millennium BC both in northern (Fattovich, 1987) and southern Ethiopia/northern Kenya (Joussaume, 2007; Lynch and Robbins, 1978; Lynch and Donahue, 1980). Although more dates are needed from the southern Ethiopian and northern Kenyan areas, it is nevertheless clear that this 'cultural continuity' extends beyond northern Ethiopia.

Somali traditions, Cushitic institutions, Christianity and Islam

The broader perspective that these sources offer is essential to the present study. The hiatus between the Aksumite and the Zagwe rule in the eleventh and twelfth century AD is a phenomenon of great interest too. Around this time, even though the presence of Islamic missionaries from Arabia is recorded in the textual and oral historical sources of the Horn of Africa (Martin, 1974; Sihab ad-Din, 2003), the continuity of pre-Islamic practices continued in the eastern Horn of Africa, in much the same way as the indigenous pre-Christian culture continued in the Christian northern highlands of Ethiopia.

It is against the background of discussions such as these that this study presents the Somali case, a case so far missing from the regional debate about possible continuities in religious tradition. I argue that there is a continuity between the pre-Christian and pre-Islamic ideologies of 'old Cushitic' institutions, including those in the northern highlands of Ethiopia, and the Christian and Islamic beliefs that were to follow. The Oromo/Borana and the Agaw can both be used as examples of the spread and continuity of indigenous religious systems that spread across the Horn of Africa because each had the experience of both Christianity and Islam. Cultural resistance is likely to go hand in hand with cultural continuity. If this is so, then why is there continuity in some respects but change in others? When different ideologies encounter each other, what is negotiable and what is not? How can one avoid using the data automatically to track 'exchange and long-distance trade' and/or the 'innovations' of 'colonists', and instead use the evidence to identify the 'cultural negotiations and continuities' that are better explained by the indigenous ideologies themselves? Any assimilation of 'these small settler communities' with deeper local traditions would involve the local indigenous and old Cushitic highland cultures, not those of the 'colonialists'. These settler community ideas could be equally relevant to the debate about the recent discovery in the Somali region of what seems to be a type of Sabaean writing, albeit in a local style (Mire, 2015). How, then, can one begin to study these indigenous cultural continuities in their own right?

'Old Cushitic highland cultures' can only be approached, using this perspective, by comparing and contrasting them with the wider regional archaeology and ethnography of the peoples and the ritual system that ties the past to the present. What is meant by 'old Cushitic' communities? The term 'Kush' can be traced back to the Ancient Kingdom of Kush in present-day northern Sudan. According to historical records, the term has its origins in the Bible. Biblical sources say that Cush was the oldest son of Ham who was the son of Noah; this narrative has resulted in the notion that the people of northeastern Africa claim to be descended from Cush. The Cushitic languages, a branch of Afro-Asiatic languages, are spoken mainly in the Horn of Africa (Somalia/Somaliland, Ethiopia, Eritrea, Sudan, Kenya and Djibouti). The most populous Cushitic language is the Oromo language spoken by 35 million people, a group that has shown a great deal of cultural resistance (e.g. Hultin, 1994).: the word 'Oromo' denotes the peoples, who live in most of Ethiopia, eastern Somalia and northern Kenya (Huntingford, 1955). The second most populous is Somali, the official language of Somalia and Somaliland and a recognised national language of Djibouti and the Somali regions of northern Kenya and eastern Ethiopia as well as Yemen. These Cushitic languages, according to Ehret (1995), can be subdivided into different branches: east–south Cushitic, Beja and Agaw. Ehret, it should be noted, also provides a link between the Cushitic language and the Semitic.

Ethiopia's many ancient Christian monuments (Conti Rossini, 1928) have led to the often expressed view that the country was predominantly Christian. Islam in Ethiopia has received little academic interest (Abbink, 1998). Braukämper (2004) expresses eloquently the Eurocentric view on Ethiopian Christianity in his introduction:

> Ethiopia, including Eritrea, however, has always been treated by the majority of researchers as a region where Orthodox Monophysite Christianity has dominated politics and culture to such an extent that Islam did not occupy more than a peripheral position. It is a well-known fact that the Europeans of the Middle Ages searched for the 'kingdom of Prester John' in north-eastern Africa as a mighty outpost

of the Christian faith and a potential ally against the Muslim world. They admired the tenacity of Ethiopian Christianity to survive in an area almost completely isolated and surrounded by Muslim territories. In this Eurocentric view Christian Ethiopia was regarded as a specific phenomenon, presenting cultural peculiarities such as an Empire State, a sophisticated clerical structure, an indigenous literature in a script of its own and monolithic rock-hewn churches. It was therefore not conceived as a genuine part of Sub-Saharan Africa, but as an appendix of the advanced civilization of the 'Old Orient'. Consequently, in scientific research since the time of Hiob Ludolf (1624–1704), the European pioneer of Ethiopian studies, emphasis has been laid on the Habaša, the representative of Christian-dominated culture and their literature in the Semitic languages of Gəʿəz, Təgrəñña and Amharic.

(Braukämper, 2004: 1–2)

Braukämper's statement is also relevant to the archaeological research carried out in Ethiopia where the focus has been on material showing links with the classical world. Archaeologists have based such Eurocentric views on very little evidence. My own research in the Somali territories shows that, far from being confined to present-day Ethiopia, ancient Christianity in the Horn of Africa was in fact widespread across most of the Horn, including the whole Somali peninsula (Mire, 2015). Modern day Sudan (Wallis Budge, 1970), moreover, has ancient Christian states. The belief, then, that an isolated ancient Christianity existed in the northern highlands of Ethiopia surrounded by enemies, including Muslims, cannot be true and neither can the view be that it was almost completely isolated in the centuries before the rise of the Islamic Empires. It is also noteworthy (Braukämper, 2004) that there has been no major conflict between Christians and Muslims in the Horn of Africa since the mid seventeenth century, with the past 400 years characterised by religious tolerance.

This Orthodox Monophysite Christian picture can be challenged on two grounds: first, people of many different religions, including a large Ethiopian Muslim community, existed alongside the Ethiopian Christian community, and, second, 'Christianity' itself is firmly embedded within a local ritual spectrum that includes the 'old Cushitic' heritage (cf. Levine, 2000; Phillipson, 2012). So even in 'ritual' terms, as my discussion of Lalibela and Aksum will show, Christianity was supported by indigenous ideologies. Just as the indigenous pre-Islamic culture, with its belief in sacred ancestors (saints), made it easy for the Somali to adopt Sufi Islam, so the pre-Christian indigenous culture, with its similar belief in the sacred ancestors of present-day Ethiopia, made it possible for them to adopt the equally saint-based Christian faith.

Aksum, for example, is the seat of ancient Christianity in Ethiopia. Its name appears to be made up of two parts: '*Ak*' meaning water in the Cushitic languages; and *shum* – meaning a chief in Amharic (Finneran, 2007). The possible importance of this will be discussed later, suffice to say here that the name is indicative of an 'old Cushitic' highland culture embedded in a local Christianity and the wider community.

The 'old Cushitic' Christian traditions form the bedrock of this largely non-Semitic people of Ethiopia (Phillipson, 2012). Archaeologists must never overlook the extent to which different peoples interacted naturally ('Highlander Christians' and the 'Lowlander Muslims') in terms of shared continuous traditions. It is the indigenous traditional foundations in a dynamic relationship which operate alongside the 'top-down' religious transitions, whether they be Christianity or Islam. Christianity from its very beginnings demonstrates how this top-down new religion was itself in synergy with the local traditions, as can be seen from the coins minted by the earliest Christian Ethiopian kings. Modern archaeologists may need to dig deeper into the anthropology of the region to reveal the stratigraphy of change and the continuity in identity and practice that bind the past to the present. Further research has appeared exploring the idea of cultural resistance (e.g. Gonzalez-Ruibal, 2014) since 2009 when I was awarded a PhD for a thesis on the topic of this book. However, there is a striking lack of indigenous archaeology perspectives combined with adequate knowledge about the languages of the region to carry out a credible interdisciplinary work combining archaeology with folklore, linguistics and ethnography in order to provide deeper insights into local practices, rituals and symbolism. As archaeologists, we can only understand the very local character of the region's archaeology if we adopt a holistic and interdisciplinary perspective to examine change and continuity, not just in conflict but in the implicit patterns of daily life.

My intention is to demonstrate that a better understanding of the present population, the way it expresses its traditions culturally and linguistically, and its ritual systems both past and present, will all lead to a better understanding of the archaeology. I do not intend, however, to bind a culture to a particular identity or a people to just one identity: it would be impossible, irrelevant and beyond the scope of this book to attempt to trace precisely which groups were associated with which religions or traditions at any one particular time. Instead, I will consider broader groups of regional peoples to understand from a multidisciplinary perspective what they have in common in terms of historical, ritual, and symbolical practices. To gain this understanding, my primary ethnographic data relates to direct observations of the Somali and the Oromo (the populous Cushitic speakers). I also study the Semitic speakers of Ethiopia including part of the Agaw, the original populations of much of northern and central Ethiopia who some still to a degree retain their traditional religion despite other influences.

The adoption of a 'master narrative' always carries with it dangers. For example, one can rarify 'Ethiopian' Christianity in the Horn of Africa to the point where Islam comes to be seen as a hostile 'external' belief with anyone deviating from the state belief system being relegated to an inferior category. Such master narratives have also been imposed upon Muslim communities in the Horn of Africa, including those of the Somali. According to these narratives, non-official cultures became 'a mass of undifferentiated 'rest'' (to borrow a term used in 'the West and the Rest' debate). The historical accounts of authors who write about particular ethnohistories are used to strengthen this debate. Incidentally, it is worth noting that some Cushitic speaking groups in central and southern Ethiopia and northern Kenya have, with great success, resisted external influences in terms of Christianity and Islam.

It is also clear that groups reject certain labels or attributions not because the elements the attributions attach are no longer a part of their cultural system but because most of them do not *now* relate to these elements or, even, outrightly deny the validity of these characteristics, whether in the past or in the present. Myths of origins and narratives of placement ('homeland), as well as displacement, demonstrate this well. I suggest that there exists a phenomenon which I shall call 'disownership of heritage' whereby the homogenisation process, empowered over the past millennium by religious and political ideologies, eliminates certain ideas about indigenous traditional heritage.

Non-Abrahamic peoples and the monotheistic traditions

Anthropological and archaeological literature about the Horn of Africa often reduces the traditional values, practices and ideas associated with non-Abrahamic peoples to simplistic terms such as 'animism' and 'pagan' in the literature (e.g. Trimingham, 1965). This continuing 'simplistic' (a gross undervaluation in itself) reference to indigenous belief systems as 'animistic' shows a lack of respect not only for the people being talked about but also for those of our colleagues and earlier scholars who have shed a remarkable light on the study of indigenous religions in the Horn of Africa – Lambert, Bartels, Baxter, Loo, Hallpike and many more – who have written about these peoples and their cultures. The religion of the present-day Agaw people is still commonly referred to as 'Animistic and Hebraic' – meaning that only the Abrahamic religions are recognised. Are the indigenous not even worth of a name? *Waaqeffannaa*, the traditional religion of the Oromo, and the Sky-God belief of Northeast Africa, are still identified by their own names, even though their beliefs are to some degree interchangeable. Yet even these are often reduced to 'local beliefs' in the literature. Similarly, Muslims' view about the pre-Islamic era leads them to use the term *Jahili-yya* to refer to 'ignorance of the guidance from God' and idol worship. This term is loosely applied to people who are not Muslim today and/or have not been in the past.

The point I am trying to make is that it is all too easy to attribute a broad, often uninformed and mostly derogative term to groups, but labelling them as 'animist' and such does not help us to understand them. As scientists we have to investigate and give names to these non-Abrahamic ideologies and describe them to the best of our abilities. This helps to teach us to distinguish what we are observing in the archaeology and ethnography while remaining sensitive to changes, which may be important though seemingly slight. For example, when I talk about ancestral veneration as it appears in current Sufi practice, I do not mean to suggest that there is an ancestral worship in Somali society today. Instead, I am referring simply to the veneration of revered religious and/or ancestral figures, i.e. a veneration of ancestors rather than their worship. However, it may well be that people worshipped ancestors rather than revered them in the pre-Islamic past.

I also use the term 'indigenous', particularly in Chapter 5, to denote what are, in terms of beliefs, material cultural and ritual, generally seen as 'Cushitic institutions' rather than as belonging to Islam or Christianity in the Horn of Africa. The history of Ethiopia makes it abundantly clear that Christianity has been constantly challenged throughout history both by traditionalist followers of indigenous religions and by the Jewish and Muslim communities.

A second problem arises when archaeologists describing pre-Christian culture mainly discuss, with varying degrees of confidence, what they see as 'Arabian influences' and offer fanciful explanations of what is more likely to be a local practice or symbolism. It is strange to hold or show little awareness or interest for the current ethnographic and ethnohistory and local ontologies and use of landscapes, rituals, beliefs and practices beyond those associated with Islam and Christianity. Given their apparent lack of interest in, and knowledge about, the local indigenous culture they seek to describe, it is perhaps surprising how quickly they can resort to sweeping statements undermining local agency. One of the elements that seems to be ignored in the archaeology and architecture of the Horn of Africa is a deeper understanding of the phallus as a ritual symbol, designed with the sole purpose, it would seem, of demonstrating the irrelevance of that very same culture. My chief concern here lies with the phallic stones and the lack of discussion about them in Christian Ethiopia. Less controversially, perhaps, are the rock hewn churches. Understanding local ontologies helps us understand why churches or Islamic pilgrim centres appear where they appear and why they are constructed in the way they are. How can the practices involving these stones be best explained? These rituals date to before, during and after Christianity. How can Aksum be understood without a knowledge of the beliefs of the 'old Cushitic' institutions, including the Sky-God belief? It is impossible to do so. The terms 'Sabaean culture' and 'Christian' hold complex meanings. Wherein lies this complexity? The Aksumites, the Zagwe dynasties and the Solomonic dynasties all had their reasons for going back to a pre-Christian Aksumite symbolism. It becomes ever more important to find out more about what are, and were, the indigenous non-Abrahamic belief systems and about how these relate to the archaeology of the Horn – and to different local cultural encounters – at different times in the history of the region. I hope the Ritual Set will provide an interpretive model to help shed light on practices involving ritual sites and their materiality in the regional indigenous cultural traditions. Many of these beliefs and rituals date to before, during and after Christianity and Islam.

It is noteworthy that a similar Neolithic style of rock art can be found (Červiček, 1979; Brandt and Carder, 1987; Gutherz et al., 2003; Hassan, 1985) in the archaeology of much of Northeast Africa, the so-called Ethio-Sabaean style. This, surely, points to the existence of a major pre-Abrahamic belief system, one that relates to the rock art and has links to the west as far as ancient Egypt and to southern Arabia to the north of the Red Sea and the Horn of Africa. This is the east–west belt of northeastern Africa across which pastoralism led to dynamic movements not only of peoples but, clearly, of cultures and social changes across the millennia.

The notion of fertility, whether it be labelled 'old Cushitic' or just northeast African, carries with it a distinct structure and specific beliefs through ritual systems, landscapes and material culture. This book aims to make sense of these spatial, temporal and human layers, to show what endures despite the dynamics of change and to consider how, starting with the known, one can move on to study the unknown over time. Hence, the book takes as its starting point the significance of reproduction practices in Somali society and the potential for continuity in the traditions associated with the promotion of kinship, peace and prosperity. The archaeology of the Horn of Africa is, as I have shown, fragmentary and contradictory. Only a multidisciplinary perspective can reveal something of the multilayered complexity of the ritual systems that bind the present so firmly to the past.

Notes

1 The word divine is justified by *Waaq/zar/tosa* as the omnipresent God and a divine source of life, in other words, "the presence of life means the presence of *Waaq*" (Bartels, 1983: 97). I have noted sometimes the word divine is denoted as *nidir* in Cushitic languages. *Ebbe* is God in Somali but in Oromo it means the divine or something blessed, for example *lafa eeba* (a blessed place).
2 I use the term, in the same way as have Cerulli (1957) and Lewis (1998), to denote the current non-Muslim and non-Christian indigenous traditions of the Horn of Africa.
3 For a wider discussion focusing on the notion of monumentality in Africa, please see Davies's caution against the use of applying terms such as 'monument' and 'megalithic', which are imported from outside the area, to, say, the cairns in east Africa whose local social significance has been poorly studied (Davies, 2013).

Bibliography

Abbink, J. 1998. An Historical-Anthropological Approach to Islam in Ethiopia: Issues of Identity and Politics. *Journal of African Cultural*, 11(2): 109–124.

Brandt, S. A. and Carder, N. 1987. Pastoral Rock Art in the Horn of Africa: Making Sense of Udder Chaos. *World Archaeology*, 19(2): 194–213.

Braukämper, U. 2004. *Islamic History and Culture in Southern Ethiopia: Collected Essays*. Gottinger Studien Zur Ethnologie. Munster: Lit Verlag Munster.

Cerulli, E. 1957. *Somalia. Scritti vari Editi ed Inediti.* Vol. I. Roma: Istituto Poligra-fico dello Stato. P. V.

Červiček, P. 1979. Some African Affinities of Arabian Rock Art. *Rassegna di studi ethiopici*, 27: 5–12.

Conti Rossini, C. 1905. Note sugli agau: 1. Appunti sulla lingua khamta dell' Averghellé. *Giornale della Società Asiatica Italiana*, 17: 109–122.

Conti Rossini, C. 1928. *Storia d'Etiopia.* Milano: Officina d'arte grafica A. Lucini.

Ehret, C. 1995. The Eastern Horn of Africa, 1000 BC to 1400 AD: The Historical Roots. In A. J. Ahmed (ed.) *The Invention of Somalia.* Lawrenceville, NJ: Red Sea Press.

Fattovich, R. 1987. Some Remarks on the Origins of the Aksumite Stelae. *Annales d'Ethiopie*, 14.

Finneran, N. 2007. *The Archaeology of Ethiopia.* London and New York: Routledge.

Gonzalez-Ruibal, A. 2014. An Archaeology of Resistance. Materiality and Time in an African Borderland. Maryland: Rowman and Littlefield.

Gutherz, X., Cros, J-P. and Lesur, J. 2003. The Discovery of New Rock Paintings in the Horn of Africa: The Rock Shelters of Las Geel, Republic of Somaliland. *Journal of African Archaeology*, 1(2): 227–236.

Hassan, F. A. 1985. Radiocarbon Chronology of Neolithic and Predynastic Sites in Upper Egypt and the Delta. *African Archaeological Review*, 3: 95–116.

Hultin, J. 1994. The Land Is Crying: State Intervention and Cultural Resistance Among the Matcha Oromo. In D. Brokensha (ed.) *A River of Blessings: Essays in Honor of Paul Baxter.* New York: Syracuse University.

Huntingford, G. W. B. 1955. *The Galla of Ethiopia: The Kingdoms of Kafa and Janjero.* London: International Africa Institute.

Joussaume, R. (ed.) 2007. *Tuto Fela et les stèles du sud de L'Ethiopie.* Paris: Éditions Recherche sur les civilisations.

Levine, D. N. 2000. *Greater Ethiopia: The Evolution of a Multiethnic Society.* 2nd ed. Chicago and London: University of Chicago Press.

Lewis, I. 1998. *Saints and Somalis: Popular Islam in a Clan-Based Society.* Law-renceville, NJ and Asmara, Eritrea: Red Sea Press.

Lynch, M. and Donahue, R. 1980. A Statistical Analysis of Rock-Art Sites in North-west Kenya. *Journal of Field Archaeology*, 7: 75–85.

Lynch, M. and Robbins, L. H. 1978. Namoratunga: The First Archaeoastronomical Evidence in Sub-Saharan Africa. *Science*, 200: 766–768.

Martin, B. G. 1974. Arab Migration to East Africa in Medieval Times. *The International Journal of African Historical Studies*, 7(3): 367–390.

Mire, S. 2015. Mapping of the Archaeology of Somaliland: Religion, Art, Script, Time, Urbanism, Trade and Empire. *African Archaeological Review*, 32(1): 111–136.

Phillipson, D. W. 2007. From Yeha to Lalibela: An Essay in Cultural Continuity. *Journal of Ethiopian Studies*, 40(1–2): 1–19.

Phillipson, D. W. 2012. *Foundations of an African Civilization: Aksum and the Northern Horn 1000 BC to 1300 AD.* Oxford: James Currey; Addis Ababa: Addis Ababa University.

Phillipson, L. and Sulas, F. 2005. Cultural Continuity in Aksumite Lithic Tool Pro-duction: The Evidence from Mai Agam. *Azania*, 40: 1–18.

Sihab ad-Din, Ahmed, b. Abd al-Qadir b. Salam b. Uthman. 2003. *Futuh al-Haba-sha.* (Written Between 1540–1560). History of Ethiopia 1490–1889. Translated by Paul Lester Stenhouse. Annotations by Richard Pankhurst. Hollywood, CA: Tsehai.

Trimingham, J. S. 1965. *Islam in Ethiopia.* 2nd ed. Oxford: Oxford University Press.

Ullendorff, E. 1955. *The Semitic Languages of Ethiopia: A Comparative Phonology.* London: Taylor's.

Ullendorff, E. 1960. *The Ethiopians. An Introduction to Country and People.* London and New York: OUP.

Wallis Budge, E. A. 1970 [1928]. *A History of Ethiopia: Nubia and Abyssinia.* Oosterhout: Anthropological Publications.

2 Sacred landscapes, materiality and fertility rituals

The object of the historian is at all times to combine all sources that are relevant and available for the investigation and there is no value in giving a privileged position to one or the other. What is important is the question and what sources are available to answer it.

(Eric Hobsbawm, 1979)

Thus, it was that during my quest to understand indigenous[1] institutions, religious syncretism and fertility rituals in the Horn of Africa, it became clear quite early on that archaeology alone is not enough. Nor is history or anthropology (Mire, 2016a: 283). I therefore decided to use a multidisciplinary approach to study the triadic relationship between material culture, landscapes and ritual in this region. I explore this relationship by studying certain beliefs and practices relating to fertility, a subject which is of permanent concern and of paramount importance to the way of life of the people of the Horn of Africa in general and, particularly, to the Cushitic[2] speaking peoples (including the Somali, the Oromo and the Konso). This book explores the historical significance of the materials, rituals (including legends) and landscape of the twelfth-century religious centre of Aw-Barkhadle, near Hargeisa, which belongs to a Sufi Saint Sheikh Sharif Yusuf Al-Kawnayn (a.k.a. Aw-Barkhadle) who is credited with the conversion of northern Somalis to the Islamic faith in that century. This sacred site is arguably the most important Muslim pilgrimage centre in the Horn of Africa.

I suggest that not only has Aw-Barkhadle been a centre of Muslim pilgrimage since the twelfth century; it is also a ruined mediaeval town which may once have been the lost capital of the Awdal (Adal) which flourished in the early decades of the sixteenth century in an area previously known as Dogor. The few references to Saint Aw-Barkhadle in the old literature, though assuming that 'Aw Bekele' (Aw-Barkhadle) at 'Dakkar' (Doggor) must be located near Harar, do indeed link his centre with the location of the ancient Awdal capital and shed light too on the centre's significance as an ideologically important burial site for the Muslim rulers of the Ifat (Yifat) state and, particularly, for the Walashma dynasty of the thirteenth–fourteenth centuries AD, which traded with countries in the Indian Ocean region, as is shown by the pottery evidence from the Yuan dynasty in China and elsewhere. Aw-Barkhadle may have been a revered burial site not only for the Ifat rulers but also for the first rulers of Awdal who may well have settled there before going on to Harar. If so, the site would once have been the seat of Sabra'ad Din, the grandson of Sa'adadin, who ruled Zaila, the seat of the Ifat kingdom. It would not be at all surprising were the sixteenth century Awdal kingdom to have had a capital in this central or eastern part of the country: I have identified the ruins of many towns, from Berbera and Togdheer to the east all the way to the Sanaag region (Mire, 2015). Archaeological excavations will soon further illuminate the history of Aw-Barkhadle.

Furthermore, this book uncovers the site's multireligious heritage by revealing an important pre-Islamic heritage in the form of Christian burials and stelae cemeteries which include decorated and phallic gravestones and non-Islamic burial mounds (cairns) that shed light on indigenous (Cushitic) religious beliefs. These findings demonstrate a religiously syncretic ritual nature when taken in conjunction with the different rituals currently, or until recently, taking place at the site.

Drawing upon unique archaeological and ethnographic data – the latter consisting of interviews and participant observation – I present a holistic interpretation of rituals and practices at the shrine and elsewhere in the Somali region, setting these against the wider historical background of indigenous 'Cushitic institutions' and ancestral veneration.

I argue that contemporary practices carried out within the framework of Islam in the Horn of Africa also contain elements of indigenous traditions. These are exemplified both through abstract concepts originating in the belief in the Sky-God, or *Waaq*, as Eastern Cushitic speaking people refer to this ancient god, and the more tangible and specific ritual uses of shrines and landscape features such as tombs, sacred stones and enclosures, sacred water sources, hills and trees. I pay particular attention to the relationship between kinship (genealogy) and human fertility as mediated or blessed by the religious (sacred) ancestors through living healers and sheikhs/sheikhas.

I also explore the pre-Islamic ritual heritage of the Horn of Africa through comparative research in the region. The region currently lacks a locally appropriate theoretical framework within which to study its sacred landscapes, associated rituals and material culture. The book constructs such a framework through its investigation and contextualisation of symbolic landscapes, material culture and the nature of the rituals relating to these. I consider the existence and continuity of the material manifestations of ideologies other than Islam and Christianity in the Horn of Africa. I ask a question fundamental to this study: *why do popular fertility cults continue to be followed in the Horn of Africa?* My research, therefore, penetrates deep inside the rituals of non-/pre-Islamic origin and the use of the landscape, including archaeological remains. I will also shed light on the material manifestation and symbolism of fertility rituals.

An understanding of the indigenous practices and religious syncretism in the archaeological landscapes and the material culture forms the bedrock of this study. Such an understanding can be achieved by recording evidence of the contemporary ritual use of these landscapes through examining and identifying, explicitly and by inference, non-Islamic ideas and elements (such as the phallic stones and dolmens) of the landscape and their relationship with indigenous (local) practices. I therefore examine in detail the current ritual use of the landscapes and pay special attention to the significance, past and present, of ritual and ideological objects in the landscape around Aw-Barkhadle (including its mausoleum, tombs, shrines, ruined town and the surrounding hills).

According to oral accounts, Muslims have continuously used this landscape for at least the past 800 years. The site is named after the Sufi saint buried there, Sharif Yusuf Aw-Barkhadle (a.k.a Sharif Yusuf Al-Kawnayn) who, it is said, came to the area 850 years ago to convert locals to Islam by preaching the Qur'an at the site. There is also a ruined town in the sacred landscape which seems to have blossomed around the thirteenth–sixteenth century as the site's Islamic ideological significance grew. From my interviews I learnt that Aw-Barkhadle is of paramount significance as *the* pilgrim centre in northern Somalia, with thousands of people taking part in the annual commemoration ceremonies held in the mid-1960s and 1970s. Aw-Barkhadle is not only thought to have converted Somalis/Berbers (people of the Berbera region) but also people far further afield: even the peoples of the Indian Ocean from places such as the Maldives and Sri-Lanka are said to recognise Sherif Yusuf Al-Kawnayn as a saint.

As legend goes, Aw-Barkhadle took over the site from Bu'ur Ba'ayr (said to be a Jew who had a congregation at the centre) after he had won a dual against him. Aw-Barkhadle therefore offers an ideal case study with which to explore the syncretism of beliefs in the Somali past. It offers plenty of data, ethnographic as well as archaeological, and a landscape that is still actively used today for ritual purposes. In this study, I therefore refer to archaeological landscapes as areas consisting of features that have both an embedded and active ritual significance and an archaeological scientific relevance.

This material allows me to investigate, and come to understand more clearly, how these rituals can be classified as non- or pre-Islamic. Consequently, I use the archaeology of the sacred centre of Aw-Barkhadle together with its ritual landscape to illuminate the nature of the several beliefs evidenced here. By investigating the role that sacrifice and rituals such as those to do with fertility plays in creating the ritual landscape, I explore how the archaeological landscape is incorporated into contemporary ritual activity. I discover, too, the part that indigenous and local rituals play in the understanding of past ideologies and the possible continuity of practices.

My approach to the archaeology of the Horn of Africa during the twelfth to thirteenth centuries is a holistic one, particularly in relation to the material data. I use the known to discover the unknown. I investigate what Lewis referred to as a 'Cushitic substratum of Somali Mohammedanism' (Lewis, 1994a: 102).

> In interpreting Cushitic belief among the Somali, the wider literature describing the religion of the Afar, Saho, and Oromo has been drawn upon, but I do not deduce from Cushitic religion in general any belief or custom for whose independent existence among the Somali there is not reasonable evidence. It is not implied that all those features of Somali social structure whose interaction with Islam is considered are necessarily typically Cushitic, but simply that it in the pre-Islamic state of Somali society they were related to Cushitic institutions.
>
> (Lewis, 1998: 2)

I reiterate Lewis's disclaimer. He suggests that the Sufi impact on the religious structure of society and the power of Sufi sheikhs (*baraka*) is part of 'the genealogical canalisation of divine grace' (1994b: 102). I take his point of view onboard when interpreting Cushitic beliefs among the Somali, drawing on the notion of ancestral veneration to gain *baraka* and exploring only those beliefs and practices that exist among the Somali and that are associated with, or attributed to, the so called Cushitic institutions.

Aw-Barkhadle's landscape, as well as the site itself, is considered to be a major sacred centre. According to oral accounts, as noted earlier, Saint Aw-Barkhadle's relation to the site dates back about 850 years, to the twelfth–thirteenth centuries AD. Furthermore, prior to Aw-Barkhadle, the site was used by Bu'ur Ba'ayr. The notion that the site dates back earlier than Aw-Barkhadle's arrival is supported by the nature of the archaeological record which includes non-/pre-Islamic graves such as phallic grave markers, a stela marked with a Coptic cross dating to the fourth–seventh centuries, cairns, dolmens and stelae cemetery fields, with symbols.

Landscapes always have a special significance.

> Landscape everywhere in the world is a construct of human beings – whether through human ascription to it or mythological creation, or through physical actions by the humans themselves. . . . Whatever the difficulties of recognizing such special sites from the archaeological record – all societies in the past would have recognized, as do all societies in the present, some features of their landscapes (if not all the earth) as special.
>
> (Ucko, 1994: xviii–xix)

Ucko's statement is important: regardless of Aw-Barkhadle's archaeology or its material culture, locals see this landscape in its entirety as holy. Other scholars have already pointed to the potential of landscapes to shed light on the archaeology of religion and beliefs (e.g. Loubser, 2008). However, I am, as far as I know, the first (Mire, 2006) to apply the term 'sacred landscape' to a sacred area containing archaeological features; and the first to introduce it into the archaeology of the Horn of Africa and to speak of landscapes rather than sites in the medieval archaeology Somaliland (Mire, 2009).

More importantly, these archaeological features are also central to the rituals that are currently performed within the sacred space (Figure 2.1). And these rituals lead to an understanding of the symbolic use of this archaeological landscape.

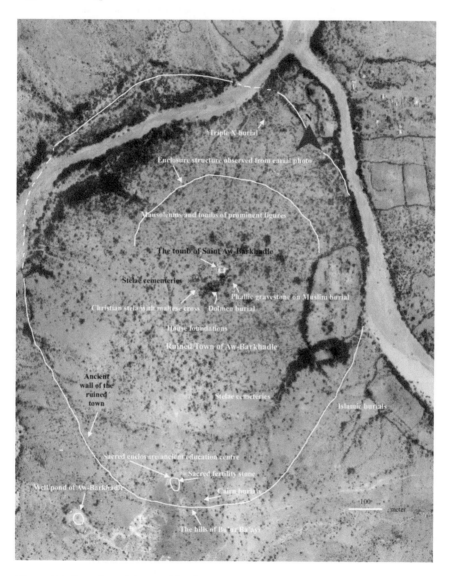

Figure 2.1 Site plan of Aw-Barkhadle

I define 'sacred landscape(s)', in the Somali context, as an area used only for ritual purposes and one where other activities are prohibited. It is significant that the Somali term *amran* can mean either 'blessed' or 'sacred'. One therefore has to study the nature of people's ritual interaction with individual objects, features or spaces in order to decide whether the word *amran* refers to something that is 'blessed' or 'sacred'. Sometimes a behaviour or an object (for example a tree) may be sacred or blessed and still be allowed to feature in a non-ritual context, while for other features or spaces only ritual interaction is allowed. The landscape of Aw-Barkhadle is considered *amran* and only ritual activities are permitted to take place here. And not only is the landscape sacred; an even greater degree of sanctity is attributed to the mausoleum of Saint Aw-Barkhadle itself (Figure 2.2), a place where people are required to take off their shoes before entering. When I use the word 'sacred' to refer to trees, stones, water sources and materials, it is because there is evidence that these objects have a sacred meaning for the local people today.

Incidentally, this is not the only sacred landscape in Somaliland; others exist at the pilgrimage centres of Sheikh Ishaaq, Sheikh Samaroon, Sheikh Iise, Sheikh Harti and Sheikh Daarood. And the reuse of particular sacred places by different religions is common around the world: the Dom of the Rock in Jerusalem, for example, is sacred to both Jews and Muslims.

Figure 2.2 The Mausoleum of Saint Aw-Barkhadle

Western scholars have not been able to study Aw-Barkhadle. This is probably because there is very little opportunity for non-venerating foreigners to gain access to sacred centres. Ritual sites in Somalia have been inaccessible to Westerners for a variety of reasons. I. M. Lewis has told me that he was chased away when he tried to walk into the Aw-Barkhadle site in the mid-1950s (pers. comm. June 2006). I have also learnt that not only is Aw-Barkhadle inaccessible to Westerners; it is also protected from non-venerating Somalis. However, as a Somali and as a woman, I have been able not only to visit the site but also to penetrate deep into its cultural depths.

This opportunity has enabled me to discover the archaeology of the site that Lewis (1998) was unable to report. I have found evidence to suggest a continuity in the ritual use of Aw-Barkhadle from pre-Islamic times to the present and evidence of overlapping burial traditions over the centuries. A relative dating system, based on a comparison between Islamic and non-Islamic burials, supports this argument. The pre-Islamic types of mounds are called *taalo* and *araweelo* (Figure 2.3), and similar mounds excavated elsewhere reveal a clearly non-Islamic culture, given the evidence of their grave goods, body positions and the layout of the graves (which do not face Mecca). As noted previously, Aw-Barkhadle also yielded a Christian burial *in situ*, with a Christian cross marked on its gravestone (Figure 2.4).

Figure 2.3 Burial mounds or cairns, also known locally as *Araweelooyin* at Aw-Barkhadle

Figure 2.4 A Coptic Christian cross marked gravestone *in situ* at Aw-Barkhadle

Locals may also be reluctant to let foreigners come to the site because of their belief that non-Muslim groups (regional or foreign) may try to appropriate the site. Oral records, for example, tell of a former Jewish presence at both Aw-Barkhadle and Lukuud, another sacred site, and the archaeology might be able to support this account as permission has now been given to excavate during the coming year. There was certainly a local knowledge of Judaism. The archaeology has uncovered the existence of two gravestones engraved with the Star of David in the Dhubato area, 30 minutes' drive from the Aw-Barkhadle site (Figure 2.5a). In addition, what appears to be a star of David with images of what looks like a menorah and other symbols (Figure 2.5b and Figure 2.5c) have been found at the Da'awaleh/Dawa'aleh rock shelter at Dhaymoole. I have pictures of artefacts dug up by a farmer in the Berbera region showing small tablets cut in the shape of hands with fingers carved out and engraved with the star of David and menorahs and other symbols. More rock engravings of the Star of David are reported in the Caynaba district in the Sool region of Somaliland. If these are of Jewish origin, this would suggest the possible coexistence of people of different religions in the Somali region, as is seen today amongst Ethiopia's Christian, Muslim and Beta Israel (popularly known as Falasha) communities.

Figure 2.5a A gravestone marked with the Star of David, found in Dhubato area

Figure 2.5b Da'awaleh rock art site includes a symbol believed to be a Menorah

Figure 2.5c What looks like Star of David rock art Dawaaleh Dhaymoole

Furthermore, evidence of a more recent Jewish presence can be found in the Jewish quarters (*Sakadda Yuhuuda*) in Hargeisa and Berbera, which are said to belong to old Jewish communities, some thought to have fled from Yemen. These claims suggest that an awareness persists of a recent time when many more religious practices existed than do at present. In ancient times, it is possible that there were Jewish communities living in areas of the Somali territory (Figure 2.5d), perhaps migrants from Arabia or offshoots of the Beta Israel and Falasha communities which reside in present-day Ethiopia. Despite these many echoes of Judaism, the distribution of Christian burials in Somaliland suggests that the Christian communities were bigger than the Jewish (Mire, 2015). A practice observed at Aw-Barkhadle (see Chapter Three) of painting a Christian cross on the foreheads of worshippers during the *ziyara* (pilgrimage) perhaps echoes recent syncretic practices at the site.

I have also come across references to Bu'ur Ba'ayr as King Mohamed Haniif of the Yibir. Some say he was a Muslim Yibir but not a 'proper' Muslim and that he practised witchcraft, something of which many Yibir are (historically) accused. Even though the bigger Somali clans acknowledge that the Yibir are good tanners and skilled in masonry, they are generally looked down upon in Somali society. They are not allowed to intermarry with other Somali clans, only with other 'outcast' clans (Kirk, 1905). The elders I have interviewed from the Yibir claim that the name 'Yibir' is one given to them by the dominant Somali clans. They, however, call themselves Beesha (people of) Mohammed Haniifa and claim that they are descended

Figure 2.5d Alleged Jewish burials at Aw-Barkhadle

from an Arab sheikh, Mohammed Ahmed Bin Haniif, who settled at Aw-Barkhadle in order to spread Islam to the rest of the Somali population. This statement is not recorded by Kirk (ibid.) who reports they are called 'Yibir' and makes no mention of the idea of Haniif being an Arab who spread Islam, despite this being a common *raison d'etre* for all claimed Arab lineage founders. According to the literature I have read, it is only ever Aw-Barkhadle that is associated with this legend of an Arab sheikh who spreads Islam. The dominant Somali clans, however, tell a different story: according to them, the Yibir are grouped together with the Gabooye community which includes the Tumaals and the Madhibaans. The M. Haniifa elders say that these three clans have formed a brotherhood because of the discrimination they suffer within Somali society. All three clans, of course, firmly adhere to Islam and speak Somali – and are in no way physically different from the rest of the Somali community.

The available literature sheds little light on how these three clans originated, although the Tumaal are said to have had some contact with the Mijerteen clan (ibid.). I met the leaders of the M. Haniifa community, including the Suldaan of the Haniifa clan, in Hargeisa in the summer of 2017, to discuss my research into the Aw-Barkhadle centre and the legend of Bu'ur Ba'ayr. They gave me a copy of Kirk's article and pointed me towards other references. Kirk (ibid.) talks about how he gained the trust of the members of the three clans by managing to speak to them on his own without an external interpreter. He discusses the 'secret dialects' of the Yibir (traditionally leather workers, 'sorcerers' and 'jugglers') and of the Madhibaan (known as 'hunters of game') (ibid.: 2). Révoil has noted that the Madhibaan in the Nugaal Valley were equipped with a bow called *gaboi'o* and poisoned arrows (*qaanso*) and a sling (*waraf*) (Révoil, 1882). Impressed by their skills as surgeons, he wrote '*[L]es midgans sont les plus ingénieux des bédouins*' (ibid.: 325) ('the Madhibaan are the most ingenious of the nomadic Somalis'). Despite their skills, however, the three clans of the Gabooye are considered to be 'Sab' (outcasts) while the rest of Somali society considers itself to be 'Gob' (gentry), with the 'Gob' creating the 'Sab'. Kirk reports that the Somali attribute slightly different negative qualities to these three clans (Kirk, 1905): he records that the Tumaal (traditionally blacksmiths who made arrows, lance heads and fish hooks etc.) 'are not actively disliked'. Both the Tumaal and the Madhibaan are less excluded than the Yibir. The Tumaal are believed to have once been a part of the Somali clans but through intermarriage to have come to be excluded as 'outcasts' (Kirk, 1905). That they once belonged to this region is signified in the use of the name 'Xabaalo Tumaalood' (the 'Cemetery of Blacksmiths') to mark an archaeological cemetery site on the Berbera Road nearby (Mire, 2015).

According to Kirk, the Yibir are believed to be 'pariahs' who serve under chiefs as 'jesters' and 'jugglers' (Kirk, 1905). This may, however, no longer be the case as I have never personally heard a Somali person referring to the Yibir as 'jesters' nor seen them in that role myself. However, at marriages, births and certain festivals they do have a distinct role to play, not least in the production of amulets, leather ornaments and traditional art.

> Whereas all other Somalis have recognised territories and watering-places for each tribe or subtribe, these three outcast tribes are a scattered people of no fixed home, who often attach themselves in small groups or families as 'abbans' or servants, to the various Somali tribes all over the country. Meanwhile, the latter will not recognise them as of Somali birth, nor will they eat or intermarry with them.
>
> (ibid.: 91)

Somali society certainly discriminates against the indigenous Bantu and the descendants of enslaved peoples, a legacy of slavery activity in action (Besteman, 1999). However, Eno and Kusow (2014: 91) observe a different kind of discrimination against the Gabooye community:

> The hate discourse used against the Yibir, Gabooye, and Tumal outcast communities is premised on assumption of their supposed *unholy origin* [my italics] and their engagement in occupations and social activities that are despised by the so-called Somali noble groups.

I will return later to the Somalis' claim that their origins are grounded in holiness as I want to explore this idea in more detail when discussing the notion of divine kinship which is central to this book. However, just as a similar claim to a sacred descent in the northern Ethiopian highlands is used, both intentionally and unintentionally, to mark sophistication and to legitimise the dominance of the Christian faith, so the dominant Somali clans use blood lineage and their assumption of an origin in the Islamic bloodline to mobilise or subjugate sections of the wider Somali society.

It may never be known how 'Mohamed Haniif', a lineage founder of the Muslim Yibir, became denoted to 'Bu'ur Ba'ayr', the supposedly infamous 'wicked' 'pagan'/'Jew' whom, according to legend, Aw-Barkhadle defeated in order to Islamise the Somalis. However, the Haniifa I have met explained to me that a clue to the original role of the Yibir may lie in the *samanyo* or compensation, traditionally called *anasnimo*, which is received at a child-birth or a wedding. The Yibir, he suggested, might have been a Somali com-munity responsible for collecting the type of taxes known as *yegibiri*. Those who paid these taxes received a piece of wood to show that they had paid. According to the current Haniifa Suldaan and other elders of the commu-nity, these tax collectors came to be known as Yibir, a name which derives from *yegibiri* or *gibiri*, both words meaning tax in the Amhara language.[3] Given the social complexity evident from the archaeology, it seems likely that the people who lived in this ancient ruined town would once have had to pay taxes.

However, the *samanyo* is nowadays paid not as a tax but as a means of gaining a blessing or avoiding a curse, the threat of which is said to have been every bit as powerful in the past as it is perceived to be today:

> In return for the fee the Yibir gives the Somali a charm, 'Makharam,' consisting of a piece of his sacred tree, sewn in a piece of leather. The effect of a persistent refusal is the curse of the Yibir, supposed to result in a violent death to the refusing party or deformity in his child.
>
> (Kirk, 1905: 91–108)

The elders of the Yibir clan in Hargeisa also refuted another legend about Bu'ur Ba'ayr, that he as ritual leader slept with the bride on every one of the six nights of the wedding. They offered me their own explanation for this story. At that time, they say, the consummation of the marriage was not allowed to take place if the girl was having her period. Haniif, as their religious leader, would have the task of confirming that the bride was not menstruating at the time. He is said to have done this by seating the bride on the fertility stone (Figure 2.6) in the sacred enclosure (Figure 2.7) to see if she stained the stone. If she did, then she had to wait for six nights in his compound before the consummation could take place. I will later discuss the issue of blood, purity and ritual, or symbolic intercourse, as it is linked

Figure 2.6 The fertility stone (*dhagaha dhalka*) at the sacred enclosure at Aw-Barkhadle

Figure 2.7 Sacred enclosure at Aw-Barkhadle

in specific societies of the Eastern Cushitic speaking peoples. This story about the Yibir, however, serves as a reminder that there may be a number of possible interpretations for this rather controversial belief and some doubts about the authenticity of the dominant Somali clans' ideas about the Yibir and the first nights of a marriage.

The Yibir themselves have a very different account of their origins as reported by Kirk (ibid.: 91–108) who relays the 'literal translation of the Yibir original, as dictated to me by a leading Yibir'. His account goes as follows:

> Long ago there was a priest who lived in a place alone. The unbelievers of old and the Moslems who lived among them were at war. Now the priest was a great man, and the unbelievers came to him and said, 'Give us an herb.' 'Why do you wish it?' he said, and they answered, 'We will kill with it these Moslems.' Then he said, 'It is much money, which, if you do not give me, I will not give you my herb.' Thus, they paid for the herb one hundred pieces of silver and one hundred camels, and he handed them the herb. Then the Moslems went out on a raid, and the unbelievers also went out on a raid. For two hundred rains, they lived in a place, and the place they went to was never found. Then the Moslems died there, and (the unbelievers attacked the old priest, and he died), and his property was looted. The priest had a young boy, who had left the place, and he and four others lived together. The boy was called Mohammed Haniif, and he became a priest, and used to (asuwano yu difadin jirei). While he was there and (o asuquano difadsha), a great priest came to him, called AuBakhardli, who said, 'How is it that you remain there and are a priest?' And he answered 'Are you better Mussulman than I?' And he said, 'I am.' Then he said, 'Show me why you are a better Mussulman.' And he said, 'I can pass through that place; do you do so.' Then he passed through beneath the great hill, and when he reached the other side, Au-Bakhardli said, 'Come back through the hill.' And while he was coming through, AuBakhardli said, 'O hill, seize him.' Then the hill came together, and the place where he went through could not be seen. And so in the middle of the hill the priest died, and there died the priest of our tribe.

It is important to note that although this version differs greatly from the one currently prevalent, the bottom line is the same: as evident from the following conclusion, it rationalizes the compensation;

> Then the boys that he begat said, 'You have killed our father, give us something for it.' And Au-Bakhardli [sic] said as follows: 'Shall I give you one hundred camels to-day, or shall I pay you for every boy begotten of a Somali one ewe, and at a marriage shall I pay you one piece of silver?' And the sons said, 'Give us for your sons an ewe, and at a marriage a piece of silver. Hereafter by this agreement we will receive that for the blood money.' By that agreement we receive our payment, we Yibirs. When the money and the ewe are paid to us we give in return a small piece of wood, thus we earn our living.

Kirk also mentions other versions of this story including the one that suggests that Haniif was removed because he conducted 'all kinds of sexual licence'. Another version is that Mohammed Haniif could tell the future and predicted the arrival of Sheikh Ishaaq from Arabia, warning the local Gala Suldaan. When Sheikh Ishaaq arrived, he married Hamida, the daughter of a local leader called Somal; he then summoned his cousin Aw-Barkhadle from Arabia to remove Haniif and converted the people to Islam.

A wife sometimes features in Haniif's story too. According to the leaders of the Yibir, he had a wife called Hanfeley (Xanfeley). The Somalis have a saying, which the Yibir leaders I spoke to dismissed as absurd, that if a Yibir person dies they are never buried; instead they disappear in a whirlwind or smoke. However, this saying was supported in the Yibirs' account given to Kirk (1905) in which Haniif's wife Hanfeley is believed to have disappeared near Harar or Adari, transformed into smoke. Kirk notes that a tomb was built on the spot where she was last seen, near Harar. Four sacred trees grow in front of Hanfele's tomb. And the *makharam* wood is cut from these sacred trees in an important tree-cutting ceremony (ibid.).

The legends suggest that, regardless of Haniif's personal religious orientation, different beliefs were being followed at this centre at the time of Aw-Barkhadle's visit. The archaeology visible at the site supports this notion.

It is noteworthy that what is frequently referred to as 'witchcraft' in colonial or Abrahamic Africa often contains within it elements of indigenous belief systems and practices. Aw-Barkhadle is a place where offerings are made to saints and *Baraka* is sought. In the time of Bu'ur Ba'ayr, the legend says that Haniif practiced 'witchcraft'. However, there is a very close similarity in both Somali and Oromo between the word for witchcraft (*fal fala/fall* in Somali and *fallfala* in Oromo) and the word for sacrifice (*falat'ne*) and the ritual offerer (*falata*). Haniif was, it seems, offering up sacrifices rather than practising witchcraft. But the coincidences of language have allowed those who today follow different religious beliefs to stigmatise unfairly the traditional pre-Islamic or non-Islamic/non-Christian religious notions.

Pre-Christian and pre-Islamic religions have not been systematically studied in the Horn of Africa (Ethiopia, Eritrea, Somalia, northern Kenya and Djibouti). The region is populated by mostly (Eastern) Cushitic speaking peoples. Anthropologists have only referred to what they call the Cushitic religion or Cushitic institutions (e.g. Cerulli, 1957; Hallpike, 1972; Lewis, 1998; Loo, 1991). Some very useful insights and observations are provided by Bartels (1983) and Hallpike (1972). Often Western anthropologists, familiar with monotheistic religions and unfamiliar with the indigenous institutions, understandably focus on Christianity and Islam, paying very little attention to indigenous religions or ritual systems. And neither do archaeologists. The present study attempts to fill in some of these gaps.

Classifications such as 'Hamitic' and 'Semitic' originate from the names of the biblical sons of Noah; Ham and Sem and are found in linguistic studies of the languages of the Horn of Africa. It is debatable, to say the least, whether these will stand up to scientific scrutiny (for example, the use of terms such as 'Kushitic'/'Cushitic' to describe the 'Hamitic' speaking people, Ehret, 1995; Trimingham, 1965). It is also unclear from some of the litera-ture about the Horn of Africa whether the term 'Cushitic' is being used to refer to an ethnic group, a language or a religion. When used to denote an ethnic group, it will refer to the whole of the Horn of Africa, i.e. a popula-tion of over 100 million 'Cushitic'/'Kushites' (e.g. Trimingham, 1965: 16). Used in the linguistic context, it may exclude the Amhara and Tigrai on the grounds that these groups currently speak languages that are categorised as 'Semitic'. In terms of religion, it leads Levine to use the ubiquity of the Sky-God (known through the variations of the cognates *Waaq*, *tosa* and *zar*) to talk about 'Greater Ethiopia'. Levine concludes

> That the Amhara culture is not *sui generis* but must be viewed as part of the broader culture area of Greater Ethiopia, is indicated, dramati-cally and paradigmatically, by the fact that cognates of all three of these names have been used by the Christian Amhara to designate various supernatural forces.
>
> (2000: 48)

My contribution to this debate is to ask whether the Amhara and the Tigrai also worshiped the Sky-God. The site of Aksum was probably populated by Tigrai and Cushitic groups; 'Aksum' is a combination of *Ak* (mean-ing 'water' in the Cushitic languages) and *šum (shum)* meaning 'chief' in Amhara/Tigrai; so 'Aksum' comes to mean 'chief of water' or 'water chief' (Finneran, 2007). If *Ak* is a reference to *Waak/Waaq*, I suggest in Chapter Six of this book that the name might actually refer to the religious nature of the centre itself and specifically to the type of pre-Christian religion that was practised there and which gave rise to the name Aksum (Chief of water). I propose, moreover, that the word Aksum might also mean the Sky-God or the God of Rain (water). If it does, then this would suggest that it would be wrong to limit the spread of the Sky-God religion to its distribution amongst present-day Cushitic speaking groups (a presumption which carries with it all the pitfalls associated with attempting to define cultural areas). Instead, its ancient roots possibly lie in the Horn as a whole (perhaps even extend-ing to current day Sudan, Nubia and adjacent Red Sea regions). If this is so, then I will need to construct my Ritual Set by drawing upon evidence not only from the archaeology found within the current territories of the cur-rent Cushitic speaking peoples. I will need also to look beyond these areas, recognising the fluidity of ideas – ideas that are rooted in an area through time and that adhere to divine fertility through a set of beliefs and associated fertility practices, landscapes and material culture.

It is not an easy task to identify the pre-Abrahamic religions of the 'Cushitic institutions'. The ideology and religion that emerge from a study of the practices common to the present-day peoples of the Horn reveal a religion that was to become marginalised and followed only by groups who had themselves often become isolated and vulnerable as a result of the Christian and Islamic conversions. The identification of these early religious practices is further complicated by their religious syncretism within the partly Christian and partly Islamic communities.

I will nevertheless focus on the institutions that are loosely considered to be Cushitic ones, i.e. those which refer to the Sky-God, *Waaq*, (a.k.a. *djar*, *Waaqa*, or *waga*) (e.g. Paulitschke, 1888; Conti Rossini, 1905; Almeida, 1954; Cerulli, 1957; Loo, 1991; Levine, 2000). I adopt a mainly linguistic and religious perspective to define the term in order to understand the relationship between groups of people and the ritual systems that join the past with the present. In so doing, I remain mindful of the dangers of essentialising ideas about what is or not 'Cushitic'. I tread cautiously when referring to what others have termed the 'Cushitic religion' or 'Cushitic Institutions'.

In defining this pre-Islamic and pre-Christian belief in the Horn of Africa, it is worth noting that another pre-Islamic and pre-Christian religion existed in the region, the 'Sabaean-religion'. This religion is thought to have influenced the cultures of the Horn of Africa from the early first millennium BC (Phillipson, 1997). The Sabaean religion also has a heaven-god, *ather* (*azhar*) in the southern Arabian kingdoms (Serjeant, 1976, and as noted by Levine, 2000). Found mainly on the shores of the Red Sea, it gave rise to a complex relationship of cultural, religious and social interaction and influence between people of the Horn of Africa and southern Arabia (Kobishchanov, 1979). However, as Phillipson (2012) and Fattovich (1987) both argue, the Aksumite culture had its foundations in distinctly African traditions.

When discussing the 'old Cushitic' religion and the characteristics credited to it by others (e.g. Paulitschke, 1888; Conti Rossini, 1905; Almeida, 1954; Cerulli, 1957; Loo, 1991; Bartels, 1983; Hallpike, 1972; Levine, 2000), I identify and examine those rituals and materials (including landscape features) which I believe are associated with this ancient religion's ritual system. Hence, my examination focuses on a set of artefacts and landscape features associated with ideas of fertility. I identify certain specific materials and associated religious ideas found within the present practices and perceptions of the local peoples of the Horn of Africa and which are supported by the archaeological material at sites such as Aw-Barkhadle. I attempt to make sense of this configuration of materials through the Ritual Set, described later in the book. I suggest that the identification of a particular set of materials does not of itself provide evidence of the Cushitic religion(s). Indigenous regional religious practices and their association with particular societies in both the past and the present play their part too.

My aim, as I have already explained, is to create a locally appropriate theoretical framework, one which will use this study's discoveries and analyses to explore for the first time the connections between regional rituals, practices, material culture, concepts and landscapes from both an indigenous and a comparative perspective and across both time and space.

My notion of a Ritual Set recognises the co-occurrence of a set of materials and features associated with fertility and an ancestral veneration in the local context of the Aw-Barkhadle landscape. I also make use of the relevant linguistic sources, historical linguistics and the ethnohistory of the region. Alongside these sources, I have chosen to study the data from relevant archaeological sites in the Horn of Africa in the belief that the Ritual Set is a methodology that can be applied elsewhere to improve our understanding of particular configurations of archaeological data elsewhere. I identify a locally appropriate theoretical framework and apply it to a particular configuration of the type of archaeology found at sites such as Aw-Barkhadle. I anchor this archaeology in the ethnography and ethnohistory of the Horn region and within the continuity that I claim for the practices identified. It sadly remains the case in Africa that local ontologies and the cultural context seldom play a part in archaeological interpretation (e.g. Andah, 1995; Posnansky, 2013) due mainly to a lack of knowledge about indigenous institutions and the local languages.

As I have already noted, I make no attempt to match any one single linguistic culture with any one particular material culture in the region; I am well aware that this would be impossible. More importantly, perhaps, I am always aware of the possibility that traditions and practices can change through time – and that even languages can too. I also do not exclude the possibility that notions similar to those associated with the northeast Africans or Cushitic groups may be found in a non-Cushitic speaking group or elsewhere in Africa.

A few studies have already tried to identify the fundamental links that join the peoples of the Horn of Africa. Of particular relevance here is a chapter by Levine on the foundations of unity in 'Greater Ethiopia' (Levine, 2000) and Cerulli's comments (Cerulli, 1957) on the collective traditions of the Horn of Africa. Trimingham (1965) suggests that the Amhara and Tigrai were originally Cushitic speaking people but argued that their language has become 'semitised' as a result of South Arabian influence. I also note Phillipson's view that such 'Semitic' influences were greatly limited (Phillipson, 2012; cf. Fattovich, 1987). Furthermore, groups such as the Guraghe exist today who speak a language classified as 'Semitic' while at the same time sharing many practices (such as that of the Sky-God religion) followed by the Cushitic speaking peoples who surround them. I realise, above all, that archaeology needs to tap into the sociological, anthropological and linguistic studies that can provide so much more information about the ethnography and ethnohistory of the peoples of the Horn of Africa.

Rituals and practices syncretised with new religions such as Christianity and Islam seem to have led to practices that are specific to cultural areas

(Cerulli, 1957; Lewis, 1994a, b, 1998). Although old beliefs are assimilated and slightly altered, their commonalities remain visible.

I suggest that there are certain shared characteristics that run throughout the rituals followed by these groups and that these are linked to a ritual system of a fertility ideology with reproductive activities involving human beings, animals and crops. These shared characteristics can be recognised in the rituals practiced in Aw-Barkhadle and the continuity with the past that is demonstrated in the way that certain landscapes are still used today. Sometimes, too, seemingly abandoned and long forgotten ruins are considered by the locals to be 'alive and kicking': when surveying areas I assumed to be neglected, people would often vividly describe their importance to me. Even after a highly disruptive civil war, it seems to me that a continuity survives with barely a falter. For Aw-Barkhadle, the continuity of the land is revealed to its visitors through its features: the mausoleum of Saint Aw-Barkhadle (Figure 2.2), the hill of Bu'ur Ba'ayr, (Figure 2.8), the enclosure (Figure 2.7), the imposing ancient burials; all these compel the viewer to contemplate a timeless landscape and, irrespective of religion, to pay respect to the ancestors' presence.

Ethnographers and anthropologists such as I. M. Lewis (1998) have summarised the general information available about saints in Somali society. Many questions, however, remain unanswered. Lewis, for example, when

Figure 2.8 The Hill of Bu'ur Ba'ayr at Aw-Barkhadle site

talking about the distribution of Sufi saint cult practices, seems unable to find any explanation for the spread of Sufi saint traditions or for why their centres emerged where and when they did:

> The demonstration of effective connections and lines of communication for the potential spread of ideas (and cult practices) does not explain why they [the cults of Sufi saints] arose in their particular places of origin when they did, nor why they appealed to other sections of society in the centres to which they were carried.
>
> (Lewis, 1996: 151)

I would argue, in response to Lewis's uncertainty, that the common Islamic notion of a place of practice – that a religious place is where you make it, as long as your worship of Allah is genuine – makes it easy for Muslims to adopt or appropriate any space (even one belonging to another religion) as their own sacred space; they do this, for example, for their daily prayers.

What emerges from the current study, however, is that location is a key factor in terms of promoting continuity within the overall trajectory of any change in belief (whether it be belief in a Sky-God or in Christianity[4] or Islam). This process is more adaptive than extinctive and location plays a key role in the ideological justification of one religious power in place of another. Aw-Barkhadle clearly demonstrates one such pre-Islamic ideological triumph, but one achieved though adoption rather than total transformation.

Serjeant (1976: 62) wrote, in relation to Arabian pre-Islamic shrines: 'It is of course no uncommon thing for tombs to lie outside a town, as for instance west of Ansab in 'Awlaqi area; these shrines [pre-Islamic shrines] may become the centre of important cults'. I suggest this is certainly true at Aw-Barkhadle, and this study will present further comparisons between South Arabia's own ritual syncretism and the Islamisation process. From a holistic point of view, however, archaeological features at Aw-Barkhadle seem to form part of contemporary ritual life and a living composition of cultural heritage.

Anthropologists have often failed to recognise the significance of indigenous institutions in the practice of the monotheist religions. Dismissive attitudes towards the 'pagan' and sometimes perceived polytheistic institutions of the Horn of Africa are commonplace in the ethnography of the Horn. Trimingham has even referred to Cushitic religions as 'barbarian religious heritage' (1965: 54). Such bias, whether intentional or not, upholds the heritage of monotheistic religions while at the same time reducing the pre-Christian and pre-Islamic indigenous religions to relics of a savage past. It ignores their current cultural relevance.

Archaeologists too should be aware that ever since Ethiopia's Christianisation there has been a process of syncretism of not only religious space but also practices and ideas within and beyond churches. They must engage with relevant anthropological and ethnographical observations, data and research while remaining ever mindful of the potential pitfalls in the use of ethnography (Lane, 1994; Beach et al., 1997; Brück, 1999; Goody, 1966; Insoll, 2001, 2004; Hall, 1997; Ingold, 2013; Kobyliński, 1994; Radcliffe-Brown, 1951). Both anthropologists and archaeologists tend to avoid each other's domains, and this leads to an inability to construct a holistic history of the peoples of the whole of northeast Africa.

There are still all too few attempts to contextualise world religions and previous or contemporary indigenous religions within the broader themes of religious knowledge (cf. Edwards, 2005: 112; e.g. Alexander, 1979; Hays-Gilpin, 2008; Robertson Smith, 1894; Stewart and Shaw, 1994). This contextualisation is much-needed. In relation to the Horn of Africa, the archaeology and history of religion needs to take account not only of the anthropology of religion but also of the practice of world religions, such as Islam and Christianity, within northeast African society. However, except for an acknowledgment of the existence of certain rain-making ritual activities of sheikhs and the *ziyara* of Sufi Saints, there is currently a lack of in-depth studies of ritual practices or ritual systems or, for that matter, of women's rituals.

Susan Kent has noted:

> Some ethno-archaeologists and ethnographers do not recognize the impact of restricting their interviewees to only males or to only females. Others fail to take into account the biases male Western ethnographers, explorers, and colonialists had about gender, biases that unintentionally influenced their interpretations of non-Western societies.
>
> (Kent, 1998: 14)

More recent studies (e.g. Nelson and Rosen-Ayalon, 2001) have also illustrated this point. African archaeology, a field that has systematically undermined the contributions of its female South African, American and European pioneers and practitioners for decades (Weedman, 2001), seems still to care less about African women's knowledge about 'male topics' such as ancient history, ancient state-building and ideologies. Even in the twenty-first century, the contributions of indigenous archaeologists and particularly black women, are being undermined. A recent paper on the 'sacred spaces' and 'ritual' objects such as incense burners in the archaeology of Somaliland (González-Ruibal and Torres, 2018) completely omits to mention the notion of 'sacred landscapes,' 'sacred enclosures' or my relevant discussion of the role of incense burners – which I first developed in my PhD (awarded 2009) and also discussed in my more recent studies (Mire, 2016b, 2015a and b). The same paper, which also discusses pastoral and urban trade settlements, equally omits to mention the published work of Jama (1996), a Somali archaeologist (trained in the US and Sweden) who studied the relationship between coastal urbanism, hinterland pastoralists and long-distance trade in the Somali peninsula.

Male anthropologists active within the Horn and particularly within Somali society seem reluctant to study women and do research with indigenous women. However, the fact that women are ignored by white male anthropologists (with the exception of Helander (1996a, 1996b) and Cassanelli (1982)) may also be due to some degree to the local cultural values and sentiments to which they are subjected. In general, Somalist scholars continue to give only men's views on social topics: nationalism, nation-building processes, the oral archives of local history (including poetry) and *waddaads* (religious men). This inevitably results in a heavily male-dominated official version of Somali history, anthropology and ethnohistory. Somali women are walking schools and encyclopaedia that teach children, both boys and girls, from a young age everything about life and educate them in multiple (traditional) sciences. Women's role in society is only fragmentally reported; (white) female anthropologists seem to limit their discussions to female craft production (Fullerton and Adan, 1995) and the practice of *zar* (Luling, 1991) and *dhikri* (Declich, 2000; Kapteijns and Omar, 1996, 2007). The late Swede Bernhard Helander (1996a, b) is, to my knowledge, the only white male anthropologist to have studied gender; he worked for the agriculturalist Rahanween clan in southern Somalia and was married to a local Somali woman. Only a few women have challenged the dominant perceptions of the various characteristics and ethnic homogeneity of the Somali (e.g. Besteman, 1999; Declich, 1996; Tiilikainen, 2010 and, to some degree, Luling, 2002). It is the commitment of these anthropologists and many others across East Africa (e.g. Moore, 1996; Boddy, 1982; James, 1988 to mention but a few) that has inspired me to seek to understand better the role that women and men and gender play in this part of Africa. I am keen, through this book, to catch the attention of all types of scholars, male, female, white, non-white, African or Africanists, and to engage with the issues surrounding gender in the history of the Horn of Africa.

I have interviewed female as well as male authorities and I have asked them all the same questions, for example *'Who was Aw-Barkhadle and what history do they believe that it is important to understand in order to explore and unravel the history of the Somali people as a whole?'* I was interested to find that both men and women shared a similar perspective when speaking from a position of authority. However, it is practices rather than mere words that reveal true roles and genuine problems: social concepts always go beyond the dominant narratives. True discovery lies only within the space that connects time, cognition and experience.

Anthropological studies not only lack insight into female societies and their social and cultural significance in the context of the Horn of Africa; they also generally study gender through the lens of the world religions. Given my own research perspectives, I agree with Hassan: 'In our exploration of the archaeological dimensions of gender we cannot rely solely on the totalizing, stereotyping views of women and men developed and perpetuated within the Judeo-Christian-Islamic tradition and the commercial-industrial experience' (Hassan, 1998: 262). Hassan further argues:

> As archaeologists, we must also seek to trace the genealogy of the social, psychological and cognitive differentials between men and women, and to uncover the impact of major cultural transformations of the conceptual constructs of women and men, as well as their roles and status in society.
>
> (ibid.: 265)

Moreover, he continues:

> Gender categorization has evolutionary, historical, and regional dimensions that are dynamic and active. It is neither fixed nor final. Gender may be viewed as the outcome of cultural processes that involve the interaction between different biologically constituted individuals in different circumstances. . . . Gender is entangled in its ideological, religious, organizational, psychological, behavioural, communicative, and material domains.
>
> (Hassan, 1998: 266)

My aim in studying fertility rituals is to clarify and expose the complex relationships that go beyond biological differences and derive instead from ideologies. Marxist concepts of ideology and social relations (Marx, 1930; Miller and Tilley, 1984; Parker-Pearson, 1984) can go some way towards understanding the notion of fertility ideology in past societies, as this book will explore further. However, my research deals with a religious ideology and with a ritual system which is profoundly intertwined both with inevitably perennial factors like death and birth and with a concept of divine kinship which inherently controls sacred fertility. The ritual system I talk about is inevitably part and parcel of the regional kinship system.

As I understand it, the criticism of religious ideologies and institutions by Durkheim (2001), Spencer (1882), Marx (1930) and others during the nineteenth and twentieth centuries paved the way for critical anthropological research into religion, symbolism and rituals; it inspired the seminal works of anthropologists and sociologists such as Lévi-Strauss (1963), Geertz (1993) and Hubert and Mauss (1964). Religion plays a crucial role in the identification of what it is to be human and in the pathways of human history, as is shown by the abundance of disciplines like anthropology, sociology, theology and psychology, all of which have advanced theoretical thinking through the use of empirical data. By contrast, archaeology as a discipline has not yet generated its own theoretical framework within which to study past religions; it has been restricted to importing ideas from other disciplines (cf. Edwards, 2005: 110; Renfrew, 1994: 3; Davis, 1989; Gibbon, 1984). The work of scholars whose expertise is deepened by not

only the multidisciplinary perspectives they apply but also a linguistic proficiency of the specific culture they study often provides a unique opportunity
for understanding inner meanings of the material at hand. By understanding indigenous material culture better, we can appreciate ancestral practices and continuing symbolic and political connotations linking the past
(e.g. Morphy, 1991). Yet, in archaeology in general and African archaeology particularly, the problem remains despite the discipline having such
great opportunities to create alternative histories and to challenge master
narratives through the application of multidisciplinary approaches (Atalay,
2006; Schmidt and Patterson, 1995; Tonkin, 1992; Tonkin et al., 1989;
Vansina, 1973). Even in the case of African archaeology, it appears that
all too often far too little attempt is made to draw on the data from ethnographic research and other disciplines. This remains so despite the presence
of so many indigenous beliefs that are crying out for a multidisciplinary
approach to the continent's religious and ritual material.

I would like to emphasise here that my aim is not to identify a religion
per se. Asad reminds us that 'there cannot be a universal definition of religion not only because its constituent elements and relationships are culturally specific, but because that definition itself is the historical product of a
discursive process' (Asad, 1983, 1993: 29). Islam and the Orient have been
essentialised for centuries (Said, 1978). Asad argues that religions such as
Islam are made up of discursive traditions rather than of complete defin-
able structures of ideas governing all aspects of everyday life (the 'Orien-
talist' view) or of a validation of all diverse mixes (the cultural relativist
approach). I understand this to mean that a rite, for example, which in one
context would be viewed as an Islamic practice, might be viewed quite dif-
ferently in another. Sufism is the traditional form of Islam in Somali society,
but in the last few decades Salafi Islam has been advancing, leading to a
debate amongst Muslims about what Islam is and what it is not. If the world
religions can thus be regarded as discursive traditions, as Said proposes,
then the possibility of defining the structure of the pre-Islamic religions will
necessarily become even more elusive, and this will remain the case even
when there are people alive today who are still following some of the traditional beliefs. This is because these followers of tradition are not isolated;
they have often been assimilated (sometimes through force) into the superficially dominant construct.

The ritual site of Aw-Barkhadle appears to reflect many ideologies. This
is confirmed by the contested heritage of the rituals and material remains
revealed at the site and by the contested landscape within which it sits.
Three groups lay claim to this sacred centre. Legend has it that the Yibir (or
as they call themselves the Beesha Mohammed Haniifa), a clan considered
by the dominant Somali clans to have had non-Somali cultural affinities, lost
their ancestor and religious leader Mohamed Haniif (a.k.a. Bu'ur Ba'ayr)
when he was captured inside the hill at Aw-Barkhadle about 850 years ago.
Recently, too, the Haniifa have been prevented from using the site for ritual

purposes. The Sufis, the second group to lay claim to the site, have always, it seems, regarded the Yibir as a problem. As already noted, the Sufis now live at the site and represent the majority of the Somalis; they venerate Saint Aw-Barkhadle (a.k.a. Sheikh Sharif Yusuf Al-Kawnayn). And more recently, the new Salafi culture, which disapproves of Sufism and the veneration of the tombs, has begun to discourage people from worshipping at such sites in general.

Notes

1 The term *indigenous* here denotes the non-Islamic and non-Christian local traditions of the Horn of Africa. It is a term many anthropologists have used to describe the traditional Cushitic institutions of the Horn of Africa.
2 The book cannot provide an exhaustive list of the characteristics of all Cushitic or even Eastern Cushitic speaking peoples. I only mention some of the main groups. I do not for example discuss the Rendille or Gabra, the Saho, Afar etc. Similarly, the historical and sociopolitical relationships between these groups – beyond the shared beliefs and practices – lie beyond the scope of this book. For example, although there is much to say about the complex relationships between the Rendille, the Borana, the Gabra and the Somali in Northern Kenya I focus in this book only on the main Eastern Cushitic groups.
3 The use of Amhara words still occurs in the western region where Somali farmers in Gabiiley and westwards use Amharic names for the months of the year when referring to farming and harvest activities.
4 According to recent archaeological discoveries (Mire, 2015), Christianity seems to have existed in Somali territory prior to Islam. Christian archaeological scripts and burials are found in northern Somalia and other parts of the Somali territories, including at Aw-Barkhadle.

Bibliography

Alexander, J. A. 1979. The Archaeological Recognition of Religion: The Examples of Islam in Africa and 'Urnfields' in Europe. In B. C. Burnham and J. Kingsbury (eds.) *Space, Hierarchy and Society*. Oxford: British Archaeological Reports. BAR International Series 59.

Almeida, M. 1954. *Some Records of Ethiopia, 1593–1646*. Edited and translated by C. F. Beckingham and G. W. B. Huntingford. London: Hakluyt Society.

Andah, B. W. 1995. Studying African Societies in Cultural Context. In P. R. Schmidt and T. C. Patterson (eds.) *Making Alternative Histories: The Practice of Archaeology and History in Non-Western Settings*. Santa Fe, NM: School of American Research Press.

Asad, T. 1983. Anthropological Conceptions of Religion: Reflections on Geertz. *Man*, 18(2): 237–259.

Asad, T. 1993. *Genealogies of Religion: Discipline and Reason of Power in Christianity and Islam*. Baltimore: John Hopkins University Press.

Atalay, S. 2006. Indigenous Archaeology as a Decolonizing Practice. *American Indian Quarterly*, 30(3 & 4): 280–310.

Bartels, L. 1983. *Oromo Religion: Myths and Rites of the Western Oromo of Ethiopia. An Attempt to Understand*. Berlin: Dietrich Reimer Verlag.

Beach, D., Bourdillon, M. F. C., Denbow, J., Hall, M., Lane, P., Pikirayi, I. and Pwiti, G. 1997. Review Feature: Snakes and Crocodiles: Power and Symbolism in Ancient Zimbabwe by T. N. Huffman. *South African Archaeological Bulletin.* 52 (166): 125–138.

Besteman, C. L. 1999. *Unrevalling Somalia: Race, Violence and the Legacy of Slavery.* Philadelphia, PA: University of Pennsylvania Press.

Boddy, J. 1982. Womb as Oasis: The Symbolic Context of Pharaonic Circumcision in Rural Northern Sudan. *American Ethnologist*, 9(4): 682–698.

Brück, J. 1999. Ritual and Rationality: Some Problems of Interpretation in European Archaeology. *European Journal of Archaeology*, 2(3): 313–344.

Cassanelli, L. V. 1982. *The Shaping of Somali Society: Reconstructing the History of a Pastoral People, 1600–1900.* Philadelphia, PA: University of Pennsylvania Press.

Cerulli, E. 1957. *Somalia. Scritti vari Editi ed Inediti.* Vol. I. Roma: Istituto Poligrafico dello Stato. P. V.

Conti Rossini, C. 1905. Note sugli agau: 1. Appunti sulla lingua khamta dell' Averghellé. *Giornale della Società Asiatica Italiana*, 17: 109–122.

Davis, W. 1989. Towards an Archaeology of Thought. In I. Hodder (ed.) *The Meaning of Things: Material Culture and Symbolic Expression.* London: Unwin Hyman.

Declich, F. 2000. Sufi Experience in Rural Somali: A Focus on Women. *Social Anthropology*, 8(3): 295–318.

Durkheim, É. 2001. *The Elementary Forms of the Religious Life.* Translated by C. Cosman. Oxford: Oxford University Press.

Edwards, D. N. 2005. The Archaeology of Religion. In M. Diaz-Andreu, S. Lucy, S. Babić and D. N. Edwards (eds.) *The Archaeology of Identity: Approaches to Gender, Age, Status, Ethnicity and Religion.* Oxon: Routledge.

Ehret, C. 1995. The Eastern Horn of Africa, 1000 BC to 1400 AD: The Historical Roots. In A. J. Ahmed (ed.) *The Invention of Somalia.* Lawrenceville, NJ: Red Sea Press.

Eno, M. A. and Kusow, A. M. 2014. Race and Caste Prejudice in Somalia. *Journal of Somali Studies*, 1(2): 91–118.

Fattovich, R. 1987. Some Remarks on the Origins of the Aksumite Stelae. *Annales d'Ethiopie*, 14.

Finneran, N. 2007. *The Archaeology of Ethiopia.* London and New York: Routledge.

Fullerton, A. and Adan, A. 1995. Handicraft of the Somali Woman. In L. Prussin (ed.) *African Nomadic Architecture; Space, Place and Gender.* Washington, DC: Smithsonian Institute.

Geertz, C. 1993. *The Interpretation of Cultures.* London: Fontana Press.

Gibbon, G. 1984. *Anthropological Archaeology.* New York: Columbia University Press.

Goody, J. 1966. Religion and Ritual: The Definitional Problem. *The British Journal of Sociology*, 12: 142–164.

González-Ruibal, A. and Torres, J. d. 2018. The Fair and the Sanctuary: Gathering Places in a Nomadic Landscape (Somaliland, 1000–1850 AD). *World Archaeology*, 50(1): 23–40.

Hall, R. L. 1997. *An Archaeology of Soul: North American Indian Belief and Ritual.* Urbana: University of Illinois Press.

Hallpike, C. 1972. *The Konso of Ethiopia: A Study of the Values of an Eastern Cushitic People.* Oxford: Clarendon Press.

Hassan, F. A. 1998. Toward an Archaeology of Gender in Africa. In S. Kent (ed.) *Gender in African Prehistory.* Walnut Creek, CA: AltaMira Press.

Hays-Gilpin, K. 2008. Archaeology and Women's Ritual Business. In D. S. Whitley and K. Hays-Gilpin (eds.) *Belief in the Past: Theoretical Approaches to the Archaeology of Religion*. Walnut Creek, CA: Left Coast Press.

Helander, B. 1996a. The Hubeer in the Land of Plenty: Land, Labour and Vulnerability Among a Southern Somali Clan. In C. Besteman and L. V. Cassanelli (eds.) *The Struggle for Land in Southern Somalia*. Boulder and London: Westview Press and Haan.

Helander, B. 1996b. 'Rahanweyn Sociability: A Model for Other Somalis? In R. J. Hayward and I. M. Lewis (eds.) *Voice and Power*. London: SOAS.

Hobsbawm, E. J. 1979. An Historian's Comment. In B. C. Burnham and J. Kinsbury (eds.) *Space, Hierarchy and Society*. Oxford: British Archaeological Reports. BAR International Series 59.

Hubert, H. and Mauss, M. 1964. *Sacrifice: Its Nature and Function*. Translated by W. D. Halls. Chicago: Chicago University Press.

Ingold, T. 2013. *Making: Anthropology, Archaeology, Art and Architecture*. London and New York: Routledge.

Insoll, T. (ed.). 2001. *Archaeology and World Religion*. London: Routledge.

Jama, A. D. 1996. *The Origins and Development of Mogadishu AD 1000 to 1850*. Uppsala: Uppsala University Press. Studies in African Archaeology 12.

James, W. R. 1988. *The Listening Ebony: Moral Knowledge, Religion and Power Among the Uduk of Sudan*. Oxford: Oxford University Press.

Kapteijns, L. and Omar, M. A. 1996. Sitaat: Somali Women's Songs for the "Mothers of the Believers". In K. W. Harrow (ed.) *The Marabout and the Muse: New Approaches to Islam in African Literature*. pp. 124–141. Portsmouth, NH: Heinemann.

Kapteijns, L. and Omar, M. A. 2007. Sittaat: Women's Religious Songs in Djibouti. Halabuur. *Journal of Somali Literature and Culture*, 2(1–2): 38–48.

Kent, S. 1998. Gender and Prehistory in Africa. In S. Kent (ed.) *Gender in African Prehistory*. Walnut Creek, CA: AltaMira Press.

Kirk, J. W. C. 1905. The Yibirs and Midgans of Somaliland, Their Traditions and Dialects. *Journal of African Society*, 4: 91–108.

Kobishchanov, Y. M. 1979. *Axum*. University Park and London: The Pennsylvania State University Press.

Kobyliński, Z. 1994. Ethno-Archaeological Cognition and Cognitive Ethno-Archaeology. In I. Hodder (ed.) *The Meaning of Things: Material Culture and Symbolic Expression*. London: Unwin Hyman.

Lane, P. 1994. The Use and Abuse of Ethnography in the Study of Southern African Iron Age. *Azania*, 29: 51–64.

Levine, D. N. 2000. *Greater Ethiopia: The Evolution of a Multiethnic Society*. 2nd ed. Chicago and London: University of Chicago Press.

Lévi-Strauss, C. 1963. *Structural Anthropology*. New York: Basic Books.

Lewis, I. 1994a. *Blood and Bone: The Call for Kinship in Somali Society*. Lawrenceville, NJ: Red Sea Press.

Lewis, I. 1994b. *People of the Horn of Africa: Somali, Afar and Saho*. London: IAI/ Haan.

Lewis, I. 1996. *Religion in Context: Cults and Charisma*. Cambridge: Cambridge University Press.

Lewis, I. 1998. *Saints and Somalis: Popular Islam in a Clan-Based Society*. Lawrenceville, NJ and Asmara, Eritrea: Red Sea Press.

Loo, J. van de. 1991. *Guji Oromo Culture (with the Collaboration of Bilow Kolo)*. Berlin: Dietrich Reimer Verlag.

Loubser, J. H. N. 2008. Discontinuity Between Political Power and Religious Status: Mountains, Pools and Dry Ones Among Venda-Speaking Chiefdoms of Southern Africa. In D. S. Whitley and K. Hays-Gilpin (eds.) *Belief in the Past: Theoretical Approaches to the Archaeology of Religion*. Walnut Creek, CA: Left Coast Press.

Luling, V. 1991. Some Possession Cults in Southern Somalia. In I. M. Lewis, A. Al-Safi and S. Hurreiz (eds.) *Women's Medicine. The Zar-Bori Cult in Africa and Beyond*. Edinburgh: International African Institute.

Marx, K. 1930. *Capital*. London: J. M. Dent.

Miller, D. and Tilley, C. (eds.). 1984. *Ideology, Power and Prehistory*. Cambridge: Cambridge University Press.

Mire, S. 2006. Gaashaan, Somali Shield. In K. Lagat and J. Hudson (eds.) *Hazina: Traditions, Trade and Transition in Eastern Africa*. Nairobi, Kenya: National Museums of Nairobi.

Mire, S. 2009. *Divine Fertility: Sacrifice and Sacred Landscapes in the Horn of Africa and the Significance of the Site of Aw-Barkhadle, Somaliland*. Unpublished PhD diss., University College London.

Mire, S. 2015. Mapping of the Archaeology of Somaliland: Religion, Art, Script, Time, Urbanism, Trade and Empire. *African Archaeological Review*, 32(1): 111–136.

Mire, S. 2016a. Somalia: Studying the Past to Create a Future. In B. Rodrigue, L. Grinin and A. Korotayev (eds.) *From Big Bang to Galactic Civilizations: A Big History Anthology*. pp. 279–288. Delhi: Primus Books.

Mire, S. 2016b. "The Child That Tiire Doesn't Give You, God Won't Give You Either" – the Role of Rotheca myricoides in Somali Fertility Practices. *Anthropology and Medicine*, 23(3): 311–331.

Moore, H. L. 1996. *Space, Text and Gender. An Anthropological Study of the Marakwet of Kenya*. 2nd ed. Cambridge and New York: Cambridge University Press.

Morphy, H. 1991. *Ancestral Connections: Art and an Aboriginal System of Knowledge*. Chicago: Chicago University Press.

Nelson, S. M. and Rosen-Ayalon, M. (eds.). 2001. *In Pursuit of Gender: Worldwide Archaeological Perspectives*. Lanham, MD: AltaMira Press.

Parker-Pearson, M. 1984. Economic and Ideological Change: Cyclical Growth in the Pre-State Societies of Jutland. In. D. Miller and C. Tilley (eds.) *Ideology, Power and Prehistory (New Directions in Archaeology)*. Cambridge: Cambridge University Press.

Paulitschke, P. 1888. *Ethnographie Nordost Afrikas, I. Die materielle Cultur des Danâkil, Galla und Somâl II. Die geistige Cultur des Danâkil, Galla und Somâl*. Vol. 2. Berlin.

Phillipson, D. W. 1997. *Ancient Ethiopia. Aksum: Its Antecedents and Successors*. London: British Museum Press.

Phillipson, D. W. 2012. *Foundations of an African Civilization: Aksum and the Northern Horn 1000 BC to 1300 AD*. Oxford: James Currey; Addis Ababa: Addis Ababa University.

Posnansky, M. 2013. Present: Past. *South Carolina Antiquities*, 45: 47–49.

Radcliffe-Brown, A. R. 1951. The Comparative Method in Social Anthropology. *Journal of Royal Anthropological Institute*, 51: 15–22.

Renfrew, C. 1994. Towards a Cognitive Archaeology. In C. Renfrew and E. W. Zubrow (eds.) *The Ancient Mind: Elements of Cognitive Archaeology.* Cambridge: Cambridge University Press.

Révoil, G. 1882. *La Vallée du Darror: Voyage aux Pays Çomalis Dis Mois à la Cote Orientale D'Afrique.* Paris: Challamel aîné.

Robertson Smith, W. 1894. *The Religion of the Semites: The Fundamental Institutions.* London: A. and C. Black.

Said, E. W. 1978. *Orientalism.* London: Routledge & Paul Kegan.

Schmidt, P. R. and Patterson, T. C. (eds.). 1995. *Making Alternative Histories: The Practice of Archaeology and History in Non-Western Setting.* Santa Fe, NM: School of American Research Press.

Serjeant, R. B. 1976. *The South Arabian Hunt.* London: Luzac.

Spencer, H. 1882. *The Principles of Sociology.* Vol. I. New York: D. Appleton and Company.

Stewart, C. and Shaw, R. 1994. Introduction: Problematizing Syncretism. In C. Stewart and R. Shaw (eds.) *Syncretism/Anti-Syncretism: The Politics of Religious Synthesis.* London: Routledge.

Tiilikainen, M. 2010. Sitaat as Part of Somali Women's Everyday Religion. In M. L. Keinänen (ed.) *Perspectives on Women's Everyday Religion.* Stockholm: Acta Universitatis Stockholmiensis.

Tonkin, E. 1992. *Narrating Our Pasts. The Social Construction of Oral History.* Cambridge: Cambridge University Press.

Tonkin, E., McDonald, M. and Chapman, M. 1989. Introduction. In E. Tonkin, M. McDonald and M. Chapman (eds.) *History and Ethnicity.* London: Routledge.

Trimingham, J. S. 1965. *Islam in Ethiopia.* 2nd ed. Oxford: Oxford University Press.

Ucko, P. J. 1994. Forward. In D. L. Carmichael, J. Hubert, B. Reeves and A. Schanche (eds.) *Sacred Sites, Sacred Places.* London: Routledge. One World Archaeology 23.

Vansina, J. 1973. *Oral Traditions: A Study in Historical Methodology.* Translated by H. M. Wright. Harmondsworth, Middlesex: Penguin University Books.

Weedman, K. 2001. Who's "That Girl": British, South African, and American Women as Africanist Archaeologists in Colonial Africa (1860s-1960s). *African Archaeological Review*, 18(1): 1–47.

3   Material culture, fertility and sacrifice at the sacred landscape of Aw-Barkhadle

This chapter discusses ritual activities at the sacred landscape of Aw-Barkhadle.[1] This landscape includes the tomb of Saint Aw-Barkhadle and spaces for rituals, ritual offerings and other material culture and culturally important natural features. I investigate the symbolic meaning of such data by studying the context and role of ritual objects, architectural features and other material elements such as trees, stones and wells. The rituals are divided into the official *ziyara* (pilgrimage), rain-making rituals and some discreet, sometimes even secret, fertility rituals relating to human reproduction. I suggest how the ritual uses of this landscape may shed light on the non- and pre-Islamic indigenous institutions of this region.

According to the oral history, the Islamic community at Aw-Barkhadle dates back to the twelfth century AD. It is also believed that a pre-Islamic community worshipped at the site before the arrival of Sharif Yusuf Barkhadle ('Sharif Yusuf the blessed one'), to whom the site is dedicated. It is a pilgrimage site for this Muslim saint who is also known as Sharif Yusuf Al-Kawnayn ('Sharif Yusuf of the World') and Sharif Yusuf al-Ikhwaan (Yusuf of the Brethren). The site has also become known by the name Aw-Barkhadle, and I use this name when referring to it and its landscape, including the pre-Islamic landscape. I refer to Sharif Yusuf Barkhadle as Aw-Barkhadle throughout.

The discussion of fertility rituals presented in this chapter is derived entirely from the data collected at Aw-Barkhadle. It is intended to elucidate what takes place only at Aw-Barkhadle and only in the present day. The following chapter (Chapter Four) extends the discussion beyond the site itself to contextualise its practices within the wider fertility rituals that take place more generally in Somali society.

Archaeological discoveries at a living and sacred landscape

The pilgrim centre of Aw-Barkhadle is located near present day Aw-Barkhadle town, a 30-minute drive on the Berbera road, northeast of Hargeisa (Figure 1.1). The landscape of Aw-Barkhadle is decorated with acacia bushes, hills and a *wadi* (*doox/tog*) which floods every year and separates the town of Aw-Barkhadle (Figure 2.1; Figure 2.2) from the sacred Aw-Barkhadle pilgrim centre. The *wadi* itself is a few hundred metres away from the sacred centre. Several thousand visitors may come to stay in the town during the few days of the official annual celebration. People come mainly by car but many also walk long distances to arrive there.

The significant visible archaeology is estimated to cover an area of at least four square kilometres (see Figure 2.1). About one and half square kilometres around its mausoleum[2] contain dense archaeological remains. These include the foundations of house structures (Figure 3.1), the ruins of an ancient town wall and numerous burials reflecting different religious styles. About 750 metres of the ancient town wall is clearly visible above ground (Figure 2.1). However, by using a drone it is possible to trace almost all the wall three kilometres around the Mausoleum of Aw-Barkhadle. This wall crosses what is locally known as the Bu'ur Ba'ayr Hill, located about 700 metres south of the mausoleum. Almost the same distance again separates the tomb from the present-day town of Aw-Barkhadle.

The ruined town is still visible as several structures remain, including some which may have been mosque foundations and house walls. The burials reflect at least four possible traditions (Figure 2.1). Walking around the immediate vicinity of Saint Aw-Barkhadle's tomb one can see 28 other Muslim tombs of varying age (Figure 3.2), identified through their typical

Figure 3.1 House and mosque foundations

Figure 3.2 Muslim graves

Islamic orientation and/or their Islamic inscriptions; at least one Christian burial with a cross carved on its headstone (Figure 2.4) and other graves which are said to be Jewish because of their perceived distinct orientation to Jerusalem rather than Mecca and burials (Figure 2.5d) similar to the Ethiopian Muslim stelae traditions (Figure 3.3). There is also what appears to be a dolmen type of burial with large stone slabs (Figure 3.4). A few cairns and burial mounds (Figure 2.3), locally known as *araweello* or *taalo*[3] (cairns), can also be found on the Buʿur Baʿayr Hill. The *araweellooyin* (pl.) are placed on the southeastern side of the hill. The *Muriid* (the custodian of the shrine of Aw-Barkhadle) suggested to me that these cairns are pre-Islamic burials and that this type of burial is traditionally associated with earlier pre-Islamic societies. Illicit diggers looking for grave goods have dug up one of the *araweellooyin* (looting is a widespread problem discussed elsewhere, for example Mire, 2011). The vast number of different kinds of potsherds scattered across the area indicate long-term habitation. The results of a preliminary surface pottery analysis, which is expected to shed light on Aw-Barkhadle's chronology, will be presented in a separate publication with an account of the results of the excavations planned for 2018–2020.

So far, I have resisted the temptation to carry out any archaeological excavation. This is still a sacred landscape and I have to take into consideration

Figure 3.3 Potentially Islamic or decorated stelae for writing Arabic or the Qur'an

Figure 3.4 Pre-Islamic dolmen burial at Aw-Barkhadle

the views of the local community. I also want to focus on the sacred land-scape as a whole and on its significance for the people today. Although this may limit my ability to do a direct chronological assessment, I have been able to do some comparative analysis using other sacred landscapes in the Horn of Africa. Furthermore, I am interested in the multi-temporal perspec-tive. Today, as the community of Aw-Barkhadle grows more aware of the site's archaeological significance, I will continue to work in partnership with them to protect the site against looters and to promote an awareness of the potentially contested heritage that it represents. In short, my focus so far has been on doing a comparative analysis of rituals, material culture (including the surface archaeology and ritual features) and the landscape.

The archaeological excavations I plan to do in the future will add another layer of understanding to the chronology and the nature of archaeological features such as the city wall, the dolmen, the grave marked with the Coptic cross stone, the ruined town and the mixed burials of this remarkable and striking place.

A sacred enclosure of a circle of stones is also found on the hill (Fig-ure 2.7) and within this enclosure can be found a sacred stone (Figure 2.6). Both the enclosure and the stone will be discussed later in this chapter. There is also a so-called well which lies about 800 metres southwest of Saint Aw-Barkhadle's tomb and about 150 metres west of Buʻur Baʻayr Hill. This well is said to have inherited the healing powers of the original sacred well (a miraculous creation by Saint Aw-Barkhadle) it replaced (see the following).

The Tomb (Mausoleum) of Saint Aw-Barkhadle

Islam introduced new spatial concepts into the African continent, as others have already shown (e.g. Mazrui, 1985: 820). Muslim architecture in Africa is influenced by Arab culture (Mazrui, 1984: 6). With the arrival of Islam, Mecca came to be the holy centre to which all Muslims face and towards which their sacred space is orientated. The site of Aw-Barkhadle also fol-lows this practice. It is possible to see how the Islamic concept of sacred space has interfered with the older traditions of sacred enclosures at the site. It is difficult to estimate how much space was once occupied by non-Islamic graves alone as the Islamic burials are positioned very close to what appear to be non-Islamic, Christian and possibly pre-Islamic burials. This suggests that the arrival of Islam disrupted the symbolism of the material culture and the ritual space.

The mausoleum of Saint Aw-Barkhadle (Figure 2.2) occupies an area of about 250 square metres. Within the mausoleum are a few rooms including one in the front which contains Saint Aw-Barkhadle's tomb and a room at the back with a grave dedicated to a Sheikh Ali (Figure 3.5). It is in Sheikh Ali's room that the custodian of the site, the *Muriid* (the spiritual and tem-poral custodian of the Aw-Barkhadle ritual landscape) and other sheikhs sit in the evenings to conduct the *dhikri* (the religious chanting). Most of

Figure 3.5 Tomb of Sheikh Ali

Figure 3.6 Architectural features of Aw-Barkhadle painted in green

the mausoleum is painted white. However, various features, both inside and outside, are painted green. These include the tips of the corners of the tomb and the entrance (Figure 3.6) and a domed structure with a pillar or a column, reminiscent of a cylindrical minaret or a pillar tomb (Figure 3.7). A green flag flies constantly in front of the tomb. The *Muriid* informed me that the Ottoman Egyptians, who rebuilt Saint Aw-Barkhadle's tomb in the mid-nineteenth century, introduced the green colour which is currently regarded as a symbol of Islam.

On top of the cylindrical pillar (or minaret) above the dome there is an arrow-shaped metal object pierced through a crescent or half-moon metal

Figure 3.7 Aw-Barkhadle mausoleum's domed structure with a pillar

piece Figure 3.8a and Figure 3.8b). On another grave, there is a crescent (*qaanso*) moon-shaped symbol in metal placed on top of the cylindrical structure above a tomb similar to that on the tomb of Saint Aw-Barkhadle (Figure 3.9). These symbols reoccur inside other tombs at Aw-Barkhadle.

Three gravestones on the corners of the tomb of Saint Aw-Barkhadle have the same form, being shaped like a stele with a pointed tip (Figure 3.19). However, one gravestone structure is remarkably shaped in a two-step shape. Each of the two marked corners of this tomb are joined by an extra gravestone structure (Figure 3.9). Two of the middle additional gravestones are shaped like stelae as the three corners and two extra middle gravestones are cylindrical with a very narrow top, resembling generally the cylindrical minaret/superstructure of the dome of the mausoleum.

The mausoleum of Saint Aw-Barkhadle is surrounded by at least 28 other tombs, all painted white. Some have remarkable gravestones conveying the idea of minarets though they are not cylindrical. There are substructures (foundations) of triangular as well as square shapes. Some of the substructures are annexed with two- or four-stepped square or rectangular shaped tops (Figure 3.10). Although the structures of the tombs follow the general style of tomb building found in the Somali territory, the top or the annexed top structures display various styles, from domed ceilings to conical roofs or square or rectangular tops with four gravestones.

Figure 3.8a Crescent-shaped iron pole atop a pillar of Aw-Barkhadle

Figure 3.8b A tomb with a phallic stone next to a tomb with a combination of crescent-star iron ornament at Aw-Barkhadle

Figure 3.9 A gravestone structure shaped in a four-step shape at Aw-Barkhadle

Figure 3.10 A grave with two- or four-stepped square- or rectangular-shaped tops

Many have four corners indicating gravestones and are shaped like ste-lae and have soft edges, reminiscent of some of the Ethiopian stelae near Aksum, particularly the Gudit Stelae field (Figure 3.11). Furthermore, not all tombs have gravestones annexed to them; some are simple domes, others are more elaborate polygons (Figure 3.12). A couple of tombs are shaped like step-pyramids. With the exception of only two, the tombs surrounding the mausoleum of Aw-Barkhadle are no more than about two metres in width and about one metre above ground. All tombs seem to have niches – a square space – carved into their sides to hold incense burners (Figure 3.12).

The stelae found at Aw-Barkhadle demonstrate varying styles of stone erection and alignment traditions. With the Islamic tombs, for example, the practice here is to place two grave stones at either end of an east–west aligned grave. The size of these stones varies amongst the notable Muslim graves. Within a few metres of each grave is a circular or rectangular wall enclosure of one to two metres surrounding the grave with an open entry space about one metre in width. These walls are formed of piled stones which are sometimes held in place by lime plaster. The space between the tomb and the wall is either a plastered floor (for the rectangular more elabo-rate graves) or a sand floor (for a more circular basic tomb). This space is for the *dawaafa* (ritual circumambulation, *tawaaf* in Arabic). Thesiger (1935:

Figure 3.11 A phallic gravestone from Gudit Stelae field, Ethiopia

Figure 3.12 A polygonal grave at Aw-Barkhadle

Figure 3.13 An incense burner (*girgire*)

10–11) reported a similar grave construction in use amongst the Muslim Dankali and the Madima in eastern Ethiopia.

The religious figures buried at Aw-Barkhadle

The people buried at Aw-Barkhadle come from different backgrounds, genders and places of origin (Figure 2.1). There are currently about 50 Islamic tombs including some that may be merely dedications to sheikh(s) rather than actual burials. These prominent tombs include the tombs of female sheikhas and these are all intentionally positioned behind Saint Aw-Barkhadle's mausoleum. Although some Muslim male burials can also be found behind his mausoleum, the location of the women's graves probably follows Islamic traditions of the spatial division of gendered space. An example of this is to be found in female worshippers praying behind, rather than alongside, the men in congregations at worship.

Sheikh Rooble,[4] who at the time was the temporary keeper of the key to the tomb of Saint Aw-Barkhadle, and Sheikh Aw-Sa'iid, the brother of the *Muriid*, provided me with information about the people allegedly buried at the site (see Appendix 2). Amongst the prominent burials lies the tomb of the architect Sheikh Mohamed 'Hindi' who was responsible for the rebuilding of Saint Aw-Barkhadle's mausoleum in the nineteenth century. He is buried in front of the mausoleum and is said to have come from Gujarat, India. He was one of the few buried at Aw-Barkhadle to have a mausoleum built around his tomb. Another equally prominent burial is that of a governor of the British Protectorate of Somaliland, Sheikh Muuse 'Igare (see appendix 2).

The lists of names provided by the local sheikhs suggest the presence of Ottomans, Gujaratis and Arabs, all testifying to the political, religious and sociocultural status of the site. There seems to be a tradition that elites will allow themselves to be buried there: when I was at the site in 2007, a British-Somali was buried in the Aw-Barkhadle landscape, having requested this before his death.

However, when asked when the site was first used and by whom, my interviewees always replied about '850 years ago' and 'by Bu'ur Ba'ayr', who was a Jew, and of the Yibir clan'. According to the oral history of Aw-Barkhadle, Sheikh Isaaq, who is the founder of the Isaaq clan, and Sheikh Yusuf (Saint Aw-Barkhadle) both came from Arabia to the area of Aw-Barkhadle at the same time (about 850 years ago). This date is interesting because historical records suggest that migrant Hadramis from Hadramaut and Yamanis from Arabia arrived in this region in about AD 1250 (Martin, 1974: 370). Martin writes:

They can often be followed from their places of origin to the regions where they intermarried with important African . . . women, carved new places for themselves in local societies, and then died. If they were members of Sufi orders, as was frequently the case, of the 'Alawiya or Qadiriya or some other brotherhood, their elaborately carved tomb slabs sometimes indicate these affiliations. When dated, they furnish a check for literary chronologies. If they are still regarded as saints by the local population . . . something about the details and continuities of religious practices, beliefs, and values can be learned.

(ibid.: 369–370)

It is believed that war and hostile environmental conditions drove people from their homelands in South Arabia to the Somali territories. Archaeologically, the Islamitization routes been reassessed for the Horn and eastern Ethiopia (Fauvelle-Aymar and Hirsch, 2004). Many of the migrants came from holy clerical families in Arabia, known as Sayyids, Sharifs and Musha'ikh (ibid.: 371), men who 'were celebrated for their excellence and sanctity' (Martin, 1974: 373). Paulitschke (1888) has recorded the lineage of Sheikh Yusuf (see Appendix 1). However, according to the legend, Sheikh Yusuf was childless, a fact acknowledged by Sheikh Isaaq and other contemporary Somali lineage founders who pledged that Sheikh Yusuf should become the religious leader of all the Somali clans. This may explain why Somali as well as Horn of Africa Muslim rulers claim to have genealogical links with Aw-Barkhadle. According to my interviewees at Aw-Barkhadle, Sheikh Yusuf was sent by God to convert the people of this region to Islam.

The accounts also suggest that there were people who refused to convert, remained 'pagan' and moved to Ethiopia or Adari (Harar). Given that Harar was also a Muslim sacred centre at about that time, it is unclear to what area any 'pagan' people could have moved. The current sheikhs, moreover, have no knowledge of the history of the Ifat or Awdal kingdoms and no one has referred to Aw-Barkhadle in connection with *xukun/boqortoonyo* (state/kingdom) or any political leadership or territorial supremacy. The religious community could only shed light on the relationship between religious conversion, prominent saints of the Sufi persuasion and lineage connections with early Arabian Muslims.

Aw-Barkhadle and the early history of Islamic States in the Horn of Africa

Christianity began to spread across the highlands of Ethiopia from about fourth century AD though many Ethiopians remained 'traditionalists', i.e. non-Christian and non-Muslim, even as late as the thirteenth–fourteenth centuries AD (Cerulli, 1957: 177–210; Trimingham, 1965: 48–76). A few centuries earlier, from about the ninth century AD, there was also a growing number of Muslims in the coastal towns on the African side of the Red Sea, particularly around the Dahlaks. This early expansion of Islam is credited to the emergence of the Islamic kingdoms in the eastern Shoa region of present-day Ethiopia and the Muslim sultanate called Makhzumi which existed in the region as early as 896–7 AD (Trimingham, 1965: 58; Cerulli, 1957). The Somali and Afar in Zeila were influenced during the seventh century by the migration of early Muslim families into this region (Cerulli, 1957; Martin, 1974). The roots of what was to become the Ifat kingdom are thought to date from this period. Ifat was founded by its earliest ruler 'Umar Walashma' who became its king in about AD 1300/1 (Trimingham, 1965: 60). This reign was called the Walashma dynasty and the earliest accounts of it date back to AD 1214–1287 (Trimingham, 1965). Its rulers traced their antecedents to the Hijaz of Arabia (perhaps via the Shoa region of Ethiopia). According to the early Arab writers their land was also called the 'land of the Jabara' in the region of eastern Ethiopia and the Somali territory. As this kingdom expanded, with the coastal town of Zeila as its main coastal centre, it was succeeded by the Awdal kingdom which included the now ruined towns of Abbasa and Old Amud (Figure 1.1). During the centuries that followed, a rapid expansion of Islam into the Somali hinterland took place leading to a number of Islamic ruined towns, which dotted medieval landscapes (Mire, 2015a, b) (Figure 3.14).

During the formation of the early Islamic kingdoms of Ifat and Awdal, it seems that one particular religious centre played an important ritual and ideological role, and that was Aw-Barkhadle. Saint Aw-Barkhadle is thought to have lived in the twelfth century, according to my interviewees, including the *Muriid*. The oral traditions suggest a connection between

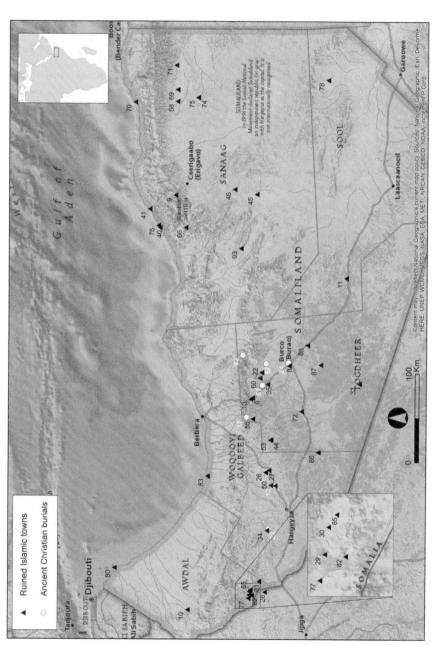

Figure 3.14 Medieval landscapes, urban centres and ruined Islamic towns in Somaliland

Saint Aw-Barkhadle and the Awdal kingdoms of the fifteenth and sixteenth centuries.

Textual material uncovered by Cerulli (1957) suggests a link between Saint Aw-Barkhadle and the earlier Walashma dynasty of the thirteenth–fourteenth centuries. In support of this link, an anonymous historical document obtained by Paulitschke offers a narrative history of Umar Walashma (Omar bin Dunja hauri), the founder of the Walashma dynasty, and his genealogy: 'Omar ben Dunja hauri ben Ahmed ben Muhammed ben Hamid ben Mahmud ben esch *Sheich Jûsuf d.i. Barkatlah* ben Muhammed ben Abdallâh' (Paulitschke, 1888: 503–504, [italics added]; see Appendix 1). Some sheikhs and sheikhas at Aw-Barkahdle believed that the Saint was childless but this is refuted by the naming of Aw-Barkhadle in the genealogy of the Walashma dynasty genealogy.

According to this genealogy, Saint Aw-Barkhadle was the fifth ancestor of the founder of the Walashma dynasty, an account made more credible by a particular king list from the Muslim Walashma dynasty (Cerulli, 1957; cf. Trimingham, 1952: 59; Lewis, 1998: 92–93) in which Yusuf Barkhadle appears as the fifth ascending ancestor of 'Umar b. Dunyahuz, the founder of the Walashma dynasty. 'Umar b. Dunyahur's reign was in the thirteenth century AD (Trimingham, 1952: 59).

It appears likely that Aw-Barkhadle was a place of political and ritual importance across the centuries. This view is supported by the reported use of the site as a burial place for the leaders of the Walashma Dynasty. For example, a chronicle from Harar, *The Tarikh al-Mujahidin*, discusses the death of Garaad Jibril who revolted against an '*Uthman*', the ruler of Harar in 1569, and mentions Aw-Barkhadle, 'the place of the great saint known as Aw Barkhadle', as the burial place of this Garaad Jibril (Trimingham, 1965; cf. Lewis, 1998; 92–93). Although his name does not appear amongst the list of the people buried at Aw-Barkhadle (a list drawn up by the resident sheikhs at my request in 2007, see Appendix 2), this does not mean that these events did not take place.

I am assuming, from the multidisciplinary data available at the site and from my own archaeological observations, that this 'place of a great saint known as Aw Barkhadle' refers to the site that is the focus of my study. The chronicle account mentioned previously suggests that the ruined town of Aw-Barkhadle belongs amongst the other ancient ruined towns attributed to the earliest recorded Muslim kingdoms in the Horn of Africa area. If it is assumed that the fifth ancestor of the thirteenth century AD ruler of Ifat was Saint Aw-Barkhadle, and if about 30 years are allowed for each generation, then it can be estimated that Saint Aw-Barkhadle might have lived around 800–900 years ago, a conclusion supported by the independent information provided by my interviewees. The link between Aw-Barkhadle and the Ifat kingdom is further supported by the existence of another sacred site dedicated to Saint Aw-Barkhadle, the Goroyo Cawl shrine (Figure 3.15) (discussed in detail later in this chapter). Goroyo Cawl is situated in what

Figure 3.15 A sacred tree and enclosure at the sacred fertility stones dedicated to Aw-Barkhadle at Goroyo Cawl, near Boorama

was once the heart of Ifat territory, between Aw-Bube (now on the Ethiopian side of the Somali/Ethiopian border) and the important ruined town of Abbasa in Somaliland. In short, a shrine dedicated to Saint Aw-Barkhadle lies at the very heart of what was once the Ifat and Awdal territory.

That the site of Aw-Barkhadle was of long-term significance is supported both by the oral accounts and by the continuity of burial evidence in the archaeological remains. Pre-Islamic early burials seem to have been left mostly undisturbed by later ones and sometimes can be found side by side with what are clearly Islamic graves. Although this does not mean that the people from non-Islamic religious backgrounds were always necessarily welcome, it does suggest that the site was esteemed as a sacred religious ground, regardless of religion. The sacred Islamic landscape appears to incorporate the non-Islamic burials too. People seem to honour the dead regardless of the ancestor's religion. Furthermore, all the people buried here are being honoured since the landscape of Aw-Barkhadle is a sacred landscape in which only ritual activity such as *ziyara* and pilgrimage is allowed.

The sixteenth-century record confirms the site's ritual significance and its historical importance. The historical evidence, according to Paulitschke (1888: 503–504), explains clearly why the Walashma leaders would want to be buried here. As noted previously, not only is Saint Aw-Barkhadle credited with having spread Islam in this region; the Walashma dynasty is also genealogically linked with Saint Aw-Barkhadle, whom they claim to be the fifth ancestor in their lineage.

I know from the oral history that the location of the Aw-Barkhadle shrine near Hargeisa was previously known as Doggor. Paulitschke names a place called 'Dakar' as the historical capital of the Awdal State and mentions 'AwBerkele' although he did not seem to have known where exactly 'Dokor,' the centre of 'AwBerkele', was located (Paulitschke, 1888). He suggested it was near Dire Dawa the regional capital of the Somali region of current day Ethiopia. This is unlikely to be the case. Given the nature of the archaeology of the Aw-Barkhadle centre, it is more plausible that Paulitschke's 'Dakar' refers to Dogor/Doggor and his 'AwBekele' refers to Aw-Barkhadle. Hence, Aw-Barkhadle's centre is most likely to have been an early capital of the Adal State. I will say a bit more about this in the next chapter. It is not, however, within the scope of this book to study this point in any further detail; instead, I will discuss this topic in a future publication following the results of the planned 2018–2020 excavations.[5] Suffice to say that both the existence of the tomb of Aw-Barkhadle as a centre dedicated to the Saint and the archaeological remains suggest that at some point in medieval times this was a major town, with a city wall (Figure 2.1) and possibly even a capital that might well predate other Awdal towns (Figure 2.1). Our planned excavation will shed light on this issue.

As noted earlier, my research focuses mainly upon the abundant and diverse data available at the site, the sources of rituals and practices and the meaning of landscapes. I have chosen not to excavate the site previously in order also to protect it from potential politically motivated destruction and looters. This has allowed me to concentrate my efforts on recording the information that is under the most immediate threat today: the oral history of this site and its current practices. This information may provide the answer to many questions, including perhaps the most important one. Why did Sheikh Yusuf Aw-Barkhadle come to this particular location in the first place?

The Somali Myth of Origin and Saint Aw-Barkhadle

The Islamic Somali Myth of Origin, which links the Somali with the Prophet Mohamed's clan, the *Quraysh* (Lewis, 1994, 1998; Mansur, 1995; Mukhtar, 1995), is central to understanding the significance of key practices such as fertility rituals and ancestor veneration. One crucial aspect of Sufi Islam is the genealogical link between followers and religious ancestors (Lewis, 1994, 1998; Trimingham, 1952; Huntingford, 1955). Lewis argues that the belief in this link facilitated Sufi Islam's success in converting traditional Somalis whose former religion (the Cushitic institution, discussed in Chapter Five) focuses heavily on ancestor worship (Lewis, 1998). In order to distinguish this version of history, which is regarded as fact by Somali people, it is essential to understand fully the Somali Myth of Origin. The site of Aw-Barkhadle is a key site in terms of this myth, as will be explored further in Chapter Four.

It is difficult to date exactly when Sharif Yusuf Aw-Barkhadle first arrived, allegedly from Arabia. However, the history and background of Saint Aw-Barkhadle (a.k.a Sharif Yusuf al-Kawnayn and Al-Kawnayn, which means 'the one of the worlds') points to the cross-continental religious status credited to Saint Aw-Barkhadle by his followers.

Burton recounts how a certain Sheikh Jami, 'a celebrated genealogist', told him that in the year A. H. 666 /AD 1266–7, Sayyid Yusuf Al-Baghdadi visited the port of Sigaro, near Berberah, which was at the time under the power of 'an infidel magician' who 'passed through mountains by the power of his gramarye'. With the aid of prayers conducted with an Arabian sheikh, Sayyid Yusuf Al-Baghdadi imprisoned the pagan in the mountain (Burton, 1966 [1898]: 101). Burton adds that the 'numerous descendants of the holy men still pay an annual fine, by way of blood money, to the family of the infidel chief' (ibid.). Burton's date of A. H. 666 is the year when Aw-Barkhadle was supposedly born (Lewis, 1998). Burton (1966 [1898]) also suggests that Sheikh Ishaaq only arrived 150 years after the 1266–7 date. According to Lewis (1998), a record exists about Saint Aw-Barkhadle which was written recently and has been held by the custodians of the shrine since 1967:

> [Saint Aw-Barkhadle] would be called Kawnayn. He would inherit the Prophet's own long robe, Solomon's ring, Moses' stick and a blessed stone. He would be born in 666AH. (1266/7 AD) and would meet 'Ammar in Baghdad on Friday between noon and evening. He would come to 'Ammar's house riding a she-camel and carrying a milking vessel. When the Sheikh came, the Prophet told 'Ammar he was to return his greeting and give him the relics entrusted to his keeping. Then 'Ammar would die. Sharif Yusuf himself would be buried in the land of the barbari, having been sent there to guide those people in the right path and to rectify their sins.
>
> (ibid.: 90–91)

No such record was found at the site in 2007. However, the verbal report given to me by the current *Muriid* echoes the information referred to by Lewis (see previous quotation) and that of Cerulli (1957). According to the current *Muriid*, the hereditary keepers, the *Muriids* of Aw-Barkhadle, have, since the eighteenth century, all come from one particular family. The *Muriid*'s claim of his family's centuries-long guardianship of the site does indeed indicate a tradition lasting for several hundred years. The *Muriid* used his *abtirsiimo* (Somali genealogical lineage tree) to provide the names of the former *Muriids* and to demonstrate his family's considerable knowledge of the site's history. People in the Hargeisa region generally recognise the authority of the *Muriid's* family; the following discussion is based on information provided by him and his first wife as well as by others linked to the site and its present ritual importance.

The following version of the story of Saint Aw-Barkhadle was told by a revered female elder of the town of Aw-Barkhadle (2007) and endorsed by the current *Muriid* of Aw-Barkhadle:

> He [Sh. Yusuf of the worlds] has been given the *risaaladii Nabiga*. [lit. the one chosen by the prophet] ('*Alayhi Salaatu Wa Salaam*); he has been given the *Qamis* of the *Nabi* [the Arabian style long gown of the prophet], the book of the *Nabi* and will come in the company of a black sheep [the black-headed sheep?], the *Kitaab* says. The *Kitaab* [the book] also says he will be 24, when he will appear with the black sheep. The *Rasuulku* [the Prophet Muhammad] says to one of his *as'haabo* [pl. from Arabic, in this context it means the Friends of the Prophet] that when a man with a black sheep appears to put on the gear; the *Qamis*, the *kitaab*, the Qur'an, *wayso* [the pre-prayer washing water container]. The *as'haab* [religious friend] asked the Prophet if he will live long enough to perform the task and the Prophet replied 'yes, the man you will meet will bury you'. He then appeared from the *toobadda* [the direction of Mecca, the *qibla*,], and the sheep sat down and the *as'haabi* [the religious friend] standing gave the things to the man, who is Sheikh Yusuf, with a sheep as he came down [from above] and he gave the sheep to the *as'haabi* [the religious friend] and at that moment the time of the *as'haab* came to an end, and the angels of Yusuf al-Kawnayn buried the *as'haabi*. After that everywhere between where the sun rises and where the sun sets, he preached the message in all peoples' languages, wherever he stayed overnight. The situation was like that. Then here [at the site of Aw-Barkhadle] Sheikh Isaaq [the founder of the Isaaq-clan] met bin Ahmed bin Hashim and Sheikh Yusuf Kawnayn, and they were *ilmo adeer* [first cousins on their fathers' side, they were the sons of two brothers]. He [Sheikh Isaaq] said to Sh. Yusuf: 'my children will venerate you'. In the region at the time there was Bu'ur Ba'ayr, the people here were *'awaan* ['pagans'] *af lagaadiin ah* [of the wrong kind of thinking]. In this situation, Sheikh Isaaq and Sheikh Yusuf came. Sheikh Yusuf Kawnayn came to the place and sat in the shade of a tree, and the spot in front of him immediately turned into a well and a pond of milk. Saint Aw-Barkhadle tried to teach Islam and a body of 3,000 people became his followers including some *jins*. Some of us who have become Muslim through Saint Aw-Barkhadle originate from the *'awaan* that Bu'ur Ba'ayr had as followers before. About 2,000 *'awaan* were the people who he tried to convert but did not succeed. These *'awaan* ['pagans'] who were once led by Bu'ur Ba'ayr were taken away since the '*Ashahaadda*' [lit. 'I give witness to', the testimony which every convert has to testify in order to become a Muslim, which means that there is

one god, Allah, and his prophet Mohamed] did not work on them. They were taken to Adari [an Afar name for Harar region, in Ethiopia; (cf. Morin, 2004: 35)], they had been taken away from here, with *qadr ilaahay* [God's will], and they are the ones that keep their hair into two bits and are *wo'oo'oobada ah* [making sound imitating prayers in a foreign language] and say '*Yaa adari*' ['oh Harar'].

What was left was Bu'ur Ba'ayr and Sh. Yusuf who sat in front of the mountain, leaning on it and put *khat (Catha edulis)* in front of Bu'ur Ba'ayr. The mountain is still here. He asked Bu'ur Ba'ayr '*burhaan max-aad haysaa?*' [what is the proof of your power?], and then Bu'ur Ba'ayr replied: 'I will make a hole in this mountain with an '*adday* [tooth brush stick], and he did that. Then Sh. Yusuf asked Bu'ur Ba'ayr to enter the hole in the mountain and this too Bu'ur Ba'ayr did. And Bu'ur Ba'ayr came out again and then Sh. Yusuf asked Bu'ur Ba'ayr to enter again and this time Sh. Yusuf said '*kum yaa ardu 'llahi!*' [Arabic, 'capture him, land of God!'], and this the mountain did; the mountain captured Bu'ur Ba'ayr and till this day he is still in the mountain.

("Elderly lady at Aw-Barkhadle town", pers. comm. 2007)

A belief exists that the Prophet would have known about the coming of Saint Aw-Barkhadle a few centuries before the actual event. Saint Aw-Barkhadle is confirmed as having 'exalted origins' through being related to the Prophet Mohammed (see Appendix 1, cf. Lewis, 1998: 91).

Furthermore, the legend persists that Bu'ur Ba'ayr[6] (a.k.a. Mohamed Haniif), was overpowered by the powers of Saint Aw-Barkhadle who trapped him inside the mountain where he is still thought to be today. And since Bu'ur Ba'ayr was killed in this way, the Yibir clan, who claim descent from Bu'ur Ba'ayr, have continued to ask for *mag* (compensation for the loss of a human life) from Sharif Yusuf Aw-Barkhadle (cf. the *Muriid* and his wife).

The elderly sheikha continued:

Yes, they asked for *mag* and Saint Aw-Barkhadle asked if they wanted *mag* that they could take at one go, all of it, or one that they would be able to take forever and ever. They replied that they wanted a compensation that they could take forever and ever. He said that I do not have children but the children of the man [Sh. Isaaq allegedly from Arabia and related to Prophet Mohamed, since he was a *Qurayshi* according to Somalis] that has cursed me so that I am unable to have children, his children will give you compensation forever. The Yibir get compensation for Bu'ur Ba'ayr from Sheikh Isaaq's descendants every time a male child is born to this clan.

During the time of Bu'ur Ba'ayr, the Yibir/Beesha M. Haniifa seem not to have been alone at the site; my interviewees talked about the site and its landscape as an area where various people of different beliefs lived. As has been already noted, the site's archaeological remains may reflect the existence of various ritual practices. And according to the legend, the wife of Sheikh Isaaq was not a Yibir (though her religion is unknown). The legend of Bu'ur Ba'ayr will be discussed in more detail later in this chapter.

The Ziyara of Aw-Barkhadle

The official ritual currently practiced at the site is the veneration (*ziyara*) of Saint Aw-Barkhadle. This takes place once a year in a commemoration known as *jima'a* Barkhadle and it occurs on the first Friday of the Muslim month of *Jumada al-Awwal* (*Jumada al Ula*). Until recently, *jima'a* Barkhadle was the most important religious commemoration in the northern Somali territory. In the 1960s and 1970s, thousands of people from all over the Horn of Africa attended this yearly event. Although this number has shrunk in the last few decades, the event is still an important occasion. Smaller but regular numbers of people come throughout the year to practice *ziyara* but during the annual commemoration large numbers arrive at Aw-Barkhadle and prepare for a three- or four-day worship of the sheikh. These visitors come with banners bearing writings praising Allah and the Sheikh. Five Saint Aw-Barkhadle pilgrimages in a lifetime are considered to be equal to one Hajj trip to Mecca. Hence, the people who come are taking part in a powerful experience; their mood is spiritual and they bring sacrificial animals and offerings; it is a mini-Hajj. In a number of important respects, Aw-Barkhadle meets the criteria required of the site of a mini-Hajj (or a poor man's Hajj).

My interviewees spoke of the Sheikh with total devotion and made it clear that the *ziyara* is a deeply rooted tradition. Some proudly told me how they had to walk for hours all the way from their homes in and around the city of Hargeisa to Aw-Barkhadle. They also walk to shrines dedicated to other sheikhs such as Sheikh Abdaal (Abgaal), again located between Hargeisa and Berbera. During the interviews, women demonstrated their deep devotion to the Sheikh by elongating their upper bodies and, putting their heads slightly to one side, raising their right hands with their index fingers pointing upwards before resting them on their hearts; Allah knows that they are telling the truth and that they are devoted to the Sheikh. When I asked why Saint Aw-Barkhadle should be so venerated, one interviewee (Sheikha, temporary keeper at Aw-Barkhadle at the time) said: 'He is The Sheikh of the religion . . . where the sun rises and where the sun sets, he is The Sheikh, which is why he is the Sheikh of *kawnka* [Kawnayn, pools].' Another added '[H]e is an *asli* [genuine] sheikh' ('Elderly lady 1 in Hargeisa', pers. comm. 2007). The feeling of genuine love for the Somali sheikhs regardless of clan is remarkable in a society that has so recently suffered a divisive civil war. The respect for sacred (*amran*) ancestors is a profound one that helps unify the Somali people.

I asked why people venerate Saint Aw-Barkhadle with the slaughter of animals they cannot spare and the burning of incense they cannot afford. One woman, astonished by my question, replied 'Without Saint Aw-Barkhadle, you and your mother and your father would not have been born with religion.' I will analyse this powerful statement later.

The material culture associated with *ziyara* includes the flags or banners of cloth (*'alamada*) brought by worshippers. These banners carry religious texts either in the form of embroidery or print. The texts read '*La ilaaha illa Allah Wa Mahammadun Rasul Allah*' ('There is only one God, and Mohammad is his Prophet'); the name, Sheikh Yusuf al Kawnayn also appears. There are signs on the banners: a crescent and a star, the signs of Islam.

The banners are mostly green and red or a mix of the two with a script of Arabic letters in white. The red colour is usually said to denote blood and sometimes signifies the sacrifice of animals for the (religious) ancestors or saints. Amongst the banners, there is one special banner, called *qiswad (qiswah)* (Figure 3.16). A similar banner covers the Sheikh's tomb at Aw-Barkhadle. The *qiswada* is made of black brocade with a printed pattern and Arabic text in gold. Some verses are from the Qur'an. Normally, *Qiswah* also covers the walls of the Ka'ba in Mecca and may reflect ancient Islamic traditions. People bring these *qiswadaha* (pl.) as offerings to Saint Aw-Barkhadle and place one on top of another on the tomb to cover it.

Figure 3.16 Qiswad of Sherif Yusuf Aw-Barkhadle tomb

When the Saint is venerated in the annual celebrations, sacrificial animals are always slaughtered. However, the gifts that people bring can vary according to the needs of the individuals and the type of blessing they seek. Women bring live animals but also incense (*foox/luubaan*) including frankincense (*yagcar*) and myrrh (*dheddin*) (Figure 3.17a and Figure 3.17b) for burning; perfumes; aromatic oils (Figure 3.18); food to cook including rice, pasta, snacks and drinks such as tea, coffee beans and coffee;[7] some even make bread. People also bring *khat* (*Catha edulis*), which is sacrificially

Figure 3.17a Frankincense (*yagcar*)

Figure 3.17b Frankincense tree growing on a rock (*Boswelia sacra*)

consumed as part of the important *dhikri* ritual. Sacrifice sharing seems to be related to the notion of *nagi* (peace, discussed in Chapter Five), and such ritual sharing can also be associated with the daily drinking of coffee or *khat* amongst the Somali and the Oromo.

I next discuss the ritual practices taking place in different parts of this landscape. I begin with the landscape of Saint Aw-Barkhadle and the materiality of *baraka*.

Figure 3.18 Perfumes and *qadarayn* aromatic oils

The sacred landscape and Aw-Barkhadle: the materiality of Baraka

The people I interviewed talked passionately about the trees, the animals and the water at and around the site; they associated it with paradise (*bar-waaqo*). One interviewee elaborated on the spiritual experience of the landscape of the *ziyara*:

> Oh, Aw-Barkhadle with all the flags and the drumming, oh. The place is beautiful! The place is full and so much is happening! The acacia trees, the river [*wadi*] and the people. You eat so much. You just feel peaceful and you just want to sleep.
>
> (an elderly woman in Hargeisa)

The women I spoke to talked about the water running (*durdur*, pouring rain) and emphasised the fertility of this landscape. Some referred to the experience as 'paradise' and one interviewee was explicit about how the place made her feel: 'Ooh you will get goose bumps of seeing all that, the growing *c'aday* trees, *dihda* (rain falling) and also the *'ulima* [religious experts] that are buried there' (an elderly woman in Hargeysa, 2007).

The experience of Aw-Barkhadle is associated with a sense of well-being. Somalis traditionally hold ceremonies involving dancing and singing during times of good rain. They do not perform traditional dances during droughts or the non-rainy seasons. Hence, they are not merely appreciating the fertility of the landscape of Aw-Barkhadle; they consider it to be a representation of the prosperity that they seek from the blessing of the sheikhs. It is therefore essential that the experience at Aw-Barkhadle lives up to people's expectations and that it reaffirms their beliefs.

I wanted to understand what it was that made the landscape of Aw-Barkhadle so sacred. I asked the interviewees if there is any one particular stone (or tree or object) that made the area sacred. One replied: 'it is in that landscape there, it is all complete in there [*banaankaa*, '*halkaasey kud-hantahay*'].' I translate the Somali word '*banaanka*' (lit. the open area) as landscape. When I asked what she meant by 'it is all complete in there', she replied, 'any stone there is sacred, in the manner of "*camal calaaniya*" ["it will be what you believe"]'; or, as another interviewee stated, 'it is anywhere that God makes it, therefore it is everywhere' (an elderly woman from the Hargeisa region, 2007). This belief was confirmed by the *Muriid*, by his wife and by many sheikhs/sheikhas and elderly people.

When one says '*camal calaaniya*', it means that if one believes in something, then it is how one believes it that matters. People believe that the whole landscape that surrounds Aw-Barkhadle is sacred; a single object extracted from this landscape has no virtue of itself. An object is powerful because it is *within* the landscape. Since the landscape, including the archaeological material is sacred (*amran*), it is all part of the one significant ritual space. I understand the landscape of Aw-Barkhadle to be sacred and I consider the term 'Sacred Landscape' to be the most useful way of defining the site. A sacred (*amran*) landscape is, I suggest, an area that is purely used for ritual purpose and one which contains natural and cultural features all of which possess cultural and ritual meaning. It is also one that is regarded by local people as sacred due to its religious attributions and links with past and/or present religions and blessing (*baraka*). The sacred landscape is one in active ritual use and exemplifies the materiality of *bakara*; it contextualises ritual sacrifice, material culture and an associated landscape. I later also apply this term to the sites of Aksum and Lalibela because the concept of blessing is not, in my view, exclusive to Islam. I will argue instead that it is a notion that is intertwined with the belief in sacred ancestors across time and space.

The socialist governmental drummers at the *Ziyara* of Sharif Yusuf

It is not only large groups of people who come to the site from all over the Horn of Africa. The Somali government itself has officially taken part in the yearly *ziyara* of Aw-Barkhadle. At present, moreover, political and clan leaders pay ritual visits to their lineage founders in an attempt to seek blessing and legitimacy for political reasons. In the 2008 ceremony, for example, soldiers were also present at the site. And between 1960 and the 1980s the Somali governments even commissioned government drummers to play during the Aw-Barkhadle *ziyara*. This has since become a tradition. The military take part in other traditional events too, such as rain-prayer[8] ceremonies (*roobdoon*), to protect participating high-ranking officials

Figure 3.19 Official rain-seeking prayers (*Roobdoon* prayers) at Hargeisa stadium in 2011

(Figure 3.19). The military gather on the modern settlement side of Aw-Barkhadle. There they play the *'baamboy'* (military drums), signifying the official status of the Sheikh. This practice continued even during the time of the secular socialist Somali state which collapsed in 1991. According to my interviewees, the drums added to the rhythmic sounds at Aw-Barkhadle by making a lasting impression on their audiences and contributing greatly to the three- to four-day gathering. One of the interviewees remembers this very well: *'Baamboy* [the military drummers] are playing and it is as if the whole world is here!' (an elderly woman, 2007).

By applying the Knowledge-Centred Approach I have been able to focus on the way that knowledge comes through experiences, the way that these experiences are preserved through practice and the way that performance paves the way to a space and knowledge that can only be accessed through the movement of the ritual. The manifestations of these experiences and events on the landscape are only fleeting and leave with the pilgrims, rather like an invisible souvenir, a whisp of a scent. Even though Aw-Barkhadle may look like an insignificant, sleepy, distant and empty mausoleum, it lies at the centre of people's most sacred experiences and secret wishes. Using the Knowledge-Centred Approach brings a sense of the immediacy of the smoke of the incense and the sound of the drum. An archaeologist's discovery of an incense burner or a drum can never hope to match this.

Drums are an important ritual paraphernalia. However, in the Horn of Africa, with its common practices of *zar* drumming and dance, the ritual drums echo a sound that lies at the heart of its ancient sacred landscapes. Drums are as much a part of ritual as are the incense burners. Some of the dolmen burials at Aw-Barkhadle include stone slabs; it is hoped that future investigations will reveal whether the prehistoric 'ritual drums' found in the Soddo region of Ethiopia and Aksum are also present at Aw-Barkhadle. I have also noted that drums have been found in the churches of Lalibela. I have come to understand that ritual practice goes way back beyond the monuments of these rock hewn churches and may, like the churches themselves, relate to the African traditional drum culture, a culture that celebrates their far-reaching role in the procession, ritual and performance of so many traditional ceremonies.

Aw-Barkhadle's ancient Christian burial with a fourth century Aksumite cross

One rather curious practice takes place during the annual celebration of Aw-Barkhadle. People come to the site and paint a cross on their foreheads. The *ziyara* until recently began with this practice, which starts at the Bu'ur Ba'ayr hill where people obtain the chalk with which to make the paint. After mixing the chalk with holy water from the sacred well near the hill, they use it to paint a cross on their foreheads before proceeding to the mausoleum of Aw-Barkhadle to perform the chanting, prayer and the *dawaafa*.

It is now known that Christianity was possibly also practised in this region, and at Aw-Barkhadle too, where there is at least one burial with stelae decorated with a Christian Orthodox cross *in situ* (Figure 2.4) (see also Mire, 2015a for an account of the archaeological record of Christianity in the Somali region). This cross is remarkably similar to the cross on the shield described earlier. It is also noteworthy that ethnographic objects sometimes carry a Christian cross, whether consciously intended as a Christian symbol or rooted in a dim and distant social memory. The Christian cross also, significantly, occurs as a symbol on Somali shields. I recorded a few headrests with crosses carved on them where the head rested (Figure 3.20a) and one shield with a fourth-century Coptic Christian cross (Figure 3.20b) potentially intended to provide a ritual protection in the face of battle during the Christian era. I have also met a former female sheikha who was well known in Hargeisa. When I saw her, she could hardly speak or sit up but she was able to say a few words to me; her greatgrandchildren helped bring out her regalia (*qiswas, tusbah* and Qur'ans). This very old and frail woman let me take a picture of her face, which was tattooed with a cross on her forehead. In much the same way as the pilgrims at Aw-Barkhadle until recently put a cross on their forehead during the annual celebration of Saint Aw-Barkhadle, so this sheikha had a cross on her own forehead – but one that was tattooed rather than painted on her skin. I did not ask her about the cross as

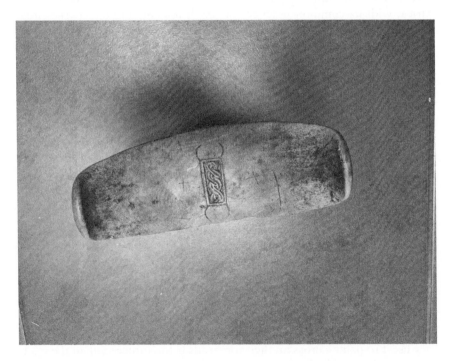

Figure 3.20a A Somali wooden headrest marked with a cross

Figure 3.20b A Somali wooden shield marked with a Coptic Christian cross

I thought it not appropriate to do so due to her age and frailty. There is what looks like an ancient Christian burial in Hargeisa region (Figure 3.20c) and according to the locals it's the place of an ancient 'Christian sheikh'. It is possible the Christian cross symbolism lingered long after ancient Christianity had disappeared amongst the Somali.

However, this meeting alerted me to the fact that symbolism can be organic and a mark of unspoken regional inter-borrowing that may reflect an ancient local tradition only faintly sensed. It may indicate remnants of a local interfaith tradition. It is common in Ethiopia to tattoo a cross and other religious symbols on the forehead, especially on women. I have also noted that in the Horn of Africa the forehead is a critical area on which to display religiosity. The Oromo Qallu wears the phallic *kallascha*[9] on the forehead (Figure 3.20d). Practicing Muslims may have a darkened spot on their forehead to mark the spot where their head touches the ground as they daily pray the *salaat* – sheikhs, in particular, become permanently marked. Males of the Jewish religion wear the *tefillin*, a charm which includes a scroll with verses from the Torah, on their foreheads when praying. These charms bear a remarkable similarity to the Quranic ones used in Somalia which are likewise made of leather and square or rectangular and sometimes also worn on the forehead. The Christian priests touch their foreheads with the processional crosses they hold in front of them, in the same manner as a woman will carry the *wagar* in front of her face after giving birth to a child.

Figure 3.20c An ancient grave shaped like a Christian cross in Hargeysa region

All the Abrahamic religions have an ancient presence in the Horn of Africa and the wider northeastern Africa and Red Sea region. Afro-asiatic languages are believed to originate from this region, and it is not surprising that the indigenous practices of its various peoples share common practices across ancient and present-day religions. It may well be that other indigenous beliefs that preceded and/or existed alongside the Abrahamic religions, such as the Sky-God or Heaven God, used charms that included different sacred and protective words or objects in place of the Abrahamic ones. One example is the Oromo phallic kallascha. Also, the *makaram/makharam* made by the Yibir included a piece of a sacred tree (known as *samanyo*) bound in a leather with four corners. Incidentally, traditional and indigenous objects, as well as Christian crosses, seem to attach an importance to the idea of four-cornered shapes.

My interviewees said that the people who lived in Aw-Barkhadle did not want to convert to Islam and so moved to 'Adari' (Harar, Ethiopia). This suggests that Cushitic traditionalists and Christian groups might have been better tolerated at Harar, in the twelfth–thirteenth century, then at Aw-Barkhadle. It may be significant that Hanfeley, the wife of Mohamed Haniif/ Bu'ur Ba'ayr, is thought to have disappeared to Adari, where her tomb is located (Kirk, 1905).

At Aw-Barkhadle, people talk about a nearby *Burco Cad Cad* (white mountain) and places with names associated with the Ethiopian people/

Figure 3.20d The Kallascha phallic headpiece of the Oromo
Source: (with permission from Eric Lafforgue)

Oromo who also lived there during the time of Bu'ur Ba'ayr. Such names include *waro miyo, waro dayo* and *waro dhaqo*. It seems coexistence has always played a role in the sacred landscape of Aw-Barkhadle.

The common practice for people to paint their foreheads with a cross that is just like the Christian cross is now not practiced, as one interviewee explained: 'It is forbidden now. It is Bu'ur Ba'ayr's people, they are the

Yibir, they are forbidden. They are not allowed now. It is a cross, infidel thing, *gaala* ['pagan'], it has been erased. Bu'ur Ba'ayr was an infidel, a Jew' ('Sheikha, at the time a temporary keeper of Aw-Barkhadle', pers. comm. 2007). Some people are clearly very sensitive about certain practices that are associated with the site. However, this attribution to the Yibir is completely incorrect as the painting was done by all visitors regardless of clan. The question arises, however, as to why the Yibir/Beesha Haniifa stand accused of these rituals when they have no association with the Jews, the 'Gala' or Christianity. Some of my interviewees associated the cross they paint on their foreheads with a ritual practised by the ancient followers of Bu'ur Ba'ayr; this is despite the fact that many others confirm that this was a common ritual at the annual ceremony at Aw-Barkhadle until only a few decades ago and had nothing to do with the Yibir clan. In fact, not only do plenty of people confirm that dominant Somalis carried out this ceremony until recently; even today, pilgrims take the chalk of Bu'ur Ba'ayr Hill to give to relatives to smear on their heads. The remarkable find of a Christian burial with a gravestone marked with a Christian Orthodox cross confirms the site's deep links with Christian concepts. Other Christian burials also exist across the country (Mire, 2015a).

It is interesting to note that the Somali word for infidel, *gaal* (*gaalo/gaala*), is used to denote 'pagans' as well as Christians or Jews. Similarly, it seems, people do not make a distinction between the star of David and a Christian cross. A similar confusion has been noted in Ethiopia where people mistakenly assume that the old pre-Christian religion had something to do with Judaism (Phillipson, 1997: 141). Somalis in the north have memories of a cross (whether the Star of David or a Christian cross or something else altogether is unclear). Archaeologically, there are finds that confirm the existence of graves and rocks marked with the Star of David or menorah as seen earlier (Figures 2.5a–c). It is uncertain whether these symbols confirm the existence of Judaism in the Somali region (although it would not be surprising at all as Judaism was prevalent in northeast Africa and the Red Sea area). However, what is certain is that materials and objects associated with ancient Judaism do exist in the Somali region too – I myself have seen what look like the menorah, the Star of David and the symbol of the hand all found separately or together in different archaeological contexts in the northern regions.

In terms of the ritual of painting crosses, it seems to matter that the white colour used comes from the soft white chalk material found at a spot on Bu'ur Ba'ayr hill. The pilgrims often take this chalk away with them and apply it on the faces of their relatives, and especially on young boys, back in the remote parts of the Horn of Africa. The myth of Bu'ur Ba'ayr will be discussed later in the chapter, but it is important to note here that Trimingham mentions Muslims in Ethiopia who sometimes chose to wear Christian amulets as protection against bad spirits (1965: 28). The Yibir, as is known, are not Jewish, but it may be that the 'Jewishness' label is used as a means of excluding them and marginalising them on the grounds of what are more likely to have been Somali ancient indigenous practices.

This attitude reveals a fair amount of hypocrisy on the part of the Somalis who all still respect traditional beliefs adopted to suit Islamic ways and rules. Kirk calls it 'Gala paganism' when it come to the Yibir, and Cerulli and Lewis label it the 'Cushitic substrata'. Kirk notes the Yibir practice of cutting the sacred trees of Hanfeley (discussed later in this chapter) and likens it to 'the old Gala paganism' (Kirk, 1905). He is not, however, saying that the Yibir are Gala; he notes that the Somali dialect of the Yibir (ibid.) shows no links with the Gala (a derogative term for the Oromo people). The Afar, too, have similar practices involving sacred stones and forehead painting. During the coronation of the Danakil king: 'Then earth from the summit of Mount Ayelu, the sacred mountain, is rubbed upon his hands, earth from beneath a large *shola* tree upon his feet, and clay from the bottom of the Awash River on his forehead.' A longer version of this account will be discussed later in this chapter. (The Dankali connect the *shola* tree with their ancestors but were rather uncertain about this link.) The sheikh is next saturated with *ghee* and the crowd fight to touch him (Thesiger, 1935: 7–8; Levine, 2000).

The contempt that the Somalis traditionally have for the Yibir is similar to the contempt that Ethiopian Christians have for the traditionalist Oromo. The 'Christian Abyssinians' hold the view that the Oromo are 'in a league with the devil' (Kirk, 1905). Both at Aw-Barkhadle and in the general discussion of Somali minority clans in the literature, the 'ignoble' vs. 'noble' savage discourse is clear and sadly serves only to devalue African indigenous philosophy, ideologies and theologies. It has also led traditional anthropologists, all too preoccupied with dominant clans and their narratives, to pay far too little attention, whether intentionally or unintentionally, to deviations from the grand narratives.

If Judaism was widespread across the Horn of Africa, as Kaplan (1992) maintains, it would not be at all surprising if it had existed in the Somali territory both before and during Christian and Islamic times. The Somali peninsula is situated in a region of the world where these Abrahamic religions took shape. Kaplan has argued that there are Jewish elements in Ethiopian Christianity (Kaplan, 1986) and this may also be the case amongst the ancient practices of the Horn of Africa. The people I interviewed at Aw-Barkhadle may be confused by what is a clearly complex syncretism of the materiality and memory of history in this ancient and living landscape.

Fertility rituals of Aw-Barkhadle sacred landscape and tombs

Female worshippers visit the tomb of Saint Aw-Barkhadle not only for the *ziyara* but also for fertility related matters. The *Muriid* often knows when women are there for fertility reasons because they arrive carrying a *qayd*, a cloth used to carry a child on the back. The Oromo use a similar cloth, *kad-dee*, sometimes made of hide, to wrap and carry a baby on the back (Loo, 1991). The *Muriid* at Aw-Barkhadle allows the women into the tomb and gives instructions for prayers. In the past, the role of the *Muriid* included directing women to the blessed fertility stone in the Aw-Barkhadle land-scape. However, the practice involving the stone has now become contro-versial, as is discussed later.

After saying a few prayers, each woman steps into the mausoleum bare-footed. She holds the corners of the tomb of Saint Aw-Barkhadle, which is covered with a green *qiswad* (*qiswah*) (Figure 3.16) upon which are written prayers in gold in the Arabic script. She recites the *Faataha* (the first *Surah* of the Qur'an) and puts the gifts she has brought in a box on a shelf while the *Muriid* pours more incense into the *girgire* (incense burner). If she has brought a *qayd*, she starts to pray again with the *qayd* on her back and this time prays for children, usually uttering: '*Sheikhow sanadkan sanadkiisa hadi Ilaahay isiiyo ilmo inshaaradii waan keenayaa siyarodaada*' meaning 'Sheikh, if God grants me a child [*ilmo* can also mean sons], the year fol-lowing this, I will bring your gifts for *ziyara*.' Then both the *Muriid* and the woman recite the selected verses of the Qur'an.

I was told that in the past there used to be inside the mausoleum of Saint Aw-Barkhadle "a wooden piece that has eyes, nose, arms that Allah has given it but are not properly visible" (an elderly woman, 2007). The women would carry this wooden piece, with its invisible eyes, arms and so on, on their backs in a *qayd*, much as they would a baby. After praying, they would put the sculpture back in its place and leave. When I took part in the *ziyara*, as a participant observer, I could see no wooden sculpture, and the cur-rent sheikha of Aw-Barkhadle, the wife of the *Muriid*, explained to me that this sculpture was no longer used as Islam prohibits figurative motifs and sculptures that resemble any living being whether animal or human. She explained that women now carry the Aw-Barkhadle Qur'an which they lift and carry in their *qayd*. When they finish praying they put it back in its place and leave. It is said that this Qur'an has replaced a very ancient Qur'an which, according to the *Muriid*, was stolen by the Said Barre regime soldiers during the civil war in 1988–1990. Furthermore, there used to be another piece of wood kept in the mausoleum of Saint Aw-Barkhadle. This was a piece thought to be from a wooden bed belonging to Aw-Barkhadle him-self and was used for fertility rituals by the women in a similar way to the wooden piece mentioned above; it is entirely possible that this is a reference to one and the same piece of wood. A divine power is ascribed to the mate-rial remains of the Sheikh so, in this context, any wood once belonging to Aw-Barkhadle would be an even more blessed medium than the wood from anything else.

After walking out of the Saint Aw-Barkhadle mausoleum, any woman looking for a blessing would do the ritual walk, *dawaafada*, around the outside of the mausoleum and those belonging to other *awliyo* (religious ancestors). Later, after giving birth, she will bring *bishaarada* (offerings) such as animals, perfume, incense and rice to the Sheikh's tomb. One of my interviewees recalls a time when she was unable to conceive a son; she performed this ritual walk for three years after giving birth to daughters only. She explained how much she wanted to have a son:

> I went there with other women and all of us wanted boys, [she counted the women's names, four other names and hers] and we all gave birth to boys the next year. I swear to God, the almighty, He is the biggest Sheikh. *Hajj* is also Sheikh Yusuf al Kawnayn. I have carried the child and kept coming and giving the *ziyara*. I slaughtered one animal every year until my son was three years old.

It is important to note the lengths to which this woman and others went to have a son. Celebratory ceremonies dedicated to the birth of boys such as the one described by the interviewee and the *waqlaal* ritual will be discussed later in the context of Somalia and the Horn of Africa.

Fertility rituals and associated sacred features at Aw-Barkhadle

A key aim of this study is to analyse the spatial practices through which ritual knowledge is enacted and transmitted so that any relationships to earlier practices can be explored. Certain features and elements in the landscape of Aw-Barkhadle seem to invite the notion of a sacred landscape and of the ritual activities that take place within it. My discussion next focuses on the elements within the landscape with which the rituals are associated. I now move on to discuss many of these elements including water, fat and stones and their roles in the rituals. Through analysing these in their proper context, it is possible to understand their meaning and the complex social, political and metaphysical messages they carry in general and, more particularly, in regard to fertility rituals.

Sacred trees and rituals at Aw-Barkhadle

The landscape of Aw-Barkhadle is relatively green and trees grow there undisturbed by human beings. Neighbouring animals wander around and graze on the vegetation. Some of the acacia trees are remarkably overgrown and even penetrate through some of the graves (Figure 3.21). These trees are generally part of the ritual repertoire and they are protected from being cut. Notions of sacred trees and their associations with supernatural powers and fertility rituals permeate the rituals of the Aw-Barkhadle landscape. I have already noted how the Yibir give a piece of sacred wood to the other Somalis when in receipt of *samayo*, a compensation. It is a practice based on the legend of Mohamed Haniif, as will be discussed later. It is interesting that the Yibir (Beesha Mohamed Haniifa) are said to have a sacred tree

Figure 3.21 Aw-Barkhadle tree growing from the belly of a Muslim grave

(Kirk, 1905). The *samayo* of the Yibir is a significant testimony to the ritual continuity of trees. If this tree is indeed the *wagar*, which is known also to be associated with Aw-Barkhadle (Mire, 2015b), then its presence is yet another testimony to the existence of a sacred tree amongst the dominant Somalis generally and the Yibir in particular.

My interviewees at Aw-Barkhadle talk about a sacred date tree. This date tree is said to have been associated with the Saint about 850 years ago. The date leaves were used for the embellishment of the graves by relatives of the deceased. Others observe similar practices in the Horn; the Danakil people to the west of Somalia/Somaliland use the date palm for decorating graves (Thesiger, 1935: 10), and the Guji Oromo and the Konso both put palm leaves in the graves of the dead (according to Hallpike, 1972; Loo, 1991; cf. Burton, 1966 [1898]). This act may signify the perpetuation of the family among the Somali and the Danakil as it does among the Guji Oromo.

Trees at Aw-Barkhadle are not only recognised for their ritual signifi-cance – one of the interviewees exclaimed passionately 'the *c'aday* trees' when describing the fertility of the landscape during the rainy season. They also play an important part as mediums in the ritual. All women requesting children, or specially boys, in their *ziyara* ritual walk, the *dawaafa*, will tie *marqaha* (a piece of cloth) or *maydhah* (the bark of an acacia tree) onto trees at Aw-Barkhadle. Thus a woman requesting a child will tear a piece of cloth or *qayd* and tie it to the tree. The sheikhs then will see the *marqaha* and pray for the woman.

When I asked what this cloth and *maydhah* on the tree meant, and why people tie *maydhah* or *marqaha* to trees, one of my interviewees simply replied 'it is the place of sheikhs and people who want children (particularly boys) will do that" ('Elderly lady 2 in Hargeisa', 2007). The description 'A place of sheikhs' is congruent with the belief in a sacred landscape, blessed by the sheikhs through the reciting of the Qur'an, ritual activities and Saint Aw-Barkhadle.

As noted above, the Somali share a myth of origin with other Cushitic speaking groups. It features a man in a tree (Luling, 1988). According to this myth, the Somalis originate from this man who came down from the sky, sat on a tree and then married a local woman (ibid.). Was this tree a sacred tree? Is this story linked to the known Cushitic traditional worship of tree-deities? I suggest later (in Chapter Five) that this Cushitic Somali Myth of Origin indicates the pre-Islamic significance of the ritual aspect of trees in a Somali context, and in the next chapter I discuss the *wagar* tree in relation to fertility, child protection and tree-deities. However, there are other accounts too of sacred trees in the Somali region. There is a holy tree at the site of Goroyo Cawl (Figure 3.15), a shrine dedicated to Saint Aw-Barkhadle in the western region Borama road, as already mentioned. This shrine also has massive fertility stones. Its holy tree might be similar to one that is mentioned by Richard Burton (Burton, 1966 [1898]). About sixteen miles from the Abbaso Fiumara, a ruined town where the Darbiyah Kola Kola's Fort lies, Burton heard a story about a fierce battle that took place 300 years ago; the two cities of Abbasa (Figure 1.1), on the Somali side of the current Ethiopian Somali border, and Aw-Bube, on the Ethiopian side of the same border, fought till both were 'eaten up' (ibid.: Chapter 5, note 148). He also added:

> At 1 P.M. we unloaded under a sycamore tree, called, after a Galla chieftain 'Halimalah,' and giving its name to the surrounding valley. This ancient of the forest is more than half decayed, several huge limbs lie stretched upon the ground, whence, for reverence, no one removes them: upon the trunk, or rather trunks, for its bifurcates, are marks deeply cut by a former race, and time has hollowed in the larger stem an arbour capable of containing half-a-dozen men. This holy tree was, according to the Somal [the Somali people], a place of prayer for the infidel, and its ancient honors are not departed. Here, probably to com-memorate the westward progress of the tribe, the Gudabirsi Ugaz or chief has the white canvass turban bound about his brows, and hence

rides forth to witness the equestrian games in the Harawwah Valley. As everyone who passes by, visits the Halimalah tree, foraging parties of the Northern Eesa and the Jibril Abokr (a clan of the Habr Awal) ['Iise and Habar Awal are Somali clans]. . . . According to Bruce this tree flourishes everywhere on the low hot plains between, the Red Sea and the Abyssinian hills. The Gallas revere it and plant it over sacerdotal graves.

The Aw-Barkhadle graves are part of a sacred landscape that includes the trees. As noted earlier, some of the trees grow out from the very heart of the graves (Figure 3.21). Burton tells us nothing about who the 'Galla chieftain' was, but it can be assumed that the Somalis of his time were not followers of the sacred tree tradition. Nevertheless, he also hastens to note that the tree's 'ancient honor' is still significant to the Somali clans who hold important events there and visit the Halimaleh tree. Kirk wonders if Halimaleh was the tree of Hanfeley (Kirk, 1905: 91–108). He quotes Burton: "[T]he Gallas are still tree worshippers, and the Somali respect this venerable vegetable as do the English their Druidical mistletoe" (ibid.).

The continuity of reverence of trees amongst Muslims in the Horn of Africa is also noted by Conti Rossini, quoted in Trimingham (1965: 260–261):

> I also observed another extravagant supervision, which we could scarcely expect from Mahomedans [Muslims]. They pay great respect to certain trees. There was a tree in Mersa which they particularly hold in great reverence. My people, desiring to sit down under its shadow, were immediately driven away, lest the *Adbar* should be angry. *Adbar* means keeper or watchman. They grease this tree and perform religious ceremonies under it. Nobody dares touch or damage the tree without risking a severe punishment.

The Gikuyu of Kenya similarly take the view that the breaking off, or damage to, a branch of the *mugumo* tree (natal fig) is a bad omen that requires a cleansing ritual (Muriuki, 1975, 2005; Kairu, 2015). Not only do people in the Horn of Africa protect their sacred trees; anyone transgressing these traditional values or violating the custom-based laws is punished. Conti Rossini has observed that in the Muslim Amhara region any touching or damaging of the tree would lead to punishment, an observation supported by Révoil who recorded that any damage to a branch of the *dange* tree by the Somali of Nugaal 'would bring the death of a close parent' (Révoil, 1882: 343). Trimingham noted an excessive syncretism of religions within the Horn (Trimingham, 1952: 28, 55). He suggests that the sacred groves around the churches in Ethiopia derived from the Agao cult (Révoil, 1882: 28, 54). The Agao, as will be discussed later, are considered to preserve the original Cushitic religion that so many Cushitic groups lost when they converted to the Abrahamic religions.

Thesiger has also noted how, in this region of eastern Ethiopia and western Somaliland, the dead are commemorated through the wooden *das*,

> large hollow cones formed of stacked tree trunks. . . . In one case four mimosa saplings had been planted in a rough square inside and joined up by thin poles placed horizontally, these poles and the trees being decorated with pieces of cloth and a sheepskin.
>
> (1935: 12)

Thesiger suggests that the trophies of 'victims' might also have been hung up on these trees. The *waqlaal* ceremony too involves hanging the bones of the sacrificial animals from the trees (Chapter 4). Thesiger seems surprised about the effort the Afar put into constructing monuments for their ancestors: "[T]hey [the Dankali] live in the crudest shelters but will carry tree trunks and large stones over very considerable distances for these monuments of the dead" (ibid.). Yet I have observed the same practice in much of the Horn of Africa: it seems that the belief in sacred ancestors, the notion of sacred fertility and the materiality of blessing (*baraka*) are sufficient to justify this kind of effort.

Ritual activity is not limited to the official veneration of the tomb of Saint Aw-Barkhadle or to women hanging *marqaha* on the trees. Furthermore, African custom-based law has preserved many indigenous philosophies, including that of the Somali *xeer* (law) *bir-ma-geydo* (discussed in Chapter 4) which protects, amongst other things, the trees that are sacred. It also extends to water.

Water and fertility rituals

At Aw-Barkhadle, one of my interviewees told me about the blessed waters, the *tog*, which provide water yearly through the rains and about the well (Figure 2.1 and Figure 3.22). Moisture is a vital element in the notion of fertility. Keeping things 'wet' (for example household leather objects) is known to be important to other Cushitic peoples, such as the Oromo and the Konso in Ethiopia, who still observe the traditional Cushitic religion (Loo, 1991; Hallpike, 1972).

> like the *dooxa* [*wadi*] here that goes all the way to Berbera, there is no special place but the waters here are all blessed by the Sheikh [referring to Saint Aw-Barkhadle]. All diseases are healed there.
>
> ("Sheikha, temporary keeper, Aw-Barkhadle", pers. comm. 2007)

It is believed that Saint Aw-Barkhadle miraculously brought a well into existence by striking the ground with his stick (some say a dagger or a spear). There are plenty such wells which are often thought to be sacred through their association with Sufi saints. The women wash at the sacred waters of

Figure 3.22 The sacred so-called well of Aw-Barkhadle

the *wadi* (*dooxa*) (Figure 2.1) and the well (Figure 3.22) (which is actually a *bali*, a man-made lake created historically by the sheikh) in order to purify, sanctify and consecrate themselves ready to receive the blessing of the Saint. They wash themselves during the night and pray for the sheikh to give them children. For the Somali, water means life; it symbolises fertility.

The well of Aw-Barkhadle must be viewed in the context of fertility rituals and the other sacred wells in the region. Some of the water sources are also naturally hot and as such are associated with the healing effect. According to one of my more prolific interviewees, the former president of Somaliland, Mr Daahir Riyaale Kahin (2007), there exists in a place called Bagay, in the western region of Jilay area, a well called 'Eel Galka Madow (the Well of the Black Cave). This is a sacred well in which the *ugaaska* (leader of the lineage) of the Gedibuursi clan traditionally took his annual coronation bath. The purpose of the bath was to wash away all the faults of the people through the washing of the lineage leader in sacred waters; through this annual royal ritual bath, the clan would prosper and the people flourish.

A leader is traditionally anointed with butter/ghee or milk, in much the same way as the bride is in her wedding bath (Chapter Four). It is also important to note that the 'Eel Galka Madow is, to my knowledge, the only sacred well that is exclusively used by the leader of the Gedibuursi clan, a man responsible for the prosperity and well-being of the entire clan. There are similarities here between the Konso priest who is the giver of life through the purification and fertility ceremonies (Hallpike, 1972) and the Somali *ugaas*. Even today, the Somali clan leaders record all male children that are born into the lineage, this being a sign that that lineage extends through each male child. Generally, all Somali traditional leaders take part in a *caleemo saar* ceremony where they are covered with leaves. *Caleemo* means leaves and the verb *saar* (not to be confused with *saar* the spirit) means to put over or cover with. The use of leaves is historically also related to the notion of sacred trees.

The Danakil people live close to the 'Iise and Gedibuursi Somali clans in northeastern Ethiopia and the northwestern Somali region including Djibouti. Similar concepts exist too amongst the Danakili, as Thesiger, who crossed Mount Jira and the 'boiling' springs, confirms (1935: 17). The hot springs are healing places associated with divinities.

Water and its sanctity together form a common pilgrimage pattern in the Horn of Africa. In Abu Menas, the sanctuary of St Menas, a World Heritage Site near Alexandria, it is reported that water was a crucial religious commodity as it was believed to possess a curative capacity (Finneran, 2002). Worshippers bring home bottles filled with water from the Zamzam well[10] in Mecca. Zamzam water, hung in bottles on the front doors of houses and businesses in the Somali region, is used to protect inhabitants from the evil eye. It is also used to treat people with various physical and mental illnesses, including infertility. And amongst the Somali and Ethiopian peoples, holy water is sprinkled on a possessed person as a form of exorcism.

Furthermore, semen is called water (*bio*) in the Somali language. Since human offspring is seen to be the result of the male's semen and the woman's womb, the semen gives life while the womb is a vessel. It is the reason why the male sexual organ is a symbol of fertility. This relationship will be explored further in relation to the discussion of the legend of Bu'ur Ba'ayr and phallic stones in the archaeological context of the Horn of Africa.

Fat (moisture) and fertility rituals

Fat is associated with fertility. The slaughter of animals and the use of their fat plays a crucial role at Aw-Barkhadle. The *Muriid* and the sheikhs, as well as the sheikhas, anoint themselves constantly with animal fat to increase their own vitality. One of the Aw-Barkhadle visitors also used *haydh* to anoint her baby boy as a fertility protection ritual. Moisture is particularly pertinent when it comes to human skin and things such as trees or objects worked from leather. When a person is possessed or cursed, Somali sheikhs or traditional healers will order the person to anoint themselves regularly in order to purify their sins and to sanctify their body, thus preventing the entry of *jins* and evil spirits. In the case of the Oromo in Ethiopia, if someone lets leather objects or their own skin dry out it can cause bad luck (Loo,

1991). If the body (and skin) is allowed to dry, then fertility (or wetness) will be lost. Within the Oromo, women's leather gowns are always kept moisturised (ibid.).

Thesiger noted a similar practice amongst the Danakil people (1935: 2) who share many customs with the Somali and the Oromo. At his coronation, the sheikh of the Budhu, who is the leader of the two clans of the Asboura and Badogalet, "is believed to receive the power of controlling rain" and he is "smeared with ghee" (ibid.: 7). The Conti Rossini's account on the greasing of the holy tree amongst the Somali is also noteworthy. I will give further Somali examples of this practice in the section on the fertility bath (Chapter 4). The sheikhs and sheikhas at Aw-Barkhadle smear themselves with fat after the ritual meals, and the Konso, another Eastern Cushitic speaking people, anoint their heads and their sacred stones with butter in the rain-making and fertility rituals (Hallpike, 1972: 262). The Somali Ramadan songs emphasise fat (*subag*) and its health benefits. I once visited the site of Aw-Barkhadle during Ramadan and the need for *subag*[11] was emphasised here too. We had to slaughter animals for the sheikhs in the name of fertility and prosperity. Fat seems not only to be associated with good health in general; it also has a significant role to play as a ritual component in the breaking of the fast. I suggest that it also has a significant part to play in fertility rituals as can be seen in the ritual of *baanashada dumarka* (discussed in Chapter Four). One of my interviewees is cited there who was asked why she tied a band of fat (*haydh*) to her son's forehead; she replied that it was so that Saint Aw-Barkhadle might bless him with fertility forever. It is a common practice among the Eastern Cushitic speakers to put a protective band on the forehead of the child, as, for example, in the use of the *injicca*, a leather band, by the Guji Oromo (Loo, 1991).

However, the Somali Yibir also use *subag* to smear on the sacred trees at Hanfeley's grave (Kirk, 1905). And the Yibir are known to be associated with the history of Aw-Barkhadle centre through their own memories and through the story of Bu'ur Ba'ayr/Mohammed Haniif and Aw-Barkhadle.

Sacred enclosure at the Bu'ur Ba'ayr hill

An open-air enclosure of stones is located on the hill of Bu'ur Ba'ayr (Figure 2.1). Stones form a circle of about 30 metres in diameter (Figure 2.7). According to my interviewees, there are many practices that have taken place at this enclosure which is understood to be both historical and sacred. The enclosure was used by Aw-Barkhadle to teach the new faith. He sat on the sacred stone (currently known as the fertility stone). He is credited with inventing a Somali name for writing the Arabic language and the holy Qur'an. The centre of Aw-Barkhadle therefore holds a revered place in the history of Somali literacy. The *Muriid* showed me a stone inside the enclosure on which could be seen a little black well in which ink was once kept (Figure 3.23).

Figure 3.23 The ink-stone with the niche for the black charcoal ink (*khad*)

People play games here too, games claimed to originate from Bu'ur Ba'ayr's time (i.e. before Islam). Some of these that particularly relate to rituals are regarded as 'wicked' by modern-day Somali Muslim society. One such game is called *Biito*. One of my interviewees in Hargeisa alleges that in Bu'ur Ba'ayr's time, naked girls played the *Biito* in front of him. The girls would sit in front of him with their legs outstretched and sing the *Biito* song and with every verse they would touch their legs in a particular order. I note here just three versions I know of this well known and ancient Somali children's song:

Version 1:

Biitooy biito,
biito xariira,
nayshay deylan,
oo daba oogan,
banbannaanis,
bankay daaqo,
bal aan soo eegee
biitooy laabo!

Version 2:

Biitooy biito,
biito xariira,
shillin baa duustay
gafanaa sheegay
sheelaa macawis

Version 3:

Kumbudhlooy,
kumbudhlaalo caddooy,
xabag geed ka baxdaay,
bilo bilo,
bilojira,
koodaar,
ka u dheer,
ee dhexaad,
ku jaboo,
ku jiqsii,
Biitooy laabo!

When the last word '*biitoy laabo*' is spoken, the person whose leg is touched must lift her knee up, keeping her foot bent. The game carries on until all but one child's leg is bent with the knee up. That last child loses the game. People say the bent legs' position would expose the little children's genitals and that it is for this wicked purpose that Bu'ur Ba'ayr invented this game. However, children – albeit fully dressed – still play this game today and there is no wickedness associated with it. Here is an example of yet another charge laid against this leader; perhaps this *biito* exposure is as false a belief as the one about Hanfeley's abduction of diseased Yibirs. Some people also suggest that the *biito* might belong to an older tradition of children's dancing going back to the Ancient Egyptians.

   This game is one of many 'iniquitous' traditions generally associated with Bu'ur Ba'ayr. And, according to the religious sheikhs and sheikhas at Aw-Barkhadle, the sacred enclosure is the ubiquitous space where all such rituals once took place.

   According to the legend, as I noted earlier, Bu'ur Ba'ayr was said to 'marry' a couple by sleeping with the bride on the first six nights of the wedding after which the bride was returned to her husband (cf. the *Muriid*; Sheikha temporary keeper; the *Muriid*'s wife, 2007). Only after Bu'ur Ba'ayr had spent these nights with her could she be considered to be married to the man. The legend also suggests that Bu'ur Ba'ayr practiced witchcraft to heal any possible illnesses that the woman might have before she married her man.

The people I interviewed suggested that when Saint Aw-Barkhadle arrived at the *landscape c.* 850 years ago, Bu'ur Ba'ayr was sitting in the enclosure and preaching his religion. This enclosure is now the sacred enclosure of Aw-Barkhadle, from where, it is said, Saint Aw-Barkhadle preached the Qur'an on the hill after incarcerating Bu'ur Ba'ayr inside.

The stone on which Bu'ur Ba'ayr is said to have sat while preaching was the fertility stone (Figure 2.6), and this was his seat in the enclosure. However, this stone is now referred to as the sacred stone of Saint Aw-Barkhadle on which *he* sat as he taught Islam and developed the Somali Arabic writing. This suggests that religious preaching continued at the enclosure after it had been taken over by Aw-Barkhadle.

The cult of Bu'ur Ba'ayr may perhaps have been based on the idea that a person could possess supernatural powers which were linked to the sacred enclosure, mountain and stone that are all still in use today, as will be explained in more detail later. Together, these form the material features in the landscape that symbolise what is today a sacred ritual landscape. The legend provides a good example of how ideas about sacred spaces can develop and how the use of sacred space can change.

If this is so, then the pre-Islamic enclosure, with its ritual and material features, might have been incorporated into the practices of a new faith. This kind of appropriation of sacred space has been found in other parts of the Horn. Aksum, itself a pre-Christian sacred space, became the centre for one of the earliest Christian communities in Sub-Saharan Africa (Phillipson, 1997). The idea that Sufi Muslim traditions similarly absorbed many of the characteristics of the pre-existing religion, thereby attracting more followers, will be discussed in Chapter Six. Certain elements of the old religions and their practices, it seems, retain their significance even today.

In Somali, an *arish* is either an enclosure made of wooden sticks or, sometimes, a whole house or hut built of the same material. The Qur'an *madarasa* or *dugsi* (school) is one such *arish*. There is a symbolic significance attached to the *arish* since Qur'an *madarasa* are traditionally built in a concrete material. Shoes are not allowed and people enter barefooted because it is considered to be a sacred space. In the sacred enclosure at Aw-Barkhadle there exists a stone (Figure 3.23) with depressions or holes with dark marks; it is uncertain when it was last used. *Khad*, which is usually made by grinding up charcoal and adding tree resin and water, is washed off the *lawh*, the wooden tablet. When a sheikh uses *khad* to write the Qur'an on a *lawh*, and the writing on the *lawh* is washed away, the water running off is collected and thought to be sacred; some people may even drink it for healing purposes. Since the ink is made of natural products (coal and resin), the black water is not seen as unclean or dangerous; on the contrary, it symbolises the sacred verses of the holy Qur'an.

I now move on from the most well known female fertility rituals to the more discrete ones. Some of these female rituals are performed in secret and are therefore not undertaken during the period of the official veneration unless they can be practiced with great discretion. These rituals, unlike those discussed above, do not take place at the tombs of the Islamic ancestors; instead, they are performed in other areas of the sacred landscape of Aw-Barkhadle. In short, these are not official rituals but ones that are relevant to, or originate from, regional indigenous practices.

The sacred fertility stone(s)

At Aw-Barkhadle, there is *dhagaha dumarka* (lit. the stone of the women) or *dhagaha dhalka* (lit. the stone of the women or the stone of fertility) (Figure 2.6; Figure 2.1), which I call a fertility stone. The sheikh, as noted earlier, used this stone when he preached the Qur'an. The *Muriid* pointed out to me that the stone has been worn down and said that this process was the result of the long occupancy of the site first by Bu'ur Ba'ayr and then by Saint Aw-Barkhadle. The official version about the historical function of the stone is that it was used as a seat, as the *Muriid* will tell any inquisitive researcher. However, as I learnt from mixing with the women who want to become pregnant, its non-official and equally historically valid use is linked to non-Islamic practices. I was told that the stone had been there in pre-Islamic times.

By spending time at Aw-Barkhadle with women, even during evening rituals, such as dhikri, in 2007, I learned more about the fertility stone and the discrete female fertility rituals that have taken place at the sacred enclosure in the past. Women usually come to Aw-Barkhadle on the day that such rituals are due to take place. They come in the name of *ziyara*. Some may already have had children but no boys. They bring gifts including a sheep and *khat* which is a flowering plant indigenous to East Africa[12] and Arabia. The *khat* is an amphetamine-like stimulant which brings excitement, sleeplessness, hallucinations, euphoria and a lack of hunger. The women bring gifts for the sheikh including incense and perfumes. The first meeting takes place in mid-afternoon, around three o'clock, in the courtyard, fenced by a sacred tree, *tugaar* (*Acacia nilotica*), at the back of the tomb of Saint Aw-Barkhadle (Figure 3.24). Afternoon prayers follow.

They next slaughter a sheep and start cooking the food. Just after sunset prayers, they all share the sacrificial food in the sacrificial enclosure next to the courtyard behind Saint Aw-Barkhadle's tomb (see plan of site). The sheep's meat at Aw-Barkhadle is divided according to tradition. The back legs and the ribs with chest meat go to the men, including the *Muriid*. The head goes to the household of the *Muriid*, and particularly to the wife. In Somali society, there is often a more rigorous and ritually significant division of meat from animals which have been slaughtered and sacrificed. In my own family in the 1980s in Mogadishu, for example, slaughtered animals were divided in a particular way between our neighbours and every year they each received the same part of the sacrificial animal meat as the year before. In return, we received the same parts back from their sacrificial

Figure 3.24 Ritual enclosure for prayers, ritual meals and meetings at Aw-Barkhadle

animals. The Konso, too, share particular ritual parts of the animals they slaughter for sacrifice (Hallpike, 1972: 102). Somalis consider the head, the stomach and the paws to be impure (cf. Cerulli, 1957: 149); women, however, do use the stomach and head to make delicacies which they consume in private.

According to Somali tradition, the men and women eat separately at Aw-Barkhadle, with the men communally eating from one large plate. After a late lunch/early dinner, the women will wash up and leave the tomb of Saint Aw-Barkhadle. The men stay sitting together in a room at the back of the mausoleum, where the tomb of Sheikh Ali is located, and start the *dhikri* and the chewing of the *khat*, in between the prayers.

The second gathering of the women proceeds to the house of the *Muriid*'s wife; she may lead the women's own *dhikri* with the rest of the group joining in with singing and clapping. Some of the women stand up and dance slowly to begin with then pick up speed as they move faster and faster. The *dhikri* lasts about an hour and a half. Soon after the *'ishaayi* (evening prayer), usually about 7.30 p.m., some women may start to walk down to the water source (the so-called sacred well), which is about 800 metres from the Aw-Barkhadle tomb and about 1.3 kilometres from where they first gathered on the town side of Aw-Barkhadle. The women walk in silence. There are usually no men around at this hour. The people nearest to them will be the men playing drums and singing *dhikri* in a concrete room at the back door of the tomb of Saint Aw-Barkhadle a few hundred metres away. Any woman wishing to become pregnant would be wise not to be seen out at night.

The women explained the ritual to me. They would wash themselves in the blessed waters of the *wadi* and the well while saying a few prayers. *'Wali'alah'ow, caafiimaad iyo caruur'isii"* 'A friend of God give me health and children.' The women continue saying this while washing their heads and arms and legs repeatedly.

The women then walk 150 metres towards the sacred enclosure near the Bu'ur Ba'ayr hill. Each sits on the sacred fertility stone in the enclosure for about five minutes and during this time prays for fertility, reciting the Qur'an and saying 'A friend of God give me health and children.' Some women will specifically ask for a boy (*I'nnan/wiil*).

Fertility rocks at Goroyo Cawl

Saint Aw-Barkhadle is associated with other sacred centres beyond the Aw-Barkhadle landscape. There is, for example, another sacred shrine, Goroyo Cawl. It lies in the western region bordering on Ethiopia, near the town of Boorama (Figure 1.1). It contains fertility stones, and rituals similar to the ones I have described at the Aw-Barkhadle sacred stone in the sacred enclo-sure take place there. The stones of Goroyo Awl are black and located next to a sacred enclosure associated with Sheikh Aw-Barkhadle (Figure 2.7). There are no settlements near the site. The Boorama Road passes close by. The Goroyo Awl black fertility stones carry engravings of the same type as those found at Dameer Gowrac at Laaso. Both have the sinuous snake/sword shapes or vague 'S' shapes and have oval depressions (Figure 3.25). There are five visible stones, the tallest being about two metres in height.

Women visit Goroyo Cawl at night and they sit on the fertility stones and pray to receive a child or a male child in much the same way as happens at Aw-Barkhadle. They use the two biggest stones, which are about two metres high, for their fertility rituals. The top of the largest and tallest stone is covered with small carved oval depressions (Figure 3.25). Furthermore, and even more intriguingly, the biggest stone also has an engraving of what seems to be a snake. Similar marks also appear on large stones in the Sanaag region. *Dhagahda Seefaha leh*, the stones with engraved sword motifs, can be found in the Dameer Gowrac mountain chain, near Laaso and about two hours' drive from the town of Berbera (Figure 1.1 and Figure 3.26). These stones are massive as the pictures show. It is possible that these too were used for fertility rituals at some point in the past. The site is set in an extraordinary landscape at the foot of the mountains. Close to the massive stones, which appear to lie around as if they had fallen randomly long ago, are some graves. The graves look very old and the orientation is not the Islamic east–west alignment; they were therefore most probably connected

Figure 3.25 The oval depressions on the black granite rocks of Goroyo Cawl rocks

to people who attached great significance to being buried close to the massive engraved stones (Figure 3.27). No one lives in the bushy areas that surround them. Nevertheless, it is possible that they are still used secretly for fertility rituals. The symbols on these massive black granite stones are similar in style to the ones found on the black fertility stones of Goroyo Cawl. Given that the latter is both a shrine dedicated to Saint Aw-Barkhadle and one where female fertility rituals still take place today, it seems more than likely that the massive black stones of Dameer Gowrac hold a similar meaning for the people of this region.

Dhaymoole, another site with potentially ritual stones, lies an hour's drive from Laaso. It is a place that is archaeologically rich in burials and spatially associated with painted and engraved rock shelters. A big red granite rock is engraved with markings in the style of Laaso and Goroyo Cawl (Figure 3.28). The people living in Dhaymoole are aware of the stones but do not report any ritual activities taking place at these stones nowadays.

The distribution of these snake-shape or vague S-shape engravings occurs on stones all over the Somali territories. Their distribution indicates that this practice of engraving was widespread in the northern part of the Somali region. It is possible that these places mark ancient hunting grounds where knives and swords would have been sharpened on these sacred fertility

Figure 3.26 Sinuous snake-like shapes on stones of Dhagaha Seefaha leh, Dameer
        Gowrac

stones and game would have been slaughtered in their sacred enclosures.
Sacred fertility stones are known to exist at both Aw-Barkhadle and Goroyo
Cawl. Dhaymoole and Laaso may also once have had sacred fertility rocks
even though these ritual practices no longer seem to take place.

The worship of stones seems also to have existed in pre-Islamic (South)
Arabia (Serjeant, 1976) where the black stone is also associated with

Figure 3.27 The massive granite stones of Dhagaha Seefaha leh, Dameer Gawrac

Figure 3.28 Dhaymoole ground-rock engraved with sinuous signs and oval shapes

fertility rituals. Does the Somali veneration of black fertility stones bear any relationship to a similar phenomenon in Arabia? People on the other side of the Red Sea are known to have offered up to deities animals which had been slaughtered at sacred stones (ibid.), in much the same way as the Konso today slaughter sheep on their phallic sacred stones to obtain fertility (Hallpike, 1972). And, echoing Serjeant's findings in Arabia, the Konso believed that by sacrificing to these deities, the rains would come. If they did not, then this would be seen as a sign that the souls of the people doing the sacrificing needed to be purified. The idea of purification can be found on both sides of the Red Sea.

Aw-Barkhadle includes a sacred fertility stone. It is a place where people slaughter animals to offer up to the divine powers even though they do not necessarily do so at the stone itself. Goroyo Cawl is an enclosure of black sacred fertility stones also used by women to slaughter animals as offerings to Aw-Barkhadle. This suggests that notions of sacred fertility associated with black stones existed on both sides of the Red Sea. Does this mean that the deities worshipped were once similar? Did the people follow the same religion(s), just as they do with Islam today? If so, does this point to shared religious trajectories in prehistorical times? It is certainly possible. I found a grave with a stele that has inscriptions of the ancient South Arabian language (Sabaean) at Shalcaw, on the Red Sea coast, in the Sanaag region (Figure 3.29, Mire, 2015a). This reveals the presence of South Arabian writing

Figure 3.29 A grave with Sabaean/Himyarite inscription at Shalcaw

on this side of the Red Sea. Excavations at sites such as Shalcaw may shed light on this issue.

The phallic stones, fertility and Aw-Barkhadle

Among the Islamic tombs surrounding the mausoleum of Saint Aw-Barkhadle, I found a phallic stone serving as one of four gravestones on the corners of a tomb (Figure 3.30a and Figure 3.30b). It was upside down and very little of it was visible. However, when I picked up a small tip from the corner of

Figure 3.30a The phallic stone of Aw-Barkhadle

Figure 3.30b The phallic stone of Aw-Barkhadle on its niche in one of the corners
    of a tomb

the tomb, I discovered that this was a phallic stone with a clear glans. It was
29 cm in height with a glans 12 cm wide; the distance below the glans was
10 cm. It had been placed on one of four corners of the grave and the niche
it was resting in had been painted green to match the gland of the stone that
rested there (Figure 3.30b). Ancient indigenous ideologies' use of the phallic to represent fertility was a common practice in northeast Africa dating

Figure 3.30c The north African regional God Osiris responsible for human, animal and crop fertility and lifeforce depicted with phallic symbolism, Ptolemaic times

Source: (copyright Rijksmuseum van Oudheden, Leiden)

back to the region's Pharaonic past, if not before. Osiris, the regional God of fertility and life force was often depicted with a phallic symbol, especially in Ptolemaic times (Figure 3.30c). Phallic symbolism can be found too in regional Somali archaeology of the last couple of millennia: a few years after I discovered the phallic symbol at Aw-Barkhadle, two more phallic stones were found at a cairn burial site in Arabsiyo, 45 minutes west of Hargeisa by an owner digging the cairn in the hope of finding gold (Figure 3.31a, Figure 3.31b for the *in situ* phallic stone at Sufi Orgome). Furthermore, looters have unearthed stone sculptures of human heads and torsos wearing complex regalia including phallic stones placed on top of their heads. These are strikingly similar to the phallic *Kallascha* of the Oromo and the Konso.[13]

Islam was initially introduced by the Arabs into all the regions conquered by the Muslims; it was a religion of the elite and it did not immediately have much of an impact on the local culture. In many parts of the world, people conquered by Islam were allowed to keep both their language and their practices just so long as they payed taxes and accepted the rule of the Arab elite. A similar process seems initially to have taken place in the Somali region too: lives changed very little and, in the hinterland, traditional practices continued alongside only a slow growth in Islamic awareness. It is therefore not surprising that Christian and other burials still occur alongside the Islamic ones in some burial grounds, in random locations. These, taken

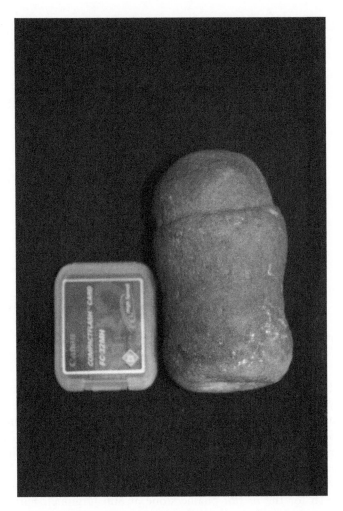

Figure 3.31a One of the Arabsiyo phallic stones

together, seem to embody a meaning for the locals, a meaning that is often layered with unspoken traditions and practices.

While doing some background research prior to excavation in 2007, I searched the collections at the British Museum for objects of Somali provenance. I found two stones labelled 'phallic gravestones' in the Curle collection of 1937. The only information attached to them stated that they were part of A. T. Curle's collection and gathered during the time that Somaliland was a British protectorate. The phallic gravestones (I and II) discovered by Curle in 1937 (Figure 3.32a and Figure 3.32b) are similar to the stone discovered at Aw-Barkhadle. Their provenance is unknown; Curle, however, is known to have travelled in the Awdal region of western British Somaliland.

Figure 3.31b Sufi Orgome phallic stone *in situ*

There is also another tomb at Aw-Barkhadle which has a corner with a space for a stone of about the same size and shape as the phallic one that I found. However, the space is now empty (Figure 3.33). Incidentally, this missing stone probably has nothing to do with Curle as he did not go to Aw-Barkhadle – his 1937 article in *Antiquity* makes no reference to Aw-Barkhadle or the Hargeisa region. The existence of phallic stones in the Hargeisa region (at Arabsiyo and Aw-Barkhadle) as well as in the Awdal region may well indicate that the practice of using phallic stones as grave

Figure 3.32a A phallic stone collected by A. T. Curle and kept at the British Museum

markers was widespread in the Somali region in pre-Islamic times. There are graves in Sanaag where phallic shaped stones are placed on top of the cairns in a circle (Figure 3.34). I further examine this practice of using phallic stones in Chapter Six and place it within a regional context that includes the Konso, the Oromo and most of the Horn of Africa.

I have found from my inspection of Curle's phallic stones from the Awdal region that one of them is the same size as the Aw-Barkhadle stone. The

Figure 3.32b A phallic stone collected by A. T. Curle and kept at the British Museum
Source: © The Trustees of the British Museum

other phallic gravestone (II) found by Curle is bigger, about 35–40 cm (Figure 3.32a and Figure 3.32b). One of the phallic stones I discovered in 2010 in Arabsiyo is the same size as the one at Aw-Barkhadle stone – but the other one is much smaller.

Furthermore, there are at Aw-Barkhadle two stones, broken into pieces, that also appear to have once been phallic. This suggests that stones like these have been destroyed intentionally or unintentionally. The fact that the

Figure 3.33 A niche for a phallic stone on a grave at Aw-Barkhadle

green painted phallic stone at Aw-Barkhadle is turned upside down, perhaps in an attempt to hide it, shows that it today does not have the meaning it might have had in the past. When I asked what the stone was for no one had any idea and it seemed to me that they were hesitant to talk about it.

The minaret-like pillar placed in a central position on the roof of the mausoleum of Saint Aw-Barkhadle is also reminiscent of a phallic grave-stone. This tradition of phallic symbolism on tombs or gravestones and

Figure 3.34 A cairn burial in Sanaag with phallic grave stones on top *in situ*

indigenous, and especially religious, architecture, occurs across the Horn of Africa. Mohammed found a few similar pillars in southern Somalia, particularly in the ancient quarters of Mogadishu (Mohammed, 1991). According to Hallpike, 'Traditionally, priests alone had phallic roof-pots on their huts' (1972: 251). The phallic symbolism of the architecture at Aw-Barkhadle will be discussed in Chapter Six; suffice to note here that it is curious that the symbol of a phallus seems to have been reconstructed into a pillar. However, a two-pronged metal stick is mounted on top of the phallic gravemarker and I was told that this two-pronged shape over the phallic grave markers of Saint Aw-Barkhadle's tomb is a Sufi mark. Sometimes it has three prongs like the sticks associated with Sufis in the region. There are also other tombs at the site of Aw-Barkhadle that have a three-pronged iron head on a stick.

Incidentally, the Konso have phallic roof-pots which are mounted with an ostrich egg (ibid.: 251). This symbolism has a dual purpose; the whiteness of the egg repels evil forces and the egg itself, according to Hallpike, may symbolise fertility. In Somali culture, iron seems to have had a similar function to that of the Konso egg whites: it is believed to repel evil spirits, a function discussed in the next chapter in relation to child protection rituals. The practice of three prongs will also be discussed in relation to other sites in the Horn of Africa. It is important here to consider the significance of the pre-Islamic notions of phallic symbols in so far as the Bu'ur Ba'ayr narrative will allow.

These stones signify a non-Islamic idea of fertility. Before describing this, it is worth first paying careful attention to the narrative of Bu'ur Ba'ayr; '*Wax la meheriyo majirin, Bu'ur Ba'ayr baa qoodhihiisa ku meherinjiray*' [There was no wedding ritual, only Bu'ur Ba'ayr married women with his penis] (Sheikha, at the time a temporary keeper at Aw-Barkhadle, pers. comm. 2007). There is as yet no written record of the phallic gravestones of Somaliland as Curle never published his finds, but it is worth considering that the phallic stones may be related to a belief in sacred semen. I noted earlier that in Somali the word 'water' is used for semen to imply its life-giving qualities. A sacred man would surely have been considered to have life-giving qualities.

The legend of Bu'ur Ba'ayr/Mohammed Haniif

I have already discussed the controversial figure of Bu'ur Ba'ayr in Chapter Two. I now want to consider how the legend associated with him can shed light on the phallic stone discovered in the Aw-Barkhadle landscape – and possibly on others recorded in the archaeology and ethnography of the Horn of Africa. The ancient belief in the Sky-God *Waaq* seems to have been strongly linked to phallic symbolism and fertility ideology in general. According to the legend, Bu'ur Ba'ayr (a.k.a. Mohamed Haniif) used to bestow marriage by sleeping with the bride for six nights before returning her to her husband; it was only after spending the first six nights with him that she would be truly married. A marriage was legitimate only if Bu'ur Ba'ayr had slept with the woman before her husband did. As one of my interviewees put it, Bu'ur Ba'ayr married women with his penis, after he slept with women for six nights ('Sheikha, temporary keeper', 2007). The legend suggests that Bu'ur Ba'ayr continued this tradition unchallenged until Sharif Yusuf came to the place which has become known as Aw-Barkhadle.

As already noted in Chapter Two, the Yibir claim Mohammed Haniif (Bu'ur Ba'ayr) as their Islamic *boqor*, a king who ruled over a wide area. However, it is possible that it is Bu'ur Ba'ayr rather than Mohamed Haniif who is attributed with the many ritual powers (*buruud*). It seems that one of these powers was that of granting fertility through the alleged wedding ritual. It is entirely possible, of course, that people are mixing two different religious heads who operated in the area at the same time, since some believe him to be 'pagan' while others think he was a good Muslim. If this is the case, and there are both a Bu'ur Ba'ayr type of leader and a Mohamed Haniif type of leader who coexisted at Aw-Barkhadle, then animosity towards the Yibir people may well have resulted in the labelling of Mohamed Haniif as Bu'ur Ba'ayr, with the latter being a healer of non-Islamic tradition. I want now to reflect on the traditions associated with this period to consider how they may shed light on the relationship between pre-Islamic belief and the present-day non-Islamic rituals of the Buʿur Baʿayr legend

1) GRANTING MARITAL LEGITIMACY AND SACRED FERTILITY

The story of Buʿur Baʿayr presents a picture of a man with supernatural powers, of one with a penis that bestows sanctity of marriage. In the views of my interviewees, his penis is considered to be the instrument of the marriage ritual. Having recorded a phallic stone at Aw-Barkhadle, I cannot help but associate it with the myth of Buʿur Baʿayr and the regional Cushitic traditions which also regard symbolic intercourse (though, as far as I know, not actual intercourse) as an element in the wedding ritual. Was the worship of phallic stones connected to Buʿur Baʿayr and his method of 'marrying' couples? The Konso are known to carry out sacrifice on top of phallic stones. Even though the Haniifa elders know nothing about the existence of phallic stones in Aw-Barkhadle or elsewhere, the dominant Somali say that Buʿur Baʿayr/Mohamed Haniif used the fertility stone (*dhagaha dhalka*) to check that the bride was not having her period (a time when she would be considered impure) during the first week of her wedding. The use of a fertility stone ritually soiled with blood is reminiscent of the Konso phallic stones (discussed later). Although it cannot be proved, it is possible that the existence of phallic stones at Aw-Barkhadle and in other parts of the Somali territories points to the continuing existence of what were originally non-Islamic traditions. Rituals such as phallic stones serving as gravestones or featuring in ritual ceremonies might well in some way or other have remained ritually important, either explicitly or implicitly, to society in general.

According to oral accounts, there existed within the tomb at Aw-Barkhadle a wooden sculpture that was used for fertility prayers; and there is also a phallic grave stone marking one of the tombs. It is therefore conceivable that there once existed the idea of a divine man (Buʿur Baʿayr or another) with the power to grant fertility. Without being able to differentiate between what is believed to have happened at Aw-Barkhadle and without being about to establish the relationship between the material found there and the narratives surrounding the site, any suggestion of such a divine man must remain speculative. However, the key to understanding the function and symbolism of such rituals may lie in wider comparisons across the Eastern Cushitic speaking regions extending as far as the Red Sea. Before considering that point, I want to look more closely at some of the evidence I have collected.

Oral reports tell how a marriage could only take place after a couple had passed though the sanctity of ritual intercourse. The union of a couple in Buʿur Baʿayr's time was legitimised through the involvement of the man who performed this (probably metaphorical) ritual intercourse. This man was held to be sacred by virtue of a divine religious presence through which the sexual relationship of the couple would be sanctified in marriage.

The purpose of the six first nights that Bu'ur Ba'ayr is said to have spent with a bride might not only be to grant marital legitimacy to the couple but also, more importantly, to grant them sacred fertility through his own sacred virility. But why would a couple bother with Bu'ur Ba'ayr when all they needed to do was to have intercourse with each other to see if they could have children on their own without his help? Perhaps it is here that the notion of divine kinship (described in Chapter Four) comes into play.

2) DIVINE KINSHIP THROUGH CONSECRATED MARRIAGE AND FERTILITY

I want to discuss further the idea of belonging to a sacred lineage, one in which the divine entity is the (founding) father of the lineage. The Oromo and the Konso, as noted later, believe that 'son of *Waaqa* has *Waaqa*'s ability.' Did the idea of divine kinship ever exist in Somali pre-Islamic society? I will investigate this issue in more detail in relation to the notion of virginity, fertility rituals and *Gudniin*/Pharaonic circumcision in the next chapter. More importantly, did a symbolic intercourse ritual offer a significant access point into a divine lineage? The concept of a divine kinship existing in the past is made more likely by the existence of ancestral worship within the pre-Islamic Cushitic institutions and the acknowledgment of sacred ancestral figures. In Chapter Five, I examine why divine kinship is important today in both Somalia and the larger Horn of Africa and how it is manifested through elaborate mythical and ritual systems that go within and beyond the current adherence to Christianity and Islam.

Gedi Baabow

In southern Somalia, Buur Hakaba (the mountain of Hakaba) is credited with pre-Islamic ritual relevance (Figure 1.1). According to the people who live there, Buur Hakaba itself is thought to possess supernatural power (cf. Kusow, 1995). There is also a rock shelter, Buur Haybe Mountain, (Brandt, 1986) which is thought to have been inhabited by deities. It is believed that there used to be a king who ruled this southern part of Somalia in a way similar to how Bu'ur Ba'ayr ruled the north. His name was Gedi Baabow. My interviewees confirm that this king is also believed to have married people by sleeping with the bride for six nights, only after which could she be wed to her groom.

There was a song mentioning 'Aw-Gedi Shambow' and marriage in Mogadishu in the 1980s. It was an old love song which describes Gedi Shambow as a hero whose wedding poems and drums are heard. The leading verse went '*Aw-Gedi Shamboowaa lagu guurihaayee*', meaning 'Me married with Saint Gedi Shambow'. Somali artist Sulfa sang this song [my translation]:

gamuunkii soo gantidaa gibilkii aay gaartaba gadoomaaye
the arrow you shoot the skin it hits falls

geesiyoow nin kuu gafay maa guuleeysahaaye, guuleeysahaayee
Oh hero, he who offends you will not win, will not win
gabayga yeeraayo guxaanka baxaayo iyo gurbaanka
The poems that are ringing, the noise sounding and drums that are
beating
aaw geedi shaamboowaa lagu guurihaaye lagu guurihaaye
Is for marrying with Aw-Geedi Shambow, marrying with
geedba geedka ka weeyn sidii loo gantoobaba adaa garataaye
The bigger the tree the better you know how to cut back
goshaan manaa gasho goofaha waa gariiraa alla waa gariiraa
If one enters your enclosure the chest shakes, yes it shakes
gabayga yeeraayo guxaanka baxaayo iyo gurbaanka
The poems that are ringing, the noise sounding and the drums that are
beating
aaw geedi shaamboowaa lagu guurihaaye lagu guurihaaye
Is for marrying with Aw-Geedi Shambow, marrying with

The song also refers to his peerless power in fighting, that he knows how to trim tall trees and how anyone who enters his enclosure will be shaking with fear. Aw-Gedi Shambow is a reference to Aw-Gedi-Baabow and the marriage rituals in which he is thought to have played a part. The sacred mountains of Buur Hakaba and Buur Heybe are also associated with similar rulers and their practices. In the name of communal fertility, during the annual commemoration of Sheikh Hussein Bali at his shrine in Annajina, Bale (in Ethiopia), women devotees kiss the closed mouths of the male followers. This also reveals a devotion and spirituality in the ritual context that is permitted to take place without censure. The practice might originate in the traditional religion of the Arsi/Oromo – the site of Sheikh Hussein is known for this mix of Oromo traditions and Islamic traditions. It may be that within the 'Cushitic institutions' issues such as symbolic intercourse and prayers for fertility were thought to be educational and uncontroversial and hence not given sexual connotations.

Cassanelli (1982) reported a phallic stone at Merka, and Mohammed (1991: 81–82) also describes a phallic monument he found in Shangaani in Mogadishu.

> Un jour, à *Muqdisho*, alors que je traversais le très vieux quartier *Shangaani* – le plus ancien avec celui de *Xamarweyne* – pour rencontrer des Sages, je découvris, au milieu d'une rue, une colonne blanche de forme phallique caractéristique.
>
> (ibid.)

This tradition of phallic grave-markers or phallic pillars featuring at prominent sites continues further down the east African coast. The ruins of Gedi and Takwa near Lamu show 'pillar tombs' as a feature of the archaeological medieval Islamic sites (Figure 3.35). I was told when I visited in June 2009 that the site is one of pilgrimage where rain-making rituals take place. This sacred site, like the Gedi site, is believed to be inhabited and protected by ancestral spirits. Since these objects are often still standing in places that have been transformed into Islamic sites, it seems that the followers of Islam have chosen to ignore rather than remove them. If the Aw-Barkhadle phallic stone is possibly associated with Bu'ur Ba'ayr, then so may these southern Somali phallic stones be associated with Gedi Babow or other similar 'old

Figure 3.35 Gedi and Takwa phallic stone making the pillar in Islamic tombs

Cushitic' practices. This may indicate that at some point in the past beliefs in a person with supernatural powers, and particularly one with the power to bring virility (signified by the phallic gravemarker), were widespread, a cult practiced all over the Horn of Africa.

Few references to kinship and male genitals can be found in metaphors, but one that does exist infers a relationship between kinship and male potency. Lewis mentions the persistence of the genealogies and notes Somalis' symbolic expression:

> In this context [patrilineal solidarity] Somali speak of patrilineal affiliation as having the strength of iron in contrast to weaker kinship ties which like thread can easily be snapped. They also compare their agnatic loyalties to testicles, a particularly apposite allusion since Somali express the fighting power of their lineages in terms of the number of penises they possess.
>
> (Lewis, 1962: 40)

The inference here is that kinship ties are as strong as iron, metaphorically speaking. In addition, patrilineal affiliation is metaphorically equalled to the number of penises (men) in a clan.

Penises are also associated with fighters and the strength of iron in discussions about the genealogical links within patrilineal Somali society. Daggers too are said to be held aloft by dancers of the 'ancient sacred dance' of *zar*, a dance thought to be associated with the Sky-God (Cerulli, 1957: 148, 157–158) in which the dancer runs into the river area and comes back with a bloody dagger. Nevertheless, it is important to remember that these phallic stones are more often associated with the idea of rain-making rather than with the heroics of slaughter. Iron, furthermore, is as much associated with rain-making as with killing an enemy. In terms of metaphors about iron, some say Saint Aw-Barkhadle used his sword to pierce the ground and create the sacred well. And Thesiger (1935: 4–5) mentions that the Danakil who live in Djibouti and northeastern Ethiopia used to 'wear the testicles of their victims around their necks' as trophies. Again, this would strengthen ideas about the potency of testicles and penises in these patriarchal societies of the Horn of Africa. Somali men wear necklaces made of one elongated stone pendent with two big beads on each side (see Révoil's account of the Somali Nugaal valley, 1882). I have heard reports of phallic stones pierced with a hole and it is possible that these and other portable phallic stones that I have seen are related to the notion of sacred fertility. The Nugaal pendants may well once have had a phallic origin and later been changed into elongated pendants.

Aw-Barkhadle fertility, sacrificial shedding of blood and the ritual hunt

Often hunting is associated with elites and royals in the societies of our current world. Yet historically it may have had a ritual significance. Certainly, as we will understand from this section, ritual hunt seems to be associated with ritual leadership and even centralisation of power and state building in the Horn of Africa. This may be why elites and royals still hunt today as a way to show virility, leadership and some sense of righteous power.

The historical role of the Beesha Mohamed Haniifa (the Yibir clan) is ritual efficacy and hunting. According to the oral history of the dominant Somali clans, the Yibir and Bu'ur Ba'ayr were said to be Jews, but there is no evidence of this, as already stated. It is useful to compare the alleged encounter of the Aw-Barkhadle and Bu'ur Ba'ayr with similar myths prevalent in the wider Red Sea region. In South Arabia, just a short boat trip over to the other side of the Red Sea, similar narratives of an encounter between Muslims and the Jewish Kings are recorded by Serjeant, who reports:

> The famous Arab king, 'Amir b. 'Abd al-Wahhab, when preparing to attack the Jewish king in Baihan, so organised matters that he sent several bodies of soldiers to go to Baihan, ostensibly to hunt; they then converged on Baihan 'from the uninhabited side' and captured the Jewish king.
>
> (Serjeant, 1976: 2)

Although this story seems to date to a few centuries later than the Bu'ur Ba'ayr era, it does show certain similarities between the accounts of non- and pre-Islamic groups in South Arabia and those at Aw-Barkhadle, similarities in both the account of the conversion and the subsequent historical narrative.

According to the inscription cited by Serjeant, offerings to God in the Hunt were made at the mountain while the Hunt took place at various mountain passes. Even more interesting, according to Serjeant, is a curious passage in this inscription which uses the word 're-join' in the sense of 'remain', meaning that offerings are made to the God 'in order that he may remain in the mountain' (1976: 31). Remembering the Bu'ur Ba'ayr legend and its tale of his capture in the mountain, and given that the Yibir still today receive the *mag* (compensation), it may be that the offerings are intended to ensure that Bu'ur Ba'ayr remains in the mountain (hill) rather than being offered to him himself, thus lifting the taboo (the *dhaim*, a curse). In the South Arabian Hunt ritual, this practice is called 'removing the taboo' (Serjeant, 1976). In the Hunt at Madudah, certain offerings are, intriguingly, made to 'remove some taboo or taint' (ibid.: 31). Equally intriguing are the similarities in the ideas of gods/religious being held captive (or captured in the case of Bu'ur Ba'ayr) in a mountain (or hill). The Oromo call such taboos *lagu* (Loo, 1991). Similarly, according to Cushitic tradition, if someone, for example, breaks off the branch of a sacred tree, it is common to spread coffee or even to slaughter a sheep in order to remove the curse (*habaar/abarsa*) of the elders and ancestors.

The Hunt ritual in Hajar Kuhlan of Baihan involves a different ritual which involves the sacrificial ritual slaughter of animals and seems relevant to the South Arabian pre-Islamic Jewish communities (Serjeant, 1976). It seems likely, moreover, that ritual hunts once took place in Somali society. Archaeological sites in Somaliland (Mire, 2008) such as rock art sites show ritualistic hunting scenes with men wearing what look like masks, carrying bows and arrows and accompanied by dogs (Figure 3.36).

Furthermore, many Eastern Cushitic groups such as the Konso, the Oromo and Sidama, who preserve the Cushitic institutions more closely than the Somali ones, have complex hunting rituals that are associated with the erection of stele or sacred stones (Bartels, 1983: 258–259; Hallpike, 1972: 153) – as indeed do Somali hunters like the Madhibaan. Often hunting ritual is associated with protecting the living and ensuring fertility by appeasing the dead: amongst peoples of southern Ethiopia, who believe in the Sky God, a ritual hunt is staged the days before or during the burial of a prominent figure, where the stela erected symbolizes the figure as well as the big game hunted. Some of the rules are very similar to the South Arabian ritual Hunt in that they involve a type of killing very much associated with fertility. The Cushitic hunt also seems to include rules involving abstaining from sexual intercourse and keeping away from the hunt sexually mature girls, women

Figure 3.36 Hunter with dogs wearing what looks like masks at Dhambalin rock art site

of childbearing age – and men (Hallpike, 1972: 153–154). The idea that women must be kept at a distance may be linked to the fact that they are not allowed to slaughter animals (Barthels 1983 and Loo, 1991; Hallpike, 1972) and in some cases not even to make animal sacrifices (Hallpike, 1972: 154). The rock art sites of Dhambalin shows numerous scenes of hunting which seem ritualistic and symbolic (Mire, 2008); they also depict goats as well as fat sheep decorated with motifs similar to necklaces and bands around their abdomens and cows with engorged udders, images later common in the Neolithic rock art of this region. The ritual killing of animals has appeared more recently, with fat sheep playing a significant part in the current practices of fertility rituals in the Horn of Africa; these are associated with appeasing spirits, as will be discussed in the next chapter.

Khat[14] is a gift that is ritually shared at Aw-Barkhadle, a practice that is also seen in a similar context in Arabia. Coffee, too, plays a role in traditional rituals and is also part of the Hunt ritual of South Arabia where it is a part of a pre-Islamic practice which includes annual sacrifice and the ritual sharing of coffee (Serjeant, 1976). No other food or drink may follow this coffee until the Hunt ritual is completed (ibid.: 46–56). If somebody breaks this rule and eats or drinks before the Hunt is completed, they are obliged to slaughter a sheep for the hunting party (the members of the Hunt group) to purify themselves from the taint (*dhaim*) (Serjeant, 1976: 56). The sheep is divided and shared. Coffee is also consumed ritually at the granting of permission to pursue the Hunt ritual (Serjeant, 1976: 46–47) and drunk at the start when the hunters venerate the tombs or domes of sheikhs (Serjeant, 1976: 50).

In the Somali context, when a woman gives birth to a child she brings *bishaarada* (the good news) and promises to bring the Saint offerings such as animals, perfume, incense and rice. There are striking similarities between a sacrificial ritual of this kind and that of the Hunt ritual as described by Serjeant (Serjeant, 1976: 27). When the Hunt is successful, a sacrifice is brought to the *Abu* (Headman of the Hunt ritual) and offered to the god(s) in the *haram*. According to the texts, the *Mansab*, the spiritual and temporal lord of the sacred enclave of Tarim, nowadays receives the same portion of meat from the Hunt ritual as would the Mansab have done in pre-Islamic times (Serjeant, 1976: 31). It is possible that the *Muriid*, as the spiritual and the temporal head of the sacred tomb of Aw-Barkhadle, the sacred enclosure, the hill and the entire sacred landscape, has inherited the role of the pre-Islamic local equivalent. The *Muriid* is the receiver of the gifts. Lewis (1998) suggested that the Somali Muslim *wadaad* inherited the role the pre-Islamic *wadaads* had had as mediators. Both the *Muriid* and the *Abu* are leaders of fertility rituals. This way the ritual efficacy gives a power to the ruling clan and has an element of territory control through rituals. The Hunt ritual is intertwined with sacred space such as landscapes, enclosures, mountains and rock – and includes phallic stones – as will be seen in the following section.

Sacred and phallic stones, rain-making and sacred enclosures

Deeds similar to the miraculous creation of wells by saints such as Aw-Barkhadle are associated with ancestors of rainmaker families in most of the Horn of Africa. Domestic animals depended on pastures and wells for their survival; often enclosures are seen to be protective spaces, sometimes marked with a sacred stone that turns them into a sacred space. The stone worship culture in the Horn of Africa noted by Trimingham (1965: 33) and others in the ethnographic reports may have an archaeological relevance too.

That the Horn places a great significance on stones is best epitomised in its stelae traditions at sites such as Aksum or the rock hewn churches of Lalibela and the portable stones (including phallic ones). As noted earlier, one can find these at Aw-Barkhadle where they are used for human fertility rituals. But one can also find enclosures for animals with sacred stones placed to protect the animals. Enclosures are meeting points, ritual space and where the sacred stone is often kept. It is common practice to sacrifice on top of stones and to pour the blood from the sacrificial animal onto them.

In Arabia, it has been noted that cattle were kept in sacred enclosures by the Mashayikh in Wahidi territory, in parts of Arabia and by the region's wells (Serjeant, 1976: 35). In his discussion about the lord of cattle (Ather), Serjeant (1976) has used philological evidence from archaeological material such as scripts (ibid.) to demonstrate that the rain god was one of the main deities in the region in pre-Islamic times. It is therefore possible to imagine that sacred enclosures for cattle and sacred animals existed in pre-Islamic South Arabia (ibid.). The study of haram by Ryckmans (1988) corresponds to the practise in South Arabia of *hawtah*, the sacred enclaves for animals and vegetation (Serjeant, 1976).

In the Wahidi territory, however, which has its own Sultanate, there are mountain hunting grounds such as the mountain of the Mansab of Kadur which belongs to the Ba Marhul Mashayikh groups. Serjeant describes how the ibex is hunted there as part of the Hunt ritual and is captured with nets. Daggers are used to disentangle the ibex from the nets (ibid.: 35). The Mashayikh 'constitute the ancient pre-Islamic aristocracy of religion, and . . . appear to have some link with rain-making' (ibid.: 38). His description of this ritual hunt is relevant to the Horn of Africa because here too can be found evidence for sacrifice and the hunting rituals in different ethnographic cases as well as archaeological scenes which depict herds of cattle with prominent and full udders (Figure 3.37, Mire, 2008). The Neolithic rock art of northeast Africa is critical to understanding the relationship between cattle as sacred animals who give life and the need for sacrificial game to facilitate the rain-making that will allow an abundance in pastures and water. Sacred enclosures and fertility pools are also found in the Horn, for example by the churches of Lalibela, as discussed later.

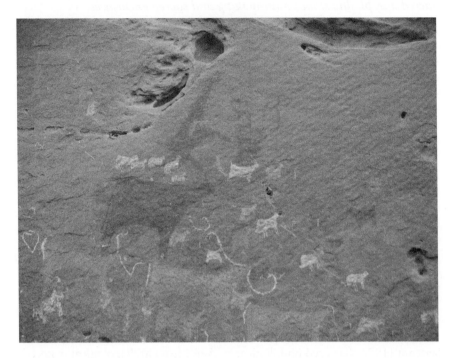

Figure 3.37 Hunting scenes are depicted with cattle with big prominent udders at Dhambalin rock art site

Rain-making figures such as Saint Aw-Barkhadle, who are considered to have miraculously created wells, are also associated with sacred enclosures. Furthermore, people are prevented from living in the sacred landscape of Aw-Barkhadle. When I inquired whether its trees and the animals are protected by law (either custom-based or religious), I was told that people know that this is a sacred area and that they are only allowed to kill animals as part of the sacrificial slaughter of domestic animals brought to the Sheikh (Aw-Barkhadle). This tradition echoes similar practices enshrined in the South Arabian Hunting laws (*qawanin*) (Serjeant, 1976; Ingrams, 1937). According to those laws, the trees and the animals in the *haram* (sacred enclosure) are protected by a divine power: the trees cannot be cut nor the animals killed (Serjeant, 1976). During the Hunt ritual, animals would be slaughtered inside the enclosure at the end of their circumambulation of the sacred space. The similarities between ritual hunting, sacred enclosures and the rules of sacrifice on both sides of the Red Sea are striking – and all performed with the intention of increasing both fertility and the rains.

The ibex and the horns of the ibex, like those of the bull, are associated with pre-Islamic gods (ibid.). Serjeant notes that the Arabic word for ibex (*wa'l*) can also mean gazelle and the word for cattle (*baqqar*) can also mean ibex (ibid.: 7).

The epigraphic evidence for the pre-Islamic division of meat in Arabia reveals: 'Now let him offer to the God a thigh (*fakhidh*) and two *muq-dums* [chest ribs] the expiation and offering in order that he may re-join the tribe' (quoted in Serjeant, 1976: 31). Serjeant notes that in present-day Tarim society a similar division of the meat of the Hunt takes place to that in pre-Islamic times (Serjeant, 1976).

Furthermore, the discovery of a phallic gravestone at Aw-Barkhadle raises interesting questions about the site's beliefs and material culture. As noted earlier, farmers digging cairns in Arabsiyo have also found phallic stones (Figure 3.31a and Figure 3.31b), as did Curle in Somaliland, and these are almost identical to the one found at Aw-Barkhadle. Phallic grave markers are found in Ethiopia too, as will be discussed later; and phallicism seems also to have existed in South Arabia:

> I cannot but conclude that this must be understood as Jabal Farj al-Lât, embodying the name of the pre-Islâmic goddess, as I have proposed in the case of two al-Nasr hills at Shabwah. Tribes such as the Saibân and Humūm are often very superficially Islamised and the significance of the name al-Lât has probably been forgotten. The phallic names of al-Zibb or al-Zubb, etc., are not uncommon in Arabia, applied to certain shapes of mountain features, and I have already recorded the famous Jabal Shummat al-'Āshiq on the pilgrim route to the Prophet Hud.
>
> (ibid.: 81)

Moreover, in South Arabia, in Al'Uqlah, hunting inscriptions have been found on stones. There are, near Al'Uqlah and Shabwah, two remote small peaks known as al-Nasr al-Qibli and al-Nasr al-Sharqi, meaning the north-ern and the eastern *Nasrs* (Eagles). Serjeant suggests that these peaks were at some point 'identified with the god *Nasr*' (Serjeant, 1976: 9). Serjeant argues that: 'There are many cases in which a rock or a small hill is identi-fied or associated with a pre-Islamic god' (ibid.). Animals were frequently slaughtered at the rock so that the blood shed at the stone would represent a significant sacrifice to that rock god (ibid.).

Some of the ideas that exist about the Buur Hakaba area echo the prac-tices that Serjeant reports from mountain peaks and hills in Arabia. Many areas in Somali territory, and even the Rendile sacred mountains in northern Kenya, include rock art like that found at Buur Hakaba. In Somali, as noted earlier, *godka jinka* refers to rock shelters. *Jin* is the devil, and since many people understand the rock art they think it is made by a *jin*. When I was doing my surveys in Somaliland I learned people referred to the caves of rock art as the place of *jin*. When I brought with me an album of rock art photos and asked if they could locate similar images, they would say '*god ka jinka* (the hole of the *jin*) that is what you are looking for' to which I would reply 'yes, I am looking for the hole of the *jin*.' Sometimes they would just say '*meesha jinka*', the place of *jin*. They say this because they believe, it seems, that the art looks a bit like something a *jin* (the devil) might have made. By contrast, the remarkable stones of Aw-Barkhadle, Goroyo Awl, Laaso and Dhaymoole, most of them black and some of them with symbols, may reflect a social memory of a pre-Islamic belief in sacred stones and associated rituals. People never talked about these particular stones as being related to *jin* (devil); instead, they referred to them as something that their ancestors had made.

I realised, however, when reading Serjeant (1976), that there might be another possible explanation as to why a location might come to be called the place of *jin*. It might lie in a reminiscence, a memory of the past, passed on through the words of 'the place/house/hole of *jin*': a memory of a non-Islamic practice, perhaps of a non-Islamic god that the Muslims had come to label '*jin*'. The holy Qur'an mentions *jins* too.

> The allusion of 'Amr, 'the son of the Servant of the Jin', is to the many animals sacrificed on the little peaks that either held the sanctuaries of al-'Uzza and al-Nasr, or which were identified themselves with these divinities; the blood flowing from the slaughtered animals turned the sides of the rock as red as brazil-wood. Another god Sa'ad worshipped at Kinanah, is described as 'a rock in a desert' upon which blood is poured.
>
> (ibid.: 10)

This notion of 'a rock in the desert' upon which blood is poured recalls the Konso practice of circumcision of the chiefs: "They stand on the sacred stone 'Shila', and the blood of their penises falls upon it. This blood, human blood, is inauspicious, and purified by animal blood, that of a sacrificial goat" (Hallpike, 1972: 293).

The sacred fertility stone of Aw-Barkhadle was also, according to the Yibir elders, associated with blood, that of the virgin's menstrual cycle, as noted earlier. Was this blood shed as a sacrifice too or was it only the blood of sacrificial animals that was offered on that stone? The ritual hunt exists in Konso culture as well:

> The Kara involves a long process of rituals which begin with the bless-ing of the elders, initiation of the young and the Haima ritual dances; then the hunt expedition, the ritual dances after the hunt, the elder's meetings to evaluate the performances of the generation, the selection, quarrying and transport of the stela and its erection.
>
> (UNESCO Konso cultural landscape file, p. 30)

Furthermore, the phallic stones of the Konso are used to position the sacrifi-cial animal so that its blood runs down the rock as the animal is slaughtered (ibid.). This raises questions as to why these phallic stones were allowed to remain at Aw-Barkhadle.

The role of wood is also intriguing. My interviewees, as noted earlier, talked about a wooden figure with anthropomorphic features that was once used in conjunction with a prayer to conceive a child. Is its disappearance the result of the Islamic non-figurative approach?

Palm trees were also worshipped within pre-Islamic Arabia on the other side of the Red Sea. Serjeant is inclined to the view that 'the palm was an object of veneration, even of worship, in pre-Islamic Hadramawt, and we know it was worshipped in Najran' (1976: 25). Najran is located in south-western Saudi Arabia near the frontier with Yemen. Did ideas about the sacred palm somehow cross over to the African side – or was the movement the other way around?

The crescent is also an important symbol both in the Horn of Africa (including northern Somalia) and Arabia where it was associated with pre-Islamic practices in pre-Islamic times (Phillipson, 1997). In Arabian pre-Islamic practice, the crescent is the emblem of the Moon God. At the rock shelter of Daa'awale, three hours' drive from Aw-Barkhadle northeast of Berbera, there are (unpublished) paintings of crescents, full moons and stars along with other geometrical and animal depictions (Figure 3.38). The stars, the half-moon and the full-moon seem, interestingly, to correlate with certain animals such as the giraffe and the tortoise. They are all painted in white, perhaps to reflect the colour of light. The star is the *awliyada*,

Figure 3.38 Crescents and full moons at Dawa'aleh rock art site in Dhaymooleh

representing religious ancestors and/or saints, according to my interviewees. Does their view echo a pre-Islamic belief in reincarnation as a star, that religious ancestors/saints would one day become stars and join the Moon God? Clearly, this is only speculation. The snake, too, appears to have been another symbol of the ancestors (both religious and non-religious), as will be discussed later.

Conclusions

In my study of fertility rituals at the archaeological landscape of Aw-Barkhadle, I have focused on the sacred and ritual meaning and function of this landscape. I have paid particular attention to ideas and rituals of fertility as practiced in what I call a 'sacred landscape'. I have explored the relationship between the archaeological landscape and current female fertility rituals and practices that are believed to date back to pre-Islamic times. I have also examined the current and pre-Islamic implications of the material evidence: a sacred enclosure, a sacred stone, a phallic stone, water sources and trees. I argue that these elements play important roles in ideas about fertility and its associated rituals as well as in ancestral veneration. I have also discovered secret female rituals that take place in various parts of the landscape such as at the sacred stone in the sacred enclosure. Women wash themselves at what is considered to be a sacred well and sit on the fertility stone and pray for a child (often a son). Other sites dedicated to Sharif Yusuf Aw-Barkhadle also contain sacred enclosures and sacred stones. The site of Goroyo Cawl has black stones with engravings that are very similar to the sites of Laaso and Dhaymoole. Were fertility stones (black, with or without carvings) widespread at some point in the past? I have found phallic stones which may relate to the alleged pre-Islamic king Bu'ur Ba'ayr. I suggest that fertility may have been granted by a divine man with a divine penis, hence the existence of phallic stones in the region.

The concept of phallic stones is relevant to Aw-Barkhadle where one phallic stone has been found *in situ* and another two possibly identified. Phallic stones from Somaliland, unprovenanced, are kept in the British Museum. Taken together, these examples suggest that the phallic stones were once a regional phenomenon.

In addition, the discovery of at least one gravestone carrying Ethiopian Orthodox Cross carvings *in situ* at Aw-Barkhadle acknowledges a past relationship between non-Muslim groups, and the site and suggests that the legend of Bu'ur Ba'ayr may not be completely without relevance.

The site of Aw-Barkhadle provides evidence of the significance of rituals in the syncretism of religions and sacred space. With its archaeology, material culture and rituals, and its legends and oral history, the site provides a great deal of data with which to shed light on significant aspects of Somali society, history, prehistory and, particularly, of indigenous practices that reach beyond Islam.

The site was once a walled town. Was this a sacred and political landscape and a burial site before it fell into ruins in perhaps the fifteenth-sixteenth centuries? This question can only be answered with excavation and accurate dating. And excavation can only take place if Aw-Barkhadle's future religious leaders agree to such procedures, and after 10 years, they have now done so and plans have been made. It appears that the pre-Islamic burial landscape of Aw-Barkhadle has been appropriated, and the new leadership legitimised, through two processes: the adoption of the physical characteristics of the old ritual burial practices and the incorporation of the ritual significance of potentially non-Islamic ideas into the daily practices of Muslim Somali society today.

When looking at the earliest city of Adal kingdom, Insoll (2017) has shown that Harar was not the earliest Islamic urban centre; for example, Harlaa preceded its sixteenth century date. However, Insoll is not sure that Harlaa can be identified with any other known historical centre in the region.

If we, however, look at Somali genealogy, Aw-Barkhadle is linked to the Islamic Walashma Dynasty, some of whose rulers are thought to be buried at Aw-Barkhadle. Paulitschke (1888) assumed that 'AwBerkele' (referring most likely to Aw-Barkhadle) in 'Dakar' (Doggor) was near Harar and that it may have been one of the capitals of the Awdal Kingdom. However, our Aw-Barkhadle site is probably AwBerkele and it is located at an ancient urban centre known as Doggor. The visible archaeology – the number of potsherds scattered, the vastness of the area (four square km) covered by the ancient burials, the city wall and the house foundations – all point to it having the great importance Paulitschke suggested for 'AwBerkele'. It seems that Aw-Barkhadle site could be the first capital of the Awdal kingdom and our planed excavations for 2020 will shed light on this issue.

In short, this is not just a sacred landscape containing archaeologically detectable remains. It is also a landscape of political and ritual significance and has been for various groups across the centuries. In the next chapter I will discuss the data on rituals that has been presented here within the broader context of Somali fertility rituals, both male and female. I will also introduce new ethnographic research on Somali fertility rituals.

Notes

1 The prefix *aw* means saint in Somali. Saint Aw-Barkhadle is Sheikh Yusuf Al-Kawnayn, see the known genealogy for Aw-Barkhadle (Appendix 1).
2 The study refers to the tomb of Aw-Barkhadle although it is actually a mausoleum inside which the tomb is placed. One of the most famous mausoleums of Islam is Taj Mahal in India, and there is a pride within Somalis that an 'Indian' architect built the Mausoleum of Aw-Barkhadle.
3 In Oromo, a grave or a tomb is called *tulluu*. *Tuul* in Somali means a heap or cairn.

4 The *Muriid* of Aw-Barkhadle was 91 in 2007 when I met him. At the age of 90 he still felt young and asked his only wife of decades (who at 70–75 years old was much younger than him) if she would let him marry a second wife. The second wife had just had her first baby by him and he was somewhat preoccupied with this event. This meant that it was the two other main sheikhs based at Aw-Barkhadle who provided me with the lists of names of the people buried there.

5 Given that this site is a living heritage it is only recently that permission has been granted to excavate particularly relevant areas of the site.

6 Mohamed Haniif is another name for Bu'ur Ba'ayr. Although he is believed to have practiced 'witch craft' and other 'wicked practices', some believe he was a Muslim.

7 Currently, coffee drinking in Somali society is in general traditionally associated with women or, in Sufi society, with both men and women. Non-Sufi men would usually not drink coffee (unless in southern Somalia's urban hotels influenced by an Italian style of life). For northern Somalis especially, encouraged by the long-distance trade across the Indian Ocean, it is tea *masala*, known also as *shah* (*chai*) that is the 'civilised' social beverage normally consumed.

8 Rain-making is a critical ritual activity in the Horn of Africa where droughts take place on a regular basis. I also noted that amongst the Eastern Cushitic languages rain has many different classifications each with a specific term. I can without any effort think of at least five words in Somali for rain (*roob, tiixtiix, bar, dixda, dhibic*). It is likely that there are many more.

9 *Kallascha* is a phallic object worn on the forehead of the Qallu, the religious leader of the traditional *Waaq* (Sky-God) belief of the Eastern Cuthistic speaking groups in the Horn of Africa. The spelling of this word differs depending on the language and transliteration. Sometimes it is written also as *kallasha, kallacca* or *hallasha*. The etymological meaning seems to be associated with sacrifice or slaughter (*qalasho* in Somali). Qallu is the sacrificer and slaughterer, the only one who is allowed to slaughter the sacred/sacrificial animal.

10 The Zamzam well, located in the Masjid Al-Haram, in Mecca, Saudi Arabia, was miraculously created by God when the prophet Ibrahim's infant son cried of thirst, according to the Qur'an.

11 Usually in Somali society fat women are preferred to skinny women; they are thought to be more fertile and healthy. The word *subag* is used in Somali slang to mean good. Somebody will say 'let's go to the cinema' and they might get the response '*Subag!*' meaning nice, in much the same way as fat in English and Swedish (*fet*) slang can mean good.

12 In 2013, the UK government made *khat* (*Catha edulis*) a class C drug under the Dangerous Drugs Act.

13 I am unable to show the pictures sent to me of these sculptures as their archaeological authenticity and current whereabouts have not yet been confirmed by specialists.

14 *Khat* (*qaad*) traditionally has a ritual significance and is associated with peace. Even today Somalis have a sitting (*fadhi*) and chew *khat* to foster or discuss peace.

Bibliography

Bartels, L. 1983. *Oromo Religion: Myths and Rites of the Western Oromo of Ethiopia. An Attempt to Understand.* Berlin: Dietrich Reimer Verlag.

Brandt, S. A. 1986. The Upper Pleistocene and Early Holocene Prehistory of the Horn of Africa. *The African Archaeological Review*, 4: 41–82.

Burton, R. 1966 [1898]. *First Footsteps in East Africa.* Edited by G. Waterfield. Travellers and Explorers Series. Praeger. New York.

Cassanelli, L. 1982. *The Shaping of Somali Society: Reconstructing the History of a Pastoral People, 1600–1900.* Philadelphia, PA: University of Pennsylvania Press.

Cerulli, E. 1957. *Somalia. Scritti vari Editi ed Inediti.* Vol. I. Roma: Istituto Poligrafico dello Stato. P. V.

Fauvelle-Aymar, F.-X., & Hirsch, B. (2004). Muslim historical spaces in Ethiopia and the Horn of Africa: A reassessment. *Northeast African Studies, 2004–2010,* 11(1), 25–54.

Finneran, N. 2002. *The Archaeology of Christianity in Africa.* Stroud: Tempus.

Hallpike, C. 1972. *The Konso of Ethiopia: A Study of the Values of an Eastern Cushitic People.* Oxford: Clarendon Press.

Huntingford, G. W. B. 1955. *The Galla of Ethiopia: The Kingdoms of Kafa and Janjero.* London: International Africa Institute.

Ingrams, W. H. 1937. A Dance of the Ibex Hunters in the Hadramaut. *Man,* 37: 12–13. London.

Insoll, T. 2017. First Footsteps in the Archaeology of Harar, Ethopia. *Journal of Islamic Archaeology,* 4(2): 189–215.

Kairu, P. 2015. Today a Sheep Will Die in Dagoretti Because a Branch Fell Off This Fig Tree. *Daily Nation.* June 19. www.nation.co.ke/lifestyle/DN2/a-branch-fell-off-a-mugumo-fig-tree-dagoretti/957860-2756998-2wj48n/index.html [accessed: 15/07/2017].

Kaplan, S. 1986. The Africanisation of Missionary Christianity: History and Typology. *Journal of Religion in Africa,* 16(3): 166–186.

Kaplan, S. 1992. *The Beta Israel (Falasha) in Ethiopia.* New York: New York University Press.

Kirk, J. W. C. 1905. The Yibirs and Midgans of Somaliland, Their Traditions and Dialects. *Journal of African Society,* 4: 91–108.

Kusow, A. M. 1995. The Somali Origin: Myth or Reality. In A. J. Ahmed (ed.) *The Invention of Somalia.* Lawrenceville, NJ: Red Sea Press.

Levine, D. N. 2000. *Greater Ethiopia: The Evolution of a Multiethnic Society.* 2nd ed. Chicago and London: University of Chicago Press.

Lewis, I. 1994. *Blood and Bone: The Call for Kinship in Somali Society.* Lawrenceville, NJ: Red Sea Press.

Lewis, I. 1998. *Saints and Somalis: Popular Islam in a Clan-Based Society.* Lawrenceville, NJ: and Asmara, Eritrea: Red Sea Press.

Loo, J. van de. 1991. *Guji Oromo Culture (with the Collaboration of Bilow Kolo).* Berlin: Dietrich Reimer Verlag.

Luling, V. 1988. The Man in the Tree. A Note on a Somali Myth. In A. Puglieli (ed.) *Proceedings of the Third International Congress of Somali Studies.* Rome: II Pensario Scientifico.

Mansur, A. O. 1995. The Nature of the Somali Clan-System. In A. J. Ahmed (ed.) *The Invention of Somalia.* Lawrenceville, NJ: Red Sea Press.

Martin, B. G. 1974. Arab Migration to East Africa in Medieval Times. *The International Journal of African Historical Studies,* 7(3): 367–390.

Mazrui, A. A. 1984. The Semitic Impact on Black Africa: Arab and Jewish Cultural Influences. *A Journal of Opinion,* 13: 3–8.

Mazrui, A. A. 1985. Religion and Political Culture in Africa. *Journal of the American Academy of Religion,* 53(4): 817–839.

Mire, S. 2008. The Discovery of Dhambalin Rock Art Site, Somaliland. *African Archaeological Review,* 25: 153–168.

Mire, S. 2011. The Knowledge-Centred Approach to the Somali Cultural Emergency and Heritage Development Assistance in Somaliland. In F. Sulas ed. Africa's Fragile Heritages. *Special Issue African Archaeological Review*, 29(1): 71–91.

Mire, S. 2015a. Mapping of the Archaeology of Somaliland: Religion, Art, Script, Time, Urbanism, Trade and Empire. *African Archaeological Review*, 32(1): 111–136.

Mire, S. 2015b. Wagar, Fertility and Phallic Stelae: Cushitic Sky-God Belief and the Site of Saint Aw-Barkhadle in Somaliland. *African Archaeological Review*, 32(1): 93–109.

Mohammed, M. A. 1991. *Histoire des Croyances en Somalie*. Paris: Annales Littéraires de l'Université de Besançon.

Mukhtar, M. H. 1995. Islam in Somali History; Fact and Fiction. In A. J. Ahmed (ed.) *The Invention of Somalia*. Lawrenceville, NJ: Red Sea Press.

Muriuki, G. 1975. *A History of Gikuyu; 1500–1900*. Oxford: Oxford University Press.

Muriuki, G. 2005. *The Sacred Mugumo Tree: Myth and Gender Construction in Gikuyu, Cosmology and Worship*. Lecture at School of Oriental and African Studies' Linguistics Department on 3rd of March 2005, London.

Paulitschke, P. 1888. *Ethnographie Nordost Afrikas, I. Die materielle Cultur des Danâkil, Galla und Somâl II. Die geistige Cultur des Danâkil, Galla und Somâl*. Vol. 2. Berlin.

Phillipson, D. W. 1997. *Ancient Ethiopia. Aksum: Its Antecedents and Successors*. London: British Museum Press.

Révoil, G. 1882. *La Vallée du Darror: Voyage aux Pays Çomalis Dis Mois à la Cote Orientale D'Afrique*. Paris: Challamel aîné.

Ryckmans, J. 1988. The Old South Arabian Religion. In W. Daum (ed.) *Yemen. 3000 Years of Art and Civilisation in Arabia*. Felix: Penguin.

Serjeant, R. B. 1976. *The South Arabian Hunt*. London: Luzac.

Thesiger, W. 1935. The Awash River and the Awsa Sultanate. *The Geographical Journal*, 85: 1–23.

Trimingham, J. S. 1952. *Islam in Ethiopia*. 1st ed. Oxford: Oxford University Press.

Trimingham, J. S. 1965. *Islam in Ethiopia*. 2nd ed. Oxford: Oxford University Press.

UNESCO. 2011. *Konso Cultural Landscape*. http://whc.unesco.org/en/list/1333 [accessed: 23/02/2016].

4   In the name of divine kinship

The fertility bath, *Bun Shuruur* (Coffee ceremony), *Baanashada Dumarka* (Nurturing of women), *Zar, Sitaat, Wagar, Gudniin Fircooni* (FGM), *Waqlaal* (Child naming ritual) and *Istunka* (Stick fight)

In this chapter I demonstrate the relationship between the notion of sacred fertility and divine kinship. I do so by analysing those practices, both the familiar and the less familiar, which form part of the domain of fertility rituals. I present a comparative analysis of these rituals in the Somali region and in the Horn of Africa and consider how they may relate to the non- and pre-Islamic ritual heritage of Aw-Barkhadle.

The rituals described in this chapter all concern fertility and its impact on men's and women's reproductive health and wellbeing both socially and culturally. The *Siti* ceremony is a unique female ritual and a veneration of religious ancestors who include female sheikhas. The *wagar* is a sacred sculpture known to safeguard fertility and children from bad spirits and illnesses (Mire, 2015b). Female circumcision (*gudniin*) is practiced widely in Somali society. The women who go to Aw-Barkhadle have usually already undergone all or some of these rituals in their passage from childhood to womanhood. The fertility rituals recorded at Aw-Barkhadle are not isolated behaviours nor are they triggered only by fertility problems. They are a part of a continuing ideology that is deeply embedded in indigenous Somali culture.

I will argue that some rituals are designed to mark stages in both men and women's fertility rites. I analyse a number of rituals, only two of which (*Siti* and spirit possession) have been discussed before by others in the context of fertility rituals and symbolism rather than in the wider context of gender, social and political issues. I want to draw upon my own ethnographic research to reach beyond female problems and spirits by discussing the *wagar, bunshuur, baanashada dumarka, waqlaal, istunka*, female circumcision and the fertility bath. The *baanashada dumarka* 'nurturing of women' is a fertility ritual which is designed to expel bad things from the body, including the spirits that possess women and interfere with their fertility, *zar*, through the insertion of herbs into the vagina (Mire, 2016b). The fertility bath takes place during Somali nomadic weddings and during the inauguration of the head of a clan or a sub-clan chief (those with, for example, the ranks of Ugas, Garaad and Caaqil) before the *caleemo saar* rituals (putting leaves on new chiefs). I argue that the *caleemo saar* too is a stage in the rituals associated with sacred fertility.

When I asked women about their veneration of Saint Aw-Barkhadle, the thoughts that seemed uppermost in their minds were the issues in their private lives that had brought them to the site. They explained why in particular they were seeking a fertility blessing. For them the context seemed all-important. Through their stories I was led to explore fertility rituals that reached beyond Aw-Barkhadle. Most of the women talked about the rituals that they had to undergo once they realised that giving birth would not be straightforward. They talked about *baanashada dumarka aan dhalin*, lit. 'nurturing of women who don't give birth', one of the many possible infertility treatments. These treatments are mostly performed by healers of a clan from a 'lower' caste or by a *calaqad*. The *calaqad* is the highest rank priestess of the *zar* cult who deals with spirit possession. She is considered to possess supernatural power and can make contact with *zar* (also known as *saar*), the spirits who, by possessing a woman, inhibit her ability to bear a child until such time as she performs their wishes.

When women have had children after undergoing the Aw-Barkhadle fertility rituals, such as sitting on the sacred fertility stone and walking the *dawaafa* in the mausoleum of Saint Aw-Barkhadle, they will also perform in their own homes other fertility rituals such as those offering further fertility protection and child protection.

One of the rituals performed during pregnancy and after childbirth is that involving a *wagar*. A *wagar* is a wooden sculpture associated with supernatural power and it is carved from a sacred tree, also called *wagar*, the African olive (*Olea europaea subsp africana*). The leaves of the sacred *wagar* tree as well as the actual worked piece of wood play a crucial part in these rituals. There is also a remarkable association between the deity which the *wagar* is thought to signify and the pre-Islamic beliefs that Bu'ur Ba'ayr and his followers are said to have followed at Aw-Barkhadle. I will discuss this later in the chapter.

I will also discuss female circumcision of the type known as Pharaonic circumcision or *gudniin* (locally known as *fara'oni*, meaning Pharaonic circumcision). All my interviewees had undergone this circumcision at an early age but not all suggested a direct relationship between this and the negative effect, intentional or otherwise, that it might have had on their fertility. I agree with Hayes (1975) and Boddy (1982) that the practice of Pharaonic circumcision is linked with a patrilineal society's desire to ensure that a child belongs to the father. It also provides an insurance that it is the blood son who will inherit the land, as Auffret (1983) maintains. I also argue that the bloodline is of crucial importance not just because it ensures this inheritance but because it also reaffirms the sacred lineage (sacred kinship in the case of the Somali) in Somalia in particular and across the Horn of Africa as a whole. I argue that Pharaonic circumcision is paramount to a kinship that claims a sacred origin. Hence, sacred ancestors of this sacred kinship grant sacred fertility. This is what I call the kinship ideology of a divine kinship in relation to the Horn of Africa. I suggest, too, that circumcision is ultimately a sacrificial shedding of the blood between the divine (the religious ancestor) and the profane (the living kin). I will argue that, originally, there is evidence to suggest that circumcision (male or female) was originally an act that took place between the human and sacred, or divine, and that it was not something that happened between one human being and another – or between female and male, as the FGM (female genital mutilation) debate largely argues.

Finally, in the light of the discoveries at Aw-Barkhadle and the fertility rituals that take place in Somali society in general, I plan to shed further light on issues, such as FGM, that are currently hotly debated. I argue that they are too often taken out of context. They must be considered alongside the rituals, some physically harmful and others less so, that are carried out on men as well as women.

The fertility bath

The purifying bath is an important ritual that is crucial to any discussions about fertility and the outcome of the marriage. A bride must undergo this purification on the night before any traditional (nomadic) wedding takes place. An old woman from the region of Haud gave me the following description.

The day before the traditional nomadic wedding, the bride is washed by other women, i.e. by female relatives and friends. This ritual bath has a number of different components, each of which holds a specific meaning. The girl is washed with water and will sometimes be taken to a sacred spring. Any available natural soap is used. Her skin is then covered with a mash made of dates. The date palm, as I noted earlier, is considered to be a sacred tree within northeast African society, and dates are considered to be one of the most sacred foods. This mash is left on her skin for long enough for the sweetness to stick to her body and the sugar to soften (exfoliate) her skin. The mash of dates is then washed off with water, or sometimes with milk, depending on how wealthy her family is, and the girl's body is moisturised with aromatic oils. This reinforces the importance of moisture in promoting fertility. Men usually prefer women who have body fat on their legs (*kub*) and hips as such characteristics epitomise the ideal beauty of a woman blessed with fertility. This description reaffirms the hourglass female body shape which is generally linked with fertility and female beauty.

The purification bath continues with the smoke from aromatic gums. The girl stands above an incense burner that is placed on the ground and puts on her wedding clothes. In this way, both her own skin and her dress are exposed to, and absorb, the aromatic smoke. A girl's first use of incense is intended to be on her wedding night and she will continue to use it for the rest of her married life, or at least until her menopause. Women who deliver babies also use a particular type of incense known as *uunsi umuleed* (delivery/postnatal incense). Smoke has a purifying importance. Incense is a ritual aroma which is used to bring blessings by attracting angels into a ritual sphere. In houses and mosques, incense is used to purify the sacred ritual space. People also use the smoke from incense to purify themselves if they have behaved immorally or suspect that harm will come to them.

The use of incense is important both before and after sexual intercourse, for two reasons. The first is to purify the woman's private parts and to create a blessed, and hence, fertile atmosphere; the second is to make the woman able to receive a child by consecrating her body through this process.

This description of the fertility bath also provides insights into the aesthetics of fertility within Somali nomadic society. The bath is thought to satisfy the human senses: sight – a beautiful bride in a bridal dress, painted with henna and wearing a gold or silver and amber necklace, with her hair plaited; smell – the aroma of incense and aromatic oils; touch – the softness of her moisturised body; and taste – the sweetness of the dates. All these are fundamental to the enhancement of the pleasure of the sexual act for both the man and the woman and increase the chance of conceiving a child. Nomadic women explained to me that the groom will smell the aroma of incense on the woman's body and hair; he can feel the smoothness of her moisturised body and taste the sweetness of the dates on her skin. All these elements – the water, the dates, the milk, the aromatic oils and the incense – are all-important in achieving a successful wedding night. They form part of a woman's feminine identity as well as enhance her childbearing potential. Incidentally, a different kind of fertility bath using milk from the *caano shub* and fresh leaves, a *calaamo saar*, forms part of the coronation ceremony of a new clan head (*Garaad*, *Ugaas* or *caaqil*), as will be discussed in Chapter Five. In that context, it is the new lineage head who will bring fertility to the clan as a whole.

The wedding celebration lasts seven days – the period of the 'honeymoon'. It ends on the seventh day with the *xeedho fur* ceremony (the opening of the *heedho* ritual container) and guests gather in front of the nomadic hut of the newlyweds. The *heedho* is a container traditionally provided by the bride's family for the wedding. It is woven and decorated with leather and cowrie shells which protect health and promote fertility. The bride will also wear items, typically a headband, that display cowries. The Oromo call cowrie *elleela* while the Somali call it *alleelo*, and they also have similar headbands, *battalaa*. The use of cowrie to protect and to encourage good health and fertility is common in the Horn of Africa. *Kuttoo* is another ornamental item, a headdress worn by the bride of the Guji Oromo (Loo, 1991). As noted later, the *ceefi* is an ornament made with cowrie shells that is used to protect an infant from the evil eye. Headdress have metaphysical as well as social and political meanings in many societies in Africa.

The *heedho* contains mashed dates mixed with herbs which are formed into a bowl shape to hold the *muqumad* (sundried, deep fried meat cubes soaked in butter). This mixture rests inside a metal container (*sati*). A complex, symbolic and ceremonial knot with a long string plays an important part in this ritual. This ceremonial knot is tied by the bride's female relatives to reassure the groom's family that the bride is a virgin. The knot can be opened only by the groom's male family members. Hence, the knot symbolises the virginity of the bride, the Pharaonic circumcision (cf. Fullerton and Adan, 1995). The groom's male family members must successfully complete this task on the last day to seal the marriage deal. Furthermore, the hourglass shape of the container symbolises the bride and the female hourglass-shaped body (*dheh yar*). The *heedho* is also veiled like the bride when it is brought into the ceremony. It is important in terms of the wedding ceremony that the men succeed in opening this *heedho* so that the male wedding guests can eat the ritual butter-soaked meat, thus demonstrating that the bride is no longer a girl but a woman, a wife, and someone who is as fertile as the meat and the butter. The act of removing the veil (*salaq*) from the *Heedho* symbolises the removal of the 'dress', and untying the knot and cutting the date cake that 'covers' the butter and the meat symbolise the act of the virginity that is being lost on the first wedding night. The undoing of the knot and the eating of the meat and butter inside the date cake symbolises the access to fertility in much the same way as the 'coffee fruits being bitten open' does for the brides of the Oromo:

> We compare this biting open of the coffee fruits with the first sexual intercourse on the wedding-day, when the man has to force the girl to open her thighs in order to get access to her vagina. By cutting open the coffee fruit herself, the woman expresses her willingness to be 'pierced' for the sake of motherhood at any sexual intercourse.
>
> (Bartels, 1983: 288)

In the Somali ceremony, a woman with a soft stick lightly hits any of the groom's male relatives (cousins) who are trying to open this complicated knot in the wrong way. As the *heedho* symbolises the bride, the male relatives must not mishandle it (her). Marriages have been cancelled because of dissatisfaction with the way the groom's family handle the *heedho*. They have to handle the bride with care and skill. However, the ceremony is for the most part a playful one in which men enjoy poems and the women sing songs for the many hours it usually takes to open a *heedho*. I maintain that the eating of the meat, fat and dates is not only symbolic of the husband's access to his wife's fertile body: it furthermore demonstrates the lineage of the groom's potential procreation. Hence, it is traditionally only the male guests (the groom's lineage) who eat the *heedho* meat. Women eat from another *heedho* that is brought to the bride's home.

In the Somali context, the fertility bath demonstrates the significance of milk, fat, sacred springs, aromatic oils, massage and incense to women's fertility. Furthermore, the *heedho* ceremony reaffirms not only the significance of virginity as symbolised by the knot but also the significance of fat, meat and dates for Somali fertility practices, in much the same way that the *bun shuruur* does (see the following section). The *heedho* containers, the veils and the cowrie and the coffee beans confirm the existence of a special material culture that has a ritual and symbolic significance in these fertility rites.

Bun shuruur /bun qalla ritual: coffee fruits, coffee and fertility

The *bun shuruur* ritual of the Somali is the Oromo equivalent of the *buna qalla* ritual (slaughtering of the coffee bean). The Somali *bun shuruur* is a prayer ritual sacrificing *bun* (coffee) to God in exchange for fertility, good health and blessings. The coffee berries/fruits with the beans inside are fried in oil (from sesame seed or olive) or *haydh* (butter, usually from cows) in an iron (*bir*) pan (*daawe*). Women utter prayers frequently during the making of the *bun shuruur/bun qalla*. The Oromo and the Somali will ask for more rain (*roob/robisa*) and cows (*sac/sa'a*). When the coffee fruits settle in a corner and burst, creating a foam (*xumbo*), they are ready to be served. They are served in a *kurbin*, a thick wooden container with a long handle, often decorated with zigzag engravings around the rim.

A spoon (*fandhaal*) is used to stir the beans and the oil. It is no coincidence that the bowl of the spoon is shaped like a vulva (Figure 4.1a) and carved so that its rims resemble the labia with lips around the bowl. The lips end at the drop or neck of the bowl in the shape of a clitoris with a hood. These spoons often have handles in the form of a stylised penis with a small truncated conical terminus in an acorn shape or even as a stylised vulva on a phallic handle (Figure 4.1b). These special spoons are now rare but are an example of the way that seemingly everyday objects can carry a symbolism which signifies their ritual function.

I have found this often to be the case. Another example of this is the distinct style of Somali headrests. These are famous for their beauty but no one has yet studied why they are shaped the way they are. I have noticed that the headrest has a phallic shape when viewed from the side (Figure 4.2a). I suggest that it is no accident that the spoon is shaped like a vulva and the headrest like a penis; it is a systematic stylistic choice that represents a fairly cognisant act of the metaphysical meaning and depiction of fertility and its aesthetics. Further research is needed to determine how this type of Somali headrest relates to the Somali spoons and what demographic or age group is associated with them and how they, perhaps unconsciously, reaffirm the ideology of fertility in the Horn of Africa. Newly wedded couples receive wedding gifts that include headrests and spoons and perhaps this is a subtle way of representing the wish for fertility (offspring).

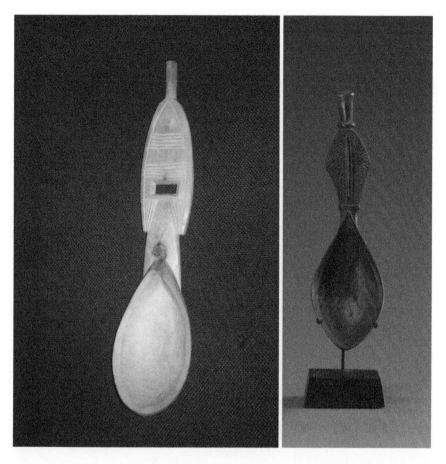

Figure 4.1a Deep foliate shape of the bowl of the spoon terminates into labia and clitoral hood and handle appears in stylized phallic shape and *Figure 4.1b* Stylized vulva on the phallic handle of a Somali spoon

Source: (*Figure 4.1b* with permission of Bonham Auction House)

The coffee ceremony or *bunsharuur/bun qalla* is another example of seemingly mundane practices that reinforce the philosophy of fertility. Sometimes during the *bun shuruur* the coffee fruits are crushed a little to let oil into the beans so that they swell and create more foam. Its preparation is a feature of the *chant* or *dhikri* gathering when everyone invited will drink coffee, eat the beans of the *bun shuruur* and moisturise their faces with butter *dhaashi* (moisturising). The *bun shuruur* is essentially a prayer ritual for fertility and wellbeing. It is part of the *zar*, the *Siti* and the *baanashada* rituals too. The *calaqad* or another ritual expert burns the incense and leads the moisturising and consuming of the coffee.

Figure 4.2a The Somali headrest in a stylized phallic shape as seen from the side

The Oromo's *buna qalla* is very similar:

> The cherry-like coffee fruits are bitten open and stewed in melted butter.
> The butter enters the fruits and reaches the beans inside. These beans
> which, because of their shape, account for the coffee fruits' use as a
> symbol of the woman: their shape is reminder of the female organ much
> as cowrie-shells are. The butter is by its very nature a symbol of the
> cow's, i.e. of female fertility. In this ritual, it is made extra tasty by the
> coffee and the coffee is made extra tasty by the butter. The result is a

Figure 4.2b The cowrie shell signifies the female sexual organ (the vulva) and fertility
Source: (copyright Eric Lafforgue)

new and even more eloquent and effective symbol of sexual intercourse. In addition, when the fruits in the end burst open they are a symbol of the hoped-for result of the intercourse: childbirth.

(Bartels, 1983: 287)

In the Oromo *buna qalla*, the word *qalla* stands for 'killing by cutting the throat' (ibid.) and it is the same in Somali. The Oromo, according to Bartels, use the word *qalla* in the context of the coffee bean to indicate that it is the symbol of a woman rather than of a bean. He argues that '[T]he verb 'to slaughter' points at a killing at which blood is shed; in this case, it refers to sexual intercourse, at which, in Matcha [Oromo] view, the woman's blood is shed' (ibid.). Both the *bun qalla* and *bun shuruur* rituals are used to bring fertility not only to human beings but also to animals and crops. In both rituals, it is obligatory to share the beans which are chewed during the prayers for rains, children and prosperity.

In Ethiopia, the coffee ceremony with its incense burning and butter is a version of the *bun qalla*. It shows how what is essentially the same tradition can vary across Ethiopia and the Horn of Africa. Women invite each other to the coffee ceremony which takes place in three stages and can last for up to nine hours. The final stage is called '*baraka*' (blessing). During the ceremony women talk about all sorts of issues. The coffee is roasted in a pan and ground in a wooden mortar before being cooked and served in *jebena* (a spherical pot with a long neck and a straw lid). The lid is both functional and symbolic: functional, in that the coffee grains are prevented from spilling out and the coffee is kept warm; and symbolic in that the straw comes from a blessed grass. Coffee is an important ritual element across the Horn of Africa which, together with cowrie shells, has a symbolic association with the female sexual organ (vulva), as Bartel has observed. Women often wear cowrie shells (Figure 4.2b) and ceremonial containers as well as adorning themselves with the shells.

Concentric circles, a pattern emulating the idea of the extension of lineage and hence a symbol of fertility, can be found on baskets, on ritual bread (*himbasha*) and on ceremonial shields (Mire, 2006). These circles also appear in the rock art of the region (Mire, 2015a).

It is a common practice in the Horn of Africa to smear faces with milk, blood, water, butter and chalk during rituals. During the *sagaalaysi* ritual (the *Siti* performance during the ninth month of a pregnancy), a woman's head is smeared with butter from the *bun shuruur* to bring about a safe delivery. Other rituals (some involving herbal medicine) stave off *umulraac* (maternal mortality, lit. 'following the delivery') during difficult or complicated deliveries. One such ritual takes place to prevent *fool-dherer*, a prolonged delivery: the woman is put onto a hard sheet which is held at each end (like a hammock) by two women and swung in a motion believed to move the baby into a delivery position. *Fool-dherer* is one of the many negative health implications of *Gudniin* (Pharaonic circumcision).

Sometimes a stillborn[1] child or a miscarriage is believed to have been caused by a female bad *jin* named *umusibiyaanad* who is widely known in the Somali region to attack pregnant women's unborn children. This malevolent spirit is usually repelled through reading the Qur'an. Today, as in the past, such malevolent spirits are driven out by specialist healers. The *baanashada* ritual includes the *umusibiyaanad* treatment.

Making women fertile: the Baanashada Dumarka

The *Baanashada dumarka* (nurturing of women) (from here on simply called *baanashada*) is a 'nurturing'/healing treatment that is arranged for women who appear to have fertility problems. It involves among other things the treatment of the spirits that are believed to have possessed the women and made them infertile. In this section, I mainly draw together new information about the *Baanashada Dumarka* ritual and its link to the butterfly bush (*rotheca myricoides*) which is locally known as *tiire* and, to a lesser extent, summarise some published findings (Mire, 2016b). I use this material to examine further the relationships between the fertility traditions of the Somali in particular and those of other Horn of Africa cultures more generally.

The ritual is led by a *calaqad* in her role as both a traditional healer and a religious head. Female ritual leadership has often only been recognised in the context of *sitaat* as sheikhas. However, they can also be the keepers of male saints' sacred pilgrimage centres. It is possible that the role of female *Muriids*, like that of their male counterparts, developed in pre-Islamic times. The *calaqad* also presides over worship, ritual sacrifice, prayers and the dancing, including when these ceremonies are associated with *zar*.

The *baanashada* takes place during a seven-day period when the women are subjected to invasive examinations including the insertion of medical plant material into their vaginas, a practice intended to heal *makaanka* (the womb). The idea is to make the uterus 'right' as one of the interviewees put it; 'the healer turned it [the womb] using two fingers.'

Five different stages of the *Baanashada* are navigated during the week of healing. First, food and drink made with *tiire* (the butterfly bush, *Rotheca myricoides*) (Figure 4.3a and Figure 4.3b) is consumed. This is intended to cleanse the body from anything that has got lodged inside it; it is called *da'arbihin/da'arbah* and involves inducing diarrhoea and vomiting. The *tiire* root features both in prepared concoctions and in drinks, food, soups (*maraq*) and tea with camel milk, all intended to ease constipation. Foods soaked in water with *tiire* are often bitter (*qadhaad*) to taste (a quality which makes it seem more like a medicine) and are frequently eaten or drunk standing up in an attempt to swallow it quickly.

The second stage is the fattening or 'nurturing' (*baanashada*) of the woman by giving her fatty food such as concentrated fat, *dihin*. A sheep is slaughtered and its bones and marrow are cooked with *tiire*. The idea is to increase the fertility fat (*haydh*). The woman regularly eats *muqumad*, sun dried, deep fried meat cubes soaked in butter. Before stage three, fenugreek is also consumed to relax tight muscles and heal any joint pain (Mire, 2016b).

Stage three involves heating the body with steam and relaxing the muscles with a full body massage so that the uterus can be examined and 'turned' to make it right:

> They [the healers] take stones and cook them in water that they then put under your skirt so that all the heat flows through your body. Then she [the healer] gives you a whole-body massage. . . . She will turn your *makaanka* if it is lying in the wrong way. She does this by putting two fingers in you and turns the *makaanka*.

After the full body massage when the body is in a relaxed state, the fourth stage requires the *tiire* to be inserted into the vagina. This invasive act is not entirely pain free. The *tiire* is covered with a film of mashed date, to

Figure 4.3a Tiire plant (*Rotheca myricoides*) known internationally as the butterfly
     bush

smoothen it. Another interviewee explained to me how the *tiire* is inserted
into the women's vagina:

> Some women use it [*tiire*] to put it in their vagina; they take a date and
> take out the stone and then replace the stone with a piece of *tiire* stick
> [about 2–3cm] in their vagina, they will keep it for days; this will lead to
> internal infection caused by the *tiire* and the date and then it will cause a
> puss and this is thought to be cleansing the bad things in there, because
> there is a puss coming out.

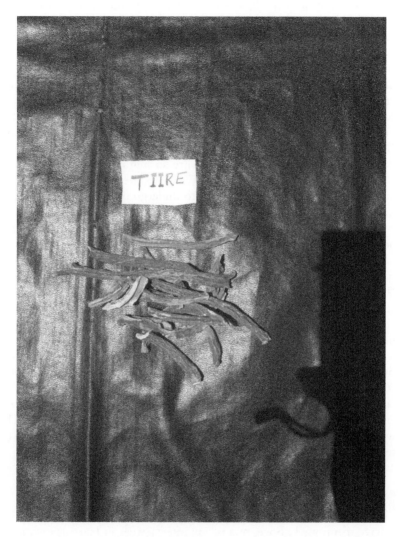

Figure 4.3b Tiire root (*Rotheca myricoides*) often included in food and remedies

It is important to note that, far from 'curing', the insertion of herbs into the vagina will more often than not leave women with further health problems. I have noted elsewhere (Mire, 2016b) that the Somali apprenticeship to become a traditional healer takes 13 years of education. This shows in what regard this knowledge is held. *Tiire* (*rothica myriocoides*) is completely poisonous and should be used only by those who have proven and tested knowledge and the privilege and right to practice. Misuse can lead to death. I also noted in my original article (Cerulli, 1957) that, after I recorded these practices in my fieldwork in Somaliland, there was a case of a Somali diaspora woman from Europe who died after seeking traditional fertility treatments in Somaliland which involved the insertion of herbs and plant parts into her vagina. She was admitted to hospital but would not disclose her ailment; sadly only after she had died were the herbs in her cervix discovered during a post-mortem (Mire, 2016b). Not only do these types of unchecked practices lead to physical suffering; they also cause other side effects such as deteriorating mental health. Yet it seems that most husbands remain unaware of the true condition of women's health, both physical and mental.

One interviewee said that Somalis have a saying '*Innan'ka uu tiire i'siin waayay, Ilaah-na i'siin maayo*', 'the boy that *tiire* does not give me, God won't give me either.' Such ideas are so ingrained in Somalis' minds that women will still come from the West, despite having access there to advanced fertility treatments, in order to undergo traditional fertility treatment back home. There is something deeply embedded inside Somali culture that allows practices such as *baanashada* and Pharaonic circumcision (discussed further below) to continue. One of my main questions in this book, as I have said earlier, is to investigate and understand why these practices are preserved.

The final treatment is *saar ka tun*, lit. 'the drumming the *zar* spirit out of the person'. The *bun shuruur* or *bun qalla* are also performed at this stage.

The women of the Madhibaan clan who are considered to possess ancient medicinal knowledge traditionally often carry out the *Baanashada*. They are also treated as an underclass by the nomadic Somali clans. Special healers commonly perform circumcision in the Horn of Africa. The Oromo have the *Ceiddeesa* who are herbalists too.

The Madhibaan perform rituals such as *baanashada*, Pharaonic circumcision and traditional surgery, the latter carried out by male healers. They collect a selection of trees and herbs called *dhirbaanta* (healing herbs) associated with the different stages of the *baanashada*.

The role of traditional healers and the historical legend of Bu'ur Ba'ayr

As I have mentioned above, one of my interviewees in Hargeisa explained that the *calaqad* will insert two fingers into the vagina and turn the uterus. The most interesting part in this procedure is the idea of ritual massage, a practice that may reflect an old tradition practiced by traditional healers in this region

I have drawn parallels between the practice of *Baanashada* and what has been said about Bu'ur Ba'ayr in terms of the 'wicked' rituals he allegedly performed to heal infertility. His marriage ritual was probably not only about sanctioning marriage but also fertility (see previous section). In the *baanashada*, the women spend a week with the healer. This idea of six nights of fertility bringing immediate healing triggers memories of Bu'ur Ba'ayr (and Gedi Shambow/Baabow) who is also said to have spent a week with the bride. The *calaqad* healer, as noted earlier, has retained a ritual authority that seems to predate Islam even though she does not appear to perform any sexual rituals. This may be because while the *calaqad* is typically a regional healer with ancestral powers, Bu'ur Ba'ayr has been singled out as conquered and defeated spirituality, as demonstrated by the duel described in an earlier chapter. Nevertheless, what the healer does during the *baanashada* bears a remarkable similarity to the legend of Bu'ur Ba'ayr and, particularly, to what regional religious heads and elders such as the Matcha elders still do. The Matcha Oromo elders smear the bride's thighs and belly with blood and coffee fruit to bless her with children (Bartels, 1983). Here are regional echoes of elders or healers intervening to promote fertility, and this links with the mention of symbolic intercourse in the legend of Bu'ur Ba'ayr. The Matcha also practice a groom and bride having intercourse through a symbolic process which is supervised by a male and a female elder. Bearing in mind these regional practices, the fingers of a healer who facilitates fertility may symbolise an ancient tradition whereby religious leaders such as Bu'ur Ba'ayr and Gedi Baabow took part in intimate rituals.

The *baanashada* integrates various rituals that are today associated with non-/pre-Islamic regional practices. It is intriguing that the last of the five stages of the *baanashada* treatment is *zar*, which deals with spirit possessions. As I explore below, this ritual aims to satisfy the spirits that potentially possess the patient and inhibit their ability to reproduce.

Waaq and Zar: spirit possessions and ancestral veneration and their relationship with fertility

Many scholars have studied spirit possessions and the cult of *Zar* in Somali society (Lewis, 1991; Luling, 1991; Boddy, 1988; Makris and Al-Safi, 1991; cf. Cerulli, 1957; Seligman, 1914). In this discussion, however, I start from a different perspective by looking at the idea of spirit possession in relation to female fertility rituals. The female visitors to Aw-Barkhadle have told me that they also go to healers for spirit possession. And *zar* is clearly a significant part of the *baanashada* treatment. It is the *calaqad* who intercedes in cases of spirit possession and is often required to do so. Hence, spirit possession in Somali society is closely linked to fertility rituals. Today, the *zar* has to a degree been replaced by the *Sitaat*. Having already described what the *calaqad* does for the patient both physically and mentally during the *Baanashada*, I want to understand more about the *zar* dance and its potential relationship with, on the one hand, ancient and current ancestral veneration and, on the other hand, an indigenous belief in the Sky-God. Although *Zar* is currently largely prohibited in the Somali territories, it is still publicly practiced in neighbouring Ethiopia. The women who used to practice *zar* are now obliged to do so secretly or to resort to the less provocative *Siti/ Sitaat* ceremony.

The dancing

The origin of the dance, according to Cerulli, lies probably in 'an ancient sacred dance' (1957: 148) relating to the Sky-God who was traditionally worshipped by the peoples of the Horn of Africa (Cerulli, 1957: 157). *Zar* has been exported to Arabia and parts of the Middle East via their ancient contact with the region historically known as Abyssinia, which at times also included the Somali region (Cerulli, 1957).

In Hargeisa, there was one particular *calaqad*, referred to as 'the Hargeisa *calaqad*' who was especially famous in the early 1970s and 1980s before her death sometime in the 1990s. The oldest amongst my interviewees remembered her and were all her patients. Her cult had a house dedicated to its practice – renowned healers often have a special house or defined areas for their ritual activity in the Horn of Africa. The *zar* of the Oromo, for example, is linked to a ceremony for the Oromo Goddess, Atete, a pre-Christian and pre-Islamic goddess associated with the myth of origin; it is in turn linked to the *ooda* tree. Another example is the *misigida*, the meeting house of the *addaraa* cult of the Guji Oromo (Loo, 1991) which is distinguished from their other ritual houses such as the *galma*. I will focus on the *calaqad*'s way of approaching the *zar*.

The Hargeisa *calaqad* was much respected in the *zar* community, which is a hierarchical one. She owned a big bull that she paraded during the ceremony to demonstrate her status and that she was owed respect. The *calaqad* used to have a special day when she would ride her *dibbi* (bull) or a horse around town, leading the dancing. Some *calaqad* also had a couple of people to beat the drums for the *zar* dancing, with the most celebrated bringing drummers imported from Ethiopia. The Hargeisa *calaqad* also had her own distinct regalia. She used to come out into the street wearing this and sit on her bull which was led by her 'Ethiopian *adoon*' (slave). It is very possible, of course, that this public progression with the bull was intended to drive away evil spirits from the town[2] as well as being for display. Often the interviewees talked about a male Ethiopian 'slave' whom the *calaqad* would keep at home to be her main drummer. The notion of ritual drumming exists in Ethiopia and 'ritual drums' formed part of the royal regalia even in Aksumite times, as I will discuss in a later chapter.

People would be recommended to the *calaqad* whose expertise spread through word of mouth. Since *zar* is a deep-rooted tradition, it is not only women who come forward for help; all kinds of people might consult a male or female *calaqad*, who will always try to help. The *calaqad* usually confirms that a person has been possessed by a spirit and lays out the necessary treatment options. Some women know right from the start that they have *zar*. One of them said 'You know it because it is in you and you get ill.'

The powers of the Hargeisa *calaqad* was such that at times even prominent politicians and businessmen have sought her help over personal issues or have consulted her about their political and economic strategies. This may explain why a powerful *calaqad* would have been able to parade publicly in the past despite the fact that *zar*, even a few decades ago, was seen as something shameful.[3]

Some of my interviewees who had been patients of this *calaqad* spoke about her in a very fond way; they regarded her work as important and wished she had still been alive to continue the healing; her absence had left a void. One of the interviewees declared:

> Yes, she slaughtered animals and the drumming oh! Dom! Dom! Dom!' Ha! [Yes!] The dancing and the hitting in the ground [fainting] would take your skin off. See [she removes the skirt upwards to show me her knees] they have recently turned dark from kneeling for the prayers but in the time of *zar* they were red and lost all their skin.
>
> ("Older lady 3 in Hargeisa", pers. comm. 2007;
> cf. "Nasra", pers. comm. 2007)

This source confirmed '*way kaa qabanaysaaa saarka*' ('she takes/grabs the *zar* from/out of you'). The *zar* ritual for fertility treatment may go on for years until there is a successful pregnancy or a final acceptance of the problem. Women often come to accept infertility as their destiny and as God's will (*qadar Allah*).

As a child growing up in Mogadishu, I witnessed many *zar* ceremonies. It is often a stressful experience for a child to see women in tears dancing and fainting since adults do not explain such matters to children. Children are not supposed to witness these events but adults often cannot keep them away. Men – all too aware of the impact of the ceremony – usually do keep away; and those who have themselves been victimised end up becoming patients too.

Many of my interviewees had been to the *calaqad* about their fertility problems. They had already worked out that something was affecting their ability to carry a child and they wanted to know what to do. They may already have assumed that they were possessed by *zar*. I was told by a woman 'So after you give his "*qoftaan*" and "*nadaafadiisa*" [gifts of adornments and perfumes] then you will get better.' It is significant that in this case 'it' (*zar*) is referred to as a male. She continued:

> You go to the *calaqad* and you say you are not well, you are ill and show where you have pain or tell her what is wrong. Then she will tell you that you have *zar*, after she has fainted she will be able to say what is wrong with you. She will be able to say exactly which one [of the *zar* types] is yours, like mine is *maame*, but there are many different ones. She will say. She treats the *zar* from many people.

When I asked whether all women get *zar*, one interviewee replied, interestingly, 'no, only the Habasha'. On being corrected and told that Somali women like her got it, she explained that it is something that comes from 'the Ethiopians and falls on us', suggesting that the affliction is both foreign and accidental. She continued to talk about it as a spirit that penetrates the body and soul. I asked if *zar* is a disease or an infection, to which she replied 'yes, it is a disease that is going around. People will say you have *zar* and the *calaqad* will tell you that you have *zar*.'

The apparent relationship between spirit possession and fertility cults is an important one: the spirits make the women childless until such time as the women can satisfy them. Potential links between *zar* and fertility may have a crucial part to play in the non- and pre-Islamic notion of *zar*. The word *zar* is said to originate from the Cushitic word *adjar* (of the Agow) which denotes the Sky-God. The *zar* is possibly, therefore, related to the dance of the *adjar*/ the Sky-God and resembles the dance of the Goddess of Atete. One of the reasons for practicing *zar* in Somali society seems to be a fear of infertility. Women do what they can to please the spirit that invades them.

Women refer to many types of *zar* spirit characters, one of them being an Ethiopian type known as *maame*. The victims of *zar* wear rings on their fingers. These are of silver with a middle stone of differing colours. Most are white but in the case of *maame* are black. Rings are just one of the many things associated with the regalia of a *zar* victim. Some women wear a necklace with many objects dangling from it that makes a noise when worn during the ritual dance. Other women have 'a stick of money'. Some have the so-called Ethiopian blanket which they wear during the ceremony and the *zar* dance. When I asked one of the interviewees when she would wear such a blanket she replied 'on *their* day' implying that the *zar* are multiple; however, in a different context the same interviewee talked about her *zar* as if it were just one person, usually a male. Many east African cultures have specific songs for spirits and spirit talk (Mire, 2016b). The Guji Oromo also have special songs for spirit possession such as the *mesmuri addaraa* (Loo, 1991). I remember the chorus of a Somali song for a *zar* spirit which offers it amber beads:

> 'wuxuu doonayaa oo uu doonayaa,
> qoor iyo qardhaas buu doonayaa'!

> 'what he [*zar*] wants more of,
> are an amulet and an amber necklace!'

Somali women often seem to practice *zar* when they are missing something, whether it be a child or a piece of adornment such as an amber necklace or even an item of clothing (such as *shaash*, a popular silk head scarf). Amber necklaces need not have much value in material terms as people sometimes use them together with amulets to protect themselves from evil spirits. Nevertheless, *zar* ceremonies are expensive rites and, as such, are more often than not practised mainly by the wealthy classes.

*The origins of Zar and a potential association
with ancestral worship*

The *Baanashada* treatment places *zar* at the centre of what might be regarded as one of its traditional roles in relation to spirit possessions. *Zar* is generally thought to have originated in Ethiopia. When asked its origin, people were quick to point out that *zar* did not originally come from 'here', meaning the Somali populated country. My interviewees instead pointed to the 'sea' and 'far away from here' and added also 'Ethiopia'. This almost feels like a defensive response from people who are suspicious of the practice and who view themselves as good Muslims who have been victimised. They see their religious affiliation to be with Arabia and not with their non-Muslim neighbours. *Zar* is seen to be a non-Islamic practice. Islam, as has been said, does not allow the recognition of possession cults which are forbidden by the religious authorities and thus mostly only practised in secret (cf. Luling, 1991).

Cerulli notes that, in Ethiopia, the name *Zar* is of non-Semitic origin. He suggests that "Zar is very probably derived from the name of the supreme divinity of the pagan Kushites, the God-Heaven called in Agau (Bilan): *djar*" (1957: 157). Linguists have already confirmed that the name *zar* (*djar*) refers to the Sky-God (e.g. Ullendorff, 1955; cf. Levine, 2000). What is intriguing about this transformation is the change in status that the Sky-God seems to have suffered during and after the Christian/Islamic conversion:

> The ancient pagan god became in a Christianized Abyssinia a malevolent genius; and in this way the animistic practices, which in the paganism of the Kushites were directed only to the minor superhuman beings, passed into Abyssinian Christianity (and then into Islam) with the proper name of God-Heaven (the Sky-God) who had been reduced to a minor rank.
> (Cerulli, 1957: 157)

Furthermore, it has been argued that ancestral worship was originally associated with the 'Cushitic institutions' (Cerulli, 1957; cf. Lewis, 1996, 1998). Others have pointed to the possible connection between the possession cults and the cult of ancestors as offering a persuasive example of religious syncretism. Luling notes that "The ancestor spirits, spirits of morality within their cultural context, can be transformed into amoral spirits outside of the context" (Luling, 1991: 130; Makris and Al-Safi, 1991: 122; cf. Cerulli, 1957: 148; Seligman, 1914).

In the Horn of Africa, there are a few named spirit possessions such as Borana, Mumbi, Mingis and Sheikh Hussein.[4] These spirits are spread out across the region and prayers are uttered to appease their relations. A special prayer called *maltu* is used to bless a sterile woman, as happens in Oromo society too (Loo, 1991). At Aw-Barkhadle, the women sheikhas also play a significant role as female spiritual healers. And *zar*, to the extent that it involves pleasing the ancestral spirits and curing infertility, is relevant to an understanding of that site.

As noted earlier, ancestral spirits can sometimes take the form of a malevolent spirit. If *zar* is the Sky-God whom the new religions have reduced to the status of a malevolent spirit, then it is likely that the *zar* dance itself may relate to ancestral worship.

It may be relevant to note that in Sudan it is believed that illness is evoked by *jins* (bad spirits); people believe in the evil eye, spirits and demons all of which are thought to represent 'a legacy of the earliest period' (Hall and Ismail, 1981: 185). In Egypt, Sudan, Ethiopia and the Swahili world, psychosomatic illnesses such as depression are treated as if they are caused by jins. The cure for such illnesses usually involves taking magical countermeasures and includes the use of charms as protection and rites of exorcism to drive the spirits away.

Although the Somali shun any suggestion of a genealogical link with their (bad) spirits, it is possible that there is a connection between the possession cults and the cult of ancestors. I suggest that while the traditional healer is associated with good things, the spirits can be associated with good and/or bad and are bad to the victim only if they are not placated. In much the same way, the spirits can interfere with fertility but also grant/give (back) fertility if satisfied. And venerated ancestral figures (spirits) are able to bless and grant sacred fertility. This point is demonstrated by a fertility ritual that is also an example of ancestral veneration, the Haawa and Fatima, the *Siti* or the *Sitaat* ceremony. *Siti* has in many ways replaced *Zar* as it is less controversial given the current political climate in much of the Horn of Africa. However, the strict Salafi adherents consider even the *Siti* to be an un-Islamic practice on account of its praise of the religious ancestors it calls upon to intercede.

The Sitaat (Abaay Siti): satisfying and honouring female religious ancestors

Siti/Sitaat or *Haawa iyo Faadumo* (Eve and Fatima/*Faadumo*/*Faatima*) is an ancestral commemoration ceremony celebrating Eve, the first woman ever to live, and Fatima, the daughter of Prophet Mohamed, along with many other renowned Muslim females. Hence, *Siti* is a strictly female practice. The *Siti/Sitaat* ceremony usually takes place when women are in their seventh month of pregnancy. Other scholars have already described elements of the *Siti/Sitaat* ceremony (Declich, 2000; Kapteijns and Omar, 1996, 2007; Tiilikainen, 2010). Here I examine this ritual from two perspectives: fertility and the veneration of sacred ancestors. The *sitaat*, I argue, sheds light on the ancestors' (and perhaps the pre-Islamic religious leaders') role in making fertility possible.

During the seventh month of pregnancy as part of a celebration of fertility, the prayers concentrate on bestowing good health on the mother and the child. There seems to be a strong belief in the protecting power of Eva or Fatima, the two most important female Islamic religious ancestors. The main purpose of the ritual is to please the ancestors so that the child will be delivered without any problems. During the ninth month of pregnancy (*Sagaalaysi*), a *Siti* performance takes place which this time is to request from the religious ancestors a safe labour. This region has one of the biggest child and maternal mortality rates (*umulraac*) in the world; in 2010, it was estimated at 1000 deaths per 100,000 live births.[5]

Siti can also be performed for reasons unconnected to fertility. For example, a woman might have a dream about an ancestor and this dream might be interpreted as a sign that she should carry out a particular task. The ancestor might be unhappy about something and appear in a dream to direct a person to do something which would please her ancestor. Some women who have had difficulties becoming pregnant or giving birth to a son have talked about a particular ancestor, most often a female, whom they think is the reason for their problem. This belief in evil spirits' interference once again echoes the fear of the *umusibiyanad* who will enter the women and kill the unborn child. In this situation women seek a sheikh (*wadaad*) who can help them to commemorate their ancestor. Some people claim that an ancestor is refusing to allow them to do something until they have performed this or that act in the ancestor's name; the act may be to sacrifice a goat or to buy clothes in the name of the ancestor.

More often than not, however, fertility is the reason people commission a *Siti* (*Haawa and Faadumo*) ceremony. Blood is shed for fertility and sustained fertility in order to stay at peace with the religious figures who are at the same time ancestors. The veneration of ancestors is a common practice within Somali society. Women interviewed for this study talk about the wish to please their female ancestors. When the *roohaan* (spirits, sometimes ancestral) appear in some way to a woman, she may seek out *herta* (*xerta*), a communion of ecclesiastical women or sheikhas, to help the ceremony organisers to perform the singing of *Nabi amaan* (songs in praise of the Abrahamic prophets) and to venerate religious ancestors.

The Herta are sheikhas who celebrate and praise important female religious ancestors. Women who wish to honour their grandmothers will commission an Eve and Fatima ceremony which focuses on female ancestors. This confirms a possible connection between the possession cults and the cult of ancestral worship. As noted by Makris and Al-Safi (1991: 122) and Seligman (1914), the ancestor spirits, though considered as spirits of morality within their own cultural sphere, can be distorted into becoming immoral spirits (Makris and Al-Safi, 1991: 122; cf. Seligman, 1914; Luling, 1991). In the next section, I describe a *Siti* performance in which I participated from its preparation stages to completion.

The Siti ceremony

A woman had a dream about her mother-in-law who had died four years ago. The woman's own mother had also died about two years previously.

The woman wanted to commemorate her own mother with a *Siti* ceremony. However, as the date of the ceremony grew closer, her mother-in-law started appearing in her dreams. In the dream, they exchanged some words; this dream kept coming back to the woman and she therefore decided to hold a *Siti* ceremony dedicated to both her mother and her mother-in-law. (In the Horn of Africa, ancestors commonly appear in the form of an apparition; and the Oromo also perform rituals when an ancestor (*ekere*) appears (Loo, 1991)).

The woman decided to hold the *Siti* the day after the Eid celebration. She told all her woman friends and relatives and, more importantly, she visited the centres of two female Sufi societies in Hargeisa and invited their members to the ceremony. They agreed to participate and perform the *Sitaat* (or *Siti*). On the day of the performance, female relatives and friends arrived at her house very early, just after the morning prayers (about 5 a.m.). Two animals were slaughtered, a goat and a sheep of female sex. The women thought that there was nothing significant in this but it is interesting to note that female animals were being offered up in a celebration of the female ancestral figures.

The animals were slaughtered at dawn by an older woman (in Somali society, it is very common for the women to slaughter animals like sheep and goats). The women stripped off the skin and did the butchering and the cooking. The livers and kidneys, considered to be a delicacy, were eaten for breakfast by the household and the women helpers at around 7 a.m. The pure meat parts of the animal are the sacrificial meat which is eaten at the actual ceremonial meal. And it is only the pure meat that is offered to neighbours and to the women helpers to take home to their families. The people (neighbours, friends and relatives) and the charities (mosques and orphanages) who receive the cooked or raw meat will praise these ancestors and pray to God that they might themselves be forgiven and blessed and welcomed into paradise at *yawm al qiyaama*, the final day of judgment.

The women of the *Herta* were the principal guests at the ceremony. They arrived at about 3 p.m. The *Sitaat* ceremony begins with the *Mowliidka nabiga* (*dhikri*). The *Herta Baha Nabi* play the Haawa and Fatima *sitaat* (*Siti* ceremony). The food containing *maraq* (soup made of boiled meat) and various dishes of fried meat, stews, saffron rice and various salad dishes are served. After this ritual food, the main meal follows with snacks such as *salool* (popcorn), *bun* (coffee), coffee beans and *timmir* (dates), as well as tea.

The *Siti* is a celebration of religious ancestors and prophets. It is possible that it is a pre-Islamic ritual too (Kapteijns and Omar, 1996, 2007; Declich, 2000). The women of the two Herta groups praised the daughters and the wives of the Prophet and other important female relatives and their friends and the important Muslim women. They then honoured the Sufi sheikhs, particularly Sheikh Sharif Yusuf (Aw-Barkhadle), Sheikh Madar Ahmed, Sheikh 'Umar, Sheikh Nuur, Sheikh Isaaq bin Ahmed al-Hashimi and Sheikh Ismail Jaberti. The final session honoured Sheikh Abdil Kadir Jeelani (in

Arabic 'Abd al-Qadir al-Hasani al-Hussaini al-Jilani) (AD 1077–1166 or AH 470–561) who was a *suni shafi/hanibali* preacher and the figurehead of the Qaadiriya Sufi order. Révoil talks about the legend of how Jabarti (also spelled as Jaberti), on his way to the Persian Gulf, found himself in the land of the Somali who were 'pagans', and he stopped to preach Islam (1882: 315–316). He was born in the Persian province of Gilan (hence his name Gilani and, in Somali, *Jeelani*) but is believed to be of the Arab bloodline of *al-ashraf*, descendants of either Hasan or Hussein, the sons of 'Ali and Fatima, the Prophet's daughter. 'Abd al-Qadir had a father descended from Hasan and a mother descended from Hussein (Arberry, 1953; Trimingham, 1965). Sh. Ismail Jaberti is also said to be from the Bani Hashim (Hashimite) clan, the Prophet's clan of the Quraishi tribe. The Darood tribe of the Somali claim to be descendants of the previously mentioned Ibrahim bin Sh. Ismail Jaberti. Like the Darood clan, the Isaaq clan claim Hashimite ancestry through Sh. Isaaq. Sh. Madar, also noted above, is also considered to be an *al-ashraf*.

Ancestral veneration involves, importantly, an aspect that I term 'divine kinship'. This is transmitted down through the Prophet Muhammad's divine lineage and enables Somalis to enjoy sacred kinship and its blessed fertility. In pre-Islamic times, as noted earlier, it would be more accurate to talk about ancestor worship than about ancestor veneration, and any such blood links would have been with pre-Islamic and pre-Christian religious figures. Ancestral worship would therefore have been directed towards sacred ancestors of the 'Cushitic institutions'.

It is important to note that no other ceremony recognises the value of women in society in the way that the *Siti* does. Apart from a reference to male religious ancestors during the *mowliidka nabiga (dhikri)*, men are totally irrelevant to this ritual and are not allowed to attend the ceremony. The men of the house eat discretely before the ceremony and then go away and avoid the house completely. The *Siti* is therefore one of the few ceremonies in which women are cleaning, cooking, preparing and serving only for the benefit of other women. The ritual is executed by women at all stages, from the preparation and slaughter of animals to cooking, consuming and performing the prayers and dances. The archaeological record may well bear witness to the ritual language used, the procession and the performance, but it can never truly capture the singing and the dancing, the sound of the drums and the smoke of incense. By attending these performances, I have been able to apply the Knowledge-Centred Approach to bring a richer interpretation to the material remains. People take away healing from these acts and the materials they use represents this healing. I was able to film the *Siti* and rewatch it to understand the context of the objects used, where they were placed and how people were interacting with them, whether it was the incense burners, the drums or the clothes they wore.

However, the most important aspect of this ritual is that living women were celebrating their female ancestors. The word ancestor (somebody who has borne a child) is crucial here because it communicates the notion of fertility. It is the present generation of women who are celebrating past generations of women in a family or lineage that stretches back to the Prophet's daughter and to the first woman (Eve). And when the *Siti* is performed for a pregnant woman, as has been noted earlier, it is also about conjuring up the ancestors' blessings for a safe delivery and about welcoming a new generation into the world. The essence of the *Siti* ceremony is arguably ultimately about celebrating the extension of a divine lineage.

The issue of a fertility related to female ancestral veneration and dedicated to the first woman of all, Eva/Eve/*Haawa*, and Fatima, the daughter of the prophet and one of the first women to be born a Muslima, clearly has a great significance for Somali women. Perhaps this links again to the Oromo and to Atete's role in the *zar* as a goddess associated with the myth of origin and fertility. There seems to be an ancient kinship tradition of a sacred ancestor who grants and/or protects fertility, a tradition with echoes going back perhaps to a pre-Islamic tradition, an idea discussed in greater detail in Chapter Five. I have already associated the *calaqad*, Bu'ur Ba'ayr and others with a similar tradition.

As mentioned earlier, the *Siti* ceremony in the later stages of pregnancy is aimed at the protection of the mother-to-be and the child by their female religious ancestors. I now turn to a discussion of the rituals that seem to have an impact on women's fertility and discuss the *wagar* ritual which also takes place before, during and after pregnancy. The *wagar* ritual also sheds some light on a possible relationship between local pre-Islamic beliefs in the Horn of Africa and current fertility rituals. I investigate the *wagar* and its significance as a sacred medium within fertility rituals and sacred landscapes. I will illuminate the religious syncretism through which an indigenous and non-/pre-Islamic practice has been appropriated and applied for fertility purposes in a Muslim society (the Somali). I am also mindful of the fact that the *wagar* is unanimously regarded as a sacred tree by most of the peoples of the Horn of Africa.

The Wagar; its relationship with Waaq, fertility and kinship

The *wagar* is a wooden object, a sculpture or figurine (Figure 4.4a and Figure 4.4b) associated with female fertility rituals in the Somali territory (Mire, 2015b). The *wagar* tree is the African olive (*Olea europaea sp. Africana*, Miskell, 2000). I found the *wagar* tree growing on some of the highest peaks of the northern Somali plateau, including the mountain ranges of Daalo and Jilib Rihin in the Sanaag region (Figure 4.5). The entire *wagar* tree is seen to be *geed amran* (a blessed/sacred tree). Although the potential pharmacological properties of this plant are unclear, the Somali believe that it is *amran* (sacred/blessed) and therefore healing. It is used for healing purposes because of its divine properties, including its aromatic qualities when burned as incense.

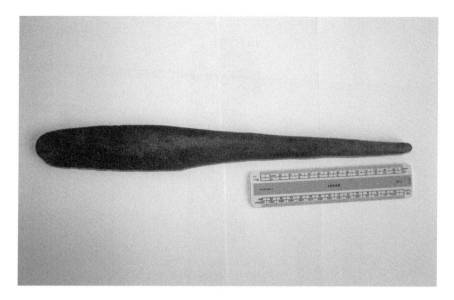

Figure 4.4a The *wagar* sculpture carved from *Olea europaea sp. Africana* native to east Africa (over 100 years old, belonging to the author's family)

The *wagar* seems to represent a wider Cushitic (pre-Islamic) symbol of a belief in sacred trees. Its shape is intriguing: it has a flat shape at the top or, sometimes, one edge with two subsequent bump shapes resembling a head or a distended big belly, an allusion to an anthropomorphic figure (Figure 4.4b). The primary role of the *wagar* in Somali female society currently is to heal infertility and ward off evil spirits. The *wagar* object appears to be the only indigenous wooden sculpture to be considered in itself a sacred object.

My maternal grandmother kept a *wagar* (see Figure 4.4a) in her private box (*kolay*) or under her bed when she was bringing up not only her own children but her grandchildren. I inherited this *wagar*, which is over 100 years old. The *wagar* is thought to provide fertility through its attributed divine qualities. It may itself represent an anthropomorphic material of a religious idol in pre-Islamic Somali culture. Women consider it to belong to an ancient tradition.

A cycle of fertility rituals: The Gubka (the burning), the Siti ceremony and the Afartanbah

In order to make themselves fertile, women are burned in the *Gub* ritual of the *wagar* (Mire, 2015b). The end-tip of the *wagar* is dipped into heated oil (such as black seed oil, *Nagela sative*) and heated on a fire. The hot end-tip of the *wagar* is then put onto the abdomen or the stomach to burn

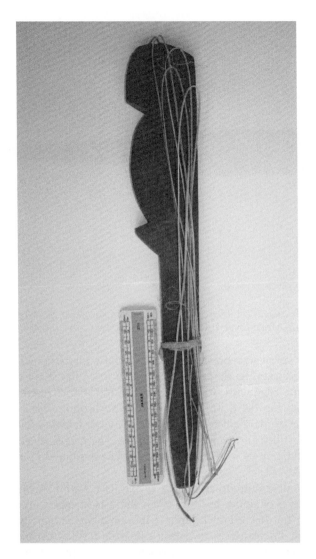

Figure 4.4b Wagar bundled with sacred grass

specific places, each three times. Healing by burning is a common practice in Somali culture. Certain childhood illnesses are treated through burning specific places on children from birth to their late teens, as I discuss later in relation to the symbols of scarification. These childhood treatments can be compared to the preventive medicine of modern vaccines.

For 40 days after the birth of her child, a woman is kept indoors except for the occasional toilet visit when she will carry a *wagar* in her hand in front of her head as she walks (Figure 4.4b). This is to protect her and her child

Figure 4.5 The sacred olive/*wagar* forests of Daalo mountains

from evil spirits. This period of seclusion also serves as a preventive measure against potential infectious diseases. This 40-day period ends with a celebration, *afartanbah*. This ritual involves what is called the *Sitaat* or the *Siti* ceremony, described above, and celebrates and thanks the religious ancestors, particularly the first Muslim woman, Faatima, the Prophet's daughter. As noted earlier, the *Siti* ceremony is also held in the seventh month of pregnancy and in the ninth month, known locally as the *sagaalaysi*. The ritual demonstrates how ancestral veneration is key to a successful birth. The *Siti* ceremony, with its 40-days' seclusion, shows similarities with the *sōgeda* ritual of the Konso (Hallpike, 1972: 296). After giving birth, the Konso women, like the Somali, remain secluded in their homestead with their babies until sometime in the third month. It is believed that evil spirits will try to kill a child if it is a boy and that he will be particularly vulnerable to harmful elements in his early weeks.

Somali society is patriarchal and based on a clan system which delineates the origin of all Somalis.[6] The regeneration of the clan is pivotal to the survival of the lineage. The (firstborn) boys, for example, are treasured because they will become the future leaders of the family and holders of important positions in the clan. Evil spirits known as *umadaha hoose* (underground beings) and s*haydaan* or *jin* (devil) are believed to attack children who consequently require protection against these evils. A *wagar* is placed near the child, usually under its bed or pillow, to stop the evil spirit from approaching.

The *wagar*, as this study will show, has an importance beyond its ability to fight spirits. All too often, African practices are not studied properly, and objects are described only in terms of their use in diverting 'spirits'. Religious syncretism is reduced to anecdotal mentions of 'spirits' which are treated as local superstitions rather than as part of a complex religious system and indigenous theology. The references to the *wagar* that I have found in the early philological ethnographic literature take the form of lists of random observations rather than ones exhibiting the cultural knowledge required to explain the value of metaphysical or logical meanings. Révoil (1882: 343) wrote:

> The ouéguer [*wagar*], simple curved and covered with engravings, would have the property of diverting bad spirits. It would be the same as *allol*, a mat of fibres and skin, that you put in front of the door of a hut. The fibres and amulets of *gaol* [tree], textile made of the bark of the acacia *goura* [tree], conjures, say the Somalis, the mortal effects of snake bites.

It is interesting to note Révoil's observation that fibre is used as a material with which to divert spirits. I have seen the *wagar* bundled together with other objects that also carry mystical powers, including fibres. There is a set of items made of materials such as iron, wood (trees) and sacred grass which are involved in the *wagar* ritual. *Wagar* leaves are also placed around the hut/house to keep the bad spirits out. These items and their symbolic meanings indicate a connection with pre-Islamic beliefs in the sacredness and spiritual power of many different elements, including fibre or grass, that cannot show up in the archaeological record.

The glow of iron is thought to 'confuse' the evil spirits. Some put eyeliner on a boy child to further confuse the spirit into thinking he is a girl.

Similarly, the Konso newborn boy may be given a girl's name to trick the spirits into thinking he is a girl (1972: 296). The Oromo paint a line under a mother's eye (*ilaanso*). In many parts of Africa, there is a complex relationship between a material and its cultural meaning (e.g. Schmidt, 1983). For example, it is recognised that iron has magical and healing powers (ibid.). In the Horn of Africa context, as noted elsewhere (Mire, 2015b), iron also has a magical power that is closely associated with fertility. Furthermore, sacred grass and palm leaves, which are also thought to have healing properties, are used to tie the *wagar* with sharp metal objects such as *tooray/bilow* (dagger), *midi*, (a knife), *musbaar* (a screw) and *makiinad*, (a razorblade). Children wear beads with protective powers around their necks and their waists.

The Somali Diaspora carry their traditional medicine with them (Mire, 2016b). There are instances where husbands have brought the *wagar* from Somaliland to their wives after the birth of a first child, especially when that child is a boy (Mire, 2015b). An interviewee who claimed she bore a child after fertility rituals at Aw-Barkhadle described to me how her child benefitted from the *wagar* rituals throughout his life, from childhood through to adulthood:

> My son also had the *hildiid* and *habasuud* [mix of herbs] tied to his arm [amulet]. Then I put the *qurbaan* [the sacrificial offerings to Saint Aw-Barkhadle]. My boy had headgear made of fat from *haydh* [fat from the stomach of animals such as sheep and goat]. The hair was removed and the *haydh* [fat masses cut into long rope-like shape] was tied to his head every year. I have now stopped since he is an adult with his own children. My son now goes on the pilgrimage to Aw-Barkhadle of his own will.

Fat and moisture, as noted in the previous chapter, play a vital part in fertility rituals. The son referred to above, whom I met, is a dedicated pilgrim of Saint Aw-Barkhadle since, as he says, this saint, blessed by God, made his life possible. Nevertheless, the *wagar*, like the amulets which contain verses of the Qur'an, are not allowed by the *Ulema* (the Muslim legal scholars) who argue that they are sinful remnants of *jahilia* practices.

The Wagar, Bu'ur Ba'ayr and the site of Aw-Barkhadle

There is an old Somali saying that refers to the *wagar* and is used by older generations: '*wagar iyo ka waasican*' which means 'even more powerful (great or extraordinary) than *wagar* and all that' (Mire, 2015b). It refers to Allah (and hence Islam) as being more powerful than whatever belief had existed before. It is used when somebody does something audacious; a mother, for example, might use it when her child comes home later than usual, '*wagar iyo ka waasican*' which in this context would emphasise the child's audacity to come home so late.

A local Sufi historian, known for his knowledge about the history of the region and Sufism, told me: "*wagar wuxuu kajoogaa sanamadii hore eela caabudijiray berigii jaahilyada, Bu'ur Ba'ayr iyo dadkiisii joogay Aw-Barkhadle*" ('*Wagar* is a remnant of the ancient idols that were worshiped in the time of paganism, by Bu'ur Ba'ayr and his people at Aw-Barkhadle'). None of my questions related either directly or indirectly to *wagar*. It is remarkable, therefore, that this interviewee, unprompted and unaware of my research into the Aw-Barkhadle, the site or the Saint, had mentioned the *wagar* and said that it was an idol that was worshiped at Aw-Barkhadle during Bu'ur Ba'ayr's era. It turned out that this was a widely held notion: the *wagar* is relevant to any discussion about the pre-Islamic character of the Aw-Barkhadle site and its sacred landscape.

The saying mentioned above is said to have been coined when Bu'ur Ba'ayr lost his duel with Sheikh Yusuf Aw-Barkhadle. If Aw-Barkhadle was able to win the dual and trap the leader of the people who believed in the *wagar*, then the new religion (Islam) must surely be greater than the religion it had replaced (*wagar/Waaq*); hence *wagar iyo ka waasican*.

An account of an anthropomorphic wooden figure that was previously kept in the mausoleum of Aw-Barkhadle and used by women for fertility rituals (Mire, 2015b) may shed some light on the true meaning of '*wagar*'. According to my interviewees, this wooden figure had been replaced by the Qur'an. Had the *wagar* once been a figure held by women in much the same way as anthropomorphic figures are said to have been in pre-Islamic times?

What deity does the *wagar* represent? The word *waga/Waǧa* (or *Waaq*) is known to signify the Sky-God, and the Konso, for example, call the wooden sculptures they erect to denote the deceased '*waga*' (Figure 4.6a) (Hallpike, 1972).

Waǧa or *Waaqa* is also the name of the Sky-God (Bartels, 1983; Hallpike, 1972; Loo, 1991; Trimingham, 1965). Historical linguistics can be useful in shedding light on the links between different words in those African societies that lack an ancient written language (Ehret and Posnansky, 1982). Both the Somali and the Konso speak a proto-South Lowland Eastern Cushitic language (Ehret, 1995). The words *wagar* and *Waǧa* (*Waaq/Waqa*) seem so similar that, at my request, Professor C. Ehret kindly carried out a reconstruction of the historical linguistics of the words *waga* and *wagar* (pers. comm. 15/06/2013). Ehret advised me that

> the words **wagar* and **Waak'* are distinct old Proto-Eastern Cushitic (PEC) roots. **Waak'* means 'rise up' and this suggests its meaning in relation to the sky and the Sky-God, while the PEC root **wagar* simply means 'olive'.
>
> (Mire, 2015b: 106)

Figure 4.6a Waga of the Konso

The Cushitic word *wagar* (known by some as *weger*) is the same word adopted in the Amharic language too; *weyeri* and *wagar* tree is *weyeri saf* (*saf* is tree in Amharic).

For many, the *wagar* is meant to symbolise a woman (Mire, 2015b). Some suggest it is reminiscent of the female body. Historically, the *wagar* also functioned as a battle weapon. It is in essence a club made of hard wood, about 2 cm in width at its narrow end and about 4–6 cm at its top. Its length ranges *between c.* 35–45 cm. As a sacred object it occupies the high moral ground, used not only to fight evil spirits but people too. It is said Allah will protect the person who holds a *wagar*.

Although the shape of the *wagar* appears to suggest the body of a plump and fertile woman, it is not supposed to look entirely like a woman (Figure 4.4b).

Powerful female figures are a part of Somali tradition: a legend has it that a long time ago, the present-day northern Somali region was ruled by

Figure 4.6b The wood and stone church of Yemrehanna Kristos church near Lalibela

a powerful female ruler, a queen Araweello. It is a fact that the numerous cairns (stone burial mounds) scattered all over northern Somalia and
Somaliland are called *araweelloyin*. Some believe these to be the graves of
this queen's 'pagan' followers in pre-Islamic times.

According to legend, this queen made men perform tricky tasks and
sterilised those who opposed her. Her own grandson killed her and took
power over the country. The currently ubiquitous *araweello* cairns came

about because anyone who passed one of her followers' cairns would throw another stone on top. Araweello is also thought to have possessed Pharaonic qualities. Ideas about a Pharaonic relationship to Somali kinship or traditions take many forms and narratives and include the *gudniin* practice. However, it may well be that people associate anything 'wicked' with non-Islamic figures like 'Araweello' or 'Bu'ur Ba'ayr' or even with the pharaohs of northeastern Africa.

Although Somalis have a patriarchal society, it is important to understand that Somali women play important social and political roles. This is even so in the realm of religion. At Aw-Barkhadle, for example, revered female sheikhas lie buried alongside male sheikhs. I have also met one permanent female *Muriid* in the Hargeisa region. This sheikha led *dhikri* with a congregation of both male and female devotees. Women in general also play a significant sociopolitical role both in the public and private domains. They usually take part both publicly and domestically in events. They control what happens in the home and their power extends to the meetings that are held there. They are an integral part of the planning, initiation and implementation of many successful political institutions. Their interests are safeguarded within the wider society. Even the most seemingly rural women can leave the nomadic camps, walk in to towns and shop and stay with relatives and friends. Anthropological records often stray far from the truth when they portray Somali women as static and domestic in their function and mobility. For the most part, such views could not be more wrong: women travel freely across the spaces that link, and reconnect with, land, relatives and new ideas.

The importance of womanhood, of powerful or religious women, of goddesses and the like, forms an intriguing aspect of the fertility cults, as the *Siti* ceremony shows. Despite this, however, Somali society remains a patrilineal one in sociopolitical terms. Whether or not the shape of the *wagar* is meant to represent a woman, one thing is clear: it is an object that is associated with women and considered to be a female object. It is possible, of course, that the *wagar* itself originally had a rather different appearance which changed to appear non-figurative during Islamic times. It can be plain or highly decorated and incised with patterns. The *wagar* may have been reinterpreted to look more ambiguous, in much the same way as the phallic grave marker at Aw-Barkhadle has been turned upside down in order, I assume, to hide its true nature. The ambiguity of the *wagar* is recalled in something that Lévi-Strauss wrote:

> A mask is not primarily what it represents but what it transforms, that is to say, what it chooses *not* to represent. Like a myth, a mask denies as much as it affirms. It is not made solely of what it says or thinks it is saying, but of what it excludes.

> (1982: 144)

Alongside its association with sacred trees and its roles as a medium for fertility, the *wagar* could represent an ancestor venerated for his or her ritual efficacy in promoting fertility amongst the Somali. Given that there is a tradition of ancestral worship within Somali Cushitic culture, the *wagar* might even symbolise the Sky-God *Waaq*. Eastern Cushitic speaking peoples regard the African olive as a sacred tree. The Oromo call it *ejersa* (Loo, 1991), probably a Guji combination of the word *wagar* and the word *saf*, meaning tree. The *wagar* is sacred to the Amhara and Tigre who call it *weyerisaf*. The Somali word wagar can also be written and pronounced as weger. It is a matter of dialects. The Guji Oromo have a sacred olive-type tree (ibid.) called *woddeesa*; and the Dorica class of the *Gada* system have a staff made of this tree. It may well be, therefore, that the *wagar* denotes the Sky-God or the deities associated with indigenous religions.

Accounts merely suggest that the *wagar* was related to Aw-Barkhadle in pre-Islamic times. Nevertheless, the idea of sacred trees and the myth of a man in a tree appears not only relevant to a myth of origin; it may also provide a clue to the very nature of *Waaq/Waqa*, as will be discussed in Chapter Five.

The divine man in the sacred tree

There are plenty of idols (*sanam*, pl. *asnaam*, from Arabic) in Somali mythology. Many people believe that Somali indigenous ancient idols correspond to ancient Egyptian Gods: *isir* who is associated with a lineage of nobleness and *bas*, who takes life. There is also *ba'al* (cf. the Canaanites of Palestine) (Mohammed, 1991). Horus (in Somali *huruse*) is symbolised by a black bird, while *wad* is considered to be an Egyptian idol that later in pre-Islamic and Islamic times became *wadaad*, the Somali sheikh. These northeast African deities contribute to the Somalis' belief that they have an ancient Egyptian heritage, a subject beyond the scope of this book. I focus here on the Sky-God, a god who dominates many of the current practices in the indigenous to the Horn of Africa and features in so many different versions of the myth of origin.

The Sky-God is associated with sacred trees – and there are several different types of them. Many Cushitic speaking peoples revere the sycamore tree (Trimingham, 1965: 260; cf. Hallpike, 1972; Révoil, 1882). Equally, the juniper is sacred to the Konso (Hallpike, 1972). Today, the veneration of trees is particularly important within Konso and Oromo society (Loo, 1991). Moreover, a belief in the Sky-God is still widespread within many groups across the eastern Horn. The Oromo hold the belief that the *ayaana* (sacred life force, destiny) inhabit the sycamore tree (*Ficus gnaphalocarpa*) and the African olive (*wagar*). The Amhara have the concept of *adbar*, the embodiment of spirits in water, trees, rocks and mountains. Conti Rossini observed the worship of trees (see above and Trimingham, 1965: 260–261). The Oromo also have local sacred trees such as the *birbirsa* (*Podocarpus gracilior*), the *bilcaano* (*Buddleja poystachia*), the *dikicca* (*Jasminum floribundum*) and *fibiro* (*Bersama abyssinia*) (Loo, 1991). Oromo daughters, as already noted, have special ceremonial sticks of wood (see in Adamson, 1967: 271). Like the *wagar* tree, the sycamore tree can also grant sacred fertility. The Oromo call it the sacred sycamore tree *ooda* and their myth of origin, which is connected to the Oromo goddess Atete, is also associated with this tree. On my way to the Yemrehanna Kristos church near Lalibela, I noted huge umbrella shaped sycamore trees. When looking at this church made of wood and stone, built in the Aksumite architectural style, I could not help but think about the sacred trees that might have been used to build it and about how these might be connected to the stone features on the Aksum obelisks that imitate horizontally laid wooden poles (Figure 4.6b). The drystone pillars of the Islamic medieval city of Abbasa include a similar construction with horizontally laid wooden poles (Figure 4.6c).

Abrahamic religious sources regard the olive and the sycamore as sacred. However, in the context of the Horn, the concept of sacred trees spreads well beyond these native species to many other trees found locally. Loo (1991), for example, notes the brittle-wood, known as *uddeesa* (*Nuxia cognesta*), as a sacred tree of the Oromo.

Eastern Cushitic speaking peoples, especially the Oromo group, the Afar, Saho and Somali (Luling, 1991), share a common myth of origin. The core of the myth is always the same; there was a man on a tree who was believed to have descended from the sky; he was discovered by a girl (a woman in some cases). He agreed to come down from the tree on condition that he

Figure 4.6c Wooden poles as part of house construction and architectural features of Abbasa ruined town

was allowed to marry the woman/girl who had found him, and it is from their union that people are descended. The common belief in the Sky-God seems to relate to the myth of the man who was sitting in the (possibly sacred) tree. It is possible that the *wagar* is a symbol of *Waaqa/Waga* (the Sky-God). This myth importantly lends support to the idea that there is a link between the notion of sacred trees and ancestral religious/divine figures. The *waga* ancestral wooden figures of the Konso have already been noted. In short, the *wagar* may be linked to sacred fertility through the medium of the blessed tree.

It is possible to understand ways in which the *wagar* appears in rituals, especially in those relating to fertility and child protection, as a means of protection against the *jin* and evil spirits. Its possible connection to the mythology of the Horn has also been mentioned. The *wagar* is in fact considered as a sacred object in its own right in most of the Horn of Africa where I have found it linked to a deity worshipped in the Aw-Barkhadle landscape. The *wagar* may have been a symbol of a divine ancestor and this ancestor may have been responsible for bestowing fertility. I will later show how ancient trees surround other sacred sites or, as I prefer to call them, sacred landscapes, such as those of Lalibela and Aksum. I suggest, therefore, that the *wagar* may symbolise the divine ancestor associated with fertility and that this divine ancestor may have been the Sky-God (Mire, 2015b). It has been said (Hallpike, 1972) that the Sky-God used to stay close by but went up to the Sky for good, leaving his other representatives (for example the *ayaana*) to remain down amongst the people. The people of the Horn of Africa certainly share a belief in an omnipresent single God removed from the everyday life whose place is taken by these *ayaana* or by other deities and by religious ancestors.

Interestingly, the concept of sacred/religious ancestors indicates a belief in genetic links between the blessed (sacred) and the people, who in turn are blessed by their blessed ancestors, and particularly by their religious ancestors. I will explore this idea in more detail later and trace its potential relevance for the region's societies in general. I now explore a possible relationship between kinship (*ab*) and *gudniin*/infibulation/Pharaonic circumcision (female genital cutting/mutilation, FGM).

Gudniin fircooni/'FGM': in the name of divine fertility and kinship?

Male circumcision is viewed as something originally related to notions of virility and sacrifice. By contrast, female circumcision (*gudniin*/FGM) has never been given any more meaningful purpose beyond virginity and sexual control. The textual evidence from Ancient Egypt infers that this practice was prevalent amongst slaves and maids though the mummified remains cannot provide conclusive evidence to support this. This inference has led to the use of the phrase 'Pharaonic circumcision' to refer to a procedure that comes not from the "civilised world" but from the 'Ancient Egyptians' and from the primitive world of 'Sub-Saharan Africans'. Because of the gross impact it has on women, researchers past and present have focused on the act as one inflicted on women by women and a confirmation of negative ideas about men's behaviour in a patriarchal society. I argue, however, that its original purpose lay primarily in the realm of religion and, only secondarily, in politics. I suggest that it is an act that reaches beyond human beings to touch the divine as well as the human. Just like some other rituals that still take place today and which I deem to be equally ancient, it is a practice rooted in sacrifice, in the sacrifice of human flesh and pain to appease the divine. Human beings create disorder, and this human act results in disorder and problems of an existential nature which require reconciliation through purification and sacrifice.

Furthermore, it is no longer enough merely to reiterate a narrative that selects one single practice and isolates it from its wider cultural ritual context, to do so would be to focus simplistically upon today's practices, ignoring the logic and ontologies of traditional societies. Anthropologists have done their best to explain female circumcision in respectful terms, but they do not understand it beyond thinking that it is about virginity. They ignore the existential and culturally specific ideologies that underpin this procedure. As a result, they leave behind a burden of assumption about barbaric acts against poor women and a lack of either a holistic understanding of the local context or an ideological history that reaches beyond current sociopolitical and economic patterns. Without a true understanding about other relevant (physical) rituals, this sort of narrative will not help eradicate FGM completely. It is essential to understand how the practice of FGM is interwoven with the other rituals to which both men and women are subjected, and in thus doing to move beyond the current economic, social and educational campaigns.

Explanations for other harmful practices concerning men, such as stick fights (*istunka*), have similarly been reduced to simple acts of male potency. I suggest that this form of male suffering has the same ideological origin as female circumcision. It appears on the surface to be an ideology that celebrates pride and honour – and as such must come from a place of individual and collective suffering for the good of both the individual and the collective good. I argue, however, that its unspoken purpose is to obtain God's blessing.

I now investigate how the practice of female circumcision may have originated. I will focus on the type of female circumcision that is known as infibulation/female genital mutilation/female genital cutting and which, in my discussion of its occurrence in a Somali context, I will call it by the Somali word *gudniin*, a name derived from *gudniin fircooni* or 'Pharaonic circumcision'. This is one of the first rituals to which a Somali woman (as a child) is subjected. Over 200 million women and girls are currently affected by this practice worldwide (UNICEF, 2016).

I will begin by trying to explain Pharaonic circumcision and how it is practiced. It is also important to explore its essentially non-Islamic nature in order to understand its persistence within the traditional societies of the Horn today.

It has already been established that the purpose of *gudniin* is not just to honour the patrilineage; it lies at the heart of the patrilineage system and the preservation of inheritance and status (cf. Boddy, 1982; Auffret, 1983). I want here to explore *why* lineage blood is important beyond general arguments about inheritance or status. I am also interested in how it relates to fertility rites and sacred ancestors and the concept of sacred descent in the Horn of Africa. I identify a 'divine kinship' ideology which refers to a blessed or sacred origin with links to religious ancestors and their ritual efficacy. I investigate the relationship between female circumcision and Somali male and female fertility rituals. I believe that an understanding of the notion of sacred fertility and sacred ancestors in the Horn of Africa will lay the foundation for investigating the persistence of FGM, or *gudniin*, in this part of Africa.

Female circumcision in Africa

The distribution of the practice of *gudniin* is interesting (Figure 4.7). It is prevalent in the states/kingdoms of the west–east belt of Sub-Saharan

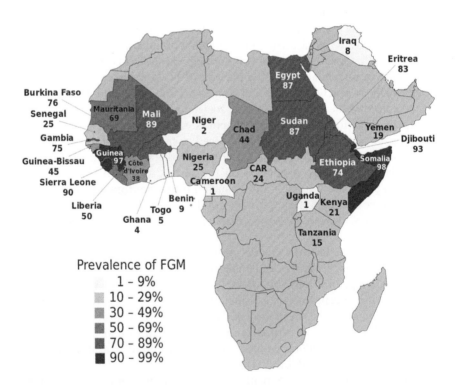

Figure 4.7 UNICEF 2013 FGM distribution map

Source: (copyright: Creative Commons)

Africa, Eritrea, Djibouti, Kenya, Somalia, Ethiopia, Egypt, Sudan, DRC, Nigeria, Burkina Faso, Mali and Senegal. It is noteworthy that the places where Pharaonic circumcision is most dominant seem to correspond to the locations of the old African kingdoms in pre-Islamic times. Countries such as Egypt, Sudan, Eritrea, Djibouti, Ethiopia, Kenya, Nigeria, Mali and Senegal which practice clitoridectomy and Pharaonic circumcision are all societies within which these practices are deeply rooted and form a fundamental part of their social institutions. It is difficult to know how long this has been the case. According to the Hosken report, ancient Egyptians practiced female circumcision (Hosken, 1993). Hayes (1975) confirms that the ancient Egyptians circumcised (via cliterodectomy) their female relatives but infibulated their female slaves to prevent them from becoming pregnant. This indicates that the ancient Egyptians knew about the practice. What was the purpose of this ritual in the past? Why did Pharaonic circumcision take place in ancient times in northeast Africa, the place where it most probably originated?

'Virgins are made, not born'

In Sudan, as Hayes noted, 'virgins are made, not born' (1975: 622). Pharaonic circumcision certifies a woman's virginity. There are five types of operation broadly referred to as female circumcision. For descriptions and details of these, see Kouba and Muasher (1985). The two most commonly practiced in the Horn of Africa are cliterodectomy/excision and Pharaonic circumcision/*gudniin*. Cliterodectomy/excision consists of 'the removal of part or all of the clitoris as well as part or all of the *labia minora*. The resulting scar tissues may be so extensive that they cover the vaginal opening' (Kouba and Muasher, 1985: 96). *Gudniin*/Pharaonic circumcision consists of:

> Cliterodectomy and the excision of the *labia minora* as well as the inner walls of the *labia majora*. The raw edges of the *vulva* are then sewn together with catgut or held against each other by means of thorns. The suturing together, or approximating, of the raw edges of the *labia majora*, is done so that the opposite sides will heal together and form a wall over the vaginal opening. A small sliver of wood (such as bamboo) is inserted into the vagina to stop coalescence of the *labia majora* in front of the vaginal orifice and to allow for the passage of urine and menstrual flow.
>
> (ibid.)

Gudniid fircooni is therefore the severest form of female circumcision; it is described as the most complete of all circumcisions since it almost totally closes the vagina through the sewing together of the *labia majora* and the partial or total excision of the clitoris and *labia minora*.

In the Somali context, *gudniin fircooni* is divided into three types; *gudniin faatima* where the top of the vagina is stitched up to 2 cm; *hooskaguddan* where the inner labia is stitched; and *gudniin kurus* where the minor labia is cut and the majora are stitched together, leaving only an opening of 5–8 mm for urinating and menstrual flow. Almost all Somali girls are cut, up to 98 per cent, and they are almost all cut by traditional cutters, most of whom have no medical training. There are two Sunna types: type one cuts the clitoris just a little and type two cuts it by half.

It is interesting that in the Somali language the word for circumcision is *gudniin* (a Somali word) and *halaalayn* (*xalaalayn*) (a Somalised Arabic word (*halaal*)). *Gudniin* denotes the act while *halaalayn* denotes not only the act but also the value of making something *halaal* (permissible). The Arabic word *halaal* also means lawful, from the Islamic law perspective. In Islam, permitted animals are slaughtered while uttering the Islamic prayer 'Bismillah' (lit. 'in the name of God'). *Halaalayn* means that the circumcision of the child is permitted even though the circumcision of girls is not an Islamic practice. But its use suggests the adoption of an Islamic phrase to describe a local indigenous tradition. The Somali word *gudniin* is the same as *guditaan*, which also means accomplishment, while *gudun* means to approve. The *Gudniin* Fatima is interestingly named after *Faadumo* (Faatima). Using words like '*halaalayn*' and '*faadumo*' is congruent with the adaption of old traditions to accommodate a new religion. I have already shown how the appropriation of a new religion's names helps conceal ancient practices that would otherwise be seen as part of *jaahiliya* (ignorance of Islam).

What are the origins of Pharaonic circumcision/*gudniin*? According to the Somali and Sudanese it is an ancient tradition dating back to the time of the Pharaonic Egyptians, hence the name Pharaonic circumcision (cf. Boddy, 1982; Barclay, 1964), and Pharaonic circumcision is indeed still widely practised in Egypt today (Yount and Carrera, 2006; Assaad, 1980; Kennedy, 1970). Furthermore, according to Kouba and Muasher (1985) and others, there is evidence for the existence of this tradition in ancient Egypt. Greek historians, first Herodotus in the fifth century BC and then the later geographer Strabo in 25 BC, both noted that male and female circumcision was practised in Egypt – although they do not go into any detail about cutting methods (Knight, 2001; Hosken, 1993; see also Hay, 1981). How long the Somalis have been practicing this custom is uncertain though many suggest that it goes back a long way. Early travellers such as Sir Richard Burton noted the practice though they do not specify to which type of circumcision they are referring (Burton, 1966 [1898]).

With the exception of Southern Arabia, Malaysia and Indonesia, female circumcision is most prevalent in the African continent. In Africa, female circumcision is found in at least 26 countries (Kouba and Muasher, 1985) where it has become a public health problem. A study of circumcision as it is practised today may lead to a better understanding of its origins.

Why (are women subjected to) Pharaonic circumcision/Gudniin Fircooni?

In the Nile valley in northern Sudan, Arab Muslim girls are subjected to Pharaonic circumcision (Hayes, 1975). Hayes writes 'The stated reason for the operation is to ensure a girl's chastity, thereby safeguarding the dignity and honour of her own and her future husband's patrilineages' (ibid.: 617). Boddy argues that, additionally, the removal of genital parts enhances femininity and de-emphasises sexuality 'for those who have undergone it and who advocate its continuance, Pharaonic circumcision is an assertive, highly meaningful act that emphasizes feminine fertility by de-emphasizing female sexuality' (Boddy, 1982: 682). Boddy suggests that the act of reproduction, rather than sexual pleasure, becomes the focus once a woman's ability to experience pleasure is removed. Hence, she argues that the 'social indispensability' of women is demonstrated by the husbands' need for the women's 'reproductive potential' through marriage (Boddy, 1982: 687). Reproduction itself may be regarded as an investment:

> Children are the capital on which male and female careers are built but at the same time kept separate, since marriages themselves are fragile and, for men, may be polygamous. It is only through marriage that men and women might inaugurate their respective, yet mutually dependent, social careers.
>
> (ibid.: 688)

In the case of the Dogon and Bambara in Mali, Séverine Auffret (1983) has suggested that farming was the sole reason for the origin of female circumcision. For the purposes of land inheritance, a patriarchal society had to be sure to whom their land belonged. Circumcision lends support to patrilineage but, as Hayes argues, it also has the effect of regulating reproduction (1975). Some have suggested that circumcision increases male sexual pleasure (el-Safi, 1970). Others argue (Knight, 2001) that it was an ancient and little practiced phenomenon that later gained social, moral and ritual justifications long after its original purpose had been forgotten.

The underlying reasons for Pharaonic circumcision

Why did Pharaonic circumcision become the custom? Did it ultimately become indispensable? Boddy rightly points out that one of the main reasons for Pharaonic circumcision is to ensure that the woman is a virgin when she marries (Boddy, 1982), but this first marriage is not the only time that a woman's virginity is relevant. Pharaonic circumcision provides the proof that the child she will give birth to will belong to her husband because he knows that she was infibulated until he penetrated her. A strong support for this line of argument is that some societies also practice a process of re-infibulation immediately after the birth of a child or when a widowed woman remarries. Re-infibulation offers a way of continuously determining who is the father of the (next) son/child to be born, thereby guaranteeing, in a very specific way, that the father's lineage's blood is extended.

Both Hayes' (1975: 622) claim 'in Sudan, virgins are made, not born' and Boddy's (1982: 687) suggestion that the 'virgin' notion has less to do with sexual self-discipline and more to do with childbearing, are significant. The first shows that a 'virgin' is physically constructed for cultural purposes. The second argument goes further in its understanding of the need to go beyond 'virgin' to an emphasis on feminine fertility (the ability to reproduce and to bear children) rather than on feminine sexuality. The ability to bear children promotes women's position as respected members of society, especially should they give birth to blood sons. The women who go from being virgins to marriage and the birth of sons attain a special social status that is denied to women who give birth only to daughters.

At the heart of any patrilineal system, the male is the rightful owner of status and most of the wealth passes to the blood son. He inherits the wealth and the responsibility for both the livelihood and the status of the family. Boddy (1982: 690) reports that Sudanese women want sons '*āwlad*' (from the Arabic word *awlad* which denotes 'children'). Auffret (1983) adds another important point: making sure the blood son inherits the family wealth or land status of his father in a patrilineal society is an economic necessity, hence circumcision becomes an economic necessity too. A similar economic argument is made by Favali (2001) regarding Eritrean pastoralists. The fact that in some cases women are re-infibulated after each child is delivered, as has been noted earlier, is further testimony to the importance of this male bloodline.

The practice of infibulation highlights the reproductive rather than the sexual aspects of the female sexual organ; it ensures a supply of virgins for a patrilineal society intent on extending male lineage; a society in which a man's role is measured by his ability to extend his lineage through fathering a blood son. Pharaonic circumcision's main rationale today may not therefore be to control women and/or their sexuality, or to increase male pleasure, or to enhance women's status locally, although these may all be clear side effects of its practice: its primary purpose is to ensure the blood extension of lineage. These ideas, however, do not explain the ideological context in which the practice may first have originated.

I will now, therefore, consider whether the origins of female circumcision are more likely to be found in an act of sacrifice to a divine power rather than in an act between human beings (or men vs. women). I will now explore the context in which the practice was introduced. I will reveal the existence of a deep-rooted and locally based logic by comparing infibulation with other physical practices.

Circumcision as a sacrifice for divine fertility and kinship –
A Somali case study

In Cushitic society, it has been suggested that female circumcision is an initiation rite (Trimingham, 1952). In some societies circumcision is associated with 'pagan' initiation ceremonies. Amongst the Cushitic speaking Afar and Beja, circumcision is an initiation ceremony for both boys and girls when they reach a certain age (ibid.: 257). In a Somali Cushitic context, it prepares girls for a life of womanhood (even though anthropologists do not recognise the act itself as an initiation ritual).

In Somali (nomadic) society, a woman gains status if she manages to perform her duty to extend *her husband's* lineage by having a son. As noted earlier, fertility rituals are intended to help her realise that same goal. I here investigate the original purposes of female Pharaonic circumcision in Somali society and examine the notions that underpin both the existence and persistence of *gudniin*.

In Sudan, it is often the older women, but not the men, who are keen on the practice of circumcision (cf. Boddy, 1982; cf. Hayes, 1975). In the Somali context, I found a similar attitude amongst Somali women but a different one amongst the men who agree, or even insist, often silently, on the continuation of *gudniin*. The patriarchal nature of Somali society perpetuates the status quo of this form of circumcision as a part of tradition.

Practically all Somali women undergo *gudniin*; and, in the urban centres, also cliterodectomy or '*Sunni*' as it is locally called (see below). This is the cutting of all or part of the clitoris together with part or all of the *labia minora* (Kouba and Muasher, 1985: 96). During the 1980s, *Sunni* became a growing practice according to the older midwives I interviewed. This may have been due to the increasingly urban lifestyle of the Somali, the growing employment of women in the private and public sector and the subsequent change in the economic power relations between husband and wife.

Gudniin fircooni, however, seems to be preferred to the *Sunni*/cliterodectomy among the urban underprivileged. This may be because poor families feel that they need to undertake *gudniin fircooni* in order to emphasise the chastity of their daughters and thereby compensate for their lack of economic status. If a girl from a poor background is infibulated her family's chance of securing a marriage will increase. Parents, too, may be willing to allow this, particularly if the potential groom's family is more economically well off. However, girls from wealthier families in the cities will be under less pressure to be infibulated. This economic aspect of *gudniin* ought not to be ignored. The midwives I interviewed for this study told me that there was a slight reduction in *gudniin fircooni* and an increase in cliterodectomy in Mogadishu in the 1980s. This may be related to social development and the improvement of women's economic rights rather than a more enlightened view regarding circumcision per se. Some of the midwives I spoke to confirmed that they were well aware of the health problems associated with the practice but that they regretfully had no choice but to circumcise their daughters when the time came: they feared for their future marriage eligibility and difficulties in securing a good marriage. As the daughters of independent and educated women are suspected of being freer, the women who are infibulated carry with them an assurance that they are respectable and beyond the reproach or judgement of others.

As a result of the ongoing war, there are millions of Somalis outside the Somali territories including some hundreds of thousands in Europe and in America. My interviewees confirmed that in these diaspora societies, female genital mutilation is not practiced as widely as in the Somali region. The increased economic security offered by these new homes might be a factor in the decline in female circumcision; there is also a growing awareness within these Western societies of the health issues of FGM, and in many places it is illegal, which helps eradicate the practice. These developments favour women's economic independence and there are ongoing domestic and international campaigns against *gudniin* in the Somali region (Mire, 2016b). At least in the West, if not in the Somali territory, it is seemingly becoming less important to perform *gudniin* to guarantee that the son who inherits is a blood son. Nevertheless, *gudniin fircooni* appears to hold an importance beyond cultural and economic arguments. It is still performed even amongst those who do not follow the tradition of bloodline inheritance. Why?

Girls from all the Somali clans traditionally undergo *gudniin*. The Somali dominant clans such as the Rahanweyn, Darood, Dir and other smaller clans have particularly epitomised kinship within an ethnicity based on blood relations (Lewis, 1994a, 2004). The procedure is performed by an underclass consisting of the so-called 'outcaste' clans like the Madhibaan (cf. Cerulli, 1957). The 'noble' clans distinguish themselves as *Somali* from the 'low caste' *Sab* clans in terms of the economic status. It is a sweeping generalisation that is not without truth to identify the difference between the *Sab* and the 'noble' clans: the *Sab* are usually held to be craftsmen/-women, smiths, hunters and farmers living between the Juba and the Shebeelle rivers; and the 'noble' clans are usually said to be the pastoralists who inhabit most of the Somali territories. Today, the dominant and the 'outcast' clans live in separated quarters in the cities, with the minority (*dadka/qabiilada laga tirade badan yahay*) clans often relegated to small overcrowded areas.

Within the mainly pastoral society of the Somali, a male child is much coveted as a means of securing family inheritance rights within the clan but, to be eligible, must be guaranteed to be the *blood* son of the husband. It is therefore important to have sons from a socio-economic viewpoint but critically important from the blood lineage perspective that they can be guaranteed genetically to be the sons of their fathers. It seems to me that this socio-economic importance comes not so much from gaining more capital (through a large number of children) as from the value of *keeping* the wealth or power within the *right* blood lineage, a view I develop below.

In terms of Pharaonic circumcision, it is not reproduction per se that is seen as relevant so much as the assurance that the son is of the father's *blood*. So, (re)infibulation may be seen in this context rather like a certificate confirming the parentage of the child and thus the guarantee that it is of the right blood. Why does it matter so much that a son is of the right blood? This is where God comes in. You may be able to trick a community into believing that a son belongs to you because your wife has given birth to him but you cannot fool God. Only the right lineage blood will ensure that God blesses the people. This blessing comes from God via the ancestors in a blessed sacred bloodline. I argue that the idea of 'noble' clans is constructed in such a way as to paint others as ungodly. This idea has sanctioned the rise of a centralised power ruling by a sacred power and dominating others whose religiosity and morals are often in doubt. Somali minority clans are subjected to such prejudice and, often, discrimination and racism, all of which support the perceived Somali notion of a sacred, and hence blessed, bloodline.

The nomadic lifestyle, too, might explain the persistence of Pharaonic circumcision within Somali society. From the point of view of the current Somali political crisis and its nation-building, the significance of the traditional ideology of kinship cannot be overestimated. Discussing ethnicity and nation building in a Somali context, Lewis (2004) argues that Somali nationalism or 'tailor-made national ethnicity' is part and parcel of a traditional society:

> It was accompanied by a pervasive system of internal *divisions based on the ideology of kinship, and hence invisible*, which carried the same emotional and subjective charge as visible ethnic distinctions elsewhere. Indeed . . . these kinship divisions, as they are formulated in Somali ideology, have many of the characteristics of *race*.
>
> (Lewis, 2004: 490) [italics added]

Aspects of Lewis' thesis on Somali pastoral social organisation certainly fit historical contexts of clanship in that society. It is impossible, however, to ignore the fact that his very narrow perception of clanship may not fit the major changes that took place in Somali pastoral politics during the last century during the colonial and postcolonial eras, as has been pointed out by Kapteijns (2004–2010: 1–25), among others. Even so, Lewis's argument for a traditional ethnonationalism within Somali society has its uses in supporting my discussion here of an ancient concept of divine kinship, a concept that has led Somalis to link their traditional lineage line right to the Prophet's line. Lewis's likening Somali kinship to the concept of a 'race' is interesting:

> Family trees (genealogies) were, and are, thus, not simply quasi-historical documents, but, essentially, the fundamental principle of personal

and social identity. From a European perspective, this is perhaps most readily understood in terms of aristocratic dynasties.

(Lewis, 2004: 491)

Aristocratic clans are usually given religious attributes. Lewis's statement above is pertinent to my argument about divine kinship: I maintain that the historical basis for the persisting practice of Pharaonic circumcision is that it supports the blood (genetic) link. This is central to traditional and indigenous concepts of descent as is the significance of such lineages:

> The concept of Somali identity, based on an awareness of common culture and language, thus preceded the development of modern nationalism. This long-standing sense of cultural uniqueness, it may be conjectured, developed in the interaction with neighbouring peoples over the centuries.
>
> (Lewis, 2004: 493)

Lewis writes 'In essence, the clan is ideologically of one blood, and it is, in short, a social, territorial, political, and to some extent religious unit' (1998: 4). This 'uniqueness', I argue, is preserved by *gudniin* which secures the continuity of a unique blood and controls a bloodline that in Islamic times goes back to the Prophet himself. In the next chapter, I will explore how this direct descent link with the divine in the Horn of Africa is observed across religions and goes back to pre-Islamic times and to the Sky-God and Christian and other deities. *Gudniin* is practiced contrary to Islam but ironically preserves that link with the prevailing divine power of the Cushitic Muslim Somali.

As I will show in the next chapter, my analysis of what I call a divine kinship seems relevant beyond the Somali cultural context. When, for example, Somalis say 'I have no *ab* or *isir* to do that', it is to the 'religious unit' that they are referring. I will further explain this saying in the following section and discuss the significance of what I believe to be a deep-rooted belief in a blessed and righteous blood.

Sacred fertility for a sacred blood

I argue that both cliterodectomy and Pharaonic circumcision are sacrifices to sacred fertility. I suggest that the idea of circumcision itself is related to sacrifice, a sacrifice made through the blood shed by the cutting of the genitals and the clitoris (itself a source of sexual pleasure) to gain sacred fertility. This may have been the case even in pre-Abrahamic times. Incidentally, in most Muslim[7] societies, male circumcision is seen as an obligation while female circumcision is regarded as a non-Islamic tradition.

The Ancient Egyptians practised circumcision, including male circumcision, as a method of sacrifice in ancient times. Since they had a system of sacred *kingship* which was based on complex kinship, it is possible that they were also intent on preserving a sacred bloodline. The Ancient Egyptians clearly practiced male circumcision as is shown by numerous depictions; they also, according to the textual evidence, carried out both cliterodectomy and infibulation. The philosopher Philo of Alexandria wrote that when the Egyptian youth reach marriageable age they are circumcised (Knight, 2001). Interestingly, this is the age when fertility as well as virginity becomes relevant. There is so far no evidence to suggest that the ancient Egyptians did *not* practise infibulation on their own girls. It may be that the need for the cliterodectomy was underpinned by the idea of sacrifice, an argument supported by the persistence of practices such as *Sunni* (cliterodectomy) which, unlike Pharaonic circumcision, clearly do not guarantee virginity. What is the point, then, of cliterodectomy?

A rich girl can afford not to be infibulated – and pricking (female genital cutting) does not ensure virginity. The reason why it is still done must be that even with a cliterodectomy blood is still shed in sacrifice so that the girl can obtain the sacred fertility she is seeking. If it is accepted that circumcision was originally not about men and women but about the human and the divine, then circumcision of any kind will be sufficient to allow the divine to bestow sacred fertility through the consecration of the circumcised person. Cliterodectomy may thus be seen as a milder form of sacrifice to obtain sacred fertility. Circumcision can be seen both as a sacrifice and a medium for sanctity. The fact that people are likely to switch to cliterodectomy, if discouraged from *gudniin*, shows that virginity per se is not the fundamental reason for the practice. Through circumcision, a child not only becomes a woman; her body is consecrated so that she can receive a sacred fertility derived from the sacred bloodline.

Interestingly, communities like the Masai stopped the practice because the Chief Moran denounced it. The Masai have replaced female circumcision with an alternative rite of passage ceremony:

> In the new ceremony, girls between the ages of 9 and 15 dress in traditional clothing that includes cow-skin black robes and crowns of beads to signify they are ready for the ritual. The girls are then taught "life lessons" – or a brief introduction to sex education – in the privacy of their huts before tribal elders bless them with milk and water. Maasai warriors show support for the alternative ceremony by butchering bulls, oxen, sheep and goats to feed the girls and the community.
>
> (Onyulo, 2016)

It is interesting that in this description can be found also the elements common to sacrifice and fertility rituals: milk and water, ancestral blessing and even the blood shed by slaughtered bulls and oxen. Some of the Pokot people in western Kenya have also stopped the practice and replaced it with a different ceremony (Al-Jazeera, 2017). However, it will take time to eradicate the practice. The Borana who live in southern Ethiopia and northern Kenya are trying to do something similar and are lobbying the Aba *Gada*, the religious leader of the traditional Borana, to ask him to denounce the practice. Much like the Somali, the Borana carry out the circumcision in secret and without any ceremony for the girls (Youth for Change, 2016).

It is noteworthy that Onyulo's account above mentions that sex education is provided for the girls in their private huts. A type of sex education is also given to a Matcha Oromo bride and groom by a female and a male elder in private and the wedding couple engage in a symbolic intercourse. The account also talks about water and milk which both feature heavily in fertility rituals. Beads, too, signify the state of womanhood to many people in the Horn of Africa, and, given that the Maasai interchange practices with their neighbours, it is possible that the Borana, for example, introduced them to circumcision. For the Maasai, sacred fertility is a ceremony involving singing and dancing, celebration and blessings for girls; it also, importantly, involves the shedding of blood through the sacrificial slaughter of cows.

It is clear when circumcision is being used as a rite of passage. Many Muslims and Christians who practice *gudniin*, however, do not regard it as such and when the practice is stopped often move from types of *gudniin/* infibulation to types of cliterodectomy. Those cultures that have used it as a rite of passage but want to stop infibulation often search for another means of marking the transition of a girl to womanhood, and, in these cases, adopt ceremonies in which, interestingly, the elders' blessing is as important as the slaughter and the shedding of blood.

It is often suggested that circumcision and having a dowry to offer provides girls with an alternative livelihood to one based on a better education and financial independence. However, as I have argued, sacred fertility, rather than economic reality, may be the primary purpose of circumcision. Sacred fertility is bestowed through a ceremony that involves an ancestral blessing and the shedding of the blood of a sacrificial animal. It is quite possible that a celebration to mark their passage into womanhood was once held for girls, both Muslim and Christian, who had also been circumcised, but if this was the case then it would have been a part of an ancient tradition rather than of their Abrahamic faith. It is for this reason that it would have been possible to do away altogether with the 'ceremony' or 'ritual' and to reinterpret it in a way that would suit the new beliefs with their social and moral inclination towards chastity and virgins.

Some Christians have now stopped the practice of circumcision altogether and replaced it with prayers to mark womanhood. The key to this lies, I believe, in the blessing and the prayer element; it is about accessing sacred fertility, even though people may not realise it. Girls are not just left alone with neither circumcision nor prayers: the act of girls becoming women is a journey to 'bless' and a journey that is both significant and religious.

In today's society, the genealogical evidence for divine kinship lies with the clans into which Somalis are divided; every one of them owns clan trees derived from the Arabian *Qurayshi* divine lineage stretching back to the Prophet Mohammed and the Hashimites. Male society demands not just a virgin per se but that any son born to their wives must be of their blood and therefore of *divine* (righteous, blessed and sacred) blood because only a divine baby can legitimately extend and head the lineage of a divine order. It follows that a woman may insist on circumcision not only because of the social status it bestows by virtue of her becoming a mother but also, more importantly, because it is an act that proves her worthy of a divine act whereby she will extend a divine bloodline. She is blessed with a fertility that comes from the divine.

It is perhaps this fear of losing the blessing by breaking the genealogical link with the sacred ancestors that has sustained *gudniin*/Pharaonic circumcision. Across religions, the people of the Horn of Africa seem to adhere to a belief in sacred descent. Why? The short answer is fertility. As an existential issue, sacrifice underpins fertility and a complex ideology, current and past. This ideology remains constant even through the transformation that comes with new ideas, religions and changed practices.

Was circumcision practised in the time of Bu'ur Ba'ayr? It is impossible to know for certain, but it is more likely than not that it was. If Bu'ur Ba'ayr (Mohamed Haniif) had indeed been checking about a bride's period and waiting for it to pass, as is suggested by the Beesha Mohamed Haniifa, then he could in this way confirm that she was not already pregnant with another man's child – and circumcision would also ensure her virginity.

Waqlaal: celebration of the birth of a boy

The Somali have a *beere* dance; it is performed when a married couple want to conceive a boy or when a boy is born. There are songs, too, that are dedicated to newborn boys and the *humbulasha* song of the Oromo and the Somali in the northeastern provinces of Kenya. Many of the peoples in the Horn of Africa sing special songs for newborn boys; and the *mote*, *hombolooleh* and *humbulasha* are sung by the Guji Oromo, as Loo notes (1991). Similar ceremonies or songs celebrating the birth of girls do not seem to be as common. Animals are slaughtered to celebrate the naming of a child, a ritual locally known as the *waqlaal*: two animals are slaughtered for a boy, one only for a girl.

This inequality between boys and girls follows current Somali traditions; a man is worth 100 camels but a woman only 50. The family gives away two-thirds of each animal slaughtered for the *waqlaal* to neighbours and to the poor. The practice of *waqlo*/*waqlaal* takes place throughout the Somali populated areas and yet remains, I believe, so far unreported. In the ritual of *waqlaal*, the customary breaking of long bones to extract marrow is forbidden. Instead, all the long bones of the animal are preserved unbroken, tied together with a string and hung on a tall tree. The idea behind this practice is to protect the child to whom the *waqlaal* ritual is dedicated. Somali men in the diaspora mark the birth of a son by sending money (up to a few hundred $US) to relatives back home who perform the ritual on behalf of the absent family. Other children born in the diaspora are carried round on the shoulders of someone special, a practice known as *garabsaar* (putting on the shoulders). In short, the tradition is still flourishing even though it has been modified over time and by dispersal through the diaspora.

Other Eastern Cushitic speaking peoples such as the Oromo also have naming rituals. The Guji Oromo (Loo, 1991) have the *maqbaasa* ritual in which the boy child is given a name and enters the *Gada* grade system with the proclamation of his father's name.

Hanging the long bones from the branches of tall tree is probably done not only to protect the bones from predators; trees are sacred and associated by various lowland Eastern Cushitic speaking peoples with the myth of origin. As has already been noted, certain trees and wooden objects seem to play a significant part in rituals associated with the protection, as well as the conception, of children. One such object is the *wagar*, discussed earlier. The Konso also make sacrifices to sacred trees for fertility. They offer up the heads of lions and other big game, putting these inside sacred trees such as the juniper (Hallpike, 1972). Furthermore, the *waqlaal* rituals and the notion of hanging bones in trees may reflect the legend of the 'Cushitic institutions' or the myth of origin (discussed in the next chapter) that is common amongst Cushitic speaking peoples: the stranger/divine man who sat on a (sacred) tree and later married a local girl and hence fathered the people living in the Horn of Africa.

It is essential to understand how the overt obsession with boys is linked to the genealogical extension of sacred blood. First, the women's bodies endure various natural and cultural modifications and interventions in order to produce a male child. And, second, there are celebrations when this male child is born and his body is protected through rituals and interventions that seem intended to prepare him for something productive, as I discuss below. The male body, as well as the female, has to endure pain in the interests of sacred fertility. For women this is via Pharaonic circumcision and for men it is via the stick fight and the ritual hunt. The stick fight is a tradition amongst some the peoples in the Horn of Africa, including the Somali, and it too involves the shedding of blood as a sacrifice for fertility.

Istunka – stick fights as a fertility sacrifice

The fact that men in the Horn of Africa carry spears and war shields has been taken to mean that the prevailing culture of the region is a patrilineal ideology about men, their virility and their fearsomeness. However, men, like women, are subject to a divine rule. Fertility is a common good and men and women are both responsible for keeping the divine happy in the interests of fertility. What often appear as fierce warrior men with spears and shields, ready to kill, have more to do with a communal existential issue than with male dominance over women. In this section I explain how even the stick fight, that most quintessential of male activities, is part and parcel of the shared fertility ideology of the region.

Istunka is a stick fight which marks the celebrations for the new year and the first harvest. It was a ubiquitous tradition until as late as the 1990s in the Somali town of Afgoi, 30 km southwest of Mogadishu. It is associated with the regional medieval Geledi kingdom. The stick fight takes place on the banks of the river Shebelle which runs through the middle of Afgoi. Men come to the meeting place carrying their sticks and reciting poems, singing and dancing. The Somali flag, banners and pictures of famous local people – such as the Suldan of the Geledi and notable elders – are displayed in the streets and thousands of people traditionally attend. The ritual is considered a vital one for rain-making and for blessing the past year and welcoming the new year. The cutting, which also mutilates the body, and the blood shedding that takes place here is, I suggest, a sacrifice for fertility.

Other Cushitic peoples such as the Guji Oromo also celebrate the new year through a feast called *bitta gaatana* (Loo, 1991). This event has persisted for many years despite criticisms from Muslims on religious grounds. Modified rain-making rituals continue to take place. In 2011, the Somaliland government organised a *roobdoon* ceremony at Hargeisa's national stadium (Figure 3.19). It was led by prominent sheikhs and attended by local men, women and children as well as the ruling elite, all united together in carrying out the ancient ritual of Somali rain-making in a Muslim context.

I will later deconstruct the hitherto only superficially understood notion of male heroism. In so doing, I will talk about the hunt ritual during which a hunter risks great danger in his quest to kill a big game animal and thereby bring fertility to his society. I will explain later how, in the case of Cushitic speaking peoples like the Oromo and Konso, this is equivalent to the act of pain that the mother endures when sacrificing her life for the extension of the lineage. The heroism of the ritual hunt is on a level with the female pain endured during childbirth. The Oromo concept of *uuma*, which denotes male fertility, is generally used to describe both human and animal fertility. The fertility of the male is often equated with the fertility enjoyed by the society in which he lives.

Somali women, of course, face far more pain than do the men in this *istunka* ritual. The unimaginable pain that female circumcision (*gudniin*) creates for women culminates in the birthing pain and the attendant complications that can lead to near death experiences, if not death. It is yet another sacrifice that the women make in the interests of *sacred* fertility and the extension of sacred blood.

Nevertheless, in this context, the pain a circumcised woman experiences in giving birth can be considered to correspond with the pain felt by man killing a big game animal, a buffalo. The act of giving birth is, of course, her third experience of pain endured as the result of her circumcision, the first being the act of cutting itself and the second the act of intercourse. Her sacrifice of female circumcision can be said to bring sacred fertility in much the same way as the ritually pure big game or stick fight can be said to bring the man his sacred fertility. This male fertility is for the common good and will be rewarded by God who will bring abundance in terms of human, crop and animal reproduction. It is believed that if the ritual hunt does not take place, and the male body modification (scarification, or lip plates amongst other Horn of Africa peoples) is not performed, and the stick fights are not held, then the rains will fail, many women will become childless and illness and famine will stalk the land.

I argue that it is this fear of disaster that underpins the continuity of *gudniin*/FGM even though people are no longer aware of the fact; its true meaning has been lost as patriarchal institutions have justified its practice in the Abrahamic interests of chastity. Seen to serve some sort of purpose, and unchallenged by even the new religions, female circumcision has continued to the point where its original ritual purpose has been lost. It is a tradition; people have a vague memory of its ritual significance and may mark its passing with the slaughter of animals, but its purpose has been reinvented. Now only the honour attached to 'virginity', and motherhood in general, are remembered. Slowly divorced from the indigenous religious ideology and diluted by new religions, this disconnection has allowed talk of this 'savage' practice to flourish in a way that is totally out of context and isolated from the rituals I have here presented, rituals which remain, in their many transformations, markers for the life cycle of human beings.

Istunka may once have been more generally widespread in the Horn of Africa than it is now and it was central to the governance of large numbers of people. The idea of sacred fertility and the divine blood lay at the heart of the inheritance of a power that would lead eventually to the extension of a lineage to create a centralised power, a state or a kingdom. Lineage heads were required to bring fertility, as the *caleemo saar* ritual shows. A successful ruler is seen to be a blessed ruler. Rain-making rituals like the *istunka*, ritual hunting and the *roobdoon* prayer ceremonies are all highly structured, with rules and roles for the religious leaders and elders. It is a system that points to the existence of an even stronger organisation in the past.

Conclusions

I have shown in this chapter the relationship between the fertility rituals taking place at Aw-Barkhadle and rituals such as the ancestral worship of *Siti*, spirit possessions, Pharaonic circumcision, child protection and fertility rituals: the ritual bath, the *baanashada* and the *wagar*. Somali male society is based upon patriarchy and kinship, and reproduction is of its very essence. Amongst the women, there is a tradition of 'treatment' and 'nurturing' for those who are childless. These Somali rituals all centre around the issue of fertility in much the same way as does the site of Aw-Barkhadle.

Linguists have shown that the word 'Zar' is derived from the Agao word *djar* and that it is identified as the Sky-God of the Agao (Cerulli, 1957; Ullendorff, 1955). I have discussed how spirit possession and *zar* and the dance of *zar* are potentially the remnants of practices associated with the worship of the Sky-God, a religion once widespread within the region. The modern ceremonies of the *Siti* as well as of the *baanashada* both feature dance, drumming and *nabi amaan*. In addition, the *zar* includes fainting, investing in spirit paraphernalia and actions designed to appease. There is the tradition of the veneration of saints (*awliyo*); people pray for the successful delivery of a child and direct these prayers to the *weli, awliyo* (ancestors). The *Siti* is one such ancestral worshipping ceremony which celebrates Haawa (Eve) and Fatima (the Prophet Mohammed's daughter) in the hope of gaining protection for mother and child.

It is difficult to know whether the important grasses used for ceremonial purposes are regarded as sacred though the *wagar* is undoubtedly a fertility object made from a sacred tree. The *wagar* is known to have existed as an object in its own right as well as representing distinctive ideas about female fertility and the protection of children who are associated with it. It is a sacred object with a symbolic meaning. In Somali oral culture, it is also known to be associated with the Sky-God. The *tiire* or the butterfly bush (*rotheca myricoides*) has been shown to play a part in the medicinal treatments for infertility and in the secret knowledge domain of the *calaqad* (the *zar* religious leader). Incidentally, although the *tiire*'s medicinal value in terms of allergies and joint pain is common knowledge in some Somali regions, it is a poisonous tree and its fertility powers are as yet untested by modern science.

Wood, trees and grasses in the Horn of Africa generally carry symbolic meanings. The *wagar* safeguards female and male fertility; it protects children, and particularly male children, from bad spirits when it is placed beneath their heads. There is a possible relationship between the idea of sacred trees, particularly the African olive, and the practice of the *wagar* and between the legend of the man in the tree coming down from heaven and the Sky-God.

I have maintained too that Pharaonic circumcision ensures that a divine (right/legitimate) blood is extended so that a lineage can be in receipt of sacred fertility (prosperity). I have argued that *gudniin*, including the cliterodectomy, is carried out for the benefit of the divine. Circumcision as a blood sacrifice may therefore have originally been intended as an act designed to please the divine and to gain access to divine fertility rather than being about the affairs of men and women: a form of sacrifice to the divine rather than something carried out between human beings. In short, divine kinship can be understood through an understanding of ancient worship and veneration as it is practised today. Ancestral worship is linked to fertility rituals whereby the (divine or religious) ancestors must be pleased so that they may grant (sacred) fertility. Only the right blood is blessed.

Confusion exists over whether *gudniin* is a religious act or not: on the one hand, the peoples of the Horn of Africa expect it to be a significant ritual, even a religious act; the blood shed by even a cliterodectomy marks a powerful and religiously important ritual, even though its original purpose has long been lost. On the other hand, it is disowned by both their Christian and Islamic faiths.

I argue that divine kinship, or sacred descent, has been important in the formation of states in Africa, across the east to western belt of early states in the Nile Valley, Nubia and Aksum. Pharaonic circumcision has perhaps played a key part in this divine kinship by its promotion of divine blood and the fertility to be gained from pleasing the gods, a fertility that includes prosperity in land, animals and crops. The present-day distribution of the FGM practice of Pharaonic circumcisions in Africa bears witness to its development in the earliest African states.

In ancient times, female circumcision would go hand in hand with those ideological and religious institutions that legitimise a certain lineage's wealth, land and power over others, that legitimise the genealogies of society itself. Ritual efficacy through successful fertility rituals and sacrifice would have helped a certain lineage to advance into prominence and take power and centralize rule. Africa hosts some of the continent's most wealthy and ancient kingdoms in its east–west belts: the Nile Valley, Nubia, Mali and the Horn of Africa. These are all strong candidates for the birthplace of *gudniin* as a method of ensuring the continuation of a sacred bloodline via divine blessing. Intermarriage between the Somali dominant clans and the 'outcast' clans is forbidden in order to preserve the pure blood that is itself linked to the idea of sacred blood.

A divine order through a divine blood that comes from, or is related to, divine deities is all-important. Pharaonic circumcision exists to ensure that a religious, right and legitimate blood is extended through sacred marriage and sacred fertility. Circumcision is not, therefore, about women or about the desires of men but rather about a relationship between the human and the divine. The practice of Pharaonic circumcision may well have been inherited originally from a divine kinship society in pre-Christian/Islamic times. The places in Africa where Pharaonic circumcision is found today certainly correspond to the places of early state formation in Africa.

In the chapter that follows, I examine further the interdependent relationship between the idea of sacred fertility and divine kinship in the ideologies of the Horn of Africa.

Notes

1 The stillborn has inspired an expression in Somali that says *mayd uur majiifo*, lit. a dead person (infant) never stays in the womb.
2 In *The Sacred Meadows*, el-Zein writes about the Lamuan *wangwana* who use the circulation of the bull to drive away a malevolent *jin* (1972: 285).
3 The original word might have been *calanqaad* ('she/he who carries the flag') since *calaqad* carries no meaning beyond being a name. *Calan* means flag while *qaad*

means to carry. Things have now changed and in a place like Hargeisa there are no longer any powerful calanqaad. Those still active work very privately, for reasons involving – but not restricted to – the growing Salafi movement which forbids many traditional practices, including *zar*.

4 Sheikh Hussein spirit is related to Sheikh Nuur Hussein Bali, a twelfth century Saint who is said to have spread Islam in the eastern Arsi Oromia region.

5 Wikimedia Commons. http://en.wikipedia.org/wiki/File:Maternal_mortality_ rate_worldwide.jpg.

6 Somalis know who they are by following the clan tree, *abtirsiimo*, the clan-lineage (the prefix *ab* meaning descendant (family), blood related etc., and *tirsiimo* meaning counting). My interviewees suggest that clan trees may extend back to the eleventh century AD or even further back in some cases and suggest a perhaps debatable longevity in these genealogies.

7 Semitic peoples adopted circumcision too: Moses' wife cut off her son's foreskin to satisfy God (Yahweh).

Bibliography

Adamson, J. 1967. *The Peoples of Kenya*. London: Collins & Harvill Press.

Al-Jazeera. 2017. *The Cut: Exploring FGM*. www.aljazeera.com/programmes/ aljazeeracorrespondent/2017/10/cut-exploring-fgm-171002112108882.html [accessed: 06/10/2017].

Arberry, A. J. 1953. *Sufism: An Account of the Mystics of Islam*. London: Allen and Unwin.

Assaad, M. B. 1980. Female Circumcision in Egypt: Social Implications, Current Research and Prospects for Change. *Studies in Family Planning*, 11(1): 3–16.

Auffret, S. 1983. *Des Couteaux contre des Femmes – de l'Excision*. Paris: Des Femmes.

Barclay, H. 1964. *Buuri al Lamaa: A Suburban Village in the Sudan*. Ithaca: Cornell University Press.

Bartels, L. 1983. *Oromo Religion: Myths and Rites of the Western Oromo of Ethiopia. An Attempt to Understand*. Berlin: Deitrich Reimer Verlag.

Boddy, J. 1982. Womb as Oasis: The Symbolic Context of Pharaonic Circumcision in Rural Northern Sudan. *American Ethnologist*, 9(4): 682–698.

Burton, R. 1966 [1898]. *First Footsteps in East Africa*. Edited by G. Waterfield. New York: Praeger. Travellers and Explorers Series.

Cerulli, E. 1957. *Somalia. Scritti vari Editi ed Inediti*. Vol. I. Roma: Istituto Poligrafico dello Stato. P. V.

Declich, F. 2000. Sufi Experience in Rural Somali: A Focus on Women. *Social Anthropology*, 8(3): 295–318.

Ehret, C. 1995. The Eastern Horn of Africa, 1000 BC to 1400 AD: The Historical Roots. In A. J. Ahmed (ed.) *The Invention of Somalia*. Lawrenceville, NJ: Red Sea Press.

Ehret, C. and Posnansky, M. (eds.). 1982. *The Archaeological and Linguistic Reconstruction of African History*. Berkeley and London: University of California Press.

el-Safi, A. 1970. *Native Medicine in the Sudan: Sources, Conception and Methods*. Khartoum: Khartoum University Press.

el-Zein, Abdul Hamid. 1972. *The Sacred Meadows: A Structural Analysis of Religious Symbolism in an East African Town*. Unpublished PhD thesis, University of Chicago.

Favali, L. 2001. What Is Missing? (Female Genital Surgeries – Gudniin, Excision, Cliterodectomy – in Eritrea). *Global Jurist Frontiers*, 1(2).

Fullerton, A. and Adan, A. 1995. Handicraft of the Somali Woman. In L. Prussin (ed.) *African Nomadic Architecture; Space, Place and Gender*. Washington, DC: Smithsonian Institute.

Hall, M. and Ismail, B. A. 1981. *Sisters Under the Sun. The Story of Sudanese Women*. London: Longman.

Hallpike, C. 1972. *The Konso of Ethiopia: A Study of the Values of an Eastern Cushitic People*. Oxford: Clarendon Press.

Hay, M. J. 1981. Review: The Hosken Report: Genital and Sexual Mutilation of Females by Fran Hosken. *The International Journal of African Studies*, 14(3): 523–526.

Hayes, O. R. 1975. Female Genital Mutilation, Fertility Control, Women's Roles, and the Patrilineage in Modern Sudan: A Functional Analysis. *American Ethnologist*, 2(4): 617–633.

Hosken, F. P. 1993. *The Hosken Report: Genital and Sexual Mutilation of Females*. Lexington, MA: Women's International Net Work News.

Kapteijns, L. 2004–2010. I. M. Lewis and Somali Clanship: A Critique. *Northeast African Studies*, 11(1): 1–23.

Kapteijns, L. and Omar, M. A. 1996. Sitaat: Somali Women's Songs for the "Mothers of the Believers". In K. W. Harrow (ed.) *The Marabout and the Muse: New Approaches to Islam in African Literature*. pp. 124–141. Portsmouth, NH: Heinemann.

Kapteijns, L. and Omar, M. A. 2007. Sittaat: Women's Religious Songs in Djibouti. Halabuur. *Journal of Somali Literature and Culture*, 2(1–2): 38–48.

Kennedy, J. G. 1970. Circumcision and Excision in Egyptian Nubia. *Man*, New Series, 5(2): 175–191.

Knight, M. 2001. Curing Cut or Ritual Mutilation? Some Remarks on the Practice of Female and Male Circumcision in Graeco-Roman Egypt. *Isis*, 92(2): 317–338.

Kouba, L. J. and Muasher, J. 1985. Female Circumcision in Africa: An Overview. *African Studies Review*, 28(1): 95–110.

Levine, D. N. 2000. *Greater Ethiopia: The Evolution of a Multiethnic Society*. 2nd ed. Chicago and London: University of Chicago Press.

Lévi-Strauss, C. 1982. *The Way of the Masks*. Translated by S. Modelski. Seattle: University of Washington Press.

Lewis, I. 1991. Introduction. In I. M. Lewis, A. Al-Safi and S. Hurreiz (eds.) *Women's Medicine. The Zar-Bori Cult in Africa and Beyond*. Edinburgh: International African Institute.

Lewis, I. 1996. *Religion in Context: Cults and Charisma*. Cambridge: Cambridge University Press.

Lewis, I. 1998. *Saints and Somalis: Popular Islam in a Clan-Based Society*. Lawrenceville, NJ and Asmara, Eritrea: Red Sea Press.

Lewis, I. 2004. Visible and Invisible Differences: The Somali Paradox. *Africa*, 74(4): 489–515.

Loo, J. van de. 1991. *Guji Oromo Culture (with the Collaboration of Bilow Kolo)*. Berlin: Dietrich Reimer Verlag.

Luling, V. 1991. Some Possession Cults in Southern Somalia. In I. M. Lewis, A. Al-Safi and S. Hurreiz (eds.) *Women's Medicine. The Zar-Bori Cult in Africa and Beyond*. Edinburgh: International African Institute.

Makris, G. P. and Al-Safi, A. 1991. The Tumbura Spirit Possession Cult of the Sudan. In I. M. Lewis, A. AL-Safi and S. Hurreiz (eds.) *Women's Medicine. The Zar-Bori Cult in Africa and Beyond*. Edinburgh: International African Institute.

Mire, S. 2006. Gaashaan, Somali Shield. In K. Lagat and J. Hudson (eds.) *Hazina: Traditions, Trade and Transition in Eastern Africa*. Nairobi, Kenya: National Museums of Nairobi.

Mire, S. 2015a. Mapping of the Archaeology of Somaliland: Religion, Art, Script, Time, Urbanism, Trade and Empire. *African Archaeological Review*, 32(1): 111–136.

Mire, S. 2015b. Wagar, Fertility and Phallic Stelae: Cushitic Sky-God Belief and the Site of Saint Aw-Barkhadle in Somaliland. *African Archaeological Review*, 32(1): 93–109.

Mire, S. 2016b. "The Child That Tiire Doesn't Give You, God Won't Give You Either" – The Role ofRotheca myricoides in Somali Fertility Practices. *Anthropology and Medicine*, 23(3): 311–331.

Miskell, J. 2000. *An Ecological and Resource Utilisation Assessment of Gacan Libra, Somaliland*. IUCN Eastern Africa Programme. Somali Natural Resources Management Programme. IUCN the World Conservation Union.

Mohammed, M. A. 1991. *Histoire des Croyances en Somalie*. Paris: Annales Littéraires de l'Université de Besançon.

Onyulo, T. 2016. Alternative to Genital Mutilation Emerges for Kenyan Maasai Girls. March 26. www.newsweek.com/female-genital-mutilation-kenya-female-circumcision-un-unicef-equality-now-439666 [accessed: 08/07/2017].

Révoil, G. 1882. *La Vallée du Darror: Voyage aux Pays Çomalis Dis Mois à la Cote Orientale D'Afrique*. Paris: Challamel aîné.

Schmidt, P. R. 1983. An Alternative to a Strictly Material Perspective: A Review of Historical Archaeology, Ethnoarchaeology, and Symbolic Approaches in African Archaeology. *American Antiquity*, 48(1): 62–79.

Seligman, B. Z. 1914. On the Origin of the Egyptian Zar. *Folklore*, 25: 300–323.

Tiilikainen, M. 2010. Sitaat as Part of Somali Women's Everyday Religion. In M. L. Keinänen (ed.) *Perspectives on Women's Everyday Religion*. Stockholm: Acta Universitatis Stockholmiensis.

Trimingham, J. S. 1952. *Islam in Ethiopia*. 1st ed. Oxford: Oxford University Press.

Trimingham, J. S. 1965. *Islam in Ethiopia*. 2nd ed. Oxford: Oxford University Press.

Ullendorff, E. 1955. *The Semitic Languages of Ethiopia: A Comparative Phonology*. London: Taylor's.

UNICEF. 2016. *Female Genital Mutilation/Cutting: A Global Concern*. New York: United Nations Children's Fund. February. www.unicef.org/media/files/FGMC_2016_brochure_final_UNICEF_SPREAD.pdf [accessed: 07/07/2017].

Yount, K. M. and Carrera, J. S. 2006. Female Genital Cutting and Reproductive Experience in Minya, Egypt. *Medical Anthropology Quarterly*, 20(2): 182–211.

Youth for Change. 2016. I Will Meet the Powerful King 'Aba Gada' to End FGM Among My Kenya's Borana Community. September 13. www.youthforchange.org/latest-posts/2016/8/31/tackling-social-norms-fgm-kenya [accessed: 08/07/2017].

5 In the name of divine fertility

Indigenous institutions and Sufi Islam in the Horn of Africa

In his account of Sufism (1953), J. A. Arberry wrote that "it is generally agreed that no religious movement can come into being or develop without having contact with other established faiths or denominations which are bound to leave their impress upon the new creation of thought and emotion." And it is without doubt possible to understand more about both the non-Islamic and pre-Islamic use of the landscape of Aw-Barkhadle and the continuity of the ritual practice conducted there by studying present-day female rituals in Somali society and the current ritual use of that landscape with its tombs, enclosures, wells and hills (Figure 2.1). This chapter therefore focuses on the ideas that underpin the Horn of Africa notion of fertility and explores further the potential relationship between kinship and ancestral worship in that region. This relationship is the key to understanding the archaeology of religion.

This chapter uses the key ideas raised by the symbolism of the materials, ritual and landscape to help make sense of the non-/pre-Islamic and non-/pre-Christian religion in this region. It takes as its example the greater Somali society (i.e. one that includes Somali populations in Djibouti, northern Kenya and Ethiopia) and uses it to investigate issues of continuity in regional fertility rituals.

It begins by investigating the relationship between Sufism, Islamic myths of origin and 'Cushitic institutions' from a Somali point of view, a topic briefly mentioned in Chapter Three. Key indigenous concepts relating to the Sky-God *Waaq* (of the Cushitic religion), ancestral worship and rain-making are discussed in more detail thereby revealing a continuity of indigenous regional practices within the sacred and ancestral landscapes and their archaeological features

In its second part, I place these observations within the context of the major groups of the Eastern Cushitic speaking people in the Horn of Africa. I identify features and objects in the ritual landscape to produce the data associated with indigenous institutions or what are termed 'Cushitic institutions' and rituals. My primary purpose is to construct a locally appropriate theoretical framework within which to interpret the symbolism associated with these landscapes, objects, and archaeological features. I rely mainly upon my own ethnographic field research and incorporate the linguistic history, ethnohistory and anthropological research of the region.

I noted in Chapter Three the significance of archaeological and landscape features and elements such as stones, enclosures, mountains (hills), water and trees. I demonstrated the symbolic significance of such landscape elements by drawing mainly on material from the Aw-Barkhadle site but also, to a lesser extent, from the site of Goroyo Cawl with its fertility stones and sacred enclosure. In Chapter Four, I sought to contextualise the Aw-Barkhadle female fertility rituals in Somali society by exploring the female and male fertility rituals that take place beyond Aw-Barkhadle and in Somali society more generally. I concluded that certain materials and practices are crucial to understanding notions of fertility and the ideology of kinship: the use of incense, trees, herbs and moisture, and their role in fertility as well as child protection rituals; the purpose of the *wagar* rituals; and the rationale behind female circumcision. I spoke of male fertility rituals such as the ritual hunt, *istunka* and *waqlaal* and suggested that female circumcision needs to be placed within its ritual and ideological contexts. I proposed that the ancestors' sacred blood is extended through fertility. Sacred fertility is granted by the ancestors in terms of blessings when the rituals are carried out successfully. Circumcision, I argue, is a sacrifice to the ancestors.

I now discuss the basis for these practices across the Horn of Africa. Deeply-rooted regional indigenous concepts are critical not only to our understanding of the regional culture but also to a contextualisation and (re)interpretation of the archaeological heritage of the Horn of Africa as a whole: the veneration/worship of ancestors, snake worship, the concept of peace and harmony, the ritual purity and the hunt ritual and the indigenous concept of the protection of the sacred (*bir-ma-geydo*).

Interactions between the Horn of Africa, the Red Sea and the Indian Ocean regions

Trade around the shores of the Indian Ocean is thought to have existed for millennia (Casson, 1989). Archaeological evidence mainly from Indus pottery (the Late Harappan phase) found in the Gulf, the Emirates and Oman (Chakrabarti, 1998: 304; Ratnagar, 1987; Potts, 1990) shows that Bahrain, Failaka (Kuwait) and the Indus were in contact with each other from as early as 2200–2000 BC. This date coincides with the Akkadian and post-Akkadian eras of Mesopotamian chronology (Chakrabarti, 1998: 309). Contact and sea trade between Egypt and Mesopotamia existed from at least the fourth millennium BC (Moorey, 1998: 193). Mesopotamia also had links with the Punjab-Gujarat and with Dilmun in Bahrain and with Magan which is thought to be present day Oman (Hourani, 1995: 6, 129; Beek, 1960). This early trade may also have extended to the Red Sea area.

These sources appear to show that Ancient Egypt's relationship with the Land of Punt (a destination for Egyptian ships of the mid second millennium

BC and thought to be situated on the African side of the Red Sea) was based on trade relations. By contrast, the pre-Axumite kingdom – a.k.a the unpronounceable word made up of the letters D'MT – and the Axumite kingdoms of what is today Eritrea and Ethiopia interacted with Egypt, particularly in Ptolemaic times, both economically and politically (Phillipson, 1997). In the first centuries BC, according to Hourani, even the Somali were taking a seafaring role and it is suggested that they were more active than the South Arabians at around this time (Hourani, 1995). Furthermore, Smith and Right (1988) have found Greek and Roman material including pottery at Raas Hafuun as well as Heis in Somaliland/Somalia.

In the fourth century AD, the Himyarites and the Sabaeans of South Arabia united to form a state. According to Hourani, there are Chinese records of a continuing Arabian (particularly Sabaean) commercial contact with countries of the Indian Ocean such as Sri Lanka, which was at this time a major commercial centre in the area (Hourani, 1995: 38–40). On the African side of the Red Sea, D'MT, the pre-Aksumite kingdom of current day Ethiopia (as well as the Somali territories), is thought to have had cultural links with South Arabia (Phillipson, 1997). Furthermore, I have discovered a gravestone with Sabaean writing *in situ* 50 metres from the beach at the coastal town of Shalcaw in the Sanaag region (Figure 3.29 and for Dhagah Kure Figure 5.1) and Sasanian pottery as well as other Indian Ocean pottery,

Figure 5.1 Dhagah Kure Sabaean and Himyarite writings

including Yuan and Ming dynasty, in the ancient ruined town of Fardowsa (Mire, 2015a). This indicates a link between the societies around the Red Sea in ancient times. Also, writings that appear to be of Himyarite character are found on various rock art sites in the Hargeisa region such as Dhagax Kurreh, near Arabsiyo, 40 minutes from Hargeisa (Figure 5.1). Furthermore, there are various objects, particularly figurines depicting human beings with Himyarite and Sabaean style and writing, that have been discovered through illicit digging in Somaliland. However, their significance as evidence remains disputed given the lack of the careful archaeological recording necessary to prove their authenticity.

Islam in Somali society

The regions around the Red Sea appear to have deep ethnic and cultural links through millennia of contact as a result of these expansions and migrations. It is important to remember that the strip of water which makes up this sea would have taken only a day or two to cross (cf. Martin, 1974: 375). It is also important to keep in mind that not only could Himyarite and Sabaean kingdoms expand towards Africa but that briefly, in the mid first millennium AD, Southern Arabia was ruled by Abyssinian kings (Hourani, 1995; King, 2004; Haldane, 1983). Ethiopian Christian rulers invaded Yemen in the time of the Prophet Muhammad (Martin, 1974 375). In 615 AD, a group of the Prophet's first followers, including family members and headed by Ja'far b. Abi Talib, fled, on the advice of Muhammad, to Ethiopia to seek the protection of the Ethiopian church from the Qurayshi traditionalists after the Prophet Muhammad's revelation of Islam (King, 2004: 10; cf. Arnold, 1929: 30; Haldane, 1983: 10; Encyclopaedia of Islam, 2005: 202; Munro-Hay, 2011: 101; Phillipson, 2012). This exodus is known as the first *hijra* in Islam though it is debated how much preaching the refugees actually did during their 13 years in Aksum. During this period, the Prophet's family came into contact for the first time with the book and the idea of the codex, and after the Prophet Muhammad's death, Salim b. Ma'qil, the client of Abu Hudhayfa, put together the Qur'an in the form of a book (*mishaf/mushaf*) (Arnold, 1929: 30). *Mushaf* is an Ethiopian word for book and this was the name adopted by Zayd b. Thabit as he copied the Qur'an into book format (Haldane, 1983: 10). It is said that about 50–60 converts joined the Prophet's family and followed them when they returned to Arabia. Even more controversially, Arabic writers of the time – the selfsame sources that both Ethiopian and foreign writers have relied on to supply other details of this *hijra* (Munro-Hay, 2011: 102–103; Encyclopaedia of Islam, 2005: 202) – tell how the ruler of Aksum himself, negesi Ashama ibn Abgar, is said to have converted to Islam. This indicates a solidarity between the two monotheistic religions, Christianity and Islam. One of the early converts and the first *mu'addin* (prayer caller) of Islam was in fact Bilal b. Rabah al Habashi, a freed slave with an Ethiopian parentage. This long-lasting and complex relationship between the peoples on both sides of the Red Sea has been overshadowed more recently by the often overemphasised perceptions of 'Arabia'/'Arabs', 'Abyssinia' and other commonplace dualisms and labels such as 'Christians' and 'Muslims'. These distinctions may to some degree be justifiable, especially in the light of the sixteenth century wars waged by the Awdal Muslim kings of the Somali region against the Ethiopian Christian kings. However, Ethiopians were for a long period after the first *hijra* exempted from *jihad* due to their historical relationship with Islam (Encyclopaedia of Islam, 2005: 202). Archaeologists, like historians, have often failed to acknowledge the complex relationships inherent in such 'dualism' narratives.

Oral history in present-day Somaliland tells how the Prophet's family came to Aksum via Zayla' where can be found potentially one of the oldest (if not the oldest) mosque in the Somali region and even in sub-Saharan Africa (see image and map of Somaliland's Islamic ruined towns in the open access article, Mire, 2015a). This mosque is called Qiblatayn because, it is said, it is orientated in two directions, one towards Jerusalem and the other towards Mecca; its name comes from the Arabic word *qibla*, meaning direction, and *qiblatayn*, two directions. It is suggested that this name testifies to its antiquity and, though there is as yet no archaeological evidence to confirm its age, many believe Zayla to be one of the oldest Muslim towns in the Horn of Africa. The existence of the mosque, it is argued, must go back to the time when the *qibla* was oriented towards Jerusalem, i.e. predating the time when Mecca became the *qibla*. According to the historical records, the town of Zayla was the first to be founded on trade links with Arabia and the Indian Ocean and was inhabited by locals as well as Arabs and, later in the sixteenth century, was occupied by Muslim armies seeking to subdue Ethiopia (Martin, 1974). My survey in 2010 revealed that the archaeological heritage of the town of Zayla includes a few remarkably old mosques which, according to the locals, date from as early as the first *hijra* (to Aksum) (Figure 5.2 and Figure 3.14). A number of locals also held collections of objects including ancient Indian Ocean coins of diverse chronological and geographical origin.

Zayla is one of many ruined towns which include those in the hinterland which flourished under Islam, including Amud and Qoorgaab, near Boorama, now hardly visible above grounds, and those that still have ruined walls and other structures such as Abbasa (Figure 4.6c), Derbiyada Cad (Figure 5.3), Eel Afwayn (Figure 5.4) Fardowsa (Figure 5.5) and Maduna (Figure 5.6). I came across some of these in my surveys in the region, and A. T. Curle recorded others including Amud and Abbasa (cf. Chittick, 1969, 1975). He made no mention, however, of the ruined town of Aw-Barkhadle. A substantial list of medieval Islamic centres and archaeological ruined towns in Somaliland is to be found along the Red Sea coast (Figure 3.14; Mire, 2015a).

Lewis states 'The coastal commercial colonies which had been founded by the Himyarite Kingdom before Islam eventually developed into the small

Figure 5.2 Ashraaf mosque in the ancient town of Zayla

Muslim states of Zeila (in its widest extension known as Adal) in Somali-land, and of Mogadishu in Somalia' (1998: 7). He fails, however, to provide any evidence for his claim that the Himyarite Kingdom founded Zeila and Mogadishu. Trimingham (1952: 58) made the same claim, also without supporting evidence. Given the lack of archaeological evidence, it is premature to conclude that the towns of Zayla and Mogadishu were founded

Figure 5.3 Derbiga Cad Cad Islamic ruined town, Awdal

Figure 5.4 God Caanood in 'Eel Afwayn Islamic ruined town

Figure 5.5 Fardowsa Islamic ruined town, Sheikh

Figure 5.6 Medieval ruined town of Maduna, Sanaag

by the Arabs. It is more likely, as Jama (1996) has suggested in relation to Mogadishu, that these ruined towns also lay alongside the ancient trade routes and hence were already in existence in some form as trade centres established through earlier trade with the hinterland. My own pastoralist grandmother set up a temporary restaurant at Xabaalu Tumaalood, on the Berbera road, as a nomad in the second quarter of the nineteenth century, and immediately, travellers congregated and built temporary market place and a sacred enclosure for prayer next to her restaurant. Jama's contribution is indeed important for understanding the organic manner of initiating trade centres that become urban centres by locals and their interaction with traders.

In terms of Mogadishu, the pottery analysis carried out by Professor Paul Sinclair, taken together with other archaeological evidence, seems to support this latter suggestion (ibid.).

The 'Arab' factor in Somali history has already been recognised by Hersi (1979) and Mukhtar (1987). These local dynasties were ruled by 'somalized Arabs or Somali strongly influenced by Arabic culture', wrote Cerulli (1957: 147). It is indeed likely that Mogadishu blossomed under Arab and Persian influences, but one must not ignore the archaeological evidence which supports the view that the Somalis came to play an important part in the Indian Ocean and Arabian trade several centuries BC. Hourani (1995) suggests, as noted earlier, that Greek textual evidence implies that it was the Somalis, rather than the Arabs, who during this time dominated the seafaring routes along the Indian Ocean and Arabia. The textual and archaeological evidence, taken together, suggest that the earliest towns along the Somali coast were more likely founded upon an indigenous network involving hinterland trade and that this may have happened even before significant Arab migrations or trade with the Somali coast. Archaeological investigations have mostly neglected indigenous material culture as they often follow only what they know or can easily check in the collections of the Western museums. Somaliland's Department of Archaeology's current and planned archaeological work will no doubt shed light on the potential local foundations of Somali coastal towns such as Zayla.

There is, then, a long-established tradition of contact and migration between both sides of the Red Sea. It is generally accepted that Islam arrived in the Somali territory immediately after the *Hijra* (Cerulli, 1957; cf. Lewis, 1998: 7; Trimingham, 1965), even if not after the first *Hijra* (noted earlier). The accounts of Arab travellers such as Ibn Battuta who travelled in the region in the fourteenth century AD shed light on the hospitality of the 'Berbers' of the medieval coastal towns of Zayla and Mogadishu (Dunn, 1989 [1325–1354]: 108–109, 232; Hourani, 1995).

In the Somali coastal region, there is an abundance of archaeological evidence to support these conclusions. Zayla, founded by Sh. Saylici, was one of many small towns developed by the Somali pastoral and trading communities which flourished through the trade that gave birth to other coastal and hinterland towns such as Heis, Maydh, Abbasa, Derbiga Cad

Cad, Qoorgaab, Fardowsa, Maduna and Amud in the western region, Aw-Barkhadle in the Hargeisa region and Fardowsa, near Sheikh (Figure 5.5). Furthermore, Somali traders might have converted to Islam within a patron-client relationship, influenced by their patrons in Arabia and in the Somali coastal towns. I have discovered Chinese pottery dating to the Yuan Dynasty of thirteenth *c.* AD and Ming Dynasty of fifteenth *c.* AD in the ruined town of Fardowsa (Figure 5.5). There are also Chinese records from the fourteenth–sixteenth century AD Ming Dynasty which reveal a cultural exchange between the Chinese and the Somali and refer to Mogadishu (Anshan, 2012; Arnoldi, 1986; Khaldun, [1406] 1989: 63; Mire, 2015a). The Somali or the people of this region seem, therefore, to have taken part in an Indian Ocean trade involving Greeks, Romans, Arabs, Chinese, Egyptians, Indians and Persians, among others.

In summary, the Indian Ocean trade and the Red Sea contacts go back approximately four thousand years and are supported by archaeological as well as textual evidence. The cultural exchange and social interactions included migrations, intermarriage between individuals from various cultural backgrounds, commodity exchange and the intermingling of lifestyles and religions. The most important issues as far as this book is concerned are the earliest interactions between Arab Muslims and Somali society and the consequent conversion to Islam, themes already introduced in Chapter Three and now developed further below.

Origins of the ideology of kinship and ancestral worship/veneration

Sufi Islam and Cushitic institutions of the societies of the Horn of Africa

Lévi-Strauss has argued that myths often exist in opposition to one another; they contradict or transform each other, and understanding any particular one without reference to another is difficult since:

> any utterance is explained with words which do not precisely figure in it, since those used by the speaker derive their meaning and importance from the fact that they were chosen in preference to others that he might have used, and to which, in commenting on the utterance, it is therefore quite in order to refer.
>
> (1982: 146)

I will now look in detail at the current myths of origin in the region and in so doing demonstrate that it is possible to make sense of their composition and meaning. I am mainly interested here in the issue of continuity in ritual practices and the reasons for their persistence. Studying the concept of fertility and the origins of the ritual(s) associated with it within the Horn of Africa is essential to understanding the potential significance of the continuity of the fertility rituals which affect both men and women. This understanding in turn leads to a critical interpretation of the archaeological elements and landscapes associated with this type of data.

Before discussing these issues, I want to examine some further developments that shed light on the depth and nature of interaction within the Horn and its adjacent regions. I do this in order to understand, from a multitemporal perspective and both ideologically and ritually, the complexity of relationships and exchange which exist within Arabia and the Indian Ocean communities. Sufism and Islam are amongst the many traditions and practices shared across this region and across time.

Sufism in the Somali Red Sea area

Sufism's arrival in the Somali Red Sea area

According to Arberry (1953: 46), Sufism first arose in Islam in the ninth century, with the first Sufi author of high rank, al-Harith b. Asad al-Muhasibi (781–837). It developed further in the twelfth and thirteenth centuries. My sources consider Sufism to be '*c'amal ilaahay*', that is 'the work of Allah' or 'Allah's doing'. According to oral traditions in northern Somalia and to the people I interviewed for my field research in Somaliland, Islam and Sufi traditions spread to Somali territory (*bilat al-Sumal*) via Arab sheikhs who crossed the Red Sea.

According to Cerulli (1957, cf. Lewis, 1998: 7), Sufism in Somalia may have arrived even earlier but this is confirmed only through the later records of the more recently formed Dervish movement. This was a religious nationalist movement that developed at the end of the nineteenth and beginning of the twentieth century as an anti-colonial struggle directed particularly against the British in Somaliland. It was led by the famous Somali hero, Sayyid Mohammed Abdullah Hassan (Beachey, 1990; Jardine, 1923; Samatar, 1982).

The Shafi'iya rite of Shariah is followed by the Somali, who are orthodox Sunnis. Within Sufism they belong to what is known as *zawiya or jama'a*, or congregations. These congregations adhere to various Orders (*tariqa*, 'The Path'). According to Arberry (1953: 52, 78), their main objective is to achieve gnosis, *ma'rifa* (lit. knowledge, spiritual knowledge) which was introduced into Sufism by Dhu 'l-Nun the Egyptian (d. 861).

The Tariiqas and their introduction to Somali society

There are four main orders (*tariiqas*) of Sufism which have 'schismatic offshoots' spreading throughout the Islamic world (Arberry, 1953: 84–92). The first Sufi Order was created by Muhyi al-Din 'Abd al-Qadir b. 'Abd Allah al-Jili (al-Jilani) who was born in Gilan in Persia in AD 1078 and lived in

Baghdad, as noted earlier. The second Order was the Suhrawardiya, named after Shihab al-Din 'Umar b. Abd Allah al-Suhrawardi who was born in AD 1144. The third Order was founded by Nur al-Din Ahmed b. 'Abd Allah al-Shadhili' who was born in AD 1196 and who was a popular Sufi scholar in north Africa. The fourth Order was the Maulawiya, named after its founder Jalal al-Din Rumi, born in AD 1273.

In today's Somali region, one finds the *tariiqas*, including Qaadiriya, Malikiya, Rashiidiya/Saalihiya and Ahmediya (cf. Cerulli, 1957: 187–195). According to my sources, these are all considered to be Sufi Muslim Orders that form part of the religion of the Prophet Muhammad. I was told that the Prophet has opened up these paths (*tariiqas*); the Prophet said '*way iga banaanyihiin*' or 'the *tariiqas* are open.' The *tariiqa*, such as Qaadiriya, Salahiya and so on are all considered to be Shaafi'iya, according to the people I interviewed.

A Shafi'te saint from Southern Arabia, Sharif Abu Bakr ibn Abd Allah al-'Aydarus (known as al-Qutb ar-Rabbanim, the Divine Axis), introduced the Qaadiriya Order, the oldest Sufi Order in Islam, into the Harar region in the fifteenth century (Trimingham, 1965). Although the Order spread into one of regions adjacent to Harar in the northern Somali region, it did not spread much into the south (ibid.). Other Orders of Sufism, Saalahiya and Rashidiya, which are thought to be more popular in the south, spread there later in the nineteenth century and early twentieth centuries.

The Somali Islamic myth of origin, divine kinship and the role of Saint Aw-Barkhadle

The history surrounding Saint Aw-Barkhadle is difficult to understand. However, the oral history I was able to collect fits well with the written records in Arabia that date to this period. These records document members of holy families moving to Ethiopian and Somali territories to take up clerical posts. Martin writes '[T]hese holy men [sayyids, sharifs and *masha'ikh*] were a sizeable contingent among the migrants' (ibid.: 371, see also el-Zein, 1972). According to my sources, Sh. Yusuf al Kawnayn (Aw-Barkhadle) was one of the *musheikhdii* (the sheikhs) who came to Somalia and taught people about Islam. Sheikh Yusuf Al-Kawnayn was believed to come from a holy family. The sheikhs I interviewed greatly respected Aw-Barkhadle (whom they refer to as The Sheikh) and admitted that they have yet to attain his *ma'rifa* (spiritual knowledge). The women I interviewed also expressed a profound adoration of Saint Aw-Barkhadle as is indicated by their response to questions about why people still make sacrifices and slaughter animals for the Saint. All the people I spoke to were surprised by the questions and were keen to enlighten me about the Sheikh. As noted in Chapter Three, one of the answers was 'Without Saint Aw-Barkhadle, you and your mother and your father would not have been born with religion.' In other words, without Aw-Barkhadle, Somalis would have been without religion as they know it today.

According to the Sufi notion of *ma'rifa*, spiritual knowledge, Sufi Orders have points of progress for the practitioner, representing perhaps the different stages of knowledge and devotion (Arberry, 1953: 14, 74–83; Trimingham, 1971). Sheikh Yusuf is referred to as a sheikh with great powers gained through the grace (*baraka*) bestowed upon him by God. Cerulli writes 'Ancient heathen magicians have been replaced by Muslim scholars, although they have kept their name *wadad* and may be also applied to magical practices. Propitiatory blessing is given as in paganism by spitting' (1957: 149). Furthermore, to be granted the *baraka*, it seems that one must be linked with a religious ancestor. As noted by Trimingham:

> The basis of the religious orders . . . in Islam is the notion that the believer who desires to attain communion with God needs the guidance of one who is experienced in the 'path' thereto, one who has been blessed by God on earth by special virtue (*baraka*), and who can act as an intermediary between the disciple and God. The founders of the *tariqas* were such guides and their spiritual *descendants inherit* their *baraka* and continue their functions to this day.
>
> (1965: 233) [italics added on the words 'descendants inherit']

Trimingham here uses the word 'spiritual descendants' to denote how spiritual power (*baraka*) is passed on. I suggest that the inheritance of divine power though the blood of the sacred lineage (kinship) is key to this argument. Martin noted 'In Arab societies, who one's father was and the identity of one's ancestors carries great weight' (1974: 369). Genealogy and kinship are important factors in the transfer of ritual power from one generation to the other.

This sacred (spiritual) kinship and ancestral veneration are, I would argue, intertwined. Within the Konso, Hallpike noted;

> It seems that senior men are respected not only for the personal qualities of wisdom and restraint which they have developed, but because they are at the same time the repository of morality and right conduct, and to this extent their status is analogous to God's. I was told for example that one's grandfather 'is like God', and their concept of God's authority is explicitly paternalistic. It is thus appropriate that it is the elders who should have the prime responsibility for blessing.
>
> (Hallpike, 1972: 135, see also p. 219)

As I noted above, it was suggested to me that Somalis would have been born without religion had it not been for Saint Aw-Barkhadle. Such a belief suggests perceptions of inheritance, or of being born with religion, as if religion was something to be passed down through lineage. Furthermore, Cerulli noted (1957: 149) that the life-giving aspect and magic of pre-Islamic traditional priests and *wadaads* was also hereditary – and so too was the office of chief itself in the religion of the Sky-God.

An understanding of Somali ancestral worship is pivotal to comprehending the Somali Myth of Origin. The former seems to have predated the latter: the Qurayshi genealogies name Sheikh Isaaq and Sheikh Darood as some of the sheikhs venerated by their descendants. Somali genealogy is clearly patrilineal. I am mindful of Andrezejewski's analysis of the importance of oral history in the study of Sufism in Somalia (Adrezejewski, 1974) and I will therefore continue to recount the local oral record as it was told to me. My male interviewees gave many versions and were very knowledgeable about the patrilineage and the history of the region. The statement made by one of my interviewees, 'Hassan's' account, reads almost like a textbook version of lineage:

> There were six *muhaajiriin* [followers of the Prophet, Mohamed, proselytizers of Islam], immigrant families, Sheikh Isse, Sheikh Isaaq, Sheikh Samaroon, Sheikh Abdirahman Sayli'i, Sheikh Abaadir, and Sheikh Yusuf Al Kawnayn [Aw-Barkhadle]. All of these sheikhs have at about the same time left their Arab homeland and come to the Somali northern region. They were Arabs. After that, some of the six were dispersed and others went to the same region. Three of them went to places that are quite close to each other, the Sheikh and Maydh areas, with about forty km in between; Sheikh Iise, Sheikh Isaaq and Sheikh Samaroon. The other three dispersed; Sheikh Abaadir went to Harar in Ethiopia, Sheikh Sayli'i ended up in Zayla and Sheikh Yusuf al-Kawnayn in Aw-Barkhadle [the site named after him], Hargeisa. The three Sheikhs had all come to places without religion [meaning 'pagan']. The three that have gone West have all left offspring. The Iise descend from Sh. Iise. Sh. Isaaq has founded the Isaaq clan. Both of them have their graves in Maydh. Sh. Samaroon is the father of the Gadebuursi clan. His grave is somewhere near Hiis.
>
> ("Hassan", pers. comm. 2007; cf. "Sufi leader", pers. comm. 2007)

With the exception of the burial site of Sh. Abaadir in the Harar region, I have visited the burial sites of the five other sheikhs: Sheikh Isaaq (Figure 5.7), Sheikh Samaroon (Figure 5.8); Sh. Iise (Figure 5.9); Sh. Sayli'i (Figure 5.10); and Sh. Sharif Yusuf Aw-Barkhadle. According to my interviewees, the Isaaq clan's mother came from the Magaal people (one of the peoples living in this region at the time of his arrival – there are still descendants of this clan living today) and Isaaaq's other wife who gave birth to his children was a *Habuusha* (an Ethiopian). It is interesting that the other wife is thought to have been a *Habuusha* since this indicates the existence of a people referred to as *Habasha* at the time. In the Horn of Africa, to identify someone as an Ethiopian probably had more to do with religion than territory, especially as today's borders are the result

Figure 5.7 Tomb of Sheikh Isaaq, Sanaag

Figure 5.8 Tomb of Sheikh Samaroon, Sanaag

Figure 5.9 Tomb of Sheikh Iise, Sanaag

of twentieth-century colonial politics. Was this woman thought to be an Ethiopian or was she referred to as an Ethiopian in order to imply that she was 'pagan', or Christian? This notion would be congruous with the myth that there were no Somali people in the area: a Somali, it seems, must be descended from the Qurayshi tribe and hence Somalis cannot predate the arrival of Sh. Isaaq, Sh. Darood and other Arab clan-founding sheikhs. Patrilineal society only accepts and records the names of the fathers, not

Figure 5.10 Tomb of Sheikh Sayli'i, Zayla

the mothers. The argument goes that the Somali people are Qurayshi, descending from the Prophet Muhammad's divine lineage. This ideology has served to eliminate not only the pre-Islamic genealogical tree on the mothers' sides but also any possibility of a Somali pre-Islamic existence. In theory, the Islamic Myth of Origin establishes a Somali as being a Muslim through the Qurayshi sacred lineage.

From a religious perspective, one must remember that:

> Since there is no God but Allah and Mahammad is His Prophet, religious prestige is connected with the Prophet's Qurayshi lineage. Thus, those in whose blood (recorded in personal genealogies) the Prophet's grace (Baraka) flows, are eminently suitable for election to the office of *khalifa*, head of an Order or of sheikh, head of congregation. Sheikhs and *khalifas*, as also the founders of the Orders themselves, have personal genealogies tracing descent from ancestors connected with the Prophet Mahammad.
>
> (Lewis, 1998: 10)

Where Lewis writes about 'those in whose blood (recorded in personal genealogies) the Prophet's grace (*Baraka*) flows', I take this to mean the sacred blood which justifies the religious figures' legitimacy to lead. Each *jama'a* is identified with the genealogy of the *khalifa* or sheikh, and even if the practitioner's genealogy is separate from the sheikh's genealogy, as noted by Lewis, that too is entailed with religious power (1998: 11).

Within the Sufi brotherhoods, the followers are also thought to possess religious power and are sometimes able to mediate disputes and thus have an impact on the tribal structure (Lewis, 1998). In such an all-encompassing relationship between followers and their identity, it is evident that no reference is here to be found to pre-Islamic Somalis in the rationale of the Somali Muslim Myth of Origin. As will be shown below, conversion to Islam has resulted in centuries of complex processes of alteration as well as the adaptation of identities, including genealogies and religions.

In summary, the Arab immigrants in southern Somalia, such as the Ashraaf (the sharifs), who descend from groups of Arab immigrant traders, are considered to be of Qurayshi origin and also perhaps linked with Sharifs from the Ba Alawi clan of Hadramaut in Arabia, who lived in the Mogadishu area (Cerulli, 1957; Martin, 1974). The Ashraaf use their Hashimite clan link with the prophet to their advantage. They function as peacemakers within groups such as the Saraman tribes in the Somali southern region; they also exist in the northern region, to where these Ashraaf seem to have spread (Cerulli, 1957; cf. Lewis, 1998: 18). Today, people generally respect the descendants of the Ashraaf due to their supposed Qurayshi origin.

Syncretism of rituals

The impacts of conversion to Islam on 'Cushitic Institutions'

This genealogical association with religious figures was also a part of the Cushitic tradition (Cerulli, 1957). According to the Sky-God belief, the religious leaders are the bringers of life (Hallpike, 1972: 252–253; Cerulli, 1957: 149; Loo, 1991). Both the Somali pre-Islamic *wadaads* and the priests of the Oromo and the Konso provide life through rituals involving purity, reconciliation and fertility. This is partly why Lewis suggests that Sufism fitted easily alongside these institutions in its focus on religious ancestors. The new *wadaads*, the men of religion of the Sufi, came over time to take on the role of the Cushitic religious leaders (Cerulli, 1957: 204–207; cf. Lewis, 1998: 14). *Wadaads* and *qadi* act as mediators between the clans and the communities. 'It is probably through the *wadaads* who issue from the *jama'a* communities that Sufism exerts its greatest influence in Somali social structure' writes Lewis (1998: 14). Sufism has a great role in the social structure not only in terms of the adaptation of religious figures and the building of *jama'a* but also in matters to do with land rights. Since the Sufi sheikhs (also known as *wadaads*) unite people across the clans, they can become involved in settling inter-clan issues regarding land. As noted earlier, the word *wadaad* is the Somali term for a religious figure (Cerulli, 1957; Lewis, 1998). The *wadaad's* role in pre-Islamic times was to mediate between the sacred and the profane.

During the period of Islam and in secular governmental institutions in the last 50 years, *wadaads* seem to mediate not only between Allah and the Muslim Somali but also between the secular (governing institutions) and the people in conflicts relating to resources. As noted by Cerulli, the community has rights beyond those enjoyed by virtue of being clan members. The Italian administration helped to strengthen the *jama'as* by appointing official *qadis* from the ranks of Sufi sheikhs (*wadaads*) (Cerulli, 1957: 207). The mediatory role of such religious men in secular institutions might echo the persistence of the fundamental ideas that Sufism also embodies (Lewis, 1998). I give examples below of syncretism and the adaptation of indigenous concepts and Cushitic genealogies, such as by those Oromo living amongst the Somali in certain areas of the Somali/Ethiopian border. This will be discussed in more detail in the following section.

The Sky-God religion

Although very little is known about its religious institutions, there is evidence to suggest that the Cushitic speaking peoples of north east Africa (cf. Paulitschke, 1888: 58; cf. Conti Rossini, 1905; Cerulli, 1957; Lewis, 1994b, 1998; Loo, 1991; Rikitu, 2001: 146; Ullendorff, 1955) shared a common belief in the Sky-God (or Heaven God), even though very little is known about its institutions. The word *Waaq (Waaq/Waaqa, waga)* refers to the Sky-God historically and today means God among the Oromo, Konso, Burji, Haddiya, Tasmai, Dasenech, Gedeo, Arbore, Elmolo, Bayso, Rendille, Afar and Somali, to mention but a few. All these groups are Eastern Cushitic speakers. It is also generally accepted that *Waaq* is associated with fertility rituals. These rituals include rain-making and are linked to crop, animal and human reproduction.

Lewis's comparison of the characteristics of the Sky-God *Waaq* and Allah is useful in terms of understanding the nature of *Waaq*. His comparison suggests both how the new religion might have translated itself into the divine quality of a local god (*Waaq*) and how the nature and power of the ancient traditional Sky-God resembles the concept of Allah:

> Although clearly delineated with greater precision, the absolute supremacy of Allah (indicated in the believer's submission (Islam) to Him) closely resembles the omnipotence of the Sky-God. As in the cult of Waaq, men are God's creatures, subject to His Will and must live in constant fear of Him and praise Him always. Similarly, to Waaq, Allah stands at the centre of His universe as its Supreme Power and Creator.
>
> (Lewis, 1998: 26)

Making sense of the possible syncretism of religions, rituals and sacred space may help to shed light on the pre-Islamic use of landscape, including the archaeological features associated with it.

Syncretism is a term, which in comparative religion refers to a process of religious amalgamation, of blending heterogeneous beliefs and practices. As such, it is an aspect of religious interaction over time. This can be seen as such a broad process that indeed every religion is syncretistic, since it constantly draws upon heterogeneous elements to the extent that it is often impossible for historians to unravel what comes from where.

(Veer, 1994: 208)

The process of syncretism is also unambiguous in other parts of the world. It is well established that many Muslims in their interpretation of Islam appropriated pre-Islamic religious elements to the extent that it is now difficult to say what is or is not Islamic (Insoll, 1999, 2003; see also Veer, 1994). Hinduism, for example, has had an influence on South Asian Islam (Forward, 1994) and it seems only natural that such processes took place in the Cushitic speaking region too. Has, then, local Somali Islam been influenced by the pre-Islamic Cushitic institutions? In attempting to answer this question, I focus not so much on the theology of the Cushitic religion as on the symbolism of the rituals, material culture and landscapes associated with its practice.

Syncretism of genealogies and names

The use of the term *Waaq* in Somali society has been noted by Cerulli (1957), Mohammed (1991) and Lewis (1998). The intermixing of Oromo and Somali groups is also longstanding and has contributed to the growth of various clans and sub-clans. For example: 'The Waaqbarre, who are attached to the Dabarre tribe, comprise three sections and have mixed traditions of connection with the Oromo Arussi and descend from a "Great Arabian Sheikh"' (ibid.: 18). Names such as 'Dabarre' and 'Waaqbarre' suggest pre-Islamic deities, the suffix *'barre'* meaning literally 'the one that worships' so that these names come to indicate the worship of *Da* or *Waaq* (see also Cerulli, 1957: 177–186). Somali Cushitic society adopted Sufism more readily than it adopted other types of Islam and some parts of the Shariah (Cerulli, 1957: cf. Lewis, 1998). This is due to the nature of the indigenous institutions and the fact that they were, importantly, compatible with a theocracy such as Sufism. I would add that the notion of a divine ancestor who grants fertility may similarly have been a local belief that was incorporated into Somali Sufi Islam.

In Muslim Somali society, the pre-Islamic Cushitic name of god, *Waaq*, corresponds directly with Allah. It is important to note that Somalis believe that the name *Waaq* is of Somali origin and not adopted from the Oromo, as Lewis confirms (1998: 136). In other words, the fact that Somalis use the name *Waaq* is not due to a post-Islamic adoption of the term *Waaq* from traditional Oromo groups; instead, it is a pre-Islamic term for God in the

Somali language as well (ibid.). In short, it is an Eastern Cushitic word (cf. Ehret, pers. com. Mire, 2015b).

The continuation in the use of the pre-Islamic name for god, *Waaq*, is due to a syncretism and Somalisation of Arabic names whereby Allah becomes *Waaq* (Lewis, 1998). In a similar way, the Islamic name Abdullaahi (the servant of Allah) has been translated into a Somali name, *BiddeWaaq*, which corresponds directly (cf. Mansur, 1995: 121). Having established that the word *Waaq* is Allah, it is remarkable that there are today 23 Somali names for God which are also used to denote Allah. It is likely that some, if not all of them, predate Islam (as *Eebe* and *Waaq* do) since they are considered to be ancient (Cerulli, 1957). They are therefore likely to have been used as names for the Sky-God. I also note that the word *eeba* in Guji Oromo means blessing (Loo, 1991: 343).

Others have already argued that pre-Islamic customs and practices have lived on (Cerulli, 1957; cf. Lewis, 1998: 136) and I will return to this later. Similarly, phenomena such as rain-making are pre-Islamic rituals that have been incorporated into Islam in much the same way as Islam has been adopted into a local traditional way of life. The discussion that follows highlights the most salient aspects of the Sky-God religion and its 'Cushitic institutions'.

The origins of the Sky-God Waaq in the Horn and an ideology of fertility

The bulk of the evidence regarding the Sky-God *Waaq* comes from an analysis of library sources. These include linguistic, ethnographic and anthropological studies into the Eastern Cushitic groups of southern and eastern Ethiopia, Eritrea, Somalia and northern Kenya. Although Somalis are Sunni Muslims, there appears to survive within Somali society traces of certain indigenous material elements, institutions and practices. This has resulted, it seems, in the syncretism of preexisting Cushitic and other practices with Islam. When studying the syncretism of ideas, it is not always easy to decide what is pre-Islamic and what is contemporaneous with Islam. It is therefore important to construe evidence *only* where the evidence is unambiguous. The Somali do not worship the Sky-God nowadays but there is evidence that they once did during and before Islamisation (Cerulli, 1957; cf. Lewis, 1994a, b, 1998). Also, as already noted, Somalis do use the word *Waaq* to refer to God (Allah). Lewis wrote,

> The form of Islam followed – Sufism (Islamic mysticism) – reflects the syncretism of Mohammedanism with the common Cushitic religion of the peoples before their conversion to the new religion.
>
> (1994a: 11)

In Chapter Four, I noted how the *zar* (spirit possession) originally denoted the Cushitic god and that it originated in the Agao name for God-Heaven *djar* which then became *zar* (Cerulli, 1957: 178; cf. Ullendorff, 1955). I also note that *tosa*, *zar* and *Waaq* are all names for the Sky-God (cf. Levine, 2000). Cerulli observed that within Somali society, *zar* is invoked as well as exorcised; 'In Somaliland only do we find, besides the exorcist rites, other ceremonies intended to procure the incarnation of the genius' (Cerulli, 1957: 153). Furthermore, I recall a Somali song for *zar* which seems to support two points: that *zar* is associated with the sky or heaven, and that it is not only a force to be driven out but also a power to be called upon: '*soo dageey soo dageey saarkii duleed oow soo dageey*' which translates 'Land! Land! The *zar* of the above/heaven. Land.' It was through the Christianisation and Islamisation of the Cushitic populations that the Sky-God became *zar*, (Cerulli, 1957: 157):

> a malevolent genius; and in this way the animistic practices, which in the paganism of the Kushites were directed only to the minor superhuman beings, passed into Abyssinian Christianity (and then into Islam) with the proper name of God-Heaven who had been reduced to a minor rank.

Thus, *zar* became the name of the 'ancient sacred dance' (Cerulli, 1957: 148) for the Sky-God. Currently there is a belief that the *zar* (the spirit) dwells in mountains, streams, rivers and springs. I suggest this echoes the relevance of fertility, including rain-making, to a belief in *Waaq*.

Common origin of the Eastern Cushitic groups and the Sky-God Waaq

The Sky-God is thought to be a common ancestor of the Cushitic speaking groups (Loo, 1991: 284; Shack, 1966; Ullendorff, 1955). The Eastern Cushitic speaking peoples are believed to have many social characteristics in common: linguistic affiliations, common origins and a shared religious past. They also enjoy a common social organisation (cf. Lewis, 1998: 1). According to the linguist Mansur (1995: 118–122), various versions of a traditional myth of origin can be found amongst the Somali and other Cushitic peoples. The myth of origin states (with minor variations) that a girl (sometimes called Faaduma/Fatima in Somali or Maryam Atete by other currently Christian Eastern Cushitic groups, such as some Oromo, Sidamo, Janjero, Bako and others inhabiting southern Ethiopia) was once grazing animals when she found a man sitting on the branches of a tree. The man came from the sky (according to most versions) and married a local woman (cf. Luling, 1988). The Konso similarly have a myth about God who 'was close to the earth. A woman was hooking down *mida* tree. The hook struck God, and God bled upon the woman' (Hallpike, 1972: 223). In this version, God is the tree that the woman strikes and bleeds.

In Chapter Three, I suggested that this legend of the man on the tree could be linked to the present-day belief in sacred trees held by the Somali and other Eastern Cushitic speaking peoples of the region. For example, the traditionalist Oromo people believe that the spirit lives in the tree and they consult it directly as well as making offerings to it (Almeida, 1954; Trimingham, 1965; Loo, 1991). The Cushitic notion of sacred trees, the association of lineages with certain trees and the worship and consultation of trees (cf. Cerulli, 1957; Conti Rossini, 1905; Burton, 1966; Loo, 1991) appear to me to be linked back to this common Cushitic Myth of Origin and the reference to a man (ancestor) in a tree.

The nature of Waaq, the Sky-God

The Sky-God exists beyond the realms of daily life and is not directly worshipped. Worship is instead directed towards the spirits on earth, their mediums and the ancestor spirits. The Cushitic religion, as already noted, has not been well researched (Bartels, 1983; Baxter, 1990; Loo, 1991; Hallpike, 1972). It is known that *Waaq* was a name for the Supreme God of the Cushitic religion, the Sky-God, as Cerulli (1957) and others report. Other names for this god, as mentioned above, seem to be the word *zar* (or *saar* in Somali) and *tosa* (cf. Levine, 2000). It is also possible that the *adbar* of the Amhara originally related to the Sky-God – as may have *Athar* (comparable to *Adjar*, the Agao word for God) too, which is believed to be the Semitic or Cushitic semitised word for the same regional god. It has been suggested that the original name for the Sky-God was actually *zar*, a name used by the Agaw, a Cushitic group in southern Ethiopia who are thought to follow the original version of this religion (Conti Rossini, 1905: 109–122; cf. Cerulli, 1957: 178–180; Ullendorff, 1955). Almeida's record from the sixteenth century mentions the Cushitic religions of the Agao:

> The Agaws of Gojam are pagans and much given to fetishism. They adore a single Creator of Heaven, whom they call Doban, but have no idols. They also worship river springs, also some species of trees and groves, sacrificing to them and offering cows, milk and butter. They bury their bodies in woods, making chambers for them and placing near heads hydromel and the cups which they were accustomed to use in drinking when alive.
> (Almeida, 1954: 20; also quoted in Trimingham, 1965: 17)

Révoil, too, wrote from the Somali Nugaal valley (1882: 343): 'I have nevertheless observed that they attach a certain veneration to the tree *ganda*, because the breakage of a branch would bring the death of a close parent.' For the traditionalist Cushitic speaking peoples, the Sky-God is regarded as a divine and almighty power. Loo furthermore suggests that 'since *Waaqa* must be the origin of male and female the deity must possess both masculine and feminine characteristics' (1991: 284). *Waaq* is metaphorically equated with the unity (oneness) of husband and wife, according to Loo. 'To trust *Waaqa* is an indication of the fundamental belief that *Waaqa*, who is the source and origin of all that exists, also cares for creation by protecting it and by bestowing it with fertility, abundance, and peace' (Loo, 1991: 284). *Waaq* grants fertility, good health, peace (*nagea*), abundance and good relations between all his creations, between nature and people and between human beings.

Incidentally, expressions for the act of giving milk as a gift in the Oromo language, particularly as documented by Loo (1991), are remarkable. Words and concepts such as *daaba* and *gumaata* refer to sharing milk. An abundance of milk (*aano* in Somali and *aanan* in Oromo), and the rituals in which milk features, form a significant part of life in the Horn of Africa. Somali chiefs are crowned with a shower of milk. A plentiful supply of such goodness depends entirely on the successful performance of rituals, offerings and ceremonies including those promoting peacemaking and fertility. It is significant to note that, incidentally, the famous Horn of Africa cows that feature in the rock art of the last three or four thousand years depicts cows always with full udders.

It is important to grasp what *Waaq* entails from the point of view of the different Cushitic groups associated with it – and to use these characteristics to highlight the relationships involved. I have found Heusch's perspective (1985) helpful in considering my Somali case study. His 'binary oppositions' or 'counterpoints' may be useful in structuring the web of Somali cultural phenomena that consist of men and women, death and life, official and private, dry and wet, fertility and infertility, circumcised and uncircumcised, divine and profane etc. Yet this metaphysical approach is not without its challenges. What role, for example, do the ancestors play in bridging the divine and the profane? Or why are 'killing and bearing' equated by some Oromo groups?

When a problem arises, for example when a woman is barren, it is recognised that this is due to *Waaq's* will. The key to resolving the problem is to sacrifice more, to keep the peace and to make *Waaq* change the situation for the better (Loo, 1991: 284–285, 155). According to the Cushitic institutions, people have a good or bad *ayaana*, the ability/destiny/quality which they bring with them at birth. If a person is close to God then he/she will have unique qualities gained through her/his prayers and sacrifices – and these qualities are divine. Given that *ayaana* is sometimes equated with *Waaqa* (the Sky-God), it is essential to understand the qualities of *ayaana* in the sayings, songs and blessings of the Guji Oromo in order to grasp fully the specific meaning(s) attributed to this God. Loo notes (1991: 145): '*ayaana* practically figures as a manifestation of the *Waaqa*-deity. It carries in these contexts the meaning of divine presence, and hence, a particularization of *Waaqa's* generative power . . . or active force in man.' As Bartels put it 'A son of *Waqa* has *Waqa's* ability' (quoted in Loo, 1991: 145; cf. Bartels, 1983; Hallpike, 1972: 135).

I suggest the statement 'A son of *Waaqa* has *Waaqa's* ability' echoes what I call a *divine* kinship, a concept that demonstrates the relationship between the divine and the follower in a way that resembles that between a father and a child. A male child is an extension of a lineage and fertility is therefore legitimately granted. This concept may be related in some way to the notion of Bu'ur Ba'ayr and Gedi Baabow and various pre-Islamic Cushitic deities who may have had divine or semi-divine attributes. At Aw-Barkhadle, I learnt that Bu'ur Ba'ayr's granting of a marriage was dependent upon his possession of the bride for the first six nights of her marriage. In Chapter Three, I suggested that the ritual intercourse noted in the Bu'ur Ba'ayr's legend had the effect of Bu'ur Ba'ayr granting fertility through this act. The Konso *poĝalla* (lineage head and priest) is, according to Hallpike, the bringer of Life: 'Life, as I have already said, is manifested for them in the fertility of women, animals, and crops; the *poĝalla* or priest is pre-eminently the bringer of Life, in his role as sacrificer' (Hallpike, 1972: 18–19). *Waaq* is an omnipresent God and a divine source of life. Bartels writes 'the presence of life means the presence of *Waaq*' (1983: 97). Did Bu'ur Ba'ayr have '*Waaqa*'s ability' to bring Life? Is this what the ritual intercourse, symbolic or otherwise, would mean?

The role of the Sky-God and mediation of Cushitic power into Muslim Baraka

Certain names denoting natural phenomena are linked with *Waaq*. *Barwaaqo*, for example, means earthly/worldly paradise, an abundance of the good things, and usually refers to prosperity linked with crops and livestock. Rain is vital for the Somali, both agriculturalists and pastoralists, and rain-making appears to be one of *Waaq's* main characteristics (Hallpike, 1972: 229; Loo, 1991). *Barwaaqo* (in Somali) denotes the 'rain of God', *bar* meaning a drop of rain. The word *barwaaqo* can also mean 'a sign of *Waaq*/God'.

The Somalis no longer worship the Sky-God (cf. Lewis, 1998: 136). Traditionally, *wadaads* mediated or transmitted *Waaq's* blessings. This blessing is now sought instead from Allah through the Muslim saints as part of 'the translation of Cushitic power into Muslim *baraka*' (Lewis, 1998: 29). The fact that rituals such as rain-making ceremonies and human fertility rituals still persist and blend in with Islam today may indicate just how deeply rooted these practices are: within Somali Muslim society, these rituals are performed by Islamic figures in accordance with traditional Cushitic customs (cf. Lewis, 1998).

There is a myth amongst the Guji Oromo that *Waaqa* (the Sky-God) was close to the earth in ancient times but gradually moved further away into the sky where he currently resides (Loo, 1991). *Waaqa* left in His place messengers to guard His creation. These messengers include birds and divine human beings close to Him who help people to know how to lead their lives. One example is the *Abba gada*, the leader of the Gada (also named the *Qallu*), and his assistants who, like other successful members of society, are considered to be blessed by *Waaqa* and so able to bless others. The purity and saintliness of a leader known in Oromo as *qallu* is critical for ritual success. Loo recalls an Oromo saying: 'The birds from *Waaqa* are like Qallu' (ibid.: 285). Today, there are birds considered to belong to saints. In Somali society, the eagle (*bas*) is associated with Sh. 'Abdiqaadir Jailaani who is the founder of the Qaadiriya Order. I myself have found a stele in the shape of a bird marking a grave at the burial site of Sufi Orgome,[1] in Bandar Wanaag near Maygaagyada in the east of Hargeisa.

> The semantic relation is eyes, seeing, sun, and light. The God's eternal constancy is compared to the centre-pole of the hut. 'May the centre-pole be as of iron.' Without support man's house collapses, but God, 'the same without the centre-pole', is full of wonder and power. According to Cerulli, in the 1930s, Somalis still sang: 'This Sky, the same unchanging, without the central-pole according to the Divine Will'. The Sky-God's belt is the rainbow, and the rains are in his keeping as gift for man; certain individuals have power over the rains through their relation to God.
>
> (Lewis, 1998: 22–23)

Lewis's observation, taken together with the Oromo saying, suggests that somebody with a divine ability (somebody with good *ayaana*, talents or skills) can pray for another with a bad *ayaana* or who is suffering a misfortune. There is another Guji Oromo saying: '*Waaqa bobaana ke'ati, booba'anan buufatini*,' 'May God keep you under my armpit, may you never go out of his armpit' (Loo, 1991: 87). This suggests *Waaq's* harmonious endorsement and protection of his followers.

The notion of the armpit reminds me of the story of how a traditional healer treated me for an unknown illness when British doctors in Hargeisa could not. The healer (*wadaad*) performed one single ritual: he put his hand under his armpit and smeared my face with his sweat – luckily, I was only one year old at the time – and with that action apparently ended months of suffering. The illness, however, had in reality started when my babysitting cousin had given me milk so hot that it burned my stomach. Yet no one attributed my healing to the aspirin I was apparently regularly taking as a treatment. The important thing is that traditional treatments possess a gravitas grounded upon the fact that they are the traditional beliefs that people have always resorted to and, most significantly, still do. Even the educated go to healers, and the *wadaad* performs a ritual that, as in my own case it seems, marks the end of the search for a cure.

Does the Oromo saying above bear any relevance to my healer's armpit? If it does, then this would suggest that the armpit of Waaq's representative on Earth, the *wadaad*, had come to symbolise the armpit of Waaq, in accordance with the Cushitic institutions. It also reminds me of another Oromo saying 'A son of *Waaqa* has *Waaqa's* ability' (Loo, 1991: 145). According to this, the *wadaad* would be practicing a skill, in this case of healing, as a son of God, in accordance with traditional Cushitic beliefs. Again, the notion indicates a kinship relationship between the divine and the healer.

I now want to consider in more detail how far, if at all, rituals of pre-Islamic origin have survived in present-day Somali society. However, it is already clear from this study's conceptualisation and outline of Cushitic ancestral veneration that elements of Cushitic origin are integrated with Islamic practice (cf. Lewis, 1998). The wider appeal that the Aw-Barkhadle cult holds today might be due to the syncretistic character of the ritual space and the rituals that intermix with Cushitic institutions, and the veneration of Saint Aw-Barkhadle might form part of the continuity of ancestor veneration that is central to pre-Islamic 'Cushistic institutions'.

The issue of ritual continuity: sacrifice and sacred landscapes

The Cushitic notion of ancestral blessing and divine kinship

Spencer suggested that the beginnings of all religions lay in ancestor worship (1882: 41). As I noted earlier in the context of indigenous religion and Sufi Islam in Somali society, there is a notion that the divine power of a religious ancestor can be inherited. 'A son of *Waaqa* has *Waaqa's* ability' (Loo, 1991: 145; cf. Bartels, 1983). Ancestral worship is, therefore, a vital ritual in the process of the transmission of *Baraka* to the next generation.

> Their descendants [the descendants of saints] often formed holy families which lived under the shadow of their saintly ancestor, inheriting his *baraka*, and exploiting it. Some remained small families attached to the shrine and thrived on the gifts of pilgrims, others in nomad areas formed the nuclei of new grouping, some (e.g. Ad Sheikh) developed into tribal groups taking the form of the society they grew up in, whilst others were scattered amongst the tribes as clans of teachers (e.g. Ad Mu'allim) or qadis and religious functionaries or wonder-workers.
>
> (Trimingham, 1965: 248)

Awliyo or '*Wali'allah*' ('a friend of God') usually refers to a Sufi saint or sheikh. In this context, a Sufi saint is someone who stands closest to God through his longstanding devotion and worship; he is someone who bestows blessings on the people who turn to him for support.

For an ancestor to bless someone, he or she must have been close to God (and a good Muslim) in life. A Somali saying goes, '*khaatimada khayr ku qadim*', 'finish your late age with goodness/blessings.' Since older people seem to become more religious with age, at the end all ancestors might come to be described as religious ancestors (*awliyo*).

I argue that ideas such as the notion of the veneration of eponymous ancestors – who were close to God and whose prayers have led to an abundance

of crops, animals and people – are indigenous ideologies that remain significant to Somalis today. This is reflected in the way Sufism has adopted these
local ideas in a way that seems to facilitate a continuity in many areas of life.

It appears to be well established that Cushitic speaking groups spend
more time in the veneration of their lineage founders through ancestor worship (e.g. Baxter, 1990; Loo, 1991). Worship at ancestor tombs is thought
to have existed within Cushitic religious practice before Islam entered this
part of the world (Lewis, 1998; Loo, 1991; Trimingham, 1965). According
to local tradition, death is seen as a transformation after which the tombs of
the dead are tended constantly and become a place of ritual (Lewis, 1998;
Thesiger, 1935). Since Cushitic tradition holds that the lineage founders are
religious men, the veneration of lineage founders becomes the most important ritual for the lineage leaders to observe (Lewis, 1998: 6). The Islamic
Sufi *ziyara* (veneration) of Sufi saints and sheikhs has now replaced the
Cushitic practice of the worship of ancestors.

Somali genealogy is, as I have already shown, another example of the
integration of Cushitic (non-Islamic) and Islamic (Sufi) practices and traditions. Somali people believe that they originate from Arabia; they claim a
divine genealogical link to the Prophet Muhammad and the Quraysh, the
Prophet's tribe. They venerate Saint Aw-Barkhadle in the belief that there
exists through him a sacred link with the Prophet Muhammad's divine
Qurayshi lineage. Hubert and Mauss wrote 'Indeed, it is in the sacrifice of
a divine personage that the idea of sacrifice attains its highest expression'
(1964: 77). They discuss the notion of 'divine personage' in relation to the
act of *sacrifice* to saints (Hubert and Mauss, 1964: 66). This notion of the
divine power of a saint is crucial in the sense that the veneration of Sufi
saints is central to Aw-Barkhadle. And, equally, the issue of sacrifice to a
divine personage to whom people relate through genealogy was a crucial
feature of indigenous Cushitic institutions.

Five visits to Aw-Barkhadle's tomb are equal to one visit to Mecca, according to my interviewees. People come from northern Kenya, Yemen, Ethiopia,
Djibouti, Eritrea and southern Somalia to take part in the annual ceremony
in the landscape of Aw-Barkhadle. Lewis noted that in 'The Muslim world
generally, pilgrimages to the shrines of such local saints are usually known
as the 'poor man's *hajj*', thus making a direct equation with pilgrimage to
Mecca' (1996: 142). Saint Aw-Barkhadle's role was a pervasive one as can
be seen from the fact that he has followers amongst Cushitic speaking peoples from places as far away as northern Kenya, an area where traditionalist
groups still follow the Sky-God.

Cerulli noted that in Somalia there is a popular notion of afterlife:

> Continuation of the material life after death and the necessity of provid-
> ing food and clothes for the dead by making sacrifices of cattle near the
> tomb and distributing meat and calicoes to poor who are said 'to cause
> the food to reach' the dead. Thence arises the custom of fixing in the
> testaments a large share of the inheritance to celebrate those ceremonies

('what one is buried with'); and the affectionate care of the sons and relatives 'to sweep the tomb' that is to make those sacrifices from time to time.

(Cerulli, 1957: 149)

I am not sure how common this practice is (or indeed if it is at all common) but Cerulli's observations provide yet another example of the continuity and complexity of beliefs in the Somali region. Burying food with the deceased is one strand of evidence for the 'Cushitic substratum of Somali Mohammedanism' (Lewis, 1994a: 102), which is the Islamisation of older religious elements such as burial integration and the sacrificial offerings made 'at former shrines of Cushitic spirits' (Lewis, 1994a: 103).

The practice of placing pots with food at the grave or in the grave for the afterlife (Lewis, 1998) is condemned by Islamic religious figures. In conventional Islam, a person is buried with only a white sheet to cover the body. It is the only object that accompanies him or her into the grave. Hence, the notion of an afterlife that requires grave goods testifies to a continuation of pre-Islamic rituals into Islamic times. As noted earlier, offerings are made to the dead. Some Oromo groups leave cups in the grave for the afterlife. Further practices of Cushitic origin also take place during the veneration of ancestors. However, these types of pre-Islamic rites such as sacrificing to the dead and offering them food etc. (cf. Thesiger, 1935: 9–12) involve public ceremonies like the ones Lewis (1998) and Thesiger (1935) described. Nowadays these rituals are performed in private at family level, as I observed in the field. It is common for Somali and Oromo families to sacrifice an animal during Islamic feasts, such as *Eid*, to honour the dead family members. Within these societies offerings to the dead are made on a weekly basis. According to Somali tradition, the spirits of the dead visit their living relatives on a Friday, a Muslim holy day. People offer coffee by giving the earth coffee, literally spilling coffee on the ground; and the family also drink coffee (*bun*) together or burn incense to purify the house from any bad spirits and to consecrate the space to welcome their dead relatives. Interestingly, coffee is not only associated with ancestors but also with fertility – and the Oromo, like the Somali, also offer coffee for the same purpose, as I have already mentioned in a previous chapter.

With the exception of ancestral veneration, sacrifice for the afterlife and secret fertility rituals take place as described in Chapters Three and Four. Furthermore, some of the female fertility cults are totally secret and only known to, and shared amongst, women who are older or still fertile. Almost nothing is revealed to the outside world. *Wagar*, in particular, is not something that all women follow. The only places where people can still find *wagar* are in the northern part of the country and among the nomadic clans of the north. There are several explanations for this. One is that Somali society conforms more closely to an official version of Islam in the cities and centres while the periphery is not subject to strict Islamic rules. Outside the cities and urban centres, people more readily coexist with their Cushitic speaking neighbours, some of whom still worship a shared Cushitic religion, a factor which contributes to the continuity of some local traditional religious practices amongst the Somali.

Ancestral veneration and snake worship in the Horn of Africa

Ancestral veneration may also be related to an ancient belief in snake worship in the Horn of Africa. Some Somali clans are associated with snakes. For example, there is a story involving a clan and a sub-clan in which the clan had made a pact with the snake. When the sub-clan founder Mahmud Saleban of the Majirteen was born and placed on a mat, a snake was found coiling itself around him (Cerulli, 1957: 78). The snake was seen as the child's protector (ibid.: 79) and the clan's ancestor (father, *aabo*). No member of the sub-clan was allowed to kill the snake, which, in turn, could not bite any of them – but if by any chance it did, then it would not poison them and their flesh was forbidden to the snake. Such totems and prohibitions can also be found amongst other Cushitic people such as the Konso whose clans are divided along religious lines (ibid.: 89–90). The association between snakes and ancestors is a widely recognised phenomenon in Somali traditional society, as I found during my fieldwork. Cerulli not only confirms that the veneration of snakes exists amongst the Muslim Somali, and particularly among the Majirteen clan, but states that this veneration might be a more widespread Cushitic practice:

> *A queste credenze sarebbe facile trovare paralleli, per esempio, presso i Galla perchè – come dicevo su – esse sono certamente connesse con la venerazione per il serpente, che è cosa generale nel paganesimo dei popoli Cusciti. È in ogni modo interessante trovare ancora così viva questa venerazione presso i Somali Migertini gia musulmani da secoli.*
> (Cerulli, 1957: 79)

Translation;

> It is easy to find parallels to these beliefs, for instance among the Galla, as I mentioned above, where these are definitely linked to the veneration of snakes, a common feature of the paganism of the Cushitic. It is, in any case, interesting to still find alive such veneration among the Majerteen clan of the Somali, who were already Muslim for centuries.
> (Cerulli, 1957: 79)

Cerulli is here suggesting that snake worship is also found amongst the Oromo groups. He suggests connections between the veneration of snakes and the 'pagan' religion of the Cushitic people. Furthermore, the *Qallu*, or religious leader, of the Oromo and the Konso wears the *kallacha*[2] on his head (Knutsson, 1967). I believe the *kallacha* to be a phallic symbol.[3] It is associated with a cobra and decorated with snakeskin. This tradition bears a striking similarity to one reported from Upper Egypt[4] where the kings were protected by a snake, *uraeus* (Hassan, 1998b). This symbol of a snake (often representing a cobra) is worn on the heads of rulers and of gods and goddesses as a symbol of divine authority.

In the Horn of Africa, I suggest, ancestral veneration and snake worship are indeed related, and in a relationship that can perhaps be traced back to the Sky-God religion. Creation myths associated with snakes are also found in the Horn of Africa (e.g. Hallpike, 1972: 251). The priests and important fertility rituals amongst the Konso involve snakes. The snake symbolises concepts of leadership and religious status as well as fertility and resurrection. As noted in Chapter Two, Aksumite culture has its roots in pre-Aksumite culture (Phillipson, 1997). Was the pre-Christian religion of the Aksum kingdom related to serpent worship? Phillipson writes;

> it is less surprising than might at first sight appear that traditional sources which, in their present form, do not predate the thirteenth century, seem to contain memories of events which took place over a thousand years earlier. . . . There are memories of serpent-worship which, as argued above, may reflect a dim memory of belief systems which prevailed in pre-Christian times.
>
> (ibid.: 141, 112)

Snake worship is clearly relevant to the archaeology of the Horn of Africa. Furthermore, it can be found in other adjacent regions too, for example in pre-Islamic eastern Arabia (Potts, 2007). In the ancient history northeast African region snake religious symbolism is prevalent (Figure 5.11).

The potential relationship between the stelae of Ethiopia and snake iconography is discussed in Chapter Six.

The landscapes of sacred Sufi centres and syncretism of space

"Sacred landscape"

Ethnographic and recent archaeological studies of religiously and ritually significant landscapes in Africa shed light on how archaeologists can make use of the data to understand continuity and significance of landscapes and beliefs (e.g. Colson, 1997; Mather, 2003; Loubser, 2008).

In her study of the plateau Tongo from Zimbabwe, Colson explained her definition of the locale of ritual in her discussions of 'places of power' and 'shrines of the land'. She associates the former with:

> permanent features of the landscape regarded as inherently sacred or the loci of spiritual power. If they are associated with particular named

Figure 5.11 Tutankhamun's mask with the snake headdress

Source: (copyright: Rijksmuseum van Oudheden, Leiden)

spirits rather than generic spirits or un-personified force, these spirits are usually mythologized as ancient heroes who existed before present political units or communities came into existence or they are conceived as spiritual forces of non-human origin.

(Colson, 1997: 52)

'Places of power' are thought to be landscapes which possess 'mountains, cliffs, caves, pools, waterfalls, hot springs, and large trees' and become 'sacred' places due to people's relationship with them and the meaning they attribute to them (cf. Colson, 1997; Scarre, 2008: 212). Aw-Barkhadle at present includes a so-called well, a 'mountain' (or rather a hill), trees and stones all credited with sacred status. These are natural features associated with the cultural attributes that people give them. 'Places of power', however, are viewed as being isolated from places of everyday activities (Scarre, 2008: 211–212). It should be noted that this is not the case at Aw-Barkhadle where its landscape was once an actively used area as is demonstrated by the ruined town walls, house structures and foundations, pottery scatters and incense burners. 'Shrines of the land', on the other hand, are:

> Built by humans and the spirits commonly associated with them are the spirits of those reputed to have first settled the locality or to have subsequently conquered and ruled it. They require offerings from those who now occupy their places, and adherence to routines established by themselves.
>
> (Colson, 1997: 52)

'Shrines of the land' indicate man-made features in the landscape, and their qualities are thought to be particularly due to the (usually named) individuals and deities associated with these features. Aw-Barkhadle generally fits the description of 'shrines of the land' though in some respects it also fits the description of 'places of power' given its hill and other natural features. This suggests that there may not always be such a clear-cut distinction between 'places of power' and 'shrines of the land' (cf. Scarre, 2008: 212). In the case of Aw-Barkhadle, it might be more appropriate to use the term 'sacred landscape', the main reason being that people without exception believe this landscape to be sacred. The fact that people are buried there and that only ritual acts are allowed there is also important. No one can own the land or build on it. Its pre-Islamic history is linked with the legend of Bu'ur Ba'ayr even though it is now known from the archaeological evidence that it was once a town with multireligious burial traditions that spanned the pre-Islamic, Christian and Islamic periods. Today the man-made lake, or well, is associated with Saint Aw-Barkhadle who is perceived to have created it miraculously; in pre-Islamic times, this *wadi* (*doox/tog*) might well have been associated with *Waaq*.

It is important to note that something that is sacred is not necessarily benign. Certain sacred trees, for example, are avoided by pregnant women, and fertile cows are never allowed to seek shade beneath them. This is to prevent the tree/spirit from damaging the woman and her child or the animal. 'Power' too is not always benign. Trees are also themselves deities so that people come to see them as either the *ayaana* (in some respects *Waaq*) rather than as *loci* for the spirits. In the Horn of Africa, the trees can give blessings not because a spirit dwells in them or they provide a home for a spirit but because they *are* the spirit (or represent *ayaana*).

Another sacred landscape is that of Goroyo Cawl. This site consists of massive natural stones, partly buried in the ground and part of the ancient mountain rock of this region. Remarkable carvings adorn the largest rock at Goroyo Cawl, as has already been noted. The site is dedicated to Saint Aw-Barkhadle. The carved symbols are undated but suggest a non-/pre-Islamic ritual significance. However, again as noted (Chapter Three) this site was, during Islamic times, dedicated to Sharif Yusuf Al-Kawnayn (i.e. Aw-Barkhadle).

The reason for suggesting that these scared fertility stones might have had an earlier significance is that they seem to be related to the already mentioned massive natural Dameer Gowrac stones near Laaso and also to those at Dhaymoole; the stones from both these sites carry the particular symbols described in Chapter Three. Goroyo Cawl, Dhaymoole and Dameer Gowrac are all associated with pre-Islamic burial traditions which locals say belong to '*khuruumihii hore*' (ancient beings) or '*khuruumihii hore oolafo wayn*' (ancient beings with big bones). These sites, associated with ancient cultures by virtue of their (currently unintelligible) rock carvings and their non-Islamic graves, are also home to present-day myths (as noted in Chapter Three) which themselves are thought to be of ancient origin. Goroyo Cawl and Aw-Barkhadle, in particular, are used both by traditionalists and by the Somali Sufi Muslims who have appropriated them in a syncretic way.

In the Horn of Africa, the rock that comes from a sacred mountain is as sacred as the mountain itself. The Aw-Barkhadle hill and the Guraali mountain of the Afar (Thesiger, 1935: 8) are amongst those regarded as sacred places. But these places are also the actual deities that they house. Similarly, trees can be deities in pre-Islamic times: the *samayo* tree of the Yibir; the *wagar* of the Somali; and *odaa*, the sycamore of the Oromo. The *zar* (spirit) is thought not just to inhabit streams, rivers and springs but to be embodied in these features themselves. This is why it is more fitting to talk about a sacred landscape than it is to talk about, say, a shrine within it: there are living sacred beings here and the objects made from them are also sacred by virtue of the living sacred landscape in which they are settled. I have already noted how, in Cushitic tradition, the actual mountain is sacred because of its character or behaviour. Some springs come from mountains. This channelling of life (water) is one characteristic that leads to mountains being perceived as being themselves deities.

Sacrifice, the sacred and syncretism

Veneration of ancestors through making sacrifices at their tombs (Lewis, 1998: 2) is a characteristic of the Sky-God religion, as I have already shown. There is evidence to show that Eastern Cushitic speakers such as the Oromo, the Somali and the Konso used to place offerings and perform rituals at sacred tombs in ceremonies that probably resembled the ones still taking place today. In 1935, Thesiger noted that containers were placed in particular parts of the tombs; and Lewis wrote about *ziyara*

> This is the structural equivalent amongst the northern nomads of the annual commemorative ritual (*siyaaro*) in honour of an eponymous lineage ancestor. This is usually held at a traditional sacred centre, often the site at which the clan founders are said to have assembled to form the original alliance.

(ibid.: 83)

In terms of the Cushitic institutions and the cult of *Waaq*, it is the annual celebration held at the tombs of the founding ancestors of lineages that has survived. In this modern-day equivalent of *ziyara* can be found echoes of the pre-Islamic ceremonies: sacred trees continue to form the focus of pilgrimage for the Oromo and other Cushitic traditionalists and these sacred tree centres all have their custodians. The trees are decorated, cattle are sacrificed and food is offered to them (Trimingham, 1965: 260).

Modern religious appropriation of sacred spaces is also evident in the fact that ancient shrines have been transformed into Christian and Muslim sanctuaries and 'high places dedicated to saints and the sacred sycamore trees to the Virgin Mary' (Trimingham, 1965: 54). Lewis confirms this: 'As in all Muslim countries, old shrines continue to command respect although the source of their power has been transferred to Islam' (Lewis, 1998: 29).

Somali Muslim saints may well have visited these places during their travels or have been associated with them in some way. Included amongst them are the sacred landscapes of Sheikh Isaaq who is the lineage founder of the Isaaq clan, Sheikh 'Iise of the Iise clan and Sheikh Samaroon of the Samaroon clan (Figures 5.7–5.9). These sacred landscapes with their burial sites and tombs of the founders of Somali clans often include sacred wells, as will be discussed in the following section.

Tombs, shrines, hilltops, caves and wells

Sites of pilgrimages and sacrifices associated with *Waaq* can be divided into three types: tombs, hills, mountains and caves. Lewis notes that 'The tombs of Somali Muslim saints "commemorate pre-Islamic figures who have been assimilated in Islam" ' (Lewis, 1998: 15). I would add that there also appears to be a pre-Islamic importance attached to the places where the Muslim tombs were built. Features such as shrines, hilltops, wells, springs and caves that were originally associated with the religion of *Waaq* may have also been attractive to new religious leaders given that they were already in use as ritual spaces and sacred landscapes.

This appropriation of sacred landscapes is a common practice among the Eastern Cushitic groups; it seems to occur within similar landscapes and/or domains and tends to involve the use of similar sacred materials. Mukhtar (1995: 13) reported traditions of 'pagan' dynasties in Southern Somalia in the Doi belt – Gedi Baabow, Dubka Baalow, Feyle Araw, Barambara – using religiously significant sites located at Bur Hakaba, Bur Haybe, Bur Gerwiine and Gelway, to name but a few. He noted a syncretism of religious space through the appropriation of earlier rituals and landscapes resulting in a re-orientation of the landscape. These pre-Islamic sites are the subject of annual pilgrimages: the landscape of Doi with its 114 mountains, for example, for the Somali Rehenwayn clan (Mukhtar, 1995: 13). Similarly, the Konso also regard hills as important to their Cushitic religious practices (Hallpike, 1972: 226–227).

Furthermore, there are crop fertility and rain-making rituals among the Rehenwayn (Helander, 1986, 1996a, b; Cerulli, 1957) which are also known to take place in these landscapes. This is further evidence of the alteration and manipulation of myths to fit new belief systems, for example in the transformation of pre-Islamic (Cushitic) ideas to accommodate Islamic or Christian views. Sites associated with pre-Islamic lineage founders and ancestors change their names to become places devoted to Islamic saints and ancestors. It would seem this adaptation to Islam brought with it a means of protecting existing political power centres as they became Islamised through the adoption of new names.

The cave site of Abka Eden and Aboy Haawa (Adam and Eve) may offer an example of this. Mukhtar (1995) reports the existence of female saints in the Doi region, namely Edeegow Shanaayti who was associated with Bur Gerwiine, Oboy Imbiyow Hassan Diinow Ala in Abdurug and Dada Ma Siti in Barawa (ibid.). Trimingham suggested that Islam absorbed the local pagan cult (1971: 28). Such accounts fit well with ideas about relationships between groups, ritual landscape and the negotiation and reinvention of genealogical relations and religious affiliation.

At Aw-Barkhadle, the appropriation of its sacred space has been legitimised through the transfer of sacred power to Sufi sheikhs and the maintenance of the rituals. The Cushitic power to promote fertility has been transferred to Islamic blessings and *baraka* and Muslim sheikhs perform rain-making prayers (*roobdoon*) and the rituals designed to help women to become fertile.

Another example of this appropriation can perhaps be found amongst the Reer Sheikh Muumin of the Rehenwayn who venerate and sacrifice for a virgin-born eponymous saint. Lewis writes 'This is tangibly displayed in the votive offering-strewn shrine and tomb itself juxtaposed with that of the earlier mystically charged Haran Madare' (1998: 87). Thesiger notes (1935: 8) too that the Danakil, almost all of whom are Muslims, still made pilgrimages to sacred mountains such as Guraali Mountain to the northwest of Aussa. The Oromo (Loo, 1991) carry out similar sacred journeys to sacred places, with peoples singing about fertility and wishing for more calves, *tapa jabbi guutu'uuti*.

The landscape of the Doi belt of Somalia provides evidence of the past and the syncretism of religion in much the same way as does the north. The ritual importance of pre-Islamic beliefs seems to continue on in a pre-Islamic landscape that is alive with substantial non-Islamic 'pagan' influences. This fusion of beliefs, justified and maintained, is the base for the social and political structure of Somali society today.

Waaq is associated with the sky, rivers, rainbows and springs. Sufi Muslim saints are also themselves associated with water. In Somali, *bali* is a water source. This Somali sheikh (Sheikh Hussein Bale) helped to spread Islam in the Bali region of southern Ethiopia (Braukämper, 2004; Lewis, 1998). *Bali yaal* means lit. 'located at the water source', a phrase incorporated into the name of Sheikh Hussain Baliyaal as his sacred landscape includes caves with water and lakes. He is still worshipped as a saint by Muslims in the Horn of Africa, including by the Somali. The association of saints with water sources implies that the saints are associated with the creation (and/or control?) of wells: many believe that these were miraculously created by various saints, including Saint Aw-Barkhadle.

Ayaana, ritual offering and compensation

Lewis (1998: 5) reported that rain-making rituals are still performed; he gave as an example the rituals carried out by Islamic religious figures within the Somali clans of the Digir and the Rahanween. Lewis also reported that religious leaders of different Digir and Rahanween (Rehenwayn) lineages were adopted into other lineages so that they might be blessed and instructed by a different successful religious leader. 'Ritual efficacy', measured by the successful outcome of blessings, is extremely important in this context as it links to the fundamental indigenous value of ancestral veneration: people adopt a lineage due to its successful eponymous ancestors. Another example of this Cushitic notion of 'ritual efficacy', also referred to as 'Cushitic power' in the literature, is inferred from the Guji Oromo's fertility rituals relating to the growth of cattle. People invite a successful cattle owner to bring a good *ayaana* (sacred life force, divine power) since he is thought to be closer to God, or more efficacious in his prayers or offerings, and therefore better able to pray for other less successful cattle owners (Loo, 1991: 148–150, 339). The notion of *ayaana* seems to have once existed in Somali society in the form *rooxaan*, spirits who were generally believed to be benign. More importantly, the meaning of the word *ayaan* in Somali is luck. Luck is close to the word destiny which is one of the meanings of the Oromo concept of *ayaana*. It is possible that after conversion the pre-Islamic Cushitic regional concept (*ayaana*) has been reduced in the case of the Somali to being simply related to 'luck'. Today the word *ayaan* means good luck or good destiny, and *ayaan darro* bad luck.

The *ayaana* concept may be comparable to the notion of pleasing God that forms the basis for the *sharh* performance during the Hunt ritual in

Southern Arabia (Serjeant, 1976: 35). This ceremony is carried out in order to stay in harmony with God and hence to obtain rains, or well-being (*ni'mah*), which itself depends on rain (Loo, 1991). The Arabian concept of *ni'mah* is close to the concept of *barwaaqo* (prosperity), discussed earlier. The Hunt ritual, as noted in Chapter Three, is essentially a rain-making ritual. Serjeant reports a saying that 'if we did not hunt, the rain would not come to us, and there would be drought' (ibid.: 36). Many amongst the Eastern Cushitic groups also carry out ritual hunting designed solely to increase fertility. Describing the *sarara*-ritual of the Matcha Oromo, Bartels argues that "killing and childbearing" are ritual acts for fertility:

> The whole sarara-ritual has to be regarded in terms of a new-year ritual, where people pray for fertility for themselves, their cattle, and their crops. It exhibits the value of killing as a universal law for men in association with fertility and generation.
>
> (Bartels, 1983: 260)

To be in harmony with God, therefore, one needs to hunt in the ritual manner by following the laws of the Hunt ritual. Only then will a game animal form an appropriate sacrifice for the god(s). The slaughter of animals for rain-making is recorded by Hallpike (1972: 153–154), Loo (1991) and Bartels (1983), among others. The notion of the slaughter of a game animal to the god(s) for rain-making is strikingly similar.

In the Somali case, the Muriid of Aw-Barkhadle and other custodians of ancestral shrines and tombs receive the *zakat* (offerings). The idea of sacrifice is deeply rooted in the desire for fertility and wellbeing and extends even within the Somali diaspora. The *Muriid* of Sh. Isaaq told me that people make offerings to the sheikh in order to ensure the wellbeing of society. When somebody commits a murder or manslaughter, the clan also pays *zakah* (or *mag*). This brings to mind the cases of the *dhaim*, 'taint', in the Hunt ritual (Serjeant, 1976), which need to be dealt with before the Hunt can take place according to the rules. After capturing Bu'ur Ba'ayr's in the mountain, Saint Aw-Barkhadle had to pay *mag* to the Yibir (Beesha Mohamed Haniifa) so that they would not curse the rest of the population. The role of this *mag* is thus to 'fix' the fault or '*dhaim*' committed against an ancestor. In present day rain-making ceremonies in Arabia, Imams bless the rain-making rituals. Rain-making is also attributed to the Prophet Muhammad who is said to have been successful in his blessing for rain. It is important to note here that these Arabian rain-making rituals are also of pre-Islamic origin; they have nevertheless been adopted into the Islamic context despite Muslim clerks' condemnation of the Hunt ritual on account of its clearly 'pagan' nature. This process of religious contestations has parallels with what has probably also taken place in the Horn of Africa.

Rain-making and the ritual hunt

Human suffering can be seen to be a form of sacrifice as I have already shown in my discussion about circumcision and *istunka*. The official and more wide-spread versions of rain-making currently involve communal prayers, as can be seen in the *roobdoon* ritual. In Somali society, sheikhs have long been associated with rain-making. One of them, Sheikh Madar, has been credited with creating a well (Figure 5.12). Sheikh Madar is a lineage founder and venerated at his shrine near Hargeisa province by his offspring as well as by others. In Arabia, interestingly, 'The ancient saint buried near Kor Saiban is known as Mawla [Lord] Matar, Lord of Rain' (Serjeant, 1976: 38). It is not certain if or how these saints are associated with each other, or if in fact they were ever related. It seems more likely that the Somali clan adopted the name of a regional sheikh famous for his success in rain-making. An inscription from South Arabia quoted by Serjeant (Serjeant, 1976: 11) credits rain to a Muslim saint, Mikayil;

> Al-Iklil, if Mikayil gives good measure, and at evening pours (rain). Watering with his flood from evening until afternoon, and none pass at night along the highway, nor go out along it in the morning to work. They sow *suhaibi* millet grain, much of it or little, or else *tahaf*-millet the stalk of which they twine into foddering twists.

(ibid.)

Figure 5.12 The well of Sheikh Madar, Hargeisa region

This may be another indication of links across the Red Sea. Furthermore, Serjeant describes the star Kalil/ al-Iklil as the *abu* of season *saif* (the first two weeks of April). Mikayil, notes Serjeant, is Michael the Archangel whom he (Serjeant) suggests is 'the Islamic successor to the pagan Shams, Lady of Maifa' who is depicted in a pre-Islamic hunting inscription (ibid.: 12). A worshipper will ask the saints and sheikhs to provide rain, a practice confirmed by Serjeant's accounts of local religious chanting. I have noted the same practice in Somali society today. An alternative explanation to the meaning of this account may be that there is a Somali clan called *Mikahil* whose ancestors are associated with rain-making. The *Mushayikh*, of the Wahidi territory in Arabia, are also associated with rain-making as mentioned earlier (ibid.: 35). It is possible that immigrants from Arabian rain-making families came to the African side of the Red Sea, perhaps long before Islam. Incidentally, the above account mentions the South Arabians growing *tahaf* (*ti'if*)-millet which grows naturally only in Ethiopia.

As Serjeant notes;

> In pre-Islamic South Arabia it may be that success in the Hunt was a sign of the favour of the God and in inscription . . . it is evident that this favour had to be sought by performing the hunt for him at the appointed time for it, and that the favour most required of the Divinity was, as is to be expected in an agricultural community, rains for the crops.
>
> (ibid.: 61)

It is noteworthy that the current practitioners of the ancient Hunt ritual include Islamised Mansabs who sometimes incorporate Islamic prayer into the Hunt ritual (ibid.). And Cerulli also notes that traditional Somali law is often closer to pre-Islamic Arabian law than it is to the Islamic. Furthermore, it may well be that ritual hunting, on both sides of the Red Sea, with their corresponding notions of ritual purity and efficacy, epitomized the kind of leadership needed to rule and unite territories. Hence, the ritual hunt seems to go hand in hand with not just bravery but also divine fertility and ritual leadership. This indicates the continuing relationship between hunting and power in general, even in the current era and globally. Ritual hunting is part of fertility ideology and may have a role also in state-formation power in the early history of northeast Africa and beyond.

In the Somali context, the rains are important for the welfare of the livestock and the crops and so in turn for the welfare of the people. At times of good rains and prosperity, the Somali and the Oromo people perform different dances. One of these, the dance locally known as *sirbikoni* or *farlooni*, the cattle dance (*lo* means cattle), celebrates the abundance of cattle.

I conclude that the hunt is a similar fertility ritual, an act between a human being and God, in much the same way as I suggest that female circumcision is best seen in the context of divine fertility, and hence as an act between the divine and the human being. The *Istunka* ritual or the stick fights of the Horn of Africa are a sacrifice and an expression of this dual relationship where the offerings are of blood and pain. So too are the fire jumping (*nairuus*) rituals associated with the beginning of the harvest and the new year.

The lack of success in rain-making is a lack of harmony with God

If a Guji Oromo farmer has bad luck with his harvest or with the health of his cattle, he will see this as a mark of his own lack of good relations with *Waaq*. He will therefore ask a successful farmer, who must clearly have a good relationship with God (and hence be close to God) to pray for him. The successful farmer will come to the farm or camp and mediate (as a sheikh would) since he is blessed by God with success. Loo (1991) discusses the lack of success with cattle and says that an Oromo would have to ask a blessed person to bless him and his herds so that he might increase the fertility (reproduction) of his herd. This practice seems similar to the Somali one of asking blessings from sheikhs or saints.

Somewhat similarly, the Somali women who fail to have children are often traditionally associated with shame and bad luck and thus rejected by their own husbands. It is imperative that the number of children is increased, particularly through the birth of sons who will extend the lineage tree. A woman who cannot give birth to a son therefore damages the clan tree. Leaving aside the shame, people also ask why the woman cannot give birth and wonder whether she is '*habaaran*' (cursed), which means that she is rejected by God. It is important to note that traditionally women would be married at a young age and that fertility issues would therefore be less prevalent. A similar concept exists among the Oromo (*abarsa*). This is further evidence, I suggest, of the significance of sacred fertility in the Horn in general and in Somali society in particular. Receiving rains and giving birth (to a boy) is to be blessed and accepted by God. Men who fail in the Hunt ritual are similarly ashamed: something is assumed to be wrong; failure is seen as a rejection by God, in much the same way as a Somali woman who fails to have children might feel rejected by God. A song goes:

> Says the maker of these verses,
> The Hunt must be held respected
> He who fails to go hunting
> By God's creatures is rejected
> (Quoted in Serjeant, 1976: 14)

The Hunt has a religious purpose in the Horn of Africa, just as it did in pre-Islamic Southern Arabia. It is a sacrifice made to the ancestors to gain blessing and fertility. Its heroes are admired not just for the act of killing but for risking their lives in sacrifice. The Oromo hunting and hero songs *gerarsa* (Somali *geraar*) have special orientations. The *gerarsa jiliba* is a song for hunting antelopes, and *gerarsa fardo'o* a song about the horses which often accompany hunters. A possible portrayal of these hunt rituals is clearly depicted in hunting scenes in the rock art in Somaliland, such as at Dhambalin and Laas Geel. Hunting takes place near lakes where the animals come to drink. The Guji sing special songs for expeditions returning from hunting at Lake Abaya (or *gerarsa boole*). The Guji sing *gerarsa nama nama ijeessa* for a hunter who has killed an enemy and women sing the *soomp'ne* song for men who have killed a buffalo. Not only do the Guji Oromo sing different songs for different hunting outcomes (Loo, 1991); they give their hunters different names/titles to mark the different degrees of risk involved in their hunting. A hunter who kills two large game animals, for example, is awarded the title *misoo*.

If the laws (*qawaniin*) of the Hunt are not respected there is a risk of a *dhaim* or 'taint', according to Serjeant. This *dhaim* results from bad moral conduct which is the reason the Hunt ritual will fail (ibid.: 15–18). Serjeant speculates whether the *Ashraf*, a family known to be of Yemenite origin, were associated with the Hunt ritual as 'a group that deals with cases of *dhaim* or "taint"' (Loo, 1991: 16). There are also Somali *Ashraaf* groups who are Arab immigrants and considered to have once been part of the group that was responsible for the conversion of many Somalis to Islam. Their descendants today are also considered significant from a religious point of view and usually enjoy a high religious status in society (cf. Lewis, 1998). However, whether and how the *Ashraaf* discussed by Serjeant are related to the groups that migrated from Arabia to the Somali coast remains uncertain, although some connection remains possible. They are known in Somali society as the *Mushayikh*, *Sheikhash* (sheikhs) as they seem to have been in Arabia (cf. Martin, 1974). The word 'taint' is associated with contamination and the disharmony that is caused by such a defect. The Somali word *nagi* means the exact opposite: it denotes harmony, a quality much sought after in fertility rituals, as I will describe in more detail below.

Indigenous concept of peace in the Horn of Africa: the notion of Nagi

In South Arabia, the word *tib* (perfume), like *naqi* and *bari*, is associated with notions of purification, (re)conciliation, being trouble free, at ease and with goodness of heart and of good faith (Serjeant, 1976: 62). In pre-Islamic times, temples were purified with perfume or incense burning, according to Serjeant (ibid.). The notion of *tib* reminds me of an experience I had in the Somali region. My team of five and I stopped after a couple of days travelling to wash at a *wadi*. We got back to our vehicle and I got my perfume out of my bag and put it on. The men in the back seats immediately said how nice it smelled. I merely said a simple 'thanks'. However, the lady sitting next to me reacted immediately by reaching for my perfume and handing it to the men who put it on. Then everyone, including the lady, said '*Allahu musali calaa sayidinaa Muhammad*' (Allah prays on our *Sayyid* Moham-med) and recited other verses asking for God's blessing. I had already been aware of the ritual significance of sharing incense smoke as it burns in the burner but this event in the car confirmed to me that perfumes are the mod-ern equivalent of incense (and it does not matter if it is *pour homme* or *pour elle*). Incense is usually ritually shared amongst the congregation by passing around the burner so that everyone can breathe in its smoke. Perfumes are also passed around after a collective meal, including the '*Eid* meal to mark the end of the month of Ramadan month. In the evenings, Somali house-holds burn incense or *uunsi* as a way to harmonise the home environment. In ways such as these, everyday cultural habits reveal a deeper concept of community, harmony and peace.

The ritual sharing of items associated with sacredness is a common prac-tice. When such sharing takes place, some Cushitic people say the word '*nagi*' (peace). Somali and Oromo men routinely share *khat* which is also consid-ered to be a ritual substance. One of the men will give a bundle of *khat* to each member of the group, asking them '*ma nagi ba?*' (is it peace/abun-dance?); and each man when receiving the bundle replies '*wa nagi*' (yes, it is peace/abundance). Is *nagi* the same word as *naqi* which is used in the same sense as *tib* in Arabia, as noted by Serjeant (1976)? Since the letters *q* and *g* are sometimes interchangeable, it is possible that the words are the same. If Serjeant's *naqi* is equivalent to the Somali notion of *nagi*, does it relate to the concept of *Barwaaqo* [lit. drop of *Waag* (god), meaning paradise/abundance on Earth, wellbeing] in Somali society? And to the notion of *ayaana* among the Oromo? In Southern Arabia, the concept of *bari* is also used as *tib* or *naqi* (ibid.). In the Hunt ritual, coffee and the meat of the Hunt game are shared (ibid.) in a similar way to the sharing of *khat* and perfumes in similar rituals. Furthermore, the procedure reminds me of the notion of reconciliation asso-ciated with the division of the meat of the Hunt. The custom of al-*habarish* (Serjeant, 1976: 63) is the sharing of the meat of the Hunt ritual amongst the hunters: one person cuts up the meat and gives each person a piece and then starts the process again after the first serving has been consumed.

Serjeant makes one reference to Somali society and it comes, interestingly, in the context of his experience of sharing the meat of the Hunt ritual:

> Meat is still sent about rather more freely than one might imagine, for our Somali *ayah* in the late forties used regularly to receive meat from Somaliland. It was dried on a line in the sun, cut with the line of the grain, and immersed in a can of ghee.
>
> (Serjeant, 1976: 64)

Serjeant also describes meat sent to London from Somaliland during the time of the British Protectorate. The Somali gift of meat he describes is

called *muqumad* and it is common for this to be sent from the Somali territories to the Somali diaspora. It is tempting to suggest that the *muqumad*
may be a remnant of a similar ritual of meat sharing in the Somali region
which echoes the Hunt ceremony in Arabia. *Muqumad* is used on special
occasions such as weddings, as has already been noted, and during *Baanashada* (see Chapter Four) to nourish the pregnant woman or someone's
recovery after an illness.

In summary, fertility is of such importance that *nagi* must be reached to
achieve it and maintained, like *ayaana*. If 'taint' is present or comes into
existence then people must be reconciled with each other and/or with God
by purifying themselves and their space. This practice is also confirmed by
other Eastern Cushitic groups such as the Konso (Hallpike, 1972: 253).
When a crime is committed that requires purification, Somali society goes
beyond ritual and beyond beliefs in purity and the interference of bad
omens: Somali custom-based law (*xeer*) comes into play to treat the crime
as one committed against protected entities which can bring bad luck to,
and a curse upon, the whole community.

Bir-ma-geydo: the protection of the sacred by custom-based law

One of the rules protecting important subjects and entities is the law and
concept of *bir-ma-geydo* which translates as 'iron should not enter' or 'forbidden for the weapon'. What is forbidden for the weapon is termed *bir-
ma-geydo* and includes a list of protected entities/subjects, including people,
animals, water sources and trees. Originally, it was a concept associated
specifically with human beings and sacred animals and trees. However, it
was later extended to prohibit the slaughter of certain animals such as those
who were pregnant (*irmaan*) or of a fertile age. In war time, *bir-ma-geydo*
covers women and children who are traditionally protected by this custom-
based law. For a Somali society where the *bir-ma-geydo* are traditionally
protected there is always a hope of reconciliation after a war; the concept
makes future harmony possible. However, if violated, anyone who during
times of war assaults the enemy's women, children, the sick and the old will
be brought to justice and be cursed by both his enemy clan and their sup-
porters. The perpetrator and his clan will forever have a curse hanging over
them, a curse which may lead to illness or a complete loss of livelihood (*cay-
dhow*) and an everlasting shame as other groups join forces with his enemy.
This explains why Somalis who became Muslim did not destroy the graves
of the Christians and why they protected the sacred trees belonging to other
groups. Hence, a transgression against *bir-ma-geydo* is the Somali version
of a crime against humanity and, too, of the Statute of Rome's articles on
crimes against culture. The expression currently serves as a reminder that to
harm or mistreat children and women is an affront to Somali traditional values. *Bir-ma-geydo* still today protects the site of Aw-Barkhadle and similar

examples of sacred heritage, both tangible and intangible. The many poems, proverbs and metaphors that are associated with or illustrate this concept in the Somali language are a testimony to the central role it plays in Somali interaction with the sacred, nature and people. And moving beyond the Somali to other parts of the Horn, when the Amhara tell Conti Rossini that the *Adbar* will be angry if they sit on the sacred tree, it seems as if similar traditional customs are protecting sacred trees elsewhere too.

Conclusions

The overriding purpose of this chapter has been to examine possible ritual continuities and to ask *why* these may occur. The ideologies, indigenous ontologies and concepts underpinning transformations and continuities have been examined. The rituals at Aw-Barkhadle, as shown in Chapters Three and Four, testify to a religious amalgamation within Somali culture and the Horn of Africa. But is it as simple a process as amalgamation, or is there also a coherence of ideas? I have discussed the basis for practices and ideas. In so doing, ideas of the nature of the Sky-God, sacred landscapes, ancestral worship, snake worship, protection of the sacred (*bir-ma-geydo*) and the concept of peace (*nagi*) are amongst the concepts that have emerged as being part of a more coherent regional ideology of fertility. I have also shown how sacred kinship plays an important role in perpetuating a harmony between the divine and the human.

The rituals of the *wagar*, for example, seem also to support this notion, and their practice at Aw-Barkhadle is thought to date at least back to the Bu'ur Ba'ayr era – or to pre-Islamic times. I have attempted to make sense of the origin of these rituals and their associations with sacred materials and sites such as stones, hills, water, moisture, trees and iron in popular religion today (Islamic mysticism/Sufism). I have examined their Somali origins, ancestral worship and the origin of ideas of fertility.

I have also discussed and highlighted the relationship between the history of Sufism and Sharif Yusuf Aw-Barkhadle, a saint associated with pre-Islamic legends and sacred centres. I have scrutinised in detail the relationship between rituals and the ideas that seem to be associated with them such as *ziyara* (pilgrimage) which is widely practiced in Somali society through the ritual worship of significant ancestral religious figures, or saints, associated with the Islamic Somali Myth of Origin. I have explored Somali Cushitic society and examined the Cushitic institutions and the issue of fertility within, for example, the *Waaq* cult of the Horn of Africa. This discussion has usefully led me into an exploration of the potential continuity of rituals to do with ancestral worship, rain-making and the ritual use of the landscapes associated with what are considered by Somali society to be pre-Islamic deities. I have discovered the integration of Islamic Sufi rituals with non-/pre-existing Cushitic practices and an appropriation of pre-Islamic sacred landscapes.

In terms of syncretism, I consider that the ideas behind pre-existing practices may not necessarily change even when the name of a Muslim religious figure replaces the name of a previous pre-Islamic deity. The Sufis, for example, ignore the presence of the phallic stone at the pilgrimage site of Aw-Barkhadle and are generally unaware of what it is.

In their complete failure to recognise the non-Islamic origin of certain rituals at Aw-Barkhadle, Muslim religious figures have indeed attempted to hide non-Islamic elements by transforming their meaning to refer to Islam. The male sexual organ may well not be as taboo as the female's. A boy-birth is celebrated precisely because of his possession of a penis. A man performs the sacrifice of the hunt to level out the risks and sacrifices that the woman makes in the name of fertility. I suggest, therefore, that the symbol of male fertility is indeed less taboo, even if it is not spoken about in Somali society. I believe this explains why the phallic stone evokes so little curiosity during the veneration of ancestors at Aw-Barkhadle; local people are nowadays unaware of the purpose of phallic stones in a non-Islamic context. The Abba Gada of the Oromo and Konso still wear the phallic symbol *kallasha* (*qallacca*) on their foreheads. Perhaps Somalis wore it too in pre-Islamic times.

It is therefore apparent that Muslim Somalis have appropriated both the sacred places and practices of old religions. The religious leaders' 'solution' to persistent 'pagan' practice seems to have been to change the name of a place and to attribute it to an Islamic religious figure rather than to prevent people from continuing to practice a local tradition. Perhaps this is one of the ways in which Islam (Sufi Islam) has had to compromise in order to fit into a new context in what is a fundamentally Cushitic Somali society.

As a result, Cushitic practices of ancestral worship have continued into Islamic times in the form of *ziyara*. The sacred centres and landscape of former religions are now used by the new religion and adopted into the new ideologies in a syncretic manner, evidence of the continuation of rituals of pre-Islamic origin into Christian and Islamic times.

In these discussions, I have identified and analysed key recurring concepts of the Cushitic institutions: ancestral worship, sacred fertility and rain-making rituals. I have also shown how these ideas have been appropriated by Sufi Islam into Somali society. I have used comparative data from regional groups both in the Horn and in the adjacent Arabian region. I have bridged the historical and ethnographic data from the Horn with that of southern Arabia in relation to fertility rituals and sacred features of the landscape. And, by studying the shared practices of the peoples of the Horn of Africa, I am hoping to understand better the ideologies that bind together their landscapes, practices and material manifestations, all of which can benefit the archaeological record of the region.

In the following chapter I look in more detail at the complex relationship that exists between the Eastern Cushitic groups (including the Somalis); the elements that they have in common offer insights into the history and current day practices of the main groups in the Horn of Africa. My starting point for this discussion is the symbolic archaeology of Saint Aw-Barkha-dle's sacred landscape. I will compare this with the archaeology of Tiya, in particular, and with Lalibela and Aksum. I present what I term the Ritual Set. This can offer an integrational framework with which to bridge the gap between the meaning of the ritual acts, the ethnography and the archaeol-ogy of the region of northeast Africa.

Notes

1 Sufi Orgome, from the Isaaq, clan and sub-clan Arab, was active in the first part of the twentieth century in what was then British Somaliland. He was known for his rebellion against the British rule.
2 *Kallacha* is the head piece worn by the *Qallu* of the Oromo and Konso during ceremonies.
3 Although some disagree (e.g. Amborn, 2009).
4 Isis – the throne, the sun disc with the cow's horns, sparrow, cobra, vulture, syca-more tree – all are elements with resonant meanings and feature in the present culture of the Horn, probably perpetuated through

Bibliography

Almeida, Manuel. 1954. *Some Records of Ethiopia, 1593–1646*. Edited and trans-lated by C. F. Beckingham and G. W. B. Huntingford. London: Hakluyt Society.
Amborn, H. 2009. The Phallsification of the Kallačča: Or, Why Sometimes a Cigar Is a Cigar. In S. Ege, H. Aspen, B. Teferra and S. Bekele (eds.) *Proceedings of the 16th International Conference of Ethiopian Studies*. Trondheim: Norwegian Uni-versity of Science and Technology.
Andrezejewski, B. W. 1974. The Veneration of Sufi Saints and Its Impact on Oral Literature of the Somali People and Their Literature in Arabic. *African Language Studies*, 15: 15–53.
Anshan, L. 2012. *A History of Oversees Chinese in Africa to 1911*. New York: Diasporic Africa Press.
Arberry, A. J. 1953. *Sufism: An Account of the Mystics of Islam*. London: Allen and Unwin.
Arnold, T. W. 1929. *The Islamic Book*. Paris: The Pegasus Press.
Arnoldi, M. J. 1986. The Artistic Heritage of Somalia. In K. Loughran, J. Loughran, J. Johnson and S. Samatar (eds.) *Somalia in Word and Image*. Washington, DC: Foundation for Cross Cultural Understanding and Indiana University Press.
Bartels, L. 1983. *Oromo Religion: Myths and Rites of the Western Oromo of Ethio-pia. An Attempt to Understand*. Berlin: Deitrich Reimer Verlag.
Baxter, P. 1990. Oromo Blessings and Greetings. In A. Jocobson-Widding and W. van Beek (eds.) *The Creative Communion. African Folk Models of Fertility and the Regeneration of Life*. Uppsala: Acta Universitatis Upsaliensis.
Beachey, R. W. 1990. *The Warrior Mullah: The Horn Aflame. 1892–1920*. London: Bellew Publishing.
Beek, G. W. Van. 1960. Pre-Islamic South Arabian Shipping in the Indian Ocean – A Surrejoinder. *Journal of the American Oriental Society*, 80(2).
Braukämper, U. 2004. *Islamic History and Culture in Southern Ethiopia: Collected Essays*. Gottinger Studien Zur Ethnologie. Munster: Lit Verlag Munster.

Burton, R. 1966 [1898]. *First Footsteps in East Africa.* Edited by G. Waterfield. Travellers and Explorers Series. New York: Praeger.

Casson, L. 1989. *The Periplus Maris Erythraei.* Text with Introduction, Translation and Commentary by L. Casson. Princeton: Princeton University Press.

Cerulli, E. 1957. *Somalia. Scritti vari Editi ed Inediti.* Vol. I. Roma: Istituto Poligrafico dello Stato. P. V.

Chakrabarti, K. D. 1998. The Indus Civilization and the Arabian Gulf: An Indian Point of View. In C. S. Phillips, D. T. Potts and S. Searight (eds.) *Arabia and Its Neighbours. Essays on Prehistorical and Historical Development.* Abiel II. New Research on the Arabian Peninsula. Turnhout: Brepols.

Chittick, H. N. 1969. An Archaeological Reconnaissance of the Southern Somali Coast. *Azania,* 4: 115–130.

Chittick, H. N. 1975. An Archaeological Reconnaissance in the Horn: The British-Somali Expedition. *Azania,* 11: 117–133.

Colson, E. 1997. Places of Power and Shrines of the Land. *Paideuma,* 43: 47–57.

Conti Rossini, C. 1905. Note sugli agau: 1. Appunti sulla lingua khamta dell' Averghellé. *Giornale della Società Asiatica Italiana,* 17: 109–122.

Dunn, R. 1989 [1325–1354]. *The Adventures of Ibn Battúta. A Muslim Traveller of the Fourteenth Century.* Berkeley, CA: University of California Press.

el-Zein, Abdul Hamid. 1972. *The Sacred Meadows: A Structural Analysis of Religious Symbolism in an East African Town.* Unpublished PhD thesis, University of Chicago.

Encyclopaedia of Islam Online. 2005. Brill.

Forward, M. 1994. Islam. In J. Holm and J. Bowker (eds.) *Worship.* Themes in Religious Studies. London: Pinter Publishers Ltd.

Haldane, D. 1983. *Islamic Bookbinding.* London: World of Islam Festival Trust in Association with the Victoria and Albert Museum.

Hallpike, C. 1972. *The Konso of Ethiopia: A Study of the Values of an Eastern Cushitic People.* Oxford: Clarendon Press.

Helander, B. 1986. Notions of Crop Fertility in Southern Somalia. *Working Papers in African Studies 4,* University of Uppsala. African Studies Program (SOAS).

Helander, B. 1996a. The Hubeer in the Land of Plenty: Land, Labour and Vulnerability Among a Southern Somali Clan. In C. Besteman and L. V. Cassanelli (eds.) *The Struggle for Land in Southern Somalia.* Boulder and London: Westview Press and Haan.

Helander, B. 1996b. Rahanweyn Sociability: A Model for Other Somalis? In R. J. Hayward and I. M. Lewis (eds.) *Voice and Power.* London: SOAS.

Hersi, A. 1979. *The Arab Factor in Somali History.* Unpublished PhD diss., University of California-Los Angeles.

Heusch, Luc de. 1985. *Sacrifice in Africa: A Structuralist Approach.* Translated by L. O'Brien and A. Morton. Bloomington: Indiana University Press.

Hourani, G. F. 1995. *Arab Seafaring.* Princeton, NJ: Princeton University Press.

Hubert, H. and Mauss, M. 1964. *Sacrifice: Its Nature and Function.* Translated by W. D. Halls. Chicago: Chicago University Press.

Insoll, T. 1999. *The Archaeology of Islam.* London: Blackwell.

Insoll, T. 2003. *The Archaeology of Islam in Sub-Saharan Africa.* Cambridge: Cambridge University Press.

Jama, A. D. 1996. *The Origins and Development of Mogadishu AD 1000 to 1850.* Uppsala: Uppsala University Press. Studies in African Archaeology 12.

Jardine, D. 1923. *The Mad Mullah of Somaliland.* London: Wyman & Sons.

Khaldun, Ibn. 1989 [1406]. *Prolegomena (Al-Muqqadimma). Introduktion till världshistorien.* Translated by Ingvar Rydberg. Lund: Alhambra.

King, G. R. D. 2004. *The Codex. The Islamic Book.* Unpublished manuscript. The School of Oriental and African Studies, Department of Art and Archaeology, London.

Knutsson, K. E. 1967. *Authority and Change. A Study of the Kallu Institution Among the Macha Galla of Ethiopia.* Göteborg: Elanders.

Levine, D. N. 2000. *Greater Ethiopia: The Evolution of a Multiethnic Society.* 2nd ed. Chicago and London: University of Chicago Press.

Lévi-Strauss, C. 1982. *The Way of the Masks.* Translated by S. Modelski. Seattle: University of Washington Press.

Lewis, I. 1994a. *Blood and Bone: The Call for Kinship in Somali Society.* Lawrenceville, NJ: Red Sea Press.

Lewis, I. 1994b. *People of the Horn of Africa: Somali, Afar and Saho.* London: IAI/Haan.

Lewis, I. 1996. *Religion in Context: Cults and Charisma.* Cambridge: Cambridge University Press.

Lewis, I. 1998. *Saints and Somalis: Popular Islam in a Clan-Based Society.* Lawrenceville, NJ and Asmara, Eritrea: Red Sea Press.

Loo, J. van de. 1991. *Guji Oromo Culture (with the Collaboration of Bilow Kolo).* Berlin: Dietrich Reimer Verlag.

Loubser, J. H. N. 2008. Discontinuity Between Political Power and Religious Status: Mountains, Pools and Dry Ones Among Venda-Speaking Chiefdoms of Southern Africa. In D. S. Whitley and K. Hays-Gilpin (eds.) *Belief in the Past: Theoretical Approaches to the Archaeology of Religion.* Walnut Creek, CA: Left Coast Press.

Luling, V. 1988. The Man in the Tree. A Note on a Somali Myth. In A. Puglieli (ed.) *Proceedings of the Third International Congress of Somali Studies.* Rome: II Pensario Scientifico.

Mansur, A. O. 1995. The Nature of the Somali Clan-System. In A. J. Ahmed (ed.) *The Invention of Somalia.* Lawrenceville, NJ: Red Sea Press.

Martin, B. G. 1974. Arab Migration to East Africa in Medieval Times. *The International Journal of African Historical Studies,* 7(3): 367–390.

Mather, C. 2003. Shrines and the Domestication of Landscape. *Journal of Anthropological Research,* 59: 23–45.

Mire, S. 2015a. Mapping of the Archaeology of Somaliland: Religion, Art, Script, Time, Urbanism, Trade and Empire. *African Archaeological Review,* 32(1): 111–136.

Mire, S. 2015b. Wagar, Fertility and Phallic Stelae: Cushitic Sky-God Belief and the Site of Saint Aw-Barkhadle in Somaliland. *African Archaeological Review,* 32(1): 93–109.

Mohammed, M. A. 1991. *Histoire des Croyances en Somalie.* Paris: Annales Littéraires de l'Université de Besançon.

Moorey, P. R. S. 1998. Did Easterners Sail Round Arabia to Egypt in the Fourth Millennium BC? In C. S. Phillips, D. T. Potts and S. Searight (eds.) *Arabia and Its Neighbours. Essays on Prehistorical and Historical Development.* Abiel II. New Research on the Arabian Peninsula. Turnhout: Brepols.

Mukhtar, M. H. 1987. Arabic Sources on Somalia. *History in Africa,* 14: 141–172.

Mukhtar, M. H. 1995. Islam in Somali History; Fact and Fiction. In A. J. Ahmed (ed.) *The Invention of Somalia.* Lawrenceville, NJ: Red Sea Press.

Munro-Hay, S. A. 2011. Chinese Source for Aksumite History in the 6th and 7th Centuries AD. *Annales d'Ethiopie*, 26(1): 99–104.

Paulitschke, P. 1888. *Ethnographie Nordost Afrikas, I. Die materielle Cultur des Danâkil, Galla und Somâl II. Die geistige Cultur des Danâkil, Galla und Somâl.* Vol. 2. Berlin.

Phillipson, D. W. 1997. *Ancient Ethiopia. Aksum: Its Antecedents and Successors.* London: British Museum Press.

Potts, D. T. 1990. *The Arabian Gulf in Antiquity.* Vols. I–II. Oxford: Clarendon Press.

Ratnagar, S. 1987. Pastoralists in the Prehistory of Baluchistan. *Studies in History,* 3: 137–154.

Révoil, G. 1882. *La Vallée du Darror: Voyage aux Pays Çomalis Dis Mois à la Cote Orientale D'Afrique.* Paris: Challamel aîné.

Rikitu, M. 2001. *The Oromo of the Horn: A Cultural History.* London: Biiftuu Diiramaa Association.

Samatar, S. S. 1982. *Oral Poetry and Somali Nationalism: The Case of Sayid Mahamad 'Abdille Hasan.* Cambridge: Cambridge University Press.

Scarre, C. 2008. Shrines of the Land and Places of Power: Religion and the Transition of Farming in Western Europe. In D. S. Whitley and K. Hays-Gilpin (eds.) *Belief in the Past: Theoretical Approaches to the Archaeology of Religion.* Walnut Creek, CA: Left Coast Press.

Serjeant, R. B. 1976. *The South Arabian Hunt.* London: Luzac.

Shack, W. A. 1966. *The Gurage: A People of the Ensete Culture.* London, New York, and Nairobi: Oxford University Press.

Smith, M. C. and Wright, H. T. 1988. The Ceramics from Ras Hafun in Somalia: Notes on a Classical Maritime Site. *Azania,* 25: 115–141.

Spencer, H. 1882. *The Principles of Sociology.* Vol. I. New York: D. Appleton and Company.

Thesiger, W. 1935. The Awash River and the Awsa Sultanate. *The Geographical Journal,* 85: 1–23.

Trimingham, J. S. 1952. *Islam in Ethiopia.* 1st ed. Oxford: Oxford University Press.

Trimingham, J. S. 1965. *Islam in Ethiopia.* 2nd ed. Oxford: Oxford University Press.

Trimingham, J. S. 1971. *The Sufi Orders in Islam.* Oxford: Clarendon Press.

Ullendorff, E. 1955. *The Semitic Languages of Ethiopia: A Comparative Phonology.* London: Taylor's.

Veer, P. van der. 1994. Syncretism, Multiculturalism and the Discourse of Tolerance. In C. Stewart and R. Shaw (eds.) *Syncretism/Anti-Syncretism: The Politics of Religious Synthesis.* London: Routledge.

6 An ideology of fertility in the archaeology of the Horn of Africa

Aw-Barkhadle and beyond

Common systematic elements of the Horn of Africa

I attempted in Chapter 4 to contextualise the fertility rituals at Aw-Barkhadle within the broader context of Somali society. In Chapter Five, I further explained the relevance of sacred landscape to ancestral veneration/worship. It presented the notion of ritual efficacy in the lineage regarding obtaining fertility, the regional notion of peace and abundance (*nagi*), ideological traditions and snake worship. I pointed to the importance of understanding pre-Islamic and pre-Christian indigenous religious institutions such as the Sky-God and to the possible syncretism of religions and religious space. Now, in this chapter, I examine in detail the material manifestations of the ideas and practices I have analysed. By using data, including that drawn from Aw-Barkhadle, I identify characteristic archaeological features and other materials to construct what I call a Ritual Set that can be applied within the Horn of Africa.

The Ritual Set (Tables 6.1a-c) is a set of material and non-material manifestations and attributes which uses specific examples to shed light on the investigation and (re)interpretation of archaeological material and sites in the region. I examine how this interpretational tool can complement existing investigative methods by applying it to the site of Tiya. I believe that the ancient societies of the Horn of Africa are not as fragmented as conventional interpretations would have us believe. The region is a dynamic one with plenty of characteristics to support archaeological reinterpretation. I use the term 'the known' to refer to the elements common to the Eastern Cushitic speaking peoples (Table 6.1a). I do so only to understand the 'unknown' and not in any way to imply that all the features they have in common are specific to them. This is very much not the case. So many non-eastern Cushitic speaking peoples, past and present, have shared and still share the regional ideology that I am investigating. I have come to understand in the course of my field research in various parts of the region how far-reaching are the indigenous foundations and their expression in the Horn of Africa.

According to the literature about traditional religions in the Horn of Africa, the main religion seems to be associated with the Sky-God (though

Table 6.1a Common Elements within the Eastern Cushitic linguistic group

People	Political system/social organisation/Ideology	Area (now)	Religion (now)	T-Religion's main sacred object	Subsistence (now)	Zar/Ancestral worship/spirit illness Evil eyel Adbar Ayana	Circumcision, FGM, gudniin, cliterodectomy 'killing and bearing' concept	Place of Origin occ. O.T.	Language branch (now)
Konso	Gada-system Fertility rituals, Age-grade system	Great Rift Valley Lakes	T- Waaq (nagea, ayaana) Worship of snakes, trees, springs, stones etc.	Cow Phallic-Kallasha, Snake (ancestor, sanctity, fertility, lineage founder, myth of origin) Waga Stele, (evil spirit), sacred juniper trees (ulahita) the olive and juniper	Farming (ensete) And cattle keeping	Both women, and men (age-grade related) Blood smearing, Ghee smearing	Both men and women (some Konso don't practice FGM)	Sacred kinship (blessed ancestors/ people link to a divine/ semi divine forefather)	E. C. Lexical sim: 55% with Dirashigna,

(Continued)

Table 6.1a (Continued)

People	Political system/social organisation/Ideology	Area (now)	Religion (now)	T-Religion's main sacred object	Subsistence (now)	Zar/ Ancestral worship/ spirit illness/ Evil eye/ Adbar Ayana	Circumcision, FGM, gudnin, cliterodectomy 'killing and bearing' concept	Place of Origin occ. O.T.	Language branch (now)
Oromo (*Boorana*)	*Gada*-system Fertility rituals, Age-grade system	Southern Ethiopia and northern Kenya	P/M/X/T-*Waaq* Fertility-dominate Worship of snakes, trees, springs, stones etc.	Phallic-Kallasha *Siqqaa/ Siqqoo*, Snake Worship of tombs and sacred trees	Pastoral (mainly cattle)	Ro Tattoos	Special herbalist healers perform FGM	Divine kinship Sothern Ethiopia	E. C.
Gedeo	Clan-based, *Baallee Gada* system Fertility rituals	Shoa	T – *Waaq/ Mageno* Worship of snakes, trees, springs, stones etc.	Phallic Stele, Snake element, Evil spirit	Hoe *ensete*	Spirits (evil eye)	Special healers perform FGM	Divine kinship, genealogical blessing	E. C. lexical similarity: 60% with *Sidamo*, & 51% with *Haddiya*
Hadiyya	Fertility rituals	Shoa	P/M/T- *Waaq* (*Fandaano*) Worship of snakes, trees, springs, stones etc.	Patron Spirits, ancestor spirits, Evil spirits/ demons	Cultivation of barley and livestock breeding, more recently Hoe *ensete*	Spirit possession	Special healers perform FGM	Divine kinship genealogical blessing	E. C. 53% with *Sidamo*

Guji- Oromo	The *Gada* system, Fertility rituals	Sidamo	T- *Waaq*/ X /M, Worship of snakes, trees, springs, stones etc.	*Kallasha*, snake element, phallic	Pastoral symbolic importance of cattle and also of *ensete*	Spirits (evil eye, *buda*) Painting/ soiling with sacred chalk	Special herbalist healers perform FGM. Special meeting house	Divine kinship genealogical *blessing*	E.C.
Arsi-/Oromo	Age-grade system Clan-based, Fertility rituals	Arusi, Bale, Sidamo	M/T- *Waaq* /X Worship of snakes, trees, springs, stones etc.	Staff 'Y'-shaped, Evil spirit	Pastoral	Soiling with sacred chalk		Divine kinship genealogical *blessing*	E. C.
Matcha Oromo (*subgroup of the Borana?*)			*Waaq* X concept of *nagea/nagi*, Worship of snakes, trees, springs, stones etc. and *ayaana/ Ayaan*	*Kallasha* Important sticks, Snake material	Farming (*ensete, tef*) and cattle keeping (decreasing)	Spirit possession (incense burning to 'disable' evil spirit)	Special healers perform FGM	Acc. to myth of origin, they crossed the Ghibe river from the north Divine kinship genealogical *blessing*	E. C.
Sidam- (*a/o*)	Age-grade system Clan-based, Fertility rituals	Sidamo	T/X/M Sky-God, Worship of snakes, trees, springs, stones etc.	*Kallasha*	Farming	Spirit possession	Special healers perform FGM	southern Ethiopia genealogical *blessing*	E. C. lexical sim. 53 % with *Haddiya* & 60% with *Gedeo*

(Continued)

Table 6.1a (Continued)

People	Political system/social organisation/ Ideology	Area (now)	Religion (now)	T-Religion's main sacred object	Subsistence (now)	Zar/ Ancestral worship/ spirit illness/ Evil eye/ Adbar Ayana	Circumcision, FGM, gudniin, cliterodectomy 'killing and bearing' concept	Place of Origin occ. O.T.	Language branch (now)
Dirasha	Age-grade system? Clan-based Fertility rituals	Somali, Eastern Ethiopia Djibouti, Kenya	T/X Sky-God, Worship of snakes, trees, springs, stones etc.	Kallasha, snake	Farming Hoe ensete, Tef (Eragrotis abyssinica)	Spirit possession Mesmuri addaraa songs	Special herbalist healers perform FGM	Divine kinship genealogical blessing	E.C. 55% lexical similarity with Konso
Somali	Age-grade system, and Gadaa system amongst Darood and Rahanwayn at Jubba, Clan-based, Fertility rituals	Somali, Eastern Ethiopia Djibouti, Kenya	M(Sunni) with remnants of the concept of Waaq/ Sky-God, concept of nagea/nagi, and ayaana/ Ayaan, veneration of springs, snakes, stones, trees etc.	Sacred stones, trees, wagar, phallic stelae, Snake (ancestor, sanctity, fertility, lineage founder, myth of origin)	Pastoral, Agriculture, Urban	Spirit possession Maame, mingis, roobaan Scarification (special burning and cutting for prevention of specific diseases) Burning Soiling with sacred chalk,	Calaqaad perform FGM/gudniin Special meeting houses	Divine kinship genealogical blessing Arabia acc. to O. T. or Lake Turkana acc. to linguistics	E.C. Somali group (including Northern Somali, Benaadir, Maay, Tunni, Dabarre, Garre, Boni, Jiidu and Rendille)

Fire
jumping,
Blood
smearing,
Ghee
smearing

Abbreviations:
Acc. – according
E.C. – Eastern Cushitic
M – Muslim
O. T. – Oral Traditions
P – Protestants
T – Traditional religion
(*Waaq, Waaga, waaqa,*
etc.)
X – Orthodox Christian

Table 6.1b The symbolism and archaeological materiality and manifestation of the Ritual Set for the Sky-God belief in the Horn of Africa

Sacred Symbols in Fertility Rituals	Water, Springs, Rivers	Trees And Sacrificial flora	Mountain / hill tops ("nearer to Waaqa") rock shelters, enclosures	Stones (grave) (granite or polished)	Iron	Moisture	Zar (spirit	Ritual hunt/killing and birthing, fertility	Circumcision, FGM, gudniin and cliterodectomy: Sacrifice both men and women	Incense and Burning incense
	Healing, Cleansing Bad spirit,	Sacred wood, grasses, Coffee fruits, groves, Divine power, Healing, protective, Ass. with protective deities (ex. African olive, sycamore tree, juniper tree)	Associated with deities, religious figures	Divine power, Healing, Ass. with deities, idols	Protective power, Fertility symbol, perpetuation of the kinship Sacrifice in the 'killing and bearing' concept and rain-making	'wet=fertile', 'keep things wet and (sky-) God will make you wet', Cleansing Body/object from bad omen/ (diseases) buna qalla, bun shuruur Zar lives in springs, rivers and wells	possession, ayaana/rooxaan), ancestral spirits spirit markers Saint/ lineage founder worship/ prophets Siti, Atete	Sacrifice (risk, pain, bravery) stick fight Istunka ceremony Atete ceremony Sarara ritual Bir-ma-geydo	Ritual, rite of passage, righteous blood, lineage, age-grade markers, status markers, (noble) 'killing and bearing'	Communicating with the deities, purifying, healing, protective against evil spirit, consecration of space and body (for ritual activity/ intercourse/ conception)

material evidence	Water sources, wells, springs, *wadi*, water from sacred source kept in bottles, springs, secret pools, architectural water containers, vessels	Stelae of wood, planks Sticks (ex. *siqe, wagar, dempi*) 'branches', grass, sprouting beans on rock art/ stelae, Headrests with the cross and/ or phallic shape, Spoons with vulva bowl and/ or phallic handle, Sculpture or figurines of cattle, snake	Rock hewn ritual sites Rock art, architecture Cairns Crushed material from 'sacred mountain/ rock' included in clay for special ritual objects such as containers (pottery) and incense burners, and *zar* clay and cow hide drum, stone bracelets	Gravestones Stelae, Phallic, Polished stones, Sculpture or figurines, cattle, snake figurines and depictions Cairns Drums, Mountains	Objects of knives, dagger/ sword, needles, and metal wires but also images of knifes on stelae and rock art	Particular containers for different substances, coffee fruits (*buna qalla, bun shuruur*) Pottery or another container, Fat sources marked with stones or sacred trees, anointment of *kraal*	Bracelet and rings for *zar Waga*, Ostrich eggs and Feathers Cattle, snakes Stone bracelets Beads, Amber necklaces, Kohl needles and pots, drums, *Hirbora* (Oromo ivory ring for hunters and killers)	Depictions and physical objects: knives, *bilow* (Somali) *bilo'a* (Oromo) daggers, bow and arrows, swords both through imagery on stelae/ rock art or objects, Special necklaces, Kohl needles and pots	Special bracelets, Rings for both men and women for circumcision and on wedding, needles, surgery equipment, bone needles	Incense burners, *meershum*, frankincense, myrrh, *wagar* trees, architectural features such as niche, net-basket (*Gambis* for clothes to souk smoke), knives (for sourcing incense from tree, *beenyo* knives, Kohl needles and pots

Table 6.1c The Horn of Africa and a Ritual Set for the Sky-God belief

Sacred Symbols in Fertility Rituals and Ancestral worship (zar, siti, Atete, adbar etc.)	Water:	Sacred: trees	Stones:	Moisture:	Animals/ depictions:	Iron:	Incense: Burning,	Calendar:
	Sacred Springs, Rivers, pools Healing, Cleansing Bad spirit,	(sycamore tree, African olive) wood, grasses, groves Sacrificial flora Coffee fruit Divine power, Healing, protective, Ass. w. protective deities, killers/heroes stelae/*waga*	phallic, vulva, snake (cobra, python) Anthropomorphic, Stelae, hills, sacred enclosures, Divine power, Healing, Ass. with protective deities, killers/heroes stelae/*waga*	'wet=fertile', 'keep things wet and (sky)-God will make you wet', Cleansing Body/object from bad omen/(diseases)	Cows (divine, fertility), sheep (peace/fertility), snakes (ancestor/spirit, fertility), Bees (esp. Guji and Amarha Ostrich (feather)	Ritual hunting, Protective power, Fertility symbol, perpetuation of the kinship (male blood) (swords piercing the ground for crop or creating wells penis piercing a girl for the sake of motherhood Cutting-scarification Fire kindling/solar new year (meskel/*dabshid*)	Sanctifying, Purifying, Healing, Spiritual Medium, Enabling fertility (the Matcha Oromo use fragrant leaves/ "smoking the belly") Disabling evil spirit	Annual sacrifice and purifications with incense, water and milk stick fight/*Istunka*, Circumcision, Lip-plates, scarification Stone worship, Snake worship Smearing trees and leather with butter

Oromo (Boorana, Arsi, Guji, Matcha and Boorana)	X	X	X	X	X	X	X
Konso	X	X	X	X	X	X	X
Somali	X	X	X	X	X	X	X
Afar	X	X	X	X	X	X	X
Haddiya	X	X	X	X	X	X	X
Sidamo	X	X	X	X	X	X	X
Dirasha	X	X	X	?	X	X	X
Gedeo	X	X	X	X	X	X	X
Amhara	X	X	X	X	X	X	X
Tigre	X	X	X	X	X	X	X

this is not to say that there were not other deities as well). Ethnographic accounts mostly discuss this Sky-God belief in terms of 'Old Cushitic', 'Cushitic institutions' and the 'Cushitic religion'. Although I find that the term Cushitic has its limitations (I prefer to avoid supposedly ethnic terms), I use it as an inclusive term that reaches beyond its linguistic limits – and I am well aware of its pitfalls in this context. When I use the term 'Eastern Cushitic common elements' in Table 6.1a, I do so more to demonstrate how the present-day Muslim or Christian beliefs amongst this group should not be seen as major barriers; their obvious commonalities help to illustrate an indigenous ideology that goes way back beyond these beliefs. As such they serve as an example of larger cultural communalities, the common perspectives, cultural expressions and beliefs that are embedded in the larger population of the whole of the Horn and even extend into its adjacent regions.

The Eastern Horn of Africa populations and subsistence economies

The population of the Horn manages its social and political territories through complex sociopolitical organisations and through the successful exploitation of various types of environment (Trimingham, 1965; cf. Huntingford, 1955; Lewis, 1994a; Baxter, 1990; Loo, 1991; Legesse, 1973; Kassam and Megerssa, 1996). In terms of land, the Eastern Cushitic speaking groups inhabit almost the entire Horn of Africa (Ehret, 1976; cf. Shinn and Ofcansky, 2004). Here can be found some of the biggest Eastern Cushitic groups, as outlined in Table 6.1a. In terms of approximate geographical locations, the Guji Oromo live by the Great Rift Valley lakes; and the Boorana Oromo in southern Ethiopia and northern Kenya. The Hadia and Gedeo are based at Shoa in central Ethiopia. The Konso live with the Sidamo in the Sidamo region; and the Arusi are in Sidamo and Arusi Bale. The Dirasha inhabit southern Ethiopia. The Somali are in the Somali territories as well as (mainly) eastern and southern Ethiopia, northern Kenya, Djibouti and southeastern Eritrea.

It has been established that in terms of linguistics the Eastern Cushitic groups are very similar (Ehret, 1976; cf. Shinn and Ofcansky, 2004: 123). The Konso share 55 per cent lexical similarities with the *Dirashigna*; the Gedeo 60 per cent with the *Sidamo* and 51 per cent with the *Haddiya*; and the *Sidamo* 53 per cent with the *Haddiya* and 60 per cent with the *Gedeo* (Ehret, 1976; cf. Shinn and Ofcansky, 2004: 123). A native speaker of Sidamo, Konso, Oromo and Somali will find it easy to understand some of the common words for religious, cultural and social phenomena (see Appendix 3). In addition to this common linguistic heritage, Eastern Cushitic speaking groups share many traditions. My focus here is on the Eastern Cushitic speaking groups because of the relevance of their geographical location to my discussion. Furthermore, this geographical area brings together those wider cultures that are relevant to the Sky-God belief of the peoples of northeast Africa.

I have noted earlier that the oral traditions and the legends of the Somali and the Muslim Oromo people suggest that their origin lies in Arabia. But I have also noted that such myths of origin have been influenced by the modification of indigenous genealogies by Islamic ones. Nevertheless, most academics agree that these groups seem to originate from the Lake Turkana area (cf. Ehret, 1976; Prouty and Rosenfeld, 1994).

Table 6.1a presents the characteristics of the religious symbolism common to the Eastern Cushitic speaker.

Traditional subsistence economies are mainly based on farming, mixed or pastoral nomadism. The Eastern Cushitic speaking agriculturalist communities are mainly found in southern Somalia and southeastern Ethiopia (Ehret, 1976; cf. Shinn and Ofcansky, 2004). The Konso, the Sidamo, the Dirasha, the Gedeo and the Haddiya also cultivate ensete[1] (*Ensete ventricosum*) a.k.a false banana or Abyssinian banana. The Guji are mixed farmers and herders, involving respectively cattle and ensete; the Arsi Oromo are Eastern Cushitic pure pastoralists. There is however a great deal of interdependence within these subsistence economies during droughts[2] (Kanshie, 2002). The Boorana Oromo are mainly cattle herders. While some of the Somali are pastoralists, there are also farming communities in the riverine region of the Shebelle and Juba.

Common traditional political systems: a kinship ideology

I have already presented a basic analysis of the function of religious lineage leaders. African political systems are inspired by indigenous ideologies and practices (Fortes and Evans-Pritchard, 1940). I use the term 'sacred kinship' to describe the Cushitic institutions in their role as institutions of sacred power which claim the prerequisite genealogical links with the religious power/the divine. In relation to sacred fertility, it is important to note that 'the clan relations were maintained with *Waaq* at all levels of the social structure' (Lewis, 1998: 29–30); the relationships with (Muslim) saints are maintained through the worship of local shrines and tombs belonging to (Muslim) eponymous ancestors who can grant *baraka* after sacrifice. Thesiger noted the enormous effort to pay homage to their dead made by the Afar who carry huge blocks of stones and wood with which to build their tombs.

The nature of Somali genealogies may itself provide a clue to understanding the nature of divine kinship in the Somali past:

> The religious aspects of Somali genealogies which centre in sacrifice at the tombs of eponymous ancestors were, in pre-Islamic state of Somali society, intrinsically a part of Cushitic religion, and knowledge of the larger hierarchy of Cushitic spirit-refractions does, I think, throw light upon the nature of sacrifice to the dead, and leads to some elucidation of the *religious meanings* attached to Somali genealogies.
>
> (Lewis, 1998: 2; cf. Cerulli, 1957). [Italics added.]

The genealogical link between religious figures such as saints and their 'ritual efficacy' is of such importance to Somalis that one genealogy might adopt a saint from a different genealogy by reason of the success of his prayers. A particular saint will achieve a popularity on account of the specialist powers with which he is associated (Cerulli, 1957: 204–205; cf. Lewis, 1998: 15). One example of this is Saint Aw Hiltir (Xiltir), a saint who is said to guard people from crocodile attacks (this is clearly of relevance in an inter-riverine area) (Cerulli, 1957). The name Hiltir comes from *hil* (*xil*) meaning a task or responsibility; and from *tir/tar*, meaning able to do. The image of the crocodile calls to mind the belief that some people are able through sorcery to turn a human being into a crocodile or even to order a crocodile to kill a person in the river. Another example is Saint Aw Mad who is associated with the Rahanween clan and protects the harvest (Cerulli, 1957: 205–206). I suggest that both these examples may indicate the continued importance of the possibly pre-Islamic religious leaders/chiefs of the Cushitic institutions.

Cushitic people appear to root their kinship in their genealogical links to the religious leaders. Prophets represent the omnipresent Sky-God *Waaq* on Earth in the Cushitic religion (which is today generally identified with the traditional Oromo religion). Those Oromo who are still traditionalists trace their origin back to these prophets who are also local saints (Braukämper, 2004; Legesse, 1973, 2000). The Oromo still retain a traditional sociopolitical system based on age-sets called the *Gada*-system or *Kallu* (*Qallu*) institution (Jensen, 1936). *Kallu* has the ultimate power to elect members to progress up the steps of the age-set system which is sociopolitically important for the males. Hence, males traditionally, within these societies, dominate in religion, politics and economic power (Legesse, 1973; Prouty and Rosenfeld, 1994). Amongst the Dirasha and the Konso, for example, women are regarded as the weaker sex and, like the Guji women, are not allowed to own land (Prouty and Rosenfeld, 1994). And, amongst the Somali, women traditionally are not allowed to own camels. Nevertheless, the social organisation of many of the Eastern Cushitic speaking people promotes an egalitarian way of mutual aid exchange within society (Legesse, 1973; Levine, 2000: 138; Hallpike, 1972). This egalitarianism has survived in most of the Oromo groups and the Konso and has even recently been incorporated into the Amharic social system (Levine, 2000). The *Gada*-system is specific to the Eastern Cushitic groups and (ibid.). Similar political systems today include the *Gada* system of the Konso, the Oromo and the Guji Oromo. The Cushitic Sidamo, Arsi Oromo, Dirasha and Somali are clan-based and the Gedeo[3] incorporate some elements of the age-grade system (see Table 6.1a). The Boorana's most important custom is *gadamoji*, the initiation cycle, which lasts eight years (Adamson, 1967).

The aspects mentioned above highlight the fact that kinship is greatly esteemed by these Eastern Cushitic speakers – but then it is also by other non-Cushitic speaking peoples in the region (e.g. Levine, 2000). I have already noted that fertility rituals are a mark of how important it is that kin are represented in the political and decision-making sections of society. As part of these rituals, certain actions are commonly applied to women's bodies to enhance their fertility (see Loo, 1991 for evidence of this amongst the Borana), and an iron knife is placed behind the heads of sleeping children to protect them from contamination by evil spirits (I have also documented evidence of this practice amongst the Somali). Similarly, the Guji Oromo put *ceefi*, an ornament decorated with cowrie shells, under a child's head as a protection against *buda* (the evil eye) (ibid.).

Given the importance that fertility holds for the people of the Horn, I will now explore in more detail the specific relationship between fertility and pre-Islamic/pre-Christian beliefs.

A common pre-Christian and pre-Islamic religion in the Horn of Africa

I have read the accounts of European ethnographers in the greater Horn of Africa going back to the sixteenth century AD. Through these it is possible to discover many of the characteristics of the Cushitic traditional religion (Alvares, 1881; Almeida, 1954 [1593–1646]; Burton, 1966 [1898]; Conti Rossini, 1905; Paulitschke, 1888; Thesiger, 1935). There is documentary evidence of the existence, within and around the region, of the same groups that still live there today, and of a continuation of the same broad cultural practices. I believe that the term 'Cushitic religion' is mainly used in the literature to distinguish the Cushitic speaking traditionalists of Ethiopia from the Christian and Muslim Tigre and Amhara populations. Yet even these latter populations retain a solid foundation of indigenous beliefs and practices mixed in with their Muslim and Christian beliefs. I therefore find it problematic to use the word Cushite to define a specific material culture. I prefer to use it to describe a regional religion because many of the large traditionalist groups also happen to be Eastern Cushitic speakers. And the traditional belief in the Sky-God was still very much observed in the southern part of Ethiopia in the sixteenth century, as Alvares and Almeida's respective reports suggest. As a result, there exist even today many cultural ideologies with shared rituals and a common symbolic use of material culture and landscape (see Tables 6.1a-c), beliefs that cross both current linguistic and religious boundaries and are fundamental to the character of the Horn of Africa and northeast Africa.

The historical literature therefore supports the argument that these Eastern Cushitic speaking groups not only had a common language and a common political system but also shared common belief systems, past and present. These sources note that the Supreme Being of the Cushitic religion is the Sky-God, the creator of everything. He is worshiped by, among others, the Oromo, Konso, Gedeo, Somali, Arsi and the Sidamo (Alvares, 1881; Almeida, 1954 [1593–1646]; Bartels, 1983; Baxter, 1990; Burton, 1966

[1898]; Conti-Rossini, 1905; Hallpike, 1972; Loo, 1991; Lewis, 1994b; Luling, 1988; Paulitschke, 1888; Shack, 1966; Thesiger, 1935).

As noted earlier, the Agao people are said to follow the Cushitic religion (Ullendorff, 1955; Cerulli, 1957: 148, 157; cf. Trimingham, 1965; Lewis, 1998). Alvares (1881) mentioned that the Agao people were still largely 'pagan' in around 1520. He documented their customs in his *Some Records of Ethiopia, 1593–1646*. He noted that they adhered to a single 'Creator of Heaven' and had no idols. Like the other Cushitic speakers, they also revered river springs, sacred groves and trees. His observation provides a rare insight into the religion of the Cushitic peoples since many of the Agao have since converted to other religions though some still exist amongst them who have preserved their traditional religion. They still gather at sacred groves, notes Trimingham who adds that traces of the traditional Agao cult practices are still to be found within, amongst others, the Christian Agao (Trimingham, 1965: 17). Furthermore, as Thesiger notes, the annual coronation of the Sheikh of Budhu (the leader of two clans, the Asboura and the Badogalet) involves many of the elements that feature in the Cushitic institutions: the ritual significance of the moisture, fat, the sacred mountain, fertility, rain-making, the sacred tree and ancestor worship.

> On being invested with his office he changes his name, and is believed to receive the power of controlling rains. The Dankali [Danakil] are fully convinced that it always rains on this day, even from a clear sky. The Sheikh is clad in a red and white cloth. He is smeared with *ghee* and may not now put his feet upon the ground. He is carried in a special chair some 200 yards towards the rising sun and back. The right of carrying the chair, as of clothing him, is hereditary. On his return the chair is placed upon a bed outside his hut. Then earth from the summit of Mount Ayelu, the sacred mountain, is rubbed upon his hands, earth from beneath a large *shola* tree upon his feet, and clay from the bottom of the Awash River on his forehead. (The Dankali connect the *shola* tree with their ancestors, but were very obscure upon this point.) The Sheikh is next saturated with *ghee*, and the crowd fight to touch him.
>
> (Thesiger, 1935: 7–8)

Even today, there are Eastern Cushitic speaking groups who still practice the traditional religion. However, it is important to note that similar concepts exist beyond the boundaries of current Cushitic speakers. The Amhara, for example, use the abstract *adbar* concept for the embodiment of spirits in trees, a rock, mountains and springs and other water sources. As noted earlier, the main deity of the people of the Horn is the Sky-God and the supernatural world of local nature-spirits is linked with natural features such as mountain peaks, stones, streams and trees (Trimingham, 1965: 18; Conti Rossini, 1905: 109–122; Cerulli, 1957: 177–186; Hallpike, 1972: 134–137). Groups of Sidamo, the Boorana and Arsi Oromo, the Konso, the Agao and the Haddiya also adopt this concept (see Tables 6.1a and c). A more profound adherence to the *Waaq* cult is found amongst the Somali who are less affected by outside influences, for example those living along the Ethiopian borders of Somalia and northern Kenya (Lewis, 1998: 140). This can be contrasted with the lack of *Waaq* in the easternmost Somali part of the Horn (ibid.). There the Sky-God is known as *Eebe*.

Indeed, the research based on linguistic material and religious beliefs into the origins of the Somali suggests there was a pre-Islamic belief in the Sky-God, *Waaq* (Kusow, 1995; Mansur, 1995; Ehret, 1995; Lewis, 1994a, 1998). Part of the belief system related to the Sky-God belief was based on the sacred trees that they considered to be deities. These trees are even now thought to be religious ancestors and are still consulted when there is need of blessing; their worshippers give offerings to them as part of a variety of rituals (Mansur, 1995; cf. Kassam and Megerssa, 1996; Lewis, 1998; Loo, 1991).

The Sky-God is worshiped in fertility rituals such as rain-making in the hope that rain may fall and the people and the cattle flourish. Baxter explained the *ayaana* and 'the peace of the Borana';

> the bounty which God evinces in the gift of rain, and hence well-being, and the gift of fertility to women and to stock, and hence prosperity, must be maintained by the flow of prayer and sacrifice and that condition of consensus and active co-operation which Boran call the Peace of the Boran.
>
> (Baxter, 1990: 238)

This is similar to the role of the priest in keeping peace amongst the Konso (Hallpike, 1972: 18–19). The same can be said about the Somali *wadaad*,[4] who helps create peace and conducts fertility, rain-making and peacemaking rituals.

Many of the Eastern Cushitic groups who remain traditionalists still follow the traditional Cushitic belief in the Sky-God and the associated fertility rituals. The traditional *Waaq* belief forms the current religion of the Sidamo, Konso, Dirashe and Gedeo (Kusow, 1995; Hallpike, 1972; Ehret, 1995; Lewis, 1994b, 1998; Trimingham, 1965). The Oromo (including the Boorana, Guji and Arusi) are of mixed belief, with some traditionalists adhering to *Waaq* and others converted to Islam and Christianity (Prouty and Rosenfeld, 1994). The Hadia are similar, with some being traditionalists and others Muslim.

The Somali are Sunni Muslims, as noted earlier. There is also, however, again as noted earlier, what Lewis called a 'Cushitic substratum of Somali Mohammedanism' (1994a: 102). Many Muslims or Christians in the Horn commonly retain some traditional beliefs because these have a strong role to play in society as they are so closely tied to custom-based law and kinship (Lewis, 1994a, b, 1998; Loo, 1991). In the pursuit of sacred fertility in the context of the conversion to Islam, it seems that a syncretism of gene-alogies has taken place. I noted earlier how the Prophet's lineage has been integrated into Somali society and how the equivalence of Cushitic power and Islamic *baraka* facilitates the veneration of Muslim saints at pre-Islamic shrines (Lewis, 1998: 29; cf. Trimingham, 1965: 263).

The sites of former pre-Islamic shrines are used for the veneration of new Islamic saints since Cushitic power can be replaced by Muslim *baraka*, according to Lewis and Trimingham. The Somali/Cushitic emphasis on genealogies and the importance attached to eponymous ancestors who are celebrated at their tombs is equivalent to the Sufi genealogies, hence easing the reorientation of clan founders into becoming Islamic saints (cf. Triming-ham, 1965; Lewis, 1998: 30). Through these means, syncretism of religions is present in groups converted to both Islam and Christianity, particularly in the region's Eastern Cushitic speaking populations.

The idea of fertility is a paramount part of Cushitic institutions. Ancestral worship is related to fertility rituals since the people venerate ancestral reli-gious figures to bring them the human and animal fertility they need in their daily existence and to bring prosperity. In this context, it is the relationship of blood to a religious figure that appears to be all-important.

My interviewees did not explain why a marriage could not be consum-mated at Aw-Barkhadle during a woman's period in the time of Bu'ur Ba'ayr. It is not difficult, however, to associate this ban with ideas about purity. The groom ought not to be with the bride while she is impure and it follows from this that a marriage can only be granted at a time when there is purity. Ritual purity is important to the gift of fertility. Consummation is a fertility ritual that needs to follow the rules, and if there is even the suspicion of a taint then the ritual will not succeed in producing offspring. Furthermore, in terms of securing a divine lineage bloodline, she will not be pregnant if she is having her period and hence any offspring can only be the product of her union.

This act of confirming purity reveals a notion of sacred fertility that can only be granted through genealogical links with religious figures: Moham-med Haniif/Bu'ur Ba'ayr, the lineage founder and highest religious leader, and Aw-Barkhadle, the cousin of many of the Somali lineage founders including Sheikh Darood and Sheikh Ishaaq. In the creation of myths of origins, the Cushitic pre-Islamic and the Qurayshi Islamic join forces to create the Somali Muslim and Cushitic religious ancestors. Why, then, is it so important to have a blood link to the divine? I explore this point further below.

An ideology of sacred fertility in the northeast African institutions

I have argued that the paramount significance of Aw-Barkhadle lies in its syncretic sacred landscapes. Cushitic institutions' notions of fertility and ancestral worship (Loo, 1991) seem still to be observed by Somali Cushitic society today, albeit in a much more implicit form. The landscape of Aw-Barkhadle, it seems, can only be truly understood in the light of the analyses of fertility rituals and sacred landscapes provided earlier in this book.

Some members of Somali society regard any link between the pursuit of fertility and the veneration of the saints to be impious since they view it as belonging to a traditional ritualistic context which is not strictly Islamic. The fact that women continue these rituals (as I have shown in both Chapters Three and Four) at a time when even Sufism is threatened by recent Salafi movements is also key to this study. In Chapter Four, I attempted to describe the non-Islamic rituals and, in Chapter Five, why numerous of these rituals (cults) are still observed today. I explored in more detail the veneration of ancestors and rain-making. I suggested that the indigenous notion of fertility is a fundamental part of the Horn of Africa societies that extends beyond the current religions of Christianity and Islam. Here is an ideology that is based on the essence of life itself: reproduction. Hence, it is an ideology rooted in nature that both Islam and Christianity (and other ideologies) have had little choice but to appropriate. The ideology of fertility is a core part of the society of the Horn of Africa.

The sacred (ancestors as trees, stones or animals) therefore remain central to the search for fertility, and it is through sacrifice that a good relationship is maintained with these sacred ancestors. Even today, sheikhs and priests practice fertility and other rituals. The *roobdoon* ritual held in Hargeisa is a Muslim 'rain-making request' prayer. Women with infertility issues go to Lalibela so that priests may plunge them into its fertility pools. Sheiks, according to Lewis (1998), have replaced the role of the traditional pre-Islamic religious leaders and similar transfers of spiritual power have taken place with Christian priests. People in the Horn of Africa are not continuously drawing strict lines between their practices in terms of Christian versus Muslim or of traditional versus either Christian or Muslim. They rather live in congruence with a regional culture and deep cultural values. The new religions of course play the central role and attract the most adherents but it is also fair to say that regional cultural practices are never far beneath the surface. Amongst the people, the notion of sacrifice is paramount, from incense burning and coffee pouring on Fridays to perfuming and the ritual sharing of meat. These kinds of convergence and transformation can be better understood through material archaeology, particularly when it is combined with a multi-temporal approach such as the Knowledge-Centred Approach.

Aw-Barkhadle: symbolism and materiality of the notion of fertility

Sacred materials or materials that entail divine power are, as noted elsewhere in this book, prominent in fertility rituals including ancestral worship and rain-making. I argued in Chapter Two that there is often a lack of cultur-ally significant theoretical frameworks within which to contextualise the archaeological material from the Horn of Africa in order to understand its symbolism and that this remains the case even though the interpretation of the symbolism of material culture and beliefs has been on the archaeological agenda for at least the last couple of decades (Hodder, 1982, 1989; Renfrew, 1994; Tilley, 1984, 1989, 1991; Ucko, 1969; Marcus and Flannery, 1994; Whitley and Hays-Gilpin, 2008; Zubrow, 1994). I have suggested that by studying certain rituals it is possible to illuminate the uses of landscape and its associated material culture. By examining the potential continuity of such rituals, it may be possible to interpret the relevant archaeological data of the last 1000 years. I have found most useful those approaches which use a holistic framework. I have noted the problems inherent in the ethnographic approach and I have, in Chapter One and elsewhere, emphasised the impor-tance of using local people's memories and knowledge when studying cultural expressions, past and present (Mire, 2007, 2010, 2017). I outlined in Chap-ter Two how I would make use of the material in the chapters that followed to generate and implement a locally appropriate theoretical framework.

I have drawn four main conclusions from the material I have studied. First, the female ritual use of sacred centres today is an activity kept separate from other more general practices. Second, certain features in the cultural landscape are significant: tombs, mountains, springs, stones, trees etc. Third, there is a strong relationship between current practices and non-/pre-Islamic and pre-Christian regional religious elements. And, finally, a social organisa-tion exists which is based on a divine kinship ideology. This in turn supports an ideology of fertility and the role of women in maintaining the Cushitic (non-Islamic) rituals that serve these fundamental ideologies by preserving these rituals and their ideals. I have argued that the disturbing rituals of the *gudniin*, *istunka* and *baanashada dumarka* and the insertion of *tiire* and herbs in the vagina (as described in Chapter Four) and the *wagar* with which women burn their hips, are all, no matter how cruel they may be, important rituals supported by a kinship ideology that emphasises sacred fertility. This is truly a fertility ideology linked to sacred kinship.

The Cushitic institutions may perhaps have used divine kinship to gain sacred fertility, as the pre-Islamic cult of Bu'ur Ba'ayr, Atete, *zar* and Gedi Baabow suggests. It is not only women that seem to make use of these Cushitic practices: as noted in Chapter Five, Sufi sheikhs have themselves adopted practices such as ancestral veneration and rain-making in the sort of services previously conducted by the religious figures who grant sacred fertility.

The site of Aw-Barkhadle, as I have shown in Chapter Three, displays a triadic relationship between rituals, material culture and landscape. The area of Aw-Barkhadle contains archaeologically significant material that is easily visible. This includes surface material, house foundations, town walls and cemeteries with tombs in both Islamic and pre-Islamic styles. At least four burial traditions are evident. The rituals that take place there are historically significant since they demonstrate a continuity in local practices that stretches back beyond the time of Islam.

I now want to focus on the significance of the archaeological data found at Aw-Barkhadle. The site was important in the past when at least one ruler of Awdal was buried there, as I noted earlier; and it is still significant to Somalis today. The continuity in the ritual use of this special landscape sheds light on the pre-Islamic ritual significance of the archaeological landscape – the sacred mountain, enclosure, burial mounds and tombs – and enriches its interpretation. It provides an opportunity to explore wider questions about the syncretism of space, rituals and their associated materials in the Horn generally and in the Somali territories in particular.

I will now discuss how the possible continuity of pre-Christian and pre-Islamic regional indigenous practices can enhance our understanding of past religious beliefs and the archaeology of the Horn. The ideology of fertility, its practices and its significance, discussed in Chapter Five, provides an insight into the use and relevance of sites and landscapes both for past generations and for those living today, and both for former and current religious institutions in the Horn of Africa.

The entire landscape of Aw-Barkhadle is sacred, as noted in Chapter Three: 'it is anywhere that God makes it, therefore it is everywhere' as one of my interviewees put it. And when I asked whether it was only one particular stone that was sacred, the answer was similarly 'it is all complete in here ['*banaankaasay ku' dhantahay*'].' And when I asked why people tie cloth [*marqaha*] to the tree branches, one of my interviewees replied, simply: 'it is the place of Sheikhs.' These replies and other accounts bear witness to the power with which this landscape is endowed.

The far-reaching impact of Aw-Barkhadle allows other sacred landscapes too to be considered in the context of fertility rituals, rain-making and ancestral veneration. Here, however, I want to focus on these practices as a way of highlighting the archaeology. As an archaeological site, the Aw-Barkhadle landscape offers elements that are both intriguing and significant. These include the tombs and the ruined town to which Aw-Barkhadle belongs. They also embrace elements that the archaeologist may not necessarily recognise as archaeological data – the stones, hills, trees and water sources (Figure 2.1). I now, therefore, want to put the archaeology from the surface analysis alongside the anthropological research to show the importance of each methodology to the whole and to draw some lessons for future archaeological investigation. I adopt the Knowledge-Centred Approach and am therefore interested in multitemporality (rather than a strict chronology); and in potential continuities in practice, both ideologically and mythologically, between rituals, material culture and landscapes, including the more conventional archaeology.

A ritual set for the archaeological context: a model for the Horn?

When studying the symbolism of archaeology in the Horn of Africa, *why* is the one question more than any other that demands an answer. Sometimes, something that appears to be of very little importance can assume a new significance when people are asked *why* they are acting in a particular way or using a specific object. It is this *why* question that has driven this book. I have identified a ritual set of materials that seems to occur together in the fertility rites (Tables 6.1b-c). I have compiled this data by observing the rituals, material culture and sacred landscape at Aw-Barkhadle and by comparing these with those associated with other sacred landscapes in the Horn of Africa – archaeological sites such as Sheikh Hussen Bale, the ancient cemetery site of Tiya, Aksum and Lalibela.

Depending on the configuration chosen, the Ritual Set can be adapted to apply to a heritage stretching back over the last two or three millennia. It will be up to archaeologists and anthropologists alike to decide what form that configuration should take. Through it, they will be able to identify tangible patterns and behaviours with which to explore the possible links between space, rituals and material culture.

Other scholars, including Hamilakis (2014), have shared my concerns about associating practices and performances that may change over time to archaeological sites that probably represent a 'snapshot' in time. However, my Knowledge-Centred Approach reaches beyond both modern-day ethnographic conventions and the conventional linear perspectives of the archaeologist. Instead, I look at the arrangement of artefacts and ask how they bear witness to intangible meanings; I consider layers of time to be cyclical and rhythmical; I look for deeper meaning than the *chaine opera-toire*. Memories, skills and performance produce acts of 'doing' as well as of putting together; and the oral contributes to other unquantifiable, but no less tangible, meanings. My use of the word 'set' in the term Ritual Set reflects my belief that this collection of observations brings together connected materials, the location (the landscape) and the acts that take place there. This setting, or performance set, demonstrates a holistic approach integrating the place of ritual, the act and the material of the performance (procession). The Knowledge-Centred Approach focuses on the intangible as well as the tangible aspects of the performance of the Ritual Set – the words uttered, the movement, the senses and the scent.

I recognise, of course, that the significance of objects, materials and landscape can change through time. The need remains, however, to investigate the potential continuity of the rituals associated with materials and landscape features, including the ancestral burials. I therefore investigate the type of materials associated with the symbols designed to boost the abundance of human beings, animals and crops in the population of the Eastern Horn. In Table 6.1a, I outline a set of shared regional characteristics including sacred materials associated with the fertility rituals of the peoples of the Eastern Horn and I will discuss these in more detail below. It is worth noting that the Somali do not now seem to consider cattle per se to be sacred though they set store by some of their characteristics, in much the same way as do their neighbours.

Water sources and moisture

Wells are often located in sacred landscapes in both the Somali and Ethiopian contexts. Many Somali sheikhs are believed to possess powers to create a well miraculously, as I noted earlier. It is widely believed that sacred wells have a purifying effect. At Aw-Barkhadle there are several sources of sacred water: the *bali* (lake), an ancient well (*ceel*) (Figure 3.22) and the *wadi* (Figure 2.1). Sacred wells are associated with sheikhs and these places are usually left undisturbed and become archaeological sites as a result of the ruined towns that have grown up around them and which were often an important part of pre-Islamic and pre-Christian indigenous belief systems. However, there are also sacred wells still in use whose ritual significance remains associated with the ancestral power of clans and families still dominant today. The *ugaas* (king) of the Iise clan of the Somali is washed in a special well dedicated to him alone in the western Somali region during the *caleemosaar* ceremony, when he is decorated with leaves (see Chapter Three). Sometimes, the *ugaas* might be washed with milk (*caanoshub*) and anointed with butter. Anointment (*dhaashi*) gives *dhalaal* (a shine) and vitality. *Dhalaal* is important for fertility but also has *dhalaal* which is good for confusing bad spirits.

The Sky-God's domain is the rainbow 'The Sky-God's belt is the rainbow, and the rains are in his keeping as a gift for man; certain individuals have power over the rains through their relation to God' (Lewis, 1998:23; cf. Hallpike, 1972; Loo, 1991; Bartels, 1983).

Water is important for ridding the body and other materials of bad omens and disease but it also denotes the fertility of human beings, land and animals. Sacred wells are particularly associated with pre-Islamic deities and hence with supernatural power; any archaeologist looking for possible non-/pre-Islamic sites might bear in mind that such sites will be associated with sacred springs, wells and rivers – and trees.

Both the Somali (Burton, 1966 [1898]) and the Oromo (Loo, 1991) consider it important to keep the body and objects made from animal skin moisturised. The Guji Oromo regard keeping leather objects wet as a ritual act reflecting fertility (ibid.): the (Sky)-God will thereby keep the land, people and animals wet and fertile. They anoint the *kraal* enclosure (sacred enclosure) during a ritual called *dibayu moona'a*. Women and men eat at the Aw-Barkhadle ritual enclosure (Figure 3.24) near the tomb (not the Bu'ur Ba'ayr enclosure) and spill *maraq* and wish to be blessed, uttering *khayr'ow khayraad*. I observed a similar enclosure near the rock hewn churches at Lalibela (Figure 6.1).

Figure 6.1 Ritual enclosure for prayers, ritual meals and meetings at one of the rock hewn churches at Lalibela

Tumuli, stones/rocks, hilltops, mountains and rock-shelters

Archaeologists often regard as separate those features which may instead be interconnected: a 'hill', 'mountain', 'rock', 'rock shelter' and 'paintings/engravings'. They recognise as sites only those that show evidence of recognisable human interaction, paintings, artefacts and the like. Random hills and stones are relegated to mere landmarks, and this places limits on their interpretation. At best, there might be a recognition of a local belief in spirits dwelling in a particular area. Archaeologists may lack the relevant knowledge of local ontologies and rely instead on the certainties of a discipline that looks only at ancient artefacts in the archaeological context; they completely lack the local input, the all-important local views on traditions – and so pass by the material meanings and ideological rhythms of the past. These rhythms reach beyond the mere appearance or utility of an object; only through working outside conventional archaeological methods and theory can the limitations of this and similar disciplines be truly understood. Rather than accepting that 'archaeologists do archaeology' it is important to recognise that archaeology has its limitations and to move on beyond those constraints. After all, who is to say what archaeology is or ought to be?

The stones themselves might be deities to whom offerings are made rather than merely suitable surfaces upon which to draw. As noted earlier, the Danakil still make pilgrimages to sacred mountains, the Guraali Mountain and the Ayelu to the northwest of Aussa, where the earth from the top of the mountain, for example, will be smeared on a new chief's body (Thesiger, 1935: 8). I have already noted how pilgrims at Aw-Barkhadle start the *siyara* of the Muslim saint by collecting chalk from the Bu'ur Ba'ayr hill to paint Christian crosses on their foreheads. Similarly, the Oromo undertake the *sirisa* pilgrimages and the Somali Iise clan crown their *ugaas* on a sacred mountain (see Chapter Three). Bartels writes 'they [the Matcha Oromo] sacrifice on the top of a hill to be "nearer to Waqa"' (1983: 90). The Konso hold certain mountains and hilltops central to their religious activities and associate some with evil spirits (Hallpike, 1972: 227). It seems reasonable to assume that the animals depicted on rocks were also once sacred and that they played an integral part in the worship of the deities. The rocks, the hills and even the animals might themselves have been regarded as deities. I have noted the important hills found at Buur Hakaba in southern Somalia. The Cushitic Rendille in northern Kenya also revere a sacred mountain named Ol Lolokwe.

As I noted when discussing sacred landscapes in Chapter Five, pre-Islamic sacred landscapes have been incorporated into Sufi Islam. According to the oral traditions recorded by Mukhtar (1995) and Lewis (1994a, b, 1998), there are several pre-Islamic legends to be found across the Somali territory. If they are indeed based on fact, surviving memories of Bu'ur Ba'ayr, by the hill at Aw-Barkhadle, demonstrate the significance of Aw-Barkhadle to both the Somali population and the Islamic and non-Islamic populations of the Horn. In my survey of sacred landscapes in the Somali region, I have come across the sacred landscapes of Sh. Darood, Sh. Isaaq, Sh. Samaroon and Sh. Iise (Figure 5.7, Figure 5.8 and Figure 5.9), all of which are sacred centres that seem to include important hills and wells. They, too, are associated with the legends of pre-Islamic deities. They remain landmarks today and represent a link with the past.

Like the engraved black fertility stones of Goroyo Cawl (Figure 3.15), the Dhammer Gowrac stones (Figure 3.27) and Dhaymoole bear similar signs which suggest a connection with each other: they, too, may once have been fertility stones. These massive stones are landmarks too, like the mountains and the hills. Associated with these engraved stones are burials of a pre-Islamic nature. The local people who guided me to the site told me that the stones and burials went back a long way. Perhaps they marked an ancient trading route or a valley of the dead, like the cairns (*arawelooyin*) I noted along the Red Sea Somali coast in the mountains of the Sanaag region, including an area between Maydh and Hiis which contains the sacred landscape of Sh. Iise and Sh. Isaaq (Mire, 2015a). The fertility stones here, like those at Aw-Barkhadle, Goroyo Cawl, Dhaymoole and Laaso appear to form part of a region-wide metaphorical reproduction of the notion of sacred fertility.

The Somali worship sacred stones (Burton, 1966 [1898]: 145, n.1; Cerulli, 1957; Lewis, 1998; Trimingham, 1965) and the Aksumite culture too is known for "a highly perfected [sic] form of stone-worship" (Bent, quoted in Trimingham, 1965: 33). Tumuli building continues in the Horn of Africa; Thesiger (1935) reported that the Afar people were still building tumuli in the twentieth century and erecting stones to celebrate revenge killings; the Danakil people create piles of stones constructed around a central standing stone (cf. Morin, 2004) to serve as tombs for the dead, with the central pillar representing the ancestors. At Aw-Barkhadle, there is a dolmen (Figure 3.4), as mentioned earlier in Chapter Two. Somali tumuli in the northeastern Somali region are attributed to Queen Araweelo (Révoil, 1882: 297). I observed and documented hundreds of massive burial mounds or cairns (araweellooyin) aligned along the tops of the maintain chains between Maydh and Heis in the Sanaag region, an area known for its Roman and other long-distance trade surface and excavated items, reported by Révoil, Chittick (1975) and myself (Mire, 2015a). These mountaintop cairns may represent ancestors that in pre-Islamic times were thought to be close to God, in much the same way as in Islamic times the revered shrines of the Somali lineage founders are located in the area. It is important to note that at Aw-Barkhadle the cairns are found on the Bu'ur Ba'ayr hill. It may well be that the pre-Islamic religious ancestors were buried, or had cairn burials dedicated to them, on hilltops facing the sea in much the same way as the lineage founders of present-day Somali clans are buried by the coast. Such cairns are found not only along the coasts of the Somali Red Sea but also along the coast of the Indian Ocean starting from Ras Hafun, where there are trade posts with Roman artefacts date to third century BC (Chittick, 1975) to all the way to Ras Kambooni, on the borders of Kenya. The above mentioned coastal Heis and Maydh area massive cairns of Sanaag and other parts of the Somali region may well represent both ancient local ancestors and stone worship. Perhaps these massive hilltops burial mounds are to imitate or mark sacred mountains and indeed they are topping some of the mountains and make an spectacular view from the sea.

When I talk, therefore, about sacred fertility in northeast Africa, I am doing do so in a regional northeast African sense. I select only those cultures that demonstrate these fertility practices most clearly; and these cultures serve not as an end in themselves but as the starting point from which to explore notions of sacred fertility across time and space. In other parts of Africa, practices may differ. Amongst the Nuer, for example, the man, or even a whole lineage, is represented in certain sacrificial contexts by a spear (Evans-Pritchard, 1940, 1954).

The approach I adopt relies not just upon one tradition; it applies a broader methodology to compare and contrast across place and time. Fattovich (1987) has established that many African cultures erect stelae – so I now want to ask *why?* and to contextualise the practice both locally and regionally in order to understand the meaning behind this widespread and probably interconnected custom.

An ancestor might sometimes be represented by, say, a metal object instead of a stone slab, dolmen, stela or a cairn. The spear and the dagger intersect with the stone in producing the stela. So, the sacredness of both materials is symbolically exploited to carve a stone stela in the shape of a spearhead or to depict a spearhead or a dagger on a stone stela. Consequently, there are some cultures who depict a spear or dagger on the stone and some who work the stone into the shape of a dagger or spearhead.

Sometimes, the construction of stone slabs on sites might mark or symbolise the killing of a big animal like a lion or elephant. At other times, for example amongst the Afar and Konso, Muslim graves commemorate revenge and its casualties; here large stones, marking the victims, stand at the entrance to walled enclosures (cf. Joussaume, 1995). I suggest that the point of stones such as these is not only to record the revenge killings of an enemy but also to celebrate life and fertility, and if the dagger or spear, or their depictions, are present, then these may well carry a life-affirming message – as they do in the case of the Oromo and Somali practices. An alternative purpose might be to offer sacrifice to the ancestors. The closer to God a farmer or herder is, the more successful he will be – and he might want to erect a large stone to signify his ritual sacrifice.

Sacrifices to hills or stones may reflect the ritual need to keep things in harmony with the ancestors; those seeking sacred fertility will ritually make objects fertile by keeping them wet. Women keep their own skins or leather wet so as not to lose the fertility of their bodies or of their animals, as Loo (1991) has suggested in relation to the Guji Oromo.

I discussed the significance of stones in fertility rituals in Chapter Three. A sacred stone exists at Aw-Barkhadle upon which women sit and pray in order to receive fertility. In Arabia, I note, blood is poured onto a stone as a sacrifice to a pre-Islamic God described as 'a rock in a desert' (Serjeant, 1976: 10).

Stones might themselves be divinities with the power to grant fertility or to heal illness and to provide protection against bad omens and the evil eye etc. Fertility stones are found elsewhere in the Somali area which may once have denoted pre-Islamic deities. When people converted to Islam, their divine power was transferred to Islamic ancestral saints. The site of Aw-Barkhadle is still associated with Somalis who, though Muslim, nevertheless practice aspects of traditional Cushitic rites in much the same way as do the Oromo groups along the eastern border of Ethiopia. The engraved black fertility stones of Goroyo Cawl, near Borama on the Somali-Ethiopian border, are significant to people on both sites of the border. Furthermore, in the neighbouring Harar region, there survives a tradition of ancestor veneration through prayers offered up to stones (Thesiger, 1935; Burton, 1966 [1898]). I also came across the idea of oath-taking on the rocks during my field research in the Somali region of Ethiopia (cf. Lewis, 1998). All this evidence taken together reveals, I suggest, a widespread pre-Islamic belief in sacred stones within the Horn of Africa.

Archaeoastronomy, stelae, phallic stelae, snakes and the Sky-God

There are many stelae cemeteries at Aw-Barkhadle and most of them appear stylistically to be non-/pre-Islamic. The stelae cemeteries are characterised by graves marked by one single stelae standing alone. A few of these also have symbols engraved on them. These stelae cemeteries and the dolmens, which include a couple of pre-Islamic burials, have large flat stone slabs and a pre-Islamic dolmen (Figure 3.4). The sacred stone and the sacred enclosure of stones at Aw-Barkhadle together with the tombs with gravestones and stelae (including phallic ones, Figure 3.30a and b, Figure 3.33) are all venerated; they bear witness to the relevance of the continuity in association between the dead (ancestors) and the living.

Furthermore, there are features of Aw-Barkhadle that are similar to those found at other sites in the Horn. In what is now present-day Ethiopia, the stelae cemeteries of Aksum, Gudit, Tiya, Tuto Fela and the megaliths of Laga Oda and the Sourré in the Harar (e.g. Buxton, 1957; Azaïs and Chambard, 1931; Joussaume, 1974, 1995; Phillipson, 1997, 2000; Fattovich, 1987; Fattovich et al., 2000) suggest a megalithic tradition in the Horn that seems to go back millennia. The tumulus at Asa Ragid is flat and in the shape of a crescent, with associated piles of shells and fourth millennium BC basalt axes (Joussaume, 1995).

The material above suggests that stelae and tumulus graves exist all over this region. My own fieldwork in Somaliland located many stelae cemeteries which have much in common with the known stelae cultures in southern Ethiopia (Mire, 2015a). Many stelae cemetery sites in the Togdheer region are considered stylistically to belong to pre-Islamic times: at Da'awaleh/Dacawaleh in Saahil region, there are what appear to be depictions of a lunar system with depictions of a full moon, crescents, a number of single squares with a diagonal cross (Figure 2.5c) and a square with 28 holes believed to be a calendar of 28 days (Figure 6.2) (Mire, 2015a). And

Figure 6.2 A square with 28 holes believed to be a calendar of 28 days, at Da'awaleh rock art site in Saahil

the present-day Eastern Cushitic speaking peoples as well as other groups in Ethiopia, including the Amhara and Tigrean (Levine, 2000), keep annual calendars of religious ceremonies. I am currently working with the Oday-Ka-Sheekee cultural and folklore centre in Hargeisa on the Somali and Cushitic calendars and potential archaeological calendars in this region. The centre's group of researchers have published the first ever Somali traditional calendar, *Dabshid*, in 2016. Their work builds on that previous generations, including the Somali polymath Musa Galaal, who compiled astrological, meteorological and calendrical information from Somali culture and folklore (Galaal, 1970). Galaal recognised early the profound interest and knowledge Somali pastoralists have about the weather, stars and time, which impact their life daily. Ours is a new exciting colloborative research, which will shed light on the relationship between indigenous perceptions of time, cosmology oral and material culture, including archaeology.

Furthermore, there is a Cushitic indigenous astronomical calendar and lunar system to mark the fertility rituals that relate to harvest and irrigation (Cerulli, 1957: 211–227). Reproduction – of plant, animal and human life – is key to the rituals of the Cushitic peoples. The Somalis, too, hold a fire kindling or *istunka* festival, (Cerulli, 1957; cf. Lewis, 1998; Trimingham, 1965) where people jump over fire and beat their bodies in the belief that the heat will cure them of disease. They keep calendars for rearing livestock and for seasonal movements.

Rock art and stelae sites including possible indigenous calendars have been dated to *c.* 300 BC (Lynch and Robbins, 1978: 767). However, at one of these sites, Hildebrand et al. (2011) found pottery associated with regional Neolithic pastoralists and suggested that the site might be from around the second or third millennium BC and served as a *loci* for the mobile pastoralists. In another study, Lynch and Donahue conclude 'The Namoratunga sites on the basis of similar grave construction and mortuary routine, are closely related to sites of present day Eastern Cushitic Speaking peoples' (Lynch and Donahue, 1980: 76; for a differing view see Soper, 1982). These sites demonstrate the concept of kin and how the layout of the cemeteries is centred around this concept (ibid.): 'It is suggested that different kin groups were represented at the two sites, possibly different patrilineages. Hence, for the Namoratunga sites the art proved to be what was clearly an important key to understanding the Namoratunga mortuary routine' (ibid.: 85). Research into the megalithic site of Namoratunga would benefit from the holistic multidisciplinary approach that I later apply to Tiya rather than a simplistic random one.

I found the stelae of Ximan and Dhaambari in the Togdheer region. The Cushitic calendar kept and used by the Somali till the early twentieth century (discussed by Cerulli, 1957) may be useful, up to a point, in the interpretation of the carvings on these stones. The Cushitic calendar records the agricultural year and the seasons for the different ritual activities relating to harvest and irrigation (ibid.: 211–227). The first astrological site in East Africa is attributed to the Eastern Cushitic speaking peoples in northern Kenya:

> Namoratunga, a megalithic site in north-western Kenya, has an alignment of 19 basalt pillars that are nonrandomly oriented toward certain stars and constellations. The same stars and constellations are used by modern eastern Cushitic peoples to calculate an accurate calendar. The fact that Namoratunga dates to about 300 B. C. suggests that a prehistoric calendar based on detailed astronomical knowledge was in use in eastern Africa.
>
> (Lynch and Robbins, 1978: 766)

The Turkana people who live in the area today are Nilotic people; their indigenous religion resembles that of the Sky-God in all but name. Their god is called *Akuj* and is a supreme omnipresent god with the same attributes as *Waaq*. Incidentally, northeastern African sacred kinship, as I call it, may be in some way distantly affiliated with the Sudanic sacral *kingship* which has long been well known (Ehret, 2002: 94, italics added):

> One key feature of classical Egyptian political culture, often assumed to have begun in Egypt, can be strongly linked to the southern influences of this period. We refer here to Sudanic sacral chiefship, which entailed in its earliest versions, one especially salient custom, the sending of servants into the afterlife along with the deceased chief. The roots of later Egyptian "divine" *kingship* lay in this Sudanic innovation. If we were able to travel back in time to visit the areas along the middle Nile and Egypt in 3500 BCE we would discover there a long-extended region of sacral chiefdoms and tiny sacral kingdoms. This long belt of small polities would have encompassed both the Eastern Sahelian communities to the south along the river and their southernmost Egyptian-speaking neighbours to the north.

Ehret continues (ibid., p. 145, italics added):

> An interesting light is thrown on how a sacral leader becomes a divine ruler if one looks at this religious context. South of Egypt, under the monotheistic Sudanic religion, the later kings of Nubia and other states of the Sudan belt of Africa retained their sacral aspects but could never become viewed as gods themselves. In contrast, in Egypt, where political unification changed henotheism into polytheism, it was possible by the time of the Third Dynasty for a king to convert the claim of sacred status into a claim of being included among the gods. We can therefore speak of divine *kingship* in relation to Egyptian culture, but only of sacral *kingship* within the context of Sudanic civilization itself.

By understanding the origins of the sacred leadership and sacred ancestors we can begin to understand the underpinning ideology of divine *kinship* in northeast Africa.

As I noted earlier, historical linguists believe that origins of the Eastern Cushitic peoples lie in the Lake Turkana area. Recent dating evidence reveals that some of the Namoratunga sites are of an even greater age; it would be interesting if their carvings were associated with a proto-Eastern Cushitic calendar.

The work of Lynch and Robbins reveals that the distribution of stones at Namoratunga was not a random act but one which correlated with 'certain astronomical events, especially since present-day Eastern Cushites have a sophisticated calendar which uses the rising of seven stars or constellation in conjunction with various phases of the moon to calculate a 12-month, 354-day year' (Lynch and Robbins, 1978: 767). The rock art site of Da'awaleh is another possible calendar site, as noted above, although its relative age is not yet known. Its paintings depict the moon in its different phases, from crescent to full moon; there are also some squares with a diagonal cross in the middle dividing them into four parts and a square with 28 little squares suggesting a day calendar. I have recently discovered a few remarkable graves at Aw-Barkhadle which are constructed in a shape which may be linked with the notion of time (Figure 6.3). One grave has three cross shapes in a line. Each cross is in the shape of a set of diagonal lines which divide each square space into four parts. It is possible that the four-part square constructed by

Figure 6.3 A grave at Aw-Barkhadle with three squares with a diagonal cross dividing each square into four parts suggests 12 months of the year

stones and replicated three times along the graves represents three by four parts, i.e. the twelve months of the year. This may well be the case because the same image of the square divided into four parts of the cross is found in Da'awalah[5] (Figure 2.5c) where it includes depictions of the moon in its different phases along with a 28-day calendar.

These geometrical signs are identical to the ones seen on the Ximan stelae which also include concentric circles that, in the indigenous regional culture, represent fertility. Interestingly, the rock art of the Namoratunga area also includes concentric circles and other intriguing geometric designs that are similar to those found at the Da'awaleh site. Further study of the stelae may lead to their interpretation within a more local context.

Lewis writes about the nature of *Waaq*; 'The semantic relation is eyes, seeing, sun, and light' (Lewis, 1998: 22). There is a Somali song about the Sky-God: 'This Sky, the same unchanging, without the central-pole according to the Divine Will' (noted by E. Cerulli and quoted in Lewis, 1998: 23). Since the Sky-God is linked with the sky and the moon and rain-making, future excavations may shed light on the age of the stelae images. Both the Da'awaaleh and Namoratunga sites are known to be associated with rain-making practices and they may perhaps have links with the Sky-God belief regionally. The rock art can be relatively dated through the dates obtained from the burials associated with the stelae. Furthermore, their relationship with other stelae traditions and decorations in the Horn of Africa can be investigated further. It is indeed remarkable that the Arusi and Konso stelae recorded by Azaïs and Chambard (1931) seem similar to the Ximan stelae. It may well be that these too are associated in some way with the Cushitic calendar mentioned above, with the worship of the Sky-God, *Waaq*, and with Cushitic people's ancient rain-making and ancestral rituals.

Elsewhere in the Horn of Africa, a relationship between the rock art and the dolmens has not yet been established though Joussaume argues that there might be a link between groups of dolmens such as those found at Tchelenko and the painters of the rock art at Laga Oda in the Harar region (Joussaume, 1995: 71). Settlements belonging to these groups have yet to be found but archaeologists ought to be able to adapt their investigative techniques to discover them however ephemeral their traces may be. The pottery and lithics of the region have not been well studied (cf. ibid.). Gravestones and cairns to mark ancestral worship can, however, still be found in this region, and it should therefore be possible to use ethnographic data from the Horn of Africa to understand how such sites might once have been used in pre-Christian and pre-Islamic times.

There are ancient stelae cemeteries in the Horn: Azaïs and Chambard (1931) found many decorated ones in areas populated by the Konso and Arussi. The stones erected for the dead served not only as grave stones but also as symbols of ancestors and fertility and the preservation of the family both amongst the Oromo and the Konso (cf. Loo, 1991; Hallpike, 1972) and, as I found during my field research, amongst the Somali too. I suggest, therefore, that the erection of stelae by these (Eastern) Cushitic speaking groups might well also have been linked to *Waaq* since some of the characteristics of *Waaq* seem to point to the significance of the sacred ancestor as a centre-pole (*udub*) or the concentric circle. It is important to note that we located at the site of Ximan in Toghdheer a concentric circle on grave markers similar to the ones in the rock art of Namaratunga of Turkana region (Figure 6.4).

Figure 6.4 Toghdheer and Ximan concentric circles on grave markers similar to in the rock art of Namaratunga of Turkana region

Material evidence of the ritual use of fertility stones, including phallic stones, can be found at Aw-Barkhadle. This indicates, on the one hand, the pre-Islamic history of the site and its links with the rest of the Horn of Africa and, on the other hand, shows a continuity in use from an indigenous culture through to the present-day. One of four corners of a tomb has a phallic tombstone (Figure 3.30a) which may suggest material evidence indicating the myths of the Bu'ur Ba'ayr legend in the case that ancient indigenous fertility rituals may have been construed as 'wicked rituals'. Furthermore, phallic stones have been discovered in other parts of the Somali region, as noted in previous chapters. In 2011, a farmer found two phallic stones (Figure 3.31a) in a cairn burial; these are similar to the one found at Aw-Barkhadle and to those in the British Museum collections (Figure 3.32a, b).

This phenomenon is known to occur at other Horn of Africa sites, for example at Tuto Fela in southern Ethiopia. This site consists of a large tumulus and lies at the heart of the region where phallic and anthropomorphic stele have been found (Joussaume, 1995: 87). Some of the decorated phallic stele at Tuto Fela appear to be anthropomorphic male/female representations with respective gender specific details, a phallus/vulva etc. (ibid.) (Figure 6.5). The current practices associated with the Cushitic religion can explain the meaning of these phallic stones. Hallpike (1972: 134) writes 'the presence of the *daga deeruma*, the phallic stones in the *moras*, is a constant reminder of past achievements in battle which should be emulated today.' Also, as noted in Chapter Five, the blood of the sacrificial animal is poured on the phallic sacred stone in order to establish reconciliation during the purification rites (*ib*). The occurrence of phallic symbolism, therefore, may be seen not just as a symbol of victorious battle and masculinity but also as a symbol of reconciliation (*nageefatta/araarafatisa*) and purification. It also, according to Bartels (1983), signifies fertility which is regarded as a similarly brave action to killing (a big game) and giving birth.

Ethnographic evidence also exists, as noted earlier, for the significance of phallic symbols in the Horn of Africa. A Konso religious leader like the Oromo also bears on his head a phallic symbol, *Kallasha*, which is a symbol of power (Hallpike, 1972; cf. Legesse, 1973). Other Eastern Cushitic religious leaders of the Oromo and the Konso tie this phallic object (Figure 3.20d) onto their heads with a snakeskin. This may suggest a link between snake worship and phallic symbolism. Phillipson (2000) reported finding a snake figurine in Aksum, perhaps indicative of a snake symbolism (though little is known about the indigenous symbolism at this site). It is important to note this because ancestral worship and snake worship are related in Cushitic society, as already discussed in Chapter Five.

Some Somalis, as noted earlier, believe that certain snakes are *awliyo*, saints, or ancestral saints and when these snakes appear, it is said that they are 'paying a visit' and that they are not meant to be killed. The landscape of Aw-Barkhadle is known for its snakes which are referred to here as religious ancestors who will never bite the people they are supposed to protect.

Figure 6.5 Stela from Tuto Fela world heritage site in Soddo region of Ethiopia in a
phallic shape with stylized vulva/phallus

It is also recognised that various sacred animals such as snakes feature in
traditional beliefs (Cerulli, 1957: 78–79; Hallpike, 1972: 251–252). Snakes
also seem to be part of the repertoire of sacred beings associated with the
Cushitic belief in the Sky-God and are seen as proxies for the protectors
or founders of lineages. Snakes are depicted in the rock art of Ethiopia

(Joussaume, 1995). Insects, too, are included in the domain of the Sky-God and Lewis (1998: 23) confirms that termites and scorpions and various insects are among the animals ascribed with divine powers within the Cushitic religion. In Somali society, the scorpion is associated with fertility.

Trees and wood

I have already described how some trees are considered to be sacred at Aw-Barkhadle and other places (Figure 3.21). Through this discussion, it has become clear that trees, wood, grasses and groves can have a ritual divine power and are considered capable of healing and protecting.

Richard Burton visited the ruined town of 'Abbasa, western Somaliland, in the 1880s. and described it as a palace with stone walls and transverse layers of wooden beams (Burton, 1966 [1898]). I have already noted that wood is used in the construction of graves and buildings. Wood may also have a ritual significance because it comes from trees. Wood usually disappears eventually from the archaeological record but, when it is found, archaeologists seldom seem to attach any particular meaning to it; they consider its importance in terms of construction and dating methods but often fail to recognise its potential cultural significance. Wood, and the trees it comes from, as well as plants, ought to be considered in terms of their religious importance since, as this study argues, trees play a central part ritually in both burials and house constructions. In relation to the Agaw and their belief in the Sky-God, Almeida (1954) has noted that they bury their dead in chambers they construct in the woods. In the Somali region, as noted earlier, the dead have sometimes been buried in trees. The concept of a sacred forest also exists. It is of course possible that wood found in the archaeological context has no ritual significance whatsoever – but it may be discovered to have if its cultural associations are explored more carefully. Ethnographic evidence need not necessarily reflect the archaeology of ancient times, but sites like Tiya do show that wood features specially in the burials.

I have already noted the importance of the sacred tree, Halimaleh, near 'Abbasa. It forms part of the ritual sacred landscape of Aw-Bube and is near Goroyo Cawl, a site also dedicated to Saint Aw-Barkhadle. Like Aw-Barkhadle, Abbasa is a ruined town associated with the Awdal and Walashma Dynasty (see the map of ruined towns, Figure 2.1). The two sites, Aw-Barkhadle and Goroyo Cawl, seem to have a similar collection of features (sacred stones and sacred enclosures) and similar anthropological characteristics. Both are associated with the Sufi saint, Saint Aw-Barkhadle. The Goroyo Cawl site additionally seems to be associated with the ancestral spirits known to have links with the pre-Islamic Cushitic and an Oromo priestess called Kola. I have already noted how trees feature in the Oromo, the Danakil and the Somali commemoration of ancestors. The Konso, moreover, erect *ulahitas*, the sacred dead juniper trees, to mark the warrior grade of their *Gada*-system (Hallpike, 1972: 28). Sacred stones are sometimes replaced by sacred wood or combined with sacred dead trees (ibid.). The juniper, the sycamore and the African olive are all considered to be sacred by the Eastern Cushitic speaking peoples in general. The trees denote ancestral spirits which are worshipped, and the tree names form genealogical clan names. According to Lewis, 'In certain situations clans are described as linked to trees and animals which are addressed by maternal kinship names, but the connection does not appear to be totemic' (Lewis, 1998: 23). The worship of trees appears to be a crucial part of the old religion of the Sky-God and it is possible that the connection in the past was totemic. The Cushitic Myth of Origin involves a man in a tree (Luling, 1988). Eastern Cushitic groups such as the Sidamo and Haddiya, Konso, Oromo, Tasmai, Somali and Afar still believe in sacred trees (Trimingham, 1965: 28, 54, 183, 260–261; cf. Cerulli, 1957; Hallpike, 1972; Legesse, 1973, 2000; Lewis, 1998; Loo, 1991; Mansur, 1995: 120). Perhaps the *waqlaal* ritual is a symbolic sign of the beginnings of a people's history: the procreation of a male lineage symbolised by the bones of the child in the ancestor or the tree. The dead may take objects made of these sacred trees into the grave with them. In the Oromo societies of Ethiopia and Kenya (especially the Boorana), sacred trees include the sycamore (*ooda*) and their present practices may shed more light on those of the indigenous traditional.

People worship trees and pray to them. Trees, regarded as ancestral priests, are consulted on issues of childbirth. Oromo daughters receive ceremonial sticks (called *Siqe/siiqqee* (see Adamson, 1967: 271) from their fathers when they are married and they keep these for the rest of their life. There are other examples of these common rituals too: the ceremony of the *siqqaa*, a sacred fertility stick given to women by their fathers on their wedding day, just before the ceremony (see Kassam and Megerssa, 1996; Loo, 1991 for evidence of this as practiced amongst the Oromo); and the sacrifice of cattle during the initiation ceremony within the *Gada*-system (see Legesse, 1973; Loo, 1991; Levine, 2000). The ceremonial sticks used by the Oromo reflect both social and religious power (Kassam and Megerssa, 1996). The Oromo have another holy tree called *dampi*. The *wagar* tree and the *wagar* sculpture, discussed in Chapter Four, provide an example of a ritually significant tree in Somali society; this may be similar to the *qanafa* wood that the Oromo women wear during child delivery and the months that follow as a protection against evil spirits.

Archaeologists ought sometimes to consider trees as sites in their own right because trees as well as places can be venerated. Sacred wood, grasses and groves, too, are associated with divine power and have healing and protective abilities. The role trees play has frequently been documented in ethnographic studies in Eastern Africa. Nevertheless, archaeologists in the Horn of Africa have so far failed to mark their potential importance as regionally sacred wood. Many Cushitic speaking groups have traditions of building sacred buildings with wood and of enclosures (*moras*) made of sacred dead trees (cf. Hallpike, 1972: 28). It is important to reflect on the role of wood in other parts of the Horn such as Lalibela where it plays such an important part in church construction and may serve a ritual, as well as an architectural, purpose.

Iron and metal objects

According to the *Muriid* and his wife, Saint Aw-Barkhadle used his sword to pierce the ground and in so doing created a well. As part of his regalia, the *Muriid* carries various sharp iron objects, including a sword. I have also seen that Sufis even today still carry swords in the Somali territory (Figure 6.6). Iron is associated with rain-making and lightning and in pre-Islamic times was also linked with the Sky-God, *Waaq*, and it therefore seems that the Sufis have recognised the significance of iron within the fertility rituals such as the rain-making rituals. The same may apply too to the Cushitic *wadaad* who continued to use his regalia after conversion to Islam. Furthermore, Lewis (1998) supposes that charms and amulets were used in pre-Islamic times and suggests that their usefulness today is related to the Qur'an.

There is also a fertility symbolism associated with iron objects such as knives, daggers, pins and swords. This symbolism is related to the specific ritual context that is ascribed to sharp objects made from iron. In Somali and Oromo female society, sharp iron objects are used to ward off the evil

Figure 6.6 A Somali Sufi man carrying his sword

eye and in child protection rituals, as discussed in Chapter Four (cf. Mire, 2015b). As I have already noted, the Somali women's *wagar*, together with a sharp metal item, is tied in a bundle of grass gathered from a sacred grove to protect the babies from evil spirits while they sleep. The *kohl* (eye make-up) is applied, using a metal pin, to children to protect them from evil spirits, a widespread practice known in the Horn of Africa. This metal pin, which is rather like a hairpin, is associated with the protection against evil and forms part of the symbolic use of iron.

The Guji Oromo man will put a dagger into the ground to mark the place where his deceased father is to be buried (Loo, 1991; 150). Others have noted practices relating to the evil eye in other parts of the Ethiopian region (Finneran, 2003 in relation to iron working; Fernández, 2011 in relation to rock art). In the context of the Guji, however, the practice symbolises the perpetuation of the kinship (Loo, 1991): that the father is not dead as long as he has sons. Iron seems to have the power both to protect against evil spirits and to be a fertility symbol in that it represents the continuation of the kinship (male blood). Amongst other Cushitic speaking peoples such as the Danakil, boys are not allowed to carry a knife, an important symbol of manhood, until they have been circumcised and admitted as men into the tribe (Thesiger, 1935: 6). Even amongst the Somali, in time of revenge, knives or daggers are for men alone to use, and they symbolise the continuation of lineage by suggesting that a man with a virile strength is like iron and will be sure to produce male offspring.

The Somali Madhibaan Myth of Origin found by Kirk states that the ancestor of all the Madhibaan people was a superhuman or demigod, named Gowedi, who was 'covered' with iron from head to toe leaving only his eyes and two digits on his hands and feet visible. The Madhibaan assert that Gowedi was one of Ishaaq's sons (Kirk, 1905). His brothers took his camels and ended up in the woods feasting on a dead animal. Gowedi, killed by an Ogaden who shot an arrow into his eye, was buried in the land of the Majeereen and the Warsangeli (ibid.). What interests me here is the iron and the supernatural power of this early lineage-founding 'iron-man'. In Somali traditional sayings, moreover, the Sky-God is metaphorically associated with iron as is the centre pole of traditional houses: 'The God's eternal constancy is compared to the centre-pole of the hut. "May the centre-pole be as of iron". Without support man's house collapses, but God, "the same without the centre-pole", is full of wonder and power' (Lewis, 1998: 22–23). I associate this image, along with the stone slab that is usually laid, or the stela that is erected, as a symbol of the perpetuation of lineage. Iron is part of the sacrifice regalia in the ancestral veneration rituals. The *Muriid* of Aw-Barkhadle confirmed the relevance of iron objects to the rituals at Aw-Barkhadle and to those associated with rain-making.

Depictions of knives have also been found on rock art in Somalia (Grottanelli, 1947). Is this further evidence of the ritual slaughter of animals or even of a ritual hunt? Depictions of knives within the Horn of Africa have often been used to suggest a warrior culture but it makes more sense to ascribe them to the ritual hunt, a sacrifice for fertility. The Sufi are not known for their warrior culture; on the contrary, they have been described as *'wadaads'* (men of religion) as opposed to *'waranleh'* (warriors) (Lewis, 1961: 27–28). Their *raison d'etre* is sacred fertility, not war. The Cushitic word for knives seems to come from the same Cushitic root: *bilow* (Somali) or *bila'o* (Oromo). Warrior cultures may well exist within the Horn, but, given the Sufi's use of the sword and dagger to promote fertility and rain-making, it seems more appropriate to study the properties inherent in these objects by virtue of their *ritual* context within the Horn of Africa.

Furthermore, as noted earlier, the *istunka* ritual of the Somali farmers demonstrates how misfortune, including failing crops, famine and ill health, will follow if a fight fails to take place. This ritual involves men hitting each other with hard sticks and is a fertility ritual performed as a sacrifice to God. Furthermore, the spear is used amongst the Matcha Oromo to kill sacrificial animals and their killing is very much associated with religion, fertility and giving birth. Through these means, the Somali men are under-going a beating in which their bodies are pierced in much the same way as a women's body undergoes *gudniin* in the interests of sacred fertility. For the Matcha, the husband 'pierces' his wife's vagina with his penis during their first act of intercourse, and the fact that the bride bleeds her maiden-blood equates with the slaughter of the sacrificial sheep. It is not enough, therefore, simply to look at depictions of knives or daggers or spears or any other weapon without first considering their ritual meaning, a meaning that extends beyond the simple war/virility association. So too must iron and metal objects be seen not just for the technology they represent or the uses to which they may be put or the 'maleness' with which they are associated; their symbolic meaning may be by far the most important reason for their inclusion in a ritual context.

Pottery, incense burners and other ritual containers

Various types of incense, including frankincense and myrrh, are utilised in the Horn as has already been noted (Figure 3.17a, b). Frankincense and myrrh in particular have an important ritual significance for the people of this area. Their trade was an important one (Groom, 1981) as is also clear from the reports of the Ancient Egyptian Queen Hatshepsut's expeditions to the 'Land of Punt', as noted in Chapter Five. It is believed even today that incense has a purifying effect on both people and space making each more receptive to God's presence. By extension, incense can be seen as a medium through which communication with God (through the saints and the sheikhs) can more easily take place. Furthermore, incense is also seen to heal and protect human beings. It offers protection against evil spirits and bad omens. The Oromo and the Somali burn it during every ritual activity. It is part of fertility rituals and a part of grief, burial and prayers.

A bride must be exposed to incense fumes during the fertility bath ritual in traditional weddings (the Oromo e.g. Bartels, 1983: 272 and the Somali wedding night), as has already been mentioned. Field-walking over the site of Aw-Barkhadle has produced many surface finds which include potsherds and the broken-off handles of incense burners. Throughout the year, in the single most important sacrifice in the Somali territory, the *ziyara*, worshippers bring *fooh* (incense) for all the venerated sheikhs. And nearly all the Islamic tombs at Aw-Barkhadle have square niches built into their sides to hold the incense burner (*girgire*) (Figure 3.13).

Incense seems to be associated with purification and ritual chastity not only in the Horn of Africa but also in Red Sea Arabia (cf. Serjeant, 1976: 63). It plays an essential part too in rituals with a pre-Islamic origin such as the Hunt ritual; this ceremony can be considered unsuccessful if participants have caused a *dhaim* (a fault); if this happens, participants must use incense, among other things, to purify themselves before repeating the Hunt ritual (ibid.).

Incense is also of great importance within the fertility rituals of the Red Sea region where it is seen as a purifier and sanctifier. It is interesting to note that the meanings 'conciliatory' and 'good at heart' are associated with incense or perfume (*tib*) and in Arabia too. The significance of the *tib* as a purifying object has already been discussed in Chapter Five. Prophet Muhammad gave the name *Taibah/Tabah* (place of reconciliation) to Madinat Rasul Allah. Madina acted as a centre of reconciliation during Prophet Muhammad's time. The Zamzam well at Mecca is known as *Tibah* due to its purifying merit (Serjeant, 1976: 62).

Pottery, alongside other types of containers, is used in sacrificial meals in the Horn of Africa. Ceremonial containers, such as the Somali *heedho*, hold the sacrificial meat that is ritually consumed at weddings. Other groups in the Horn may use the word *fijaan* instead of *heedho*, as in, for example, the *filjan* used by the Amhara during the famous coffee ceremony which is itself a fertility ritual. The Oromo have particular containers for fat (butter/*ghee*) which are used on ceremonial occasions (see Appendix 3). These include pottery as well as bottles, woven containers and metal containers. As Thesiger (1935) observed, the Harar Oromo and Somali were putting food in pots placed on top of tombs as offerings to the dead. And Almeida noted how the Agaw, who bury their dead in chambers in the woods, place 'hydromel and the cups which they were accustomed to use in drinking when alive' (1954: 20).

The Somali, affected by the Islamisation that took place along the coast in as early as the ninth century, retained fewer indigenous religious ideas than did the Oromo. They use special containers (*kurbin*) for the *Bun dahaadhan* (whole coffee beans) which the Oromo also consider have magical powers. *Bundub* (roasting beans) are associated with the Friday ancestral worship of the Somali. The Somali say *bun dubow balaayo ma arko* (the roaster of coffee beans never experiences bad things). The *Qallu*, a ritual expert who mediates between people and the *Waaq* god, is believed to be in constant communication with the Waaq. The word *Qallu* comes from slaughter and it is the *Qallu* who sacrifices to God.

The Agaw, as has been noted, make offerings of cows, milk and butter to sacred springs, trees and groves. Containers found near rivers, springs and trees in places without any trace of 'settlement' signify ritual activities. These containers ought to be tested for traces of any contents they might once have contained – the residues of milk, butter, meat and the like which may signify food that can also signify ritual activity relevant to the location.

Reports on the archaeology of the Horn mention incense burners (e.g. Phillipson, 1997; Joussaume, 1995; Joussaume, 1981) but offer no interpretational framework or cultural context. At many sacred centres in the Horn such as Aw-Barkhadle, the use of incense is evident in the incense burners and distinctive sherds found. Archaeologists can understand the significance of incense and its association with ritual if they contextualise it through a study of the Ritual Set including the ethnographic evidence relating to fertility rituals.

The Ritual Set (Tables 6.1b-c) which I have constructed is mainly based upon my study in the field of practices and archaeology associated with the regions populated by the Eastern Cushitic speakers, but its applicability is not limited to them. Instead, it serves as a departure point from which to explore exchange patterns and the broader ideological relationships between regional communities: distance, proximity and length of coexistence are critical. As I have already stated, I am not equating a particular object, practice, feature or symbol with any one linguistic group; it would be unwise to do so. I am, however, recognising the ideological origins of these features in the context in which they materially occur.

African religions are seldom distinguished from each other and simplistic words like 'animist' are often used to describe them. Ethnography therefore plays an important part in helping them to be better understood. I use the Sky-God religion as a blanket term to describe many variations in belief and I am well aware that different groups, the Oromo and the Boorana for example, will each have their own individual 'take' on their religion.

Summary

It is possible to argue that the erection of stones, notions of the evil eye and some of the elements described above might well exist in other societies too. In constructing the Ritual Set I have therefore avoided basing interpretations on random objects or behaviours. I have not, for example, suggested that the discovery of incense burners in the archaeological context will automatically mean that the people who used them were practicing fertility rituals. What I do suggest is that certain clues as to the meaning of such incense burners might come from: a study of the site as a whole; a record of the potential relationships between space and objects such as stones, wood and rituals; and an investigation of culturally relevant sets of data including any available ethnographic material.

Material evidence for the ideas that surround death and burial (ancestral worship) and reproduction (fertility rituals) may well have existed in the region for long enough to be of relevance to archaeologists. The contrasting yet interconnected nature of perennial issues such as death and fertility (giving birth/creating life) can produce a continuity of sets of artefacts and associated landscape features at Aw-Barkhadle and other sacred centres in the Horn. Amongst the Cushitic speaking peoples of the Horn today, sons erect a pole from the wood of a sacred tree, or pile sacred stones upon, the tops of their fathers' graves to mark the continuity and perpetuation of the family. Knowing that this happens can help to explain the meaning of a stelae, for example, but that meaning will become far more complete once the incense burners, the iron objects, the carvings on, and of, stone, the alignments etc. are added. The point of the Ritual Set is therefore to provide the archaeologist with a springboard from which to investigate and understand the cultural context and the meaning of certain configurations of material culture.

I have chosen the word 'ritual' because it is a dynamic and meaningful description. And, as I explained earlier, I chose the word 'set' because it relates to sets of objects, to their performance and to the landscape or space within which they are arranged and constructed. The Ritual Set represents, in essence, a triadic relationship – material culture, rituals and space.

The significance of fertility rituals is rooted in the survival of the present generation and the assurance of a next generation. I conclude this about Aw-Barkhadle: God and the ancestors are worshipped and venerated, and the ancestors are well treated, to ensure that they will bless the living with fertility. To achieve these aims, the appropriation of ideas and the reuse of the religious space belonging to the sacred ancestors and the founders of an Islamic heritage (saints) appear essential; and so too does the symbolism of material culture (including religious regalia) and the relevance of the features set within its sacred landscape today.

Fertility ideology in Ethiopia – the case study of Tiya with Aksum and Lalibela

The relevance of Tiya

In the Horn of Africa there are a variety of stelae types: undecorated ones such as those at Gudit Stelae Field (Figure 3.11) (Chittick, 1974; Phillipson, 2000), and decorated ones such as those at Tuto Fela (Figure 6.7), Aksum (6.8), Tuttiti (Figure 6.9) and Tiya (Figure 6.10) (Joussaume, 1995; Joussaume, 1983). Even though the prevalence of stelae has been well documented in Africa (e.g. Fattovich, 1987, their meaning in relation to indigenous practices and symbolism of non-Muslim and non-Christian archaeology remains largely unexplored. There are many gaps, both temporally and regionally,

Figure 6.7 Tuto Fela with the crosses on the shaft of the stelae with both vulva and phallic motifs, Soddo region, Ethiopia

Figure 6.8 Aksum stelae complex, Ethiopia

Figure 6.9 Tuttiti phallic stelae field of Gedeo region, Ethiopia

Figure 6.10 Tiya stelae field, Soddo region, Ethiopia

in African archaeology (Lane and Read, 2016; Posnansky, 2009, 2017). Archaeological studies, too, have been limited by a paucity of true indigenous archaeological practices of the kind that is both independent and sufficiently resourceful to move beyond the work that Westerners so often do with locals in the name of indigenous archaeology. I noted in Chapter Two the lack of an in-depth understanding of stelae sites and their symbolism in the Horn (although some interesting points have been raised, for example by Joussaume, 1995; Godet and Pierre, 1993; Le-Quellec, 1987). Joussaume (1995) have suggested that the interpretation of the site of Tiya demands a local perspective. It is in this spirit that I attempt to approach the site with what I consider to be a regional indigenous viewpoint. I argue that the information I have so far presented in this study may be of significant use in the interpretation of sites such as Tiya.

The pottery used by the people who live today around the site of Tiya in the Soddo region of Ethiopia, the Guraghe, differs from that of the population of archaeological Tiya (Joussaume, 1995). I have already noted that, according to oral tradition, the Guraghe claim to have come originally from the Harar region, not the Tiya area (Braukämper, 2004: 66; Prout and Rosenfeld, 1994). Despite some Semitic speaking clusters, the majority of people living in southern Ethiopia today are Eastern Cushitic speaking peoples. Lewis suggests that these peoples originated from southern Ethiopia-northern Kenya, 'Since today twenty-one of the twenty-four languages of the Eastern Cushitic group are spoken in southern Ethiopia-northern Kenya' (Lewis, 1966: 39).

Given this and the fact that sixteenth century accounts talk of burial practices and rituals associated with the same peoples, it seems that Cushitic groups might have inhabited an area including the Soddo region where Tiya is located (e.g. Alvares, 1881; Almeida, 1954; 1646]; Burton, 1966 [1898]; Lewis, 1966; Paulitschke, 1888; Thesiger, 1935). Hence, the Guraghe claim of migration from Harar might be accurate on a linguistic and archaeological level. However, no matter what the pottery styles may suggest, tradition and religion remain all-important: the Guraghe practice the religion of the Sky-God and it makes sense to use this fact to explore regional ideological and material relations. The Eastern Cushitic Speakers, to take an apposite example, seem historically associated with the general region of eastern and southern Ethiopia as a whole. Their traditions and their (non-/pre-Islamic/Christian) archaeology of indigenous practices furthermore offer important insights into the site of Tiya and the practices that may have once taken place there. It is noteworthy that there are systematic cultural similarities within the dominant Eastern Cushitic speakers of southern Ethiopia, and that these commonalities are crucial to an understanding of Tiya cemetery in particular and of stelae traditions in southern Ethiopia in general. Whether or not the people who made the stelae spoke a Cushitic language is irrelevant if all their other characteristics fit within a wider pattern that identifies a major regional indigenous culture.

As noted in Chapter Five, there is much commonality between these groups. There is a relatively high lexical similarity within Eastern Cushitic speaking peoples (Ehret, 1976; cf. Shinn and Ofcansky, 2004: 123). There are distinctive words and expressions that refer to particular cultural patterns and social behaviour that are common to these groups. Words such as *Ebbe* (God), *ayaana* (destiny) and many more express similar concepts. An Oromo speaker and a Somali speaker will understand each other's words for specific phenomena, behaviour and speech as shown throughout this book. In addition to this, these groups also seem to have in common a traditional sociopolitical organisation, an age-set system (e.g. Legesse, 1973; Prouty and Rosenfeld, 1994), for example the *Gada*-system that characterises these Eastern Cushitic groups (Levine, 2000). Furthermore, as I noted earlier, the Eastern Cushitic peoples of southern Ethiopia all share a belief in the traditional deity they call the Sky-God, *Waaq*, the Supreme God of the Cushitic peoples (Bartels, 1983; Baxter, 1990; Hallpike, 1972; Lewis, 1994b; Loo, 1991; Luling, 1988).

Levine's view about the common foundations of the peoples of 'Greater Ethiopia' is compelling. I would extend his perspective to include most of the Horn of Africa. I argue that the systematic cultural elements held in common – language, religious beliefs and sociopolitical organisation – enable us to explore the ideas expressed at Tiya cemetery since these ideas seem today to encompass all the elements essential to the living and to their relationships with each other at times of death and birth. I will now explore how the ethnographic evidence regarding human fertility (kinship), animals (cattle), inheritance, wealth and burial practices can be relevant to Tiya and how this evidence is consolidated by monuments, decorations and burial practice. I will attempt, too, to provide some explanation of the symbolism manifested at this cemetery site (Figure 6.10).

Tiya, a World Heritage Site since 1981,[6] is a cemetery of decorated stelae in southern Ethiopia and it dates from the eleventh–thirteenth centuries AD (Joussaume, 1995), i.e. to before the Christianisation of this region. The site was first reported by Azïs and Chabard in their impressive volumes of text and pictures (1931); since then, Joussaume (1983, 1995) has studied it more systematically. Godet and Pierre (1993), Anfray (1982) and Le Quellec (1987) have attempted to decipher its symbolism. The conclusions that follow are based upon my understanding of the archaeology of Tiya and the interpretive thrust of the literature in general and of the inspiring and stimulating work of Roger Joussaume and his colleagues in particular.

Tiya cemetery holds about 40 stelae. Fifty tombs have been excavated, with pits generally of 1.50 metres deep and 1.80 metres wide, yielding a total of 52 individuals of whom 17 have been identified as women and 18 as men, with one infant (Joussaume, 1995: 218). The majority of the bodies, 24 in total, had been placed on a bed of wooden sticks (Figure 6.11). I will later talk about the sacred olive trees that surround both Lalibela and Aksum site and their ritual significance (Figure 6.12). At Tiya, another

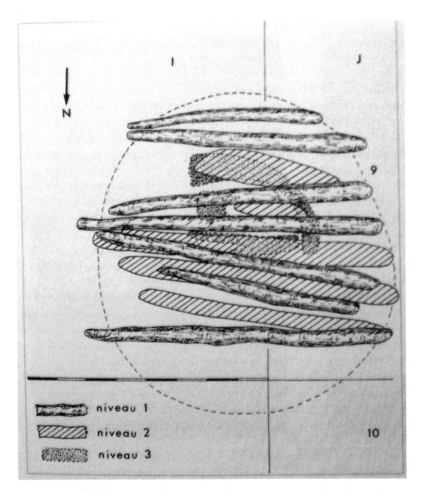

Figure 6.11 Wooden sticks that corps are laid on in the graves at Tiya (after Joussaume, 1995)

eight bodies were laid instead on a stone slab with another stone slab placed on top to close the pit. There is good reason to believe that some of the other 20 skeletons might originally have also been placed either on sticks or stones, of which some traces can still be seen (Joussaume, 1995). A secondary chamber containing the grave goods was usually placed above the pit that held the individual so that the grave goods were kept completely separate from the body. Grave goods included lithics, pottery, bovine bones, beads and iron objects (Joussaume, 1995).

Thirty-seven of the forty stelae appear to have been decorated (ibid., Figure 6.13). Seventy-two per cent of the stelae are between 2 metres and 3 metres in height with the two tallest, 4.5 metres and 5 metres in height

Figure 6.12 Sacred olive trees surround both Lalibela and Aksum sites

having, respectively, ten and nineteen *épées* (swords) incised upon them. The stelae decorations are predominantly a combination of *épées*, incised on 28 stelae and what Joussaume calls '*la triade symbolique*': tree signs, consisting of what he describes as an 'x' motif, incised on 14 of the stelae; a disk or circles on 31; a 'w' sign on 17 (Figure 6.13); and a so-called plant/vegetable sign on 33 (Figure 6.10 and Figure 6.14). Thirty-nine of the forty stelae

Figure 6.13 Knife motif, the discs, the plant sign and the zigzag or 'w' sign of Tiya stelae

have perforations on their bottom part. Only one stela was still standing when the site was first discovered by a French expedition at the end of the 1970s. This *in situ* stone revealed that the perforations had once been below ground (Figure 6.14).

A physical anthropological study of the skeletal material of Tiya was carried out to establish the ethnicity of the people buried there (Joussaume,

Figure 6.14 The diagonal cross sign of Tiya stelae

1995). The results failed to attribute ethnicity as such but showed that the remains belonged to 'Ethiopian' peoples. The pottery, however, bore similarities to that found in the settlement sites of Mito and Kere which are thought to be contemporaneous with Tiya. This lead Joussaume to conclude, quite plausibly, that the people buried at Tiya might have come from these settlements.

In his attempt to decipher the stelae decorations, Joussaume suggests that the *épées* may symbolise a warrior culture and heroes (ibid.), a tradition that to some extent still exists within the wider region today. He also argues that the plant sign is a symbol of masculinity but he lacks supporting evidence for this conclusion in much the same way as he does for his similar conclusions about the Lemo-Miya stelae. The latter are inscribed with what look like a necklace and two female breasts (fig. 197 in Joussaume, 2007: 229). Joussaume, however, argues that these cannot link with the present-day Bume and Dinka women of southern Ethiopia because they lack the 'the triade symbolique' which characterises the ramifique scarification found on such women today (see fig 183 in Joussaume, 1995: 156–158, 2007: 216).

Joussaume does not provide an explanation for the perforations on the stelae of Tiya though Godet and Pierre (1993) mention, interestingly, that local people say that the perforations might be intended to allow the dead to move through them. They do not elaborate on this concept but the hypothesis interests me because it suggests a local belief in the spiritual movement of the dead which must be provided for when making the stelae. I will discuss this in more detail below.

Joussaume further suggests that the 'x' or 'w' symbols (Figure 6.10 and Figure 6.14) (Joussaume, 1995; Joussaume, 2007) represent a person's ribs and rib cage because of the way they are positioned between the ramifique sign and the two circles. He uses the same explanation for the engravings on the upper body of the Tuto Fela stelae (ibid.) whose circles and discs he attributes to male breasts.

Joussaume argues the need for additional studies to explore how local people interpret the symbolism of Tiya. Having visited the site myself, I want to take his suggestion further and to consider its symbolism within the theoretical framework set out in this book in order to assess how its characteristics may lend themselves to a comparative regional analysis.

I want to produce a more culturally grounded ethnographic interpretation using regional practices and oral history and drawing upon other relevant archaeological regional material. Joussaume's other scholars have reflected upon some, but by no means all, ethnographic themes. I want to use the Ritual Set (Tables 6.1b-c) to discuss some of these. First, wood was clearly associated with the burials, but no explanations have been so far offered as to its purpose. Wood has a particular meaning in the burial cultures of the majority of the peoples of southern and eastern Ethiopia, as I have already noted. Second, the skeletons are buried in a foetal position which belongs to the cultural traditions of the peoples who have lived in this area for millennia. Third, the structure of the grave (two chambers one above the other, with the bottom one containing the body and the upper one holding grave goods) needs to be put into the context of local burial traditions and beliefs. And fourth, the most obvious explanation for the iconography of *épées*, knives or daggers – that it represents a warrior culture in the region – must not be taken at face value without first considering what else a knife or *épée* might signify in a *burial* context in a ritual cemetery like Tiya.

I therefore agree with Joussaume et al. that there is a need to construct an appropriate methodology with which to interpret the complex and intriguing display of symbolism at Tiya. I therefore want to apply a reflective transdisciplinary and multidisciplinary perspective, drawing upon ethnohistory, anthropology and archaeology. I believe that the Ritual Set I have developed will enhance my understanding of the symbolic meaning of materials such as trees, iron and stone within both a regional and local framework.

Foetal body position: in the tomb as in the womb

The foetal position in which 48 out of 52 bodies (ibid., fig. 79 in Joussaume, 1995) at Tiya were buried is a common practice in the Horn of Africa (Brand, 1986, 1988) and in the Somali archaeological context and elsewhere (Joussaume, 2007: 238): and also note '*en position assise ou couchée fléchie sur le côté, dans une niche latérale au fond d'un puits creusé dans le sol*' referring to the Gewada, the Konso and the Borana. Ethnographic accounts (Loo, 1991: 150) from southern Ethiopia reveal that the shape of the pit metaphorically denotes a 'womb', sometimes called *qaddaa*. This suggests that the pit and the foetal position of the Tiya burials (fig. 80 in Joussaume, 1995) represents a womb and a foetus within it. The womb is a sterile space without worldly materials and this would explain why no grave goods are present in the pit containing the body. If the lower pit represents birth, a 'womb'[7] for a foetus, then the separate upper space with its grave goods may reflect afterlife and/or rebirth. This suggestion, though unproven, is at least derived from a consideration of regional practice and abundant symbolism.

Iron objects and knives (Épées): killing equals giving birth

Joussaume recorded the recovery of iron objects such as an iron pin and a cylindrical pin shaped as a bracelet associated with a female burial yet made no attempt to interpret their meaning. Two female bodies, aged 25–30 and 30–40 respectively (for details, see tomb A25 in Joussaume, 2007: 194), however, are of particular interest. I have already noted that iron has a symbolic use amongst the Somali and the Oromo, the biggest Eastern Cushitic groups in the Horn. Of particular relevance here is its association with certain fertility rituals. Women use iron pins to paint their own eyes (particularly when pregnant) and the eyes of their children (particularly boys) with *koyl* to protect their own fertility and to ward off the evil eye from their offspring. If a woman is infertile, her lower abdomen is burnt with the tip of an iron pin in an attempt to cure her sterility. The evil spirit is tricked by the *kohl* into thinking that the boy is a girl and is confused by the way the iron shines. Women also wear iron jewellery to bewilder the spirits as the metal shines. Local information of this kind is particularly pertinent to the Tiya burials where iron pins are clearly associated with women of a fertile age. Iron objects are often placed near to, or beneath, the heads of infants to protect them from evil spirits, as is the *wagar* (Mire, 2015b). A knowledge of local customs can once again suggest a reason for the pins found near the heads of the deceased at Tiya.

Perhaps the most significant of the Tiya motifs is the *épée*, a relief found on the stelae that looks like a knife or a dagger (Figure 6.10). This symbol is incised on nearly all the 40 stelae excavated. Joussaume suggests that this symbol might refer to a warrior culture though he admits that the type of *épée* found on the stelae of Tiya in no way resembles the warrior knives known to be in use in the region. Even if *épées* do refer to a warrior culture in some contemporary cultures, it would be wrong to apply this explanation automatically to artefacts from the past. Their appearance in a ritual burial context warrants a deeper investigation.

Hunting scenes have long been a part of the artistic tradition of northeast Africa and it is possible that they were linked to the idea of ritual hunting. The art at the Neolithic rock art site of Laas Geel includes hunting scenes with anthropomorphic figures that appear to be in the shape of knives and, particularly, in the style of the flint knives of pre-dynastic Egypt (Figure 6.15 and Figure 6.16). Although these sites are dated thousands of years apart, hunting scenes and knife depictions in the rock art seem to follow an ancient African tradition of fertility rituals. The likely continuity of regional traditions is further supported by the recent discovery of east African Neolithic pastoral pottery at the stelae sites in the Horn of Africa, as noted earlier.

Returning again to the site of Tiya, there is a single stela there in the shape of a person with arms that is also suggestive of the shape of a knife (see Joussaume, 1995: 99) (Figure 6.17). It is stuck into the ground. Sufi saints, as already noted, are credited with striking the ground with their swords to bring about miracles and create wells and rain (Figure 6.6). This shape may be an example of a spearhead/knife penetrating/piercing the land. If it is, then its meaning extends beyond the superficial warrior symbolism into the realms of the present-day fertility rituals practised by Eastern Cushitic speakers such as the Oromo. Killing (a big animal) and bearing a child involve life-threatening risks both to the man who kills and the woman who gives birth. Birth and death are, moreover, closely intertwined. The Matcha Oromo say '*ilmon dhira duaf dhalata* – a son who is a real man is born for death' (Bartels, 1983: 268). A man's bravery in, for example, killing a buffalo is symbolically equal to his mother's pain when giving birth to him. If the son/man kills a big animal like the buffalo, he is given an important bracelet, '*tchatcshu*', a symbol of bravery, made of three giant snail shells held together in a string from the buffalo's skin; he then gives his mother his '*tchatcshu*' to honour the pain his mother incurred when giving birth to him.

Figure 6.15 Anthropomorphic potential 'knife figure' with bow and arrow and a
dog in a hunting scene at Laas Geel neolithic rock art site

Large animal hunters are called by a special name in Oromo, *misoo*, to
distinguish them from small animal hunters. Another link between fertility and killing is evident in the aftermath of a (for example) buffalo killing: the hunter will sacrifice a sheep to make peace with the guardian spirit
(*ayaana*) of the buffalo, and his mother and other women of her generation
will anoint him and his hunting companions with butter. ('Here we should

Figure 6.16 Anthropomorphic potential 'knife figures' at Laas Geel neolithic rock art site

Figure 6.17 The spearhead penetrating the ground at a Soddo site (After Azaïs and Chambard, 1931)

remember that butter is a symbol of female fertility' writes Bartels, 1983: 270.) Bartels further notes: 'The act of killing is seen to be in a way identical with the sexual intercourse, especially the first sexual intercourse on the wedding night' (Bartels, 1983: 271) when the bride sheds maiden-blood. In the wedding songs of the Matcha Oromo, the bride is compared with the buffalo; the bride is 'killed' (made to bleed on her wedding night), like the sheep is sacrificed, 'slaughtered'. The bride is 'sacrificed'/made to bleed in the interests of motherhood. The killing of the game is not a simple male activity but a ritual hunt with rules and regulations and a sacrifice to bring fertility to promote communal prosperity. The ritual hunt is essentially a fertility ritual. The knife is a fertility symbol, denoting the killing and slaughtering of the ritual animal (game) for fertility.

Children are still protected in this region today by placing an iron knife under their pillows when they are sleeping. The Somali do something similar with their use of a *wagar*, as do the Oromo society to protect children from the evil eye or a bad omen. The burial practices of the Guji Oromo (Loo, 1991: 150) are also of particular relevance in this context: for them, the knife symbolises the protection of the dead and the perpetuation of family. Taken together, these practices show that the symbolism of knives and iron objects found in the archaeology of this region is more likely than not to refer to fertility, the preservation of the family and sacrificial offerings to sacred ancestors. As noted earlier,Bartels (1983) too has observed fertility rituals linked to the fertility hunt.

The Somali *istunka* ritual, as we noted earlier, has the same fertility purpose as the pre-Islamic Hunt ritual in Arabia. Men come with special sticks that are intentionally carved from a blessed tree (in medieval as well as pre-Islamic times they carried heavier sticks, daggers, wore specific costumes and followed strict ritual-based rules of the fight). In Arabia, the *Abu* (Headman, a religious figure) heads the ceremony and the men of the Hunt (the hunters), with many others, including poets, form part of the ceremonial procession. Here some of the men of the Hunt 'make play with their *jambiyahs* (daggers)' (Serjeant, 1976: 29). The daggers (or knives) seem to have a ritual significance within the Hunt ritual (which is in essence a fertility ritual) which is designed to ensure that the god(s) grant rain. The ritual slaughter and offering to the god(s) take place on the sacred stones which represent the divinity(ies), and these stones are located inside the *haram*, the sacred enclosure.

The Knowledge-Centred Approach I have developed takes into account the acting out of beliefs through the medium of an object. It is not the object itself which matters but the archaeological configuration and the processes in which the object plays an active part. I suggest that the depictions of knives found at Tiya probably represent the ritual sacrifice associated with rain-making, perpetuation of kinship and fertility, both in this region and beyond this linguistic group of Eastern Cushitic speaking peoples (the Somalis, the Oromo and the Konso); they do not simply signify an appreciation of the men who kill big animals; instead, they mark something far more existentially important, the rituals of rain-making and human fertility.

The burials at Tiya might even belong to groups such as the Gorore of the Borana or the Match-Oromo – groups with a special reputation for ritual efficacy.

Ethnographic evidence from the region suggests that the daggers at Tiya, which are found in a burial context, are more likely to have a protective and reproductive symbolism than a warrior one. The role that iron objects, and particularly sharp iron ones such as iron pins and knives, play in reproductive and protective rituals is widely known and it is a role that is not just found amongst Eastern Cushitic speakers such as the Somali, Oromo and Konso; it is widespread across the Horn of Africa. Rain-making is associated with iron and, as already noted, the Sufi saints are associated with using their swords to strike and pierce the ground to create wells.

Wood, 'Planchers' and the 'vegetable' sign of Tiya stelae

Bodies in the pits in the Tiya cemetery are placed on top of shaped wooden sticks neatly in a row. As far as I know there is no explanation for the meaning of this nor any botanical study of the type of wood from which these sticks were made.

I have already noted the widespread belief in sacred trees, wood and grasses that exists in the Horn of Africa in general and amongst the Eastern Cushitic speaking groups in particular (Almeida, 1954; Burton, 1966 [1898]; Bartels, 1983; Conti Rossini, 1905; Loo, 1991; Kassam and Megerssa, 1996; Thesiger, 1935). This belief is, to my knowledge, never mentioned in studies of Tiya.

Artefacts carved out of sacred wood become sacred objects in themselves and endowed with supernatural power. Examples include the *dhanqee* (*denga* in Somali?) and the *siqqoo* amongst the Oromo and the *wagar* amongst the Somali (Mire, 2015b). Oromo fathers give their daughters the *siqqoo* when they marry to ensure their fertility (e.g. Loo, 1991). The *siqqoo* are ceremonial sticks symbolising fertility (Figure 6.18). The *siqqoo* and the Oromo male ceremonial stick both accompany their owners to the graves when they die (e.g. Loo, 1991; Bartels, 1983). Furthermore, up until recently, the *siqqoo/wagar* was placed near the heads of newborn children amongst the Eastern Cushitic groups (particularly the Borana and the Guji of Oromo and the Muslim Somali) to protect them against bad omens. Many people in the Horn of Africa, as already noted, regard the *wagar* as a sacred tree. In rituals designed to protect a child, the *wagar* is tied together with an iron knife and sacred grass and placed under the head of the child. A triple burial, a woman, man and child, has been found in tomb A5 at Tiya (Joussaume, 1995). Their bedding is composed of three layers of wooden sticks (the so-called *plancher*), and each body is accompanied by their own row of sticks.

Figure 6.18 Phallic shaped Siqqoo or siiqqee wooden stick symbol of the rights of married women of the Oromo

Source: (with permission from Eric Lafforgue)

The *plancher* upon which the bodies were placed at Tiya is best considered in the context of the role played by trees, particularly by sacred trees, in the rituals of the Horn of Africa. The beds of the dead at Tiya may have a special meaning given that the Guji Oromo, like many Somalis and others, lay the deceased on sacred grass (Loo, 1991: 90). If so, it is possible that the stone slabs found in burial chambers elsewhere serve the purpose of the '*branches*' or '*planchers*' found at Tiya and perhaps at other sites with similar beliefs.

The wooden planchers at Tiya may serve a symbolic function similar to the sacred fertility wood of *siqqoo* and the *wagar*. Some individuals are buried with their sticks, and perhaps this is what has been found with the two adults and child in Tomb A5 at Tiya. Furthermore, ethnographic evidence (Loo, 1991: 90; cf. Levine, 2000) demonstrates that ritual grass from particular trees is sometimes used in burials as a bed for the dead.

Sheikh Saint Aw-Barkhadle, moreover, once had a bed which women used to hold or touch to receive a blessing of fertility. The wooden *planchers* might be ritual items in harmony with the regional notion of sacred trees.

Incidentally, particular numbers of stones in specific context are thought to bring good luck. Lewis noted that nomadic men in northern Somali often kept three stones for good luck. Perhaps this is linked to the tradition of the *hersi* necklaces [amulet] containing three stones that men wear: a pendant consisting of one elongated stone with two round stone beads on each side, also recorded by Révoil (1882).

Equally as remarkable as the daggers is one of the symbols found on the stelae which has been referred to as the 'vegetable' sign or 'ramifique'/'bifurque' (Figure 6.10) (Joussaume et al, 1995, 2007; Godet and Pierre, 1993). It has been suggested that this symbolises masculinity. I would argue, however, that this sign would be better interpreted in the light of the tradition of sacrificial flora, sacred grass and trees associated with the fertility rituals currently practiced in the Horn of Africa.

Grass is also used amongst groups in the Horn to protect the dead from a bad afterlife, a practice that van de Loo (1991) has noted amongst the Guji Oromo. This group place sacred grass in the grave to serve as a bed for the deceased in what is obviously a significant ritual relating to the continuation of the family and the exchange of wealth (ibid.: 91). The sign of the 'ramifique' may, in the burial context, indicate continuation. This would make sense in Tiya in terms of the archaeology as the place is clearly linked to ritual and, perhaps, the blessing of the ancestors and the protection of the family and the lineage.

The sprouting or 'vegetable' sign of Tiya may therefore be associated with the regeneration of lineage. As noted earlier, the bride of the Matcha Oromo weaves a grass plate that is used on her wedding day. A male elder will smear beansprouts soaked in a slaughtered sheep's blood, together with coffee fruits, on her belly and thighs while uttering a prayer; 'Have children. May your blood sprout (into children)' (Bartels, 1983: 263). The ritual grass, the coffee beans and the sprouts form part of the customs that mark the first coitus. The Konso also sacrifice vegetables (plants) or flora (Hallpike, 1972).

In another example, the Arsi-Oromo and other pious followers and visitors of Sheikh Hussein Bali in Ethiopia, who are a mix of Muslims and Oromo traditionalists, carry a short and *bifurcated* stick called a *dhanqee*. This stick is carved from a sacred tree with special powers that is found in the valley of Qacamsaree near Annajina/Dire Sheikh Hussein. The *dhanqee* is part of the tradition of the Sky-God religion as practised by the Oromo (*Waaqeffannaa*). The Oromo trace their ancestry to one forefather and claim to have originated in Mada Walabu, an area near Dire Sheikh Hussein and part of the Soddo where Tiya is located. It is possible that the Oromo would feel affinities with the religious culture of the people who created the stelae of Tiya, given that the Sky-God religion is a region-wide belief and that sacred trees are recognised by all the people. After the conversion to, and the spread of, Islam, more sacred centres belonging to pre-Islamic Abba Muudaa were dedicated to Muslim Abba Muudaa. Traditional Islam was tolerant and adaptive to indigenous practices, including the symbol of the *dhanqee*. The sprouting symbol is now a common symbol of fertility in the Horn of Africa.

The wood used in Tiya had clearly been burned. This in itself is interesting: the tip of the *wagar*, too, is burned when it is used to cure infertility. It is also burned for its properties as a consecrating and purifying sacred tree.

When discussing the *'ramifique'* plant sign of Tiya it is important to acknowledge the many similar ideas that exist about sacred trees, grass and palms, including coffee bean sprouts. The traditional *ensete* (false banana) and coffee both grow at Tiya. The former is an essential basic food for the farmers who live in the fertile area where Tiya is situated. It was clear from my discussions with people living nearby that they wanted to keep their land fertile through rituals involving sacrifice and the protection of human and crop fertility. It is possible that the plant sign symbolises the sacrificial flora and fertility rather than masculinity. Abundant evidence has been presented both of sacrifice to trees as well as of offerings of trees/bushes/grasses during rituals mainly relating to birth, death, purification, consecration and healing. Plants are part of ritual meals and are used in many local rituals (*Bun qalla, wagar, baanashada, sitaat, istunka*, ritual baths, *waqlaal*, purification and wedding ceremonies). The plant symbolism of a region rich in sacrificial and sacred flora cannot be reduced to simple 'male' meanings. The sticks used by the followers of Sheikh Hussein Bale may be equally relevant. This sheikh, a Somali, was said to have been in the area during the thirteenth century and, like Aw-Barkhadle, is believed to have introduced and spread Islam in this part of the Horn. The bifurcation sign may represent one of the symbols of the people of Tiya which may have been preserved through syncretic transformation.

Fertility beings and bodies: zoomorphic and anthropomorphic motifs of Tiya

Depictions of female breasts, phallic stelae and motifs that seem to represent reptiles are found at Tiya and at other sites in the Horn. These require further explanation. In addition to the plant symbol, the knives and the disk, the stelae of Tiya are also decorated with the symbols 'x' and 'w', and with perforations (Joussaume, 1995). It is important to consider similar iconography from some of the other archaeological sites of stelae cemeteries.

The dressed stelae of Tuto Fela, a site in the Sidamo region of southern Ethiopia and contemporary with Tiya, carry iconography which, I conclude from my own observations, seems to suggest a snake symbol (Figure 6.19). I believe this bears a striking similarity to the shape of the 'x/H' (Figure 6.14) seen on the Tiya stelae (Plate 6.6 in Joussaume et al, 1995). I suggest, therefore, that the 'x' and 'w' are related to a *snake cult*. The pottery of Tiya provides even clearer evidence of snake motifs in an apparently ritual context (Figure 6.20a) which shows similar diagonal crosses and zigzag patterns present in the archaeology of the region. There are reptile-like sinuous motifs on stelae in Tiya and on other sites (Figures 6.20a-d.). The reptile depictions (zigzag/crosslines pattern) on the stelae in Tiya are found at ground level, close to the perforations. Some look like lizards with feet.

Figure 6.19 The heads of the Tuto Fela stela suggest a snake shape – probably cobra

Others are/have a crossline/zigzag pattern which seems to suggest serpent movement underground or just above the ground. Similar signs are prevalent in Somali rock art in general and in the engravings on grave-markers in particular. Tiya's 'historied' stelae show a zigzag line running and crossing another one in the middle of the stone with a similar zigzag line running around all the edges of the stelae. This brings to mind the shape of a snake.

Figure 6.20 A. Potential snake symbolism on pottery of Tiya (after Joussaume, 1995). and similar diagonal crosses and zigzag patterns at B. Stela of Biqqisa, Sidamo (after Azais and Chambard, 1931). C. Aw-Barkhadle diagonal cross burial and D. Tuto Fela stela with diagonal crosses

Depictions of snakes, though rare, are found at many sites in the Horn of Africa and Nubia, including Laas Geel and Dhamblain (Mire, 2008). Cows' horns are often used to imitate the shape of a snake (Dhambalin) while on other sites (for example Laas Geel) a snake is painted alongside or inside a cow. The head of a snake also seems to be linked to the phallic as a symbol of fertility (Laas Geel). The profile heads of Tuto Fela, with their tiny narrow holes for eyes and the two narrow holes below them for a nose, seem to suggest a cobra.

Given that there are 14 stelae with so called 'x' incisions and 17 stelae with 'w' suggests that the two signs may have been interchangeable. This zigzag sign is significant. I do not agree with the view (Joussaume, 1995) that this represents ribs or a rib cage. Why would a rib cage matter so much? A reptile-like animal has already been identified on one of the stelae (Figure 6.21a). Zigzags have, moreover, been found in other decorated

Figure 6.21a Reptile-like sinuous zigzag pattern depicted on a 'story' stela at Tiya

stelae cemeteries in the Somali territories (Mire, 2015a) and especially at
Aw-Barkhadle, Gidheys and Ximan. The zigzag pattern appears to denote
a snake. Interestingly, the stelae reported by Joussaume (2011) at Amorigé
in the Bui region, south of Addis Adabba, include a 'stela with a compart-
mented face'; this stela belongs to the so-called historied stelae and carries
the 'swords' (two) and the 'triad' (the ramifique, two discs and two 'w' signs
below the discs) associated with the Tiya stelae; it also includes two of the

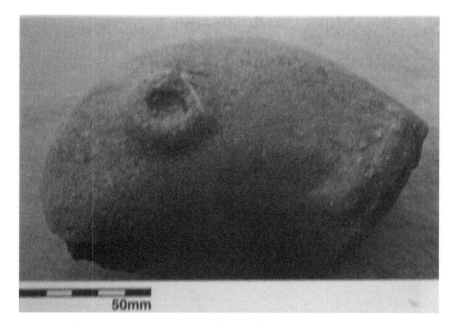

Figure 6.21b A snake figurine from Aksum (after Phillipson, 2000)

so-called w signs 'turned to the right and the left' (ibid.: 106–108). These so-called w designs each have below them 'two vertical zigzags' (Joussaume, 2011: 108). No explanation is offered for these 'ww' designs as far as I know. However, they are composed of two connected 'w' shapes as in 'ww' except that they are more rounded and resemble a serpent body in motion. These sinuous zigzags occur right below the so called two rib signs of the 'w' and face away from each other on each side of the body. The serpent-like zigzags of Amorgé therefore start below the 'w' sign and end on the horizontal line that includes two horizontal lines connected by zigzag lines (ibid., Figure 6.20a, b). This stele provides evidence that the 'w' sign and the snake-like zigzag sign may be symbolically associated and not coincidentally near each other. This aspect of snake movement is further strengthened by the depiction of the even clearer image of the reptile, with its zigzag patterns, at the base of the previously mentioned stela at Tiya. Most of the 'historied' stelae carry geometrical zigzags going in all sorts of directions and combinations (see the Silte stelae). The Amorige zigzags also end in the base of the decorated panel of the stela while those at Tiya almost always end at the base of the stone. This may shed light on the relationship between the perforation and the snake/zigzag depiction: the snakes and the ancestors would need to move through the perforations at the base of the stones underground, and hence the stelae might be intended to symbolise the ancestors themselves.

In addition to this suggestion of snake iconography, snake cult traditions are known through the ethnography and oral history of the Horn (cf. Loo, 1991: 56–57; cf. Phillipson, 1997: 141, 112). Snakes are seen as symbols of renewal and fertility. It has already been noted that the *kallacca*,[8] a phallic ritual object made of iron, is decorated with a snakeskin and signifies male fertility (Figure 3.20d) and that snakes such as cobra and pythons are also associated with male fertility (Loo, 1991). The Oromo and Konso wear the *kallacca* on their heads (ibid.). A few of the stelae found at Tuto Fela are phallic and appear also to carry snakeheads. Stelae might take the shape of a penis (phallic) and/or a snake or a knife (as at Tiya), all suggesting a relationship between this symbolism and fertility. The *Kallascha* seems reminiscent of Tuto Fela's phallic stelae. The phallic stelae are found in all parts of the Horn of Africa including the Somali region, and it may well be that the depiction of knives, snakes and phallic symbolism is more common than is realised in the archaeology of the region.

Furthermore, as has been already mentioned, certain snakes are avoided and not killed, particularly if they have entered a house to 'visit'. It is believed that saints, *awliyo*, or ancestors might 'come back' as snakes. Amongst the Oromo, as with the Somali, certain snakes, the cobra for example, have a power related to (male) fertility, the continuation of the family and resurrection. Human scarification also plays a part in medical matters and preventative healing. Stelae decoration in the Horn of Africa may well have much to tell about the practices associated with age and time, and the timing of rituals. Events taking place in the landscape are linked with fertility as it relates to lineages, animals and crops. Hence, fertility, time and medicine are essential ingredients in the indigenous ideologies concerning ritual practice and burial traditions.

The belief that people or important religious figures in society come back as saints in the form of snakes in Cushitic-Somali society has been mentioned before. A major part of the religion of the pre-Christian/pre-Islamic regional cultures involved the veneration of tombs, a process that can be seen in the annual ceremonies led by religious leaders at Aw-Barkhadle and other sites in the Horn. In addition to this ethnographic evidence, Phillipson (2000) reports finding snake figurines in Aksum (Figure 6.21b). The rock art from the Horn (see Joussaume, 1995, 2011) adds to the weight of evidence supporting the importance of snakes in the ritual context.

The perforations on the stelae of Tiya can best be studied in the light both of this evidence and of the snake's pre-Christian/Islamic importance to ancestors. Snakes are believed to move underground and the perforations at the base of the Tiya stelae may be intended to make this movement possible. The average distance between the plant sign and the perforations of the Tiya stelae is 40–45 cm; although the depth to which each was buried is not known, the size of this distance supports this interpretation. Why were perforations made on the part of the stelae that was buried underground? That these might relate to the notion of ancestor spirits moving in the form of snakes underground seems a plausible enough explanation.

Two small disks are engraved on nearly all the Tiya stelae and appear on other similar stelae in southern Ethiopia (Figure 6.14, Joussaume, 1995; Tournemire, 2003). Two discs are associated with the sign 'w' and 'x'/'H'. The Sky-God is associated with the eye and with seeing (Lewis, 1998: 22). The disks might indicate an omnipresent Sky-God who sees, is all-seeing and eternal. This idea raises issues to do with time, existence and presence. The perforation of the Tiya stelae might indeed relate to the expression of such characteristics of the supreme God, one who is responsible for the ever-important rains. The majority of the stelae in this region do, moreover, exhibit discs and circles similar to those found at Tiya and at Aksum. It may be worth asking the local people how they view these sites even though they are not the ones who created them and even though allowances have to be made for misremembered rituals. Time, however, is cyclical rather than linear; farmers may become hunters and vice versa in the space of just a few generations. Belief systems, by contrast, tend to linger in ways that can be missed if too much attention is focused on particular sites in particular areas.

The snake is a very special animal in the Horn of Africa region as is shown by the headbands of the *Kallasha*, the heads/silhouettes of the Tuto Fela and the rock art. At the same time, it is seldom spoken about and rarely depicted openly.

Joussaume (2011: 111) has noted that little is currently known about the so-called historied stelae in southern Ethiopia; these are mainly considered to be of a funerary nature. However, given the information presented above, they may perhaps best be explained in the context of the Konso and Oromo hunt ritual. The role of the *Qallu*, the ritual chief and the slaughterer (hence the name *qallu*) of ritual animals (domestic or wild) is particularly noteworthy.

The figures found in Joussaume (2011, fig. 6.5–6.8) depict the so-called stelae with compartmented faces. The swords are knives and the backs of those shown in fig. 5A and B, and 6A and B and 7A all appear to carry depictions of sheaths (with a visible band in the back of 6B, a stela from Mamo). Another characteristic that supports this theory of the ritual slaughter and the *Qallu*'s knives is the depiction of bows and arrows (Joussaume, 2011, fig. 5A, 6B and fig. 7A). In Yemen, men still carry *Jambiya*, which may have a history grounded in the ritual hunt in South Arabia (Serjeant, 1976) described above. There are also depictions of human beings and animals (see Joussaume, 2011: fig. 5A, 6 B, 7B). An image of female breasts (Figure 6.21a) lends further support to the argument that this is about fertility (Joussaume, 2011, figures 9B and 11A, B, C and D). The rock art site of Dhambalin reveals images of human beings with bows and arrows hunting with dogs (Mire, 2008). In Somali, *qaanso* (bow) and *laab/falaadh* (arrow) have a ritual significance in hunting. The shape of a *qaanso* is also associated with *qaanso roobeed* (rainbow). Bow and arrows, sometimes used as spears, are also linked to the male.

As I noted earlier, Godet and Pierre (1993) associated this 'triade symbolique' with the male and with masculinity. However, without an a deeper understanding of the cultural practices of the region, it is all too easy to associate such complex symbolism simplistically with the 'male character'. The motifs on some stelae move beyond male symbolism to include a mix of gendered images. '*Bourrelets*' knives, spears, bows and arrows appear alongside female breasts (see stela from Tite, fig. 6.7, in Joussaume, 2011: 111). Both women and men in the region can be ritual leaders or diviners. The stelae from Tite (Joussaume, 2011) also, as already noted, display the so-called bourrelet and, interestingly, also depict the so-called ribs; why would these 'ribs' be located so low down if they really were ribs? And in Figure 6.6 in the same publication, the 'plant' sign seems to be evolving into the so called 'rib' sign (the 'w', according to Joussaume, 2007). Is the so-called rib sign not really about ribs at all? The plant sign (ramifique) of Tiya appears to be similar to Tuto Fela's so-called rib signs. It is of course all too tempting to try to offer possible explanations for symbolic images – and people have done so by either focusing on specific regions of the Sidamo/Soddo and/or by seeking comparisons further afield, as in the case of the Indo-European symbolism (Le Quellec, 1987). Such temptation must be resisted: it is a trap into which will fall all those who do not possess the knowledge about regional practices or an understanding of the ethnography, history and linguistic expressions that shape these motifs and the rituals they represent.

The snake, for example, generally has a regenerative meaning in the Horn of Africa as in many other parts of the world. But why should it be depicted by these particular groups of people in this particular area? What was it in their belief systems that led them to depict the snake? In this region, the snake is often equated with safeguarding fertility. Somalis frequently wear as protection a necklace made of precious stones which sometimes has an amulet in the middle or a large stone threaded on a string. This symbol may be linked to the legend of the serpent as protector and moral guardian. Révoil mentioned finding similar objects in northeastern Somalia (1882: 344). The shining stones are precious and prescient. They are associated with both sacred stones or stone worship as well as with serpent worship in the 'Old Cushitic' culture. The serpent sees by means of these shiny precious stones in much the same way as does the ancestral spirit.

The 'historied' stelae include many specific recurring motifs that are as yet unexplained. Like those found at Tuto Fela, which seem to show both phallic and vulva elements, these stelae may be gender ambiguous. The masque (Tournemire, 2003), or 'compartmentalised' (Joussaume, 2011) heads appear to be the same for both those that possess male (discs/circles) breasts or female ones. It is important to remember that 'killing and bearing' may well have been connected in complex ways that lie outside our modern notions of gender and power relations. A notion of gender that goes beyond the narratives of heroism may help decipher the meaning of these symbols. An understanding of why the people of the Horn still modify and cut their bodies today may lead to an explanation of body modification and scarification. This may often have much to do with health, sacrifice and fertility.

The way that bodies have been modified in the present-day, or have even been exposed to pain, may provide clues to the interpretation of archaeological remains (Layton, 1989; Ucko and Rosenfeld, 1967). Scarification such as that seen on the Tuto Fela phallic stelae in the navel area (see Joussaume, 2007) appears similar to that seen on Somali children and adults today. The navel area may signify a womb (the Oromo call the womb the navel). The Somali word *xudun* for navel can also refer to a disease that affects the stomach. To cure or prevent this disease, people will cut marks on their skin resulting in scarification. Some burn lines or dots on their *xudun*. The marks on the Gorro-Shino stelae from the Soddo region[9] indicate scarification on the belly area and around the navel. Somali *dhajis* cutting, a healing ritual offering protection from the evil eye, involves making marks on the area between the sternum and the navel. To prevent this scourge, one centimetre high vertical lines are cut to form a square. Stelae in the Soddo region can be found with a tiny square showing in this area between the navel and the breasts. In addition, the *falaadh* cutting ritual (involving an arrow symbol) is another treatment designed to prevent pneumonia; it is practised by Somalis including those who live amongst the Oromo in the eastern region of the Horn (Figure 6.22). Révoil notes about the Somali that 'It is rare to meet a native who does not have the body covered with a real tattoo of burns or scarification' (1882: 330). Although current day practices of scarification are sometimes mentioned in studies about rock engraving, it is not safe to do so without conducting more in-depth ethnographic studies into the meaning and function of these designs. Only then can the findings be tentatively applied to archaeological material.

Stick fights also involve beating, which leaves permanent cut marks on the body which are regarded as a sign of bravery and sacrifice for the communal good (i.e. fertility).

Another interesting find at Tiya are the drum stelae which are not explained in Joussaume's work (1995). Drums are important in the Horn of Africa and used during significant ceremonies (Levine, 2000). Those found on archaeological sites suggest that they were as important in the past as they are today. The significance of drums and drumming in the ceremonies held at Aw-Barkhadle has already been noted. Their status there is highlighted by the fact that it is the national governmental drummers who, until recently, performed the ritual drumming at the annual pilgrimage ceremony. It is possible that in ancient times people used drums in much the same way to mark the *zar* spirit or to celebrate the Saint and other ceremonies. The people of Tiya may have used drums to accompany the regional dances and songs that were dedicated to the spirits. Moreover, drums are part of the royal regalia too and their use goes back to the traditions of Aksum (Munro-Hay, 2002: 116; Levine, 2000: 62). The Afar, Konso and Borana also use drums as royal regalia. And the ancient practice of *zar* similarly

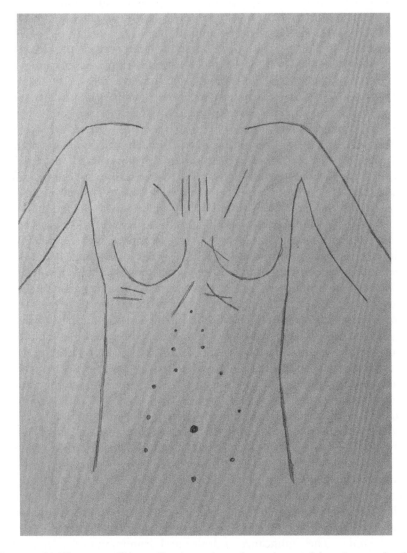

Figure 6.22 Illness-specific scarifications through cutting and burning marks for therapy and preventive medicine on a Somali woman

involves drums as a key part of *saar ka tun* 'drumming the spirit away', as noted earlier. The ancient drums of the Horn may well be linked to the Sky-God and especially to ancient dance and fertility rituals. Little is known, however, about the 'drum stelae' discovered through archaeology. They may perhaps have related to ritual and have been symbols of status or used to call upon, or ward off, spiritual beings. Stone drums are still used at Lalibela to call people to prayer. My interviewee informed me that the tree from

Figure 6.23 A stone drum from the Tiya cemetery

which the prayer calling drum is hung is a blessed one. Stone drums can also be found at Tiya, as at many other sites in Soddo region (Figure 6.23).

Incense burning, pottery and ritual containers

Incense burners have been found at the Tiya cemeteries, and the incense burning in early second millennium AD must surely have been related to the traditions then existing in the Horn of Africa. In many ancient societies, the purpose of incense is to connect the living with the dead, the gods with their followers and life with the afterlife. In northeast African societies, incense links people to the religious ancestors and saints. It also functions as a purifying substance, healing and protecting both places and people against the evil spirit. It has already been noted that all the tombs at Aw-Barkhadle have built-in spaces to hold incense burners. When doing my survey, I noticed incense burners and their broken pieces scattered on the surface in addition to those *in situ* in niches and still being actively used. At Tiya, there were reports of incense burners found inside the chambers. There has as yet been no research into their ritual significance past and present or into the possible continuities in certain kinds of ritual behaviour.

An ethno-archaeological study on the contemporary pottery of Tiya has been conducted by Cassen (1995) and links with the work of Joussaume. It focuses almost entirely on the *chaine operatoire* and attempts to link issues of technical style and design to ethnic groups. What seems to be missing in this work is a consideration of the special uses and meaning of the ancient pottery designs and how ethnography can contribute to an understanding of the function and symbolism of the pottery discovered by the archaeologists. Although Cassen (ibid.) observes how different decorations are used on different pots containing different things in the Tiya region today, he does not seem to reflect on the implication of this finding for the archaeological material other than to conclude that today's pottery differs from that used in ancient Tiya.

The Knowledge-Centred Approach I use differs from the traditional ethnoarchaeological tradition in that it is about performance and adopts a comparative reflective methodology. It begins by asking what the ceramics are used for and how this might relate to the ritual practices, religious activities and symbolism of the people to whom they belong. I have shown through my own ethnographic study that different containers, particularly ritual ones, have different purposes. The Somali container, the *heedho*, holds the *muqumad* meat as noted earlier. Its symbolism is related to circumcision and virginity as well as the fertility of a bride. The ever-important *bun qalla* of the Oromo ceremony (also known as *bun shuruur* in Somali) uses specific pots and containers. I have also talked about the Matcha Oromo girl's wedding container. The Oromo use different containers and contents in different rituals including that of today's fertility rituals (Bartels, 1983; Hallpike, 1972; Loo, 1991). The Konso bride, as already noted, produces a woven basket for her wedding night. The Konso houses, too, have a special pot (a broken one) which they place on top of the *kēgesha* (the upper part of the thatched roof of the house). 'It seems likely that the pot is seen as symbolizing fertility (a womb-like vessel), earth (the material from which it is made), women (who make and use it) and nourishment (what it contains)' (Hallpike, 1972: 289). Phallic pots are placed on the roofs of houses belonging to males and priests. The *kēgesha* itself, says Hallpike, is potentially a phallic symbol: 'Perhaps, in view of its appearance and its resemblance to the *hallasha* [*kallascha/Kallasha*], it would not be too fanciful to suggest that it is a phallic symbol, and that in conjunction with the pot it is a symbol of fertility' (Hallpike, 1972: 290). It is important to remember the number of phallic architectural features that appear generally in the archaeology of the Horn – and particularly the amount that appear as centre-poles.

Like the Somali, the Oromo, including the Boraana, have a number of ritual containers. Some are made of pottery, others of skin, wood or woven from fibre. Milk containers such as *ticcoo*, *kumburee* and *gareere* are common. One, however, is of particular interest here, the *okkele*, made of skin or wood. It is used both to collect milk from the cows and the blood from a sacrificial animal. Its material is probably symbolically linked to its use to collect sacrificial blood. In much the same way, brazil wood is chosen for its red colour because it symbolises the blood that comes from the sacrificial animals slaughtered at the sacred stones (for example see Serjeant, 1976: 6).

Horns are painted with red clay and the same clay as is used to make certain types of pottery. This clay is thought to come from fragmented sacred stones/rocks which themselves are said to be of ritual significance (Serjeant, 1976). Furthermore, there are graffiti portraying the sacred trees and animals known to have once been associated with rituals such as the Hunt ritual (ibid.: 25). An example of this can be found at Wadi Thibi. The rock there is decorated with date trees and ibex close to the tomb of Hud (ibid., see 'Fig. II' and 'Fig. III', Serjeant, 1976: 26). As Serjeant has noted, some Arabian ritual pottery speaks of disintegrated rocks and stones which are closely identified with deities and therefore considered to be of ritual significance; these objects might themselves be considered to have divine powers. In terms of ritual containers, this might mean that the material they are made of is itself considered to be sacred and symbolic of the sacrificial content they hold and for which the pot has been made. Pottery, for example, may be made from clay that comes from important stones or mountains. Wooden containers too may be carved from sacred trees. The skin of the slaughtered sacrificial animal may be used to make a container to collect sacrificial blood. The women of the Matcha, Somali and the Boorana weave containers from grass for different rituals, including wedding ceremonies. Much like the Somali Heedho, the Matcha bride makes a fibre container specifically for the fertility rituals associated with her wedding night. Special ritual containers are therefore very common across the region. The archaeologist must keep all these possibilities in mind. Investigations need to move beyond conventional ethno-archaeological approaches to reach not only the concepts that govern function, style and meaning but also the broader cultural values upon which the societies of the Horn of Africa are founded.

Other materials at Tiya

The materials presented above are not intended to be an exhaustive account of all that have been found at Tiya. As noted above, Joussaume's edited volume (1995) contains a very useful analysis of the human remains as well as the pottery and lithics found at the site. The discussion here has attempted to put into context the regional and local ideas that might be embedded in the symbolism of materials such as those found there.

Plenty more material has been found at Tiya which may be related to the idea of fertility and other rituals, for example beads, rings and bracelets. Beads are known to serve a ritual purpose in the Horn of Africa. For example, when a Somali woman marries she is given amber necklaces. Amber symbolises fertility and health across northern Africa (as my recent fieldwork in Morocco confirms). Many precious stones have meanings for the Toureg and the Berbers of northern Africa, as they do for the Somali. Thus, for both women and men, bracelets and necklaces as well as other decorations embody meanings concerning status, authority, gender, age and the like. It is interesting to note that in the song reproduced in Chapter Four which relates to spirit possession, a woman states that the spirit which has possessed her wants amulets and an amber necklace. Certain ornamentation belongs to *zar*, such as the ring with a black stone for the *maame*. As noted earlier, the son who succeeds in killing a big game animal will give his mother a special necklace to mark his successful display of a bravery that is equivalent to her bravery when she gave birth to him. The Tiya beads may hold similar complex meanings beyond being merely the beads belonging to a woman. Furthermore, the Konso *poĝalla* (lineage head and priest) possesses five bracelets (Hallpike, 1972). Many of the stelae of southern Ethiopia display lines or motifs that suggest necklaces. In this way, ethnographic material, provided it is used carefully and with due regard to context, can open up new avenues of exploration.

The Knowledge-Centred Approach reminds us that the symbols discovered through the archaeology of the Horn of Africa once formed part of spoken and performed rituals or actions and that they were not an end in themselves. They are not a language to be deciphered. Instead, they form part of a body of ideas and ideologies and it is these that need to be absorbed. To do this demands a curiosity that extends beyond archaeology's material remains. It is in this context that the Ritual Set comes into play with its use of both ethnography and comparative regional archaeology to bridge the anthropological and archaeological gaps. Where relevant, I have had to carry out my own anthropological research to fill in these gaps.

Aksum and Lalibela as sacred landscapes

Aksum and Lalibela may seem a long way away from Aw-Barkhadle and the sites in southern Ethiopia. Nevertheless, it is essential to follow the trails left by the archaeological material and by present-day behaviour to understand the connectivity between places and peoples. Only in this way can the big picture emerge of common shared foundations in the Horn of Africa and the continuity of ideas in their many forms and expressions.

Across these lands can be found the decorated stelae, dolmens and other burials that bring together the region. Current religious divisions provide few clues about the beliefs upon which these practices were founded. An engraved Coptic cross of a style typical to the fourth–seventh century marks an *in situ* burial at Aw-Barkhadle and is very similar to the Aksumite (or Coptic) cross found at Aksum (Figure 6.25, compare with Figure 2.4). Some people who are not themselves Christian have crosses tattooed on their foreheads. The cross can also be found on ethnographic objects in the Somali region (Figure 3.20a, b). Fattovich has concluded (as noted earlier): 'The Aksumite stelae can be attributed to a regional cultural tradition of Eastern Sudan and Northern Ethiopia going back to the late 3rd millennium BC' (Fattovich, 1987: 63). As he notes, other stelae traditions, including those found in southern and eastern Ethiopia, form part of an indigenous practice. Somali stelae, too, should be viewed in the light of regional practices.

Figure 6.24 Aksumite Coptic cross engraved on stone

Very little is understood, however, about either the spatial or the temporal continuity of these stelae traditions in the Horn of Africa. Many of these discoveries seem to point the way to Aksum and Lalibela: the stelae traditions, including the phallic stelae, to the former and the Christian material including the Aw-Barkhadle burial and the isolated grave designed as a cross, to the latter. Beyond Christianity lie the rituals of fertility that are part of the landscapes of both Aw-Barkhadle and Aksum.

Even in Aksum and the northern Horn

> Appreciation of continuity is hampered by the fact that, whereas Aksumite period sites have seen a fair amount of archaeological investigation, this is not yet true for those of subsequent times which have been primarily investigated by historians, including art-historians.

> (Phillipson, 2012: 247)

'It is for the period that followed the decline of Aksum and the eastward transfer of the state's capital . . . that the difficulty is most acute and essential continuity obscured' (ibid.). Phillipson argues for the breaking down of disciplinary divisions and adds '[We] have effectively no knowledge of the domestic settlements, material culture, or economic practices of the people who made these churches; remedy of this deficiency is perhaps the

Figure 6.25 A natural pool at Sameeno Furte mountain's underground cave systems and rock hewn dwellings with rock art

most urgent need of all' (ibid.). I have tried in my work to break down these disciplinary barriers by incorporating as much ethnographic, historical and oral historical work as possible while at same time trying to address the fragmentary nature of archaeological knowledge across the Horn of Africa.

The materiality of the Ritual Set includes sacred enclosures used for ritual purposes, the notion of sacred grass, sacred springs, fertility wells/pools, sacred purification waters, sacred mountains or rocks, phallic symbolism, olive trees and the olive; all these symbolic features were also present in Aksumite times.

The hewing out of ritual structures and dwelling features from mountains and the piling up of bits of rocks is essentially an ancient African tradition – and, in the Horn of Africa, a common practice. Rooms inside sacred mountains and rock art are found at Sabeeno Furte in the Sanaag region, together with scripts in ancient languages and a natural water pool inside the mountain with underground cave systems and rock hewn dwellings (Figure 6.24). The Sabeeno Furte is reminiscent of the rock hewn churches at Lalibela and its landscape is equally evocative of the Sheikh Hussein Bali landscape in Bale, Ethiopia, of its sacred caves and water sources. Bali also has sacred niches for the monks similar to those found in the churches of Lalibela. In Ethiopia, most churches are surrounded by olive trees and other ritually significant trees. I noted earlier how the Christian Cushitic speaking Agaw people surround their churches with sacred groves. Aksum and Lalibela are dotted with olive trees and with other sacred trees like the sycamore. It is very possible that the trees that are regarded as sacred in the Horn of Africa were also considered to be important at these ancient religious centres. The olive trees at Aksum and Lalibela are hundreds of years old (Figure 6.12). They are locally known as *weyeri* which is essentially the same word as *wagar*. At Lalibela, too, there exists an enclosure (Figure 6.1) used for rituals which is very like the one found next to the Aw-Barkhadle tomb (Figure 3.24) where food preparation, cooking and eating take place to this day. The Lalibela enclosure is said to be where the 'association', or ritual societies, meet, drink local beer, make offerings and pray.

The religion of the Sky-God is associated with the *wagar* and the wild olive, which is native to the Horn of Africa. Olive is a hard wood long used in house construction, furniture making and fencing. The olive tree, specifically, seems to be universally recognised as a sacred tree throughout the Horn of Africa. Akum and Lalibela, the two major ancient centres of Christianity in Ethiopia, are both surrounded by olive trees – and local people at both sites told me that olives were planted specially for ritual purposes.

I have already noted *ejersa weyersaf* and that most Ethiopian churches were originally located near olive and juniper woods. The notion of *adbar* as an entity embodied in trees, mountains, rocks and water sources may be relevant to the Sky-God too. If so, this would suggest that the pre-Islamic religion of the Horn, and principally the Sky-God belief, retained some significance during and after the conversion to Christianity, with the pre-Christian religious centre of Aksum maintaining some of its indigenous elements into the Christian era. Stones or wood are frequently incorporated into the architecture of the Horn of Africa and their potential ritual meaning ought not to be ignored. Furthermore, as already noted, there are similarities between the notion of *bir-ma-geydo* and the *Adbar* that protects the sacred tree of the Amhara. This suggests that sacred trees in the Horn are protected by custom-based law and tradition, and embedded into a sacred landscape protected by sacred beings.

The literature on Aksum and Lalibela, and Ethiopian archaeology generally, can shed light on the extent to which some sacred trees belong to a shared heritage. According to these sources, the olive is only mentioned in terms of imported oil. Only one source, it seems, mentions the use of olive branches (Munro-Hay, 1991) as fly-whisks by the 'keeper of the fly-whisks' (*aqabe tsentsen*), a practice that occurred in the Zagwé King Lalibela's time (AD 1225); this practice featured also in the ceremony of King Zara Ya'qob's coronation, which led Munro-Hay to describe it as 'very evocative of this item of Aksumite regalia' (ibid.: 116). The use of Aksumite ritual regalia like the olive branches appears to have a continuity in the Zagwé and beyond.

The wild olive tree (*Olea Africana*) is widely distributed in the dry forests of Ethiopia and Somalia. Rainfall is very low and the area is prone to droughts. It would have been very important to have evergreen forests in the altitudes where farming was feasible. The fauna depicted on the rock art of the Horn of Africa, or at least in the eastern Horn, indicate that the environment was once greener. This rock art is dotted about in the mountain chains where these dry forests are now located. Significant burials have also been found near this rock art. Olive trees are long-lived and can survive in a dry climate. In the same mountains and forests where the *wagar* grows can also be found the aromatic gums that have been traded over many millennia. The *wagar* too is used as incense; any part of the tree can be burnt to create a characteristic smoke, which is also used as an insect repellent in most of the Horn. In Ethiopia, it is also used for seasoning local traditional drinks such as '*Tela*' and '*Irgo*' (yoghurt), and its sap is used for curing skin disease and mental health problems (Bekele, 2000), and, in Kenya, a concoction of bark and root are used to treat malaria. Many of the peoples of the Horn, including the Oromo, use fragrant or aromatic trees, for example the *eddera* tree (*Hypericum revolutum*). Its fragrant leaves, called *tero* by the Guji, are often included in offerings made near graves.

The olive tree and its fruit are also important in religious contexts. Olives are mentioned several times in the Bible, both in the New and Old Testaments; and olive has also been celebrated as a blessed tree and fruit in the Holy Quran (Quran, Chapter 24 Al-Nur, Verse 35).

It is impossible to look at the many phallic stelae and the *kallasha* without considering their possible links with Aksumite architecture and even with Lalibela itself which, as noted in Chapter Two, borrows some elements of Aksumite tradition. If the phallic cult is linked to the Sky-God or Heaven God, then evidence of this can also be found in Aksum where the obelisks appear to form a part of this phallic tradition. Given that the phallic symbol became obscured during the Christian and Islamic eras, the possible marriage of this traditional religious iconography with Christianity demands a careful re-examination of the evidence available from a wider area than hitherto envisaged.

Aw-Barkhadle is known to have had both a phallic and a Christian heritage, as is shown by the practices and legends associated with the site and by the *in situ* archaeology of the Christian Coptic cross burial. Christianity itself seems to have been viewed as something 'Semitic' in the historiography of the Horn of Africa which refers to the 'Semitic' 'minority'. Nevertheless, it seems that Christianity, which now seems to have been more widespread than once thought, did, according to the evidence presented earlier, reach the northern Somali region. It is possible that both Christianity and Islam came to coexist with the Sky-God belief. It is important, incidentally, not to fall into the common trap of defining the Horn as consisting, from the start, of distinctions such as 'Somalia' and 'Ethiopia' and 'Islam' and 'Christianity'. As noted earlier '*Ak*' refers to water, as in *Waaq* (sky/rain) and God is called *shum*, an Amharic word meaning chief or lord. The resulting name, Aksum, has such complex origins and connections that it can only be understood in a context that embraces both the Sky-God belief and other possible indigenous religions in the Horn of Africa.

The centres of Aksum and Aw-Barkhadle lie at the heart of the pre-Christian religions of the Horn of Africa. Both seem to be related the Sky-God *Waaq* and both sites appear to be linked to the symbolism of the olive. Both are also associated with Christianity in the region.

Lalibela, therefore, includes the sacred landscape features demanded by the Ritual Set: sacred trees, sacred enclosures, sacred water, fertility pools, wells and healing ponds. It has the fertility pool or pond into whose sacred waters infertile women dip themselves naked (Figure 6.26). The grass that is said to cover the pool is also believed to be sacred. Furthermore, the population of Lalibela go in the early morning to collect water from the sacred spring that is kept in the sacred water reserve, and pipes from the sacred spring mouth lead to the bath house where people bring jerrycans to hold the sacred water with which to shower and purify themselves (Figure 6.27).

The landscape, activities and symbolism of Lalibela inevitably bring to mind the landscape of Aw-Barkhadle. When the Aw-Barkhadle interviewee told me 'it is all complete here' she meant that the whole landscape is sacred. Similarly, the whole landscape of Sheikh Bale is sacred. The pre-Islamic and pre-Christian religious meanings given to wells, trees, stones, cliffs, rivers, mountains and shrines have been transferred into Islamic times in a spiritual synergy. It is this synergy that produces the laws that look after human beings and offer the protection for a nature that is considered to be sacred.

Tiya's iconography, too, offers many insights into the past. However, a true understanding of a site like this is not gained through only looking at marks on rocks or through opportunistically picking examples from the

Figure 6.26 One of the fertility pools of Lalibela rock hewn churches

Figure 6.27 An official sacred water spring and shower houses at Lalibela

ethnography. It can only come from studying and comparing the many complex and diverse groups who live closely together in this region in an effort to identify the glue that binds these peoples together. The notion of sprouting or the 'vegetable' sign at Tiya seems, for example, to be linked with prosperity and the continuation of lineage. The Matcha Oromo bride on her wedding day offers a glimpse not only of the ritual uses of grass but also of the symbol of sprouting. Male elders smear beansprout, soaked in the slaughtered sheep's blood, together with coffee fruits on a bride's belly and thighs. Prayers are said to bless a girl with children: 'Have children. May your blood sprout (into children)' (Bartels, 1983: 263). There is abundant evidence in the Horn of Africa for the ritual importance of grass, coffee beans and the bean sprouts, often in the context of fertility.

Bartel has pointed out in his chapter 'Killing and Bearing' that the acts of killing and of giving birth both denote a risk, a pain and a bravery but that they also both represent sacrifice in the indigenous religions of the Horn of Africa (Bartels, 1983). In some Oromo weddings, a sheep is slaughtered to represent the 'slaughter' of the virgin bride. The bride is meant to shed blood on her first night of consummation. The knife that is used to slaughter the sheep is ritually equivalent to the penis that 'pierces' the bride. As Bartels demonstrates so clearly, 'Killing and giving birth' are intertwined in the practices of the Matcha Oromo. The spear is used to denote the penis and vice versa; and there are stelae in the shapes of both spears and phallic shapes to be found in the Horn of Africa. Just as the spear pierces the ground to create wells miraculously or to make the crops flourish, so the penis pierces the girl (virgin) in the interests of motherhood. Both acts – the piercing of the ground for crop fertility or the bride for human fertility – are carried out in the name of ritual and fertility. Just as the girl is 'killed' so the spear kills the sheep by slaughtering. Both the girl who has been slaughtered, and the sheep, are sacrificed in the interests of fertility. A similar relationship can be seen too in the fertility ritual of the Oromo and the Somali, *bun qalla* (lit. the slaughter of the coffee bean).

The material culture at Aw-Barkhadle reflects the relationship between sacred fertility and the veneration of religious ancestors. The rituals taking place in the Aw-Barkhadle landscape also offer the opportunity to create a configuration of ritual material culture in terms of perceptions of historical events, characters and practices. The Ritual Set has also been tested in relation to the interpretation of other archaeological material from the Horn. It has demonstrated how to approach and interpret the symbolic archaeology of Tiya by utilising ethnographic insights into indigenous beliefs. At this site, the bodies inside the burial pits suggest foetuses in their wombs. The wood used in the burials might be related to ideas of protection and reproduction, and of family and fertility rituals, connections supported by an abundance of ethnographic and comparative evidence.

Many writers have linked the arrow, pronged objects and phallicism to a warrior culture. However, this research suggest that such objects and imagery are not simply about a warrior culture. They have far more to do with the ritual sacrifice of game or domestic animals, with knives piercing the ground to ensure fertility and the safeguarding of lineage. This remains the case even though traditional warrior groups still exist in the Horn. The knives and the symbols are overwhelmingly associated with ritual sacrifice, fertility and divine powers. There is clear evidence within the archaeological record for phallicism. This phallicism is associated with a sacred power which, in turn, is associated with a religious leader who may be imbued with the power to grant fertility. The 'maleness' aspect of these symbols is linked to sacrifice. The erection of stelae and the depiction of knives and daggers may also be markers for the ritual hunt designed to carry out the sacrificial slaughter of animals in the interests of communal prosperity.

I have argued that iron objects are associated with fertility rituals. I have suggested that the decoration of the Tiya stelae with 'w' and 'x'/'H', disks and perforations, with their potential association with snakes, may relate to the religious worship of saints and ancestors, the continuation of family and fertility symbols. Ethnographic and archaeological records confirm the prevalence of serpent worship. Decorations such as these can be seen to relate to a complex iconography that spreads right across this part of the Horn. Sacred objects and the rituals associated with them of course require further detailed study to test the validity of the hypothesis presented here. Nevertheless, my contextualisation of the archaeological record within the groups that broadly inhabit this region can provide a first step towards a more local approach that can offer better insights into the archaeology and burial ritual practice in this part of Africa. In my attempt to build a comprehensive picture of the traditions of iconography and material culture, and of ethnographic symbolism, I have adopted a transdisciplinary approach, drawing upon disciplines such as ethnography, ethnohistory, historical-linguistics, ethno-botany and anthropology.

The collective burials in Harar at Tchercher would also benefit from this trans-disciplinary approach. These too were excavated by Joussaume et al. (1995) and contain grave goods, including spherical vases with necks. Some appear to be female graves from the type of grave goods found. Three other sites (Rare, Soure Kabana and Tchelenko) include monumental burial chambers that contain incense burners, iron arrows and daggers, copper and silver rings and copper earrings, beads of carnelian, glass, limestone, gold and silver, cowrie shells, olive-stones, eye make-up (*kohl*) and antimony (ibid.). Sites with similar finds have also been recorded in Ethiopia (Phillipson, 2000). Although Joussaume incorporates some in depth ethnographic research in his analysis, he does suggest that such work needs to be extended. He notes how little research has been done so far in most areas of the Horn, with very few tumulus or stelae sites to date studied in Eritrea, Ethiopia, Somalia/Somaliland, Djibouti and northern Kenya.

Conclusions

Earlier in this chapter, I gave details of the Ritual Set I have devised using an ethnographic and archaeological approach (Tables 6.1b-c). I then applied this model to the archaeology beyond Aw-Barkhadle and used it to interpret the symbolism of the material culture of rituals and sacred sites found within archaeological contexts in the Horn of Africa. I focused particularly on the material evidence relating to indigenous traditions and, to a lesser extent, on contexts associated with Christianity and Islam. From out of the womb of ancient indigenous and regional religion there has arisen a set of ideas reflected in practices, features and objects, all of which seem to connect the north and the west of the Horn of Africa with the south and the east. Comparative ethnography reveals much about the beliefs, practices and material culture of the site of Tiya it suggests that a knife is not about a warrior culture nor a phallic stone about male virility. Images of trees incised into rocks are linked to the uses of, and symbolism inherent in, sacred trees and grass. The art cannot be deciphered without an understanding of life and the cycle of life and health, purity and fertility. Northern Ethiopia is not a region isolated from the rest of Ethiopia or even from the rest of the Horn. By identifying the ideas and practices that the peoples of the Horn of Africa have in common it is possible to reach a deeper understanding of a shared regional heritage. The same approach applied to archaeological and ethnographic material reveals that places such as Aksum and Lalibela are not so much 'sites' as sacred landscapes. These landscapes have been shaped by the people, past and present, who have followed both a monotheistic religion and the ideology of a divine kinship and sacred fertility.

I suggest that the Sky-God religion originated in the Horn of Africa. It seems to be most clearly characterised by its phallic symbolism, a symbolism that can be traced as far back as ancient Egypt and Nubia and that survived through pre- and post-Aksumite times. The native olive tree is another feature of this religion. Its wood is burned for its aromatic scent and used as incense. The rituals associated with it suggest an ancient significance that would not have been lost on the early traders of the Horn of Africa. A trade in incense developed and expanded in the same region that the olive flourished and in areas where myrrh and frankincense grow. Amongst the civilisations of the Mediterranean and the Indian Ocean, the native olive would come to enhance this region's reputation as the seat of a mystical and ritual power. It remains unclear how far the archaeology of the wider Horn of Africa will ever be able to illuminate the long history of the native olive forests and the olive's uses in pre-Aksumite and Aksumite times.

Art history and archaeology have paid all too little attention to indigenous practices and institutions. Phallic symbolism, for example, has been either avoided for political reasons or completely misrepresented or misinterpreted. Archaeological and art historical scholarship at sites associated with an 'indigenous' culture – the stelae fields of Ethiopia, dolmens, cairns and rock art sites – have until now been dominated by environmental, ecological and economic perspectives; the study of symbolic material and local perspectives have largely been ignored. As a result, possible connections between different materials, myths and the landscapes have largely been overlooked.

Fertility ideology and divine kinship form the main synergies here. Yet archaeologists generally fail to understand the pre-Abrahamic and traditional belief systems of this region. And there is a lack of historical and archaeological knowledge, and depth, within the anthropological community. The research presented in this book is intended to fill this gap. Its aim is to use both anthropology and archaeology to bring about a deeper knowledge and insight into the past and present societies of this region.

Notes

1 Ensete is a multi-purpose, drought resistant plant (Karlsson and Dalbato, 2013).
2 Kanshie, K. T. 2002. *Five thousand years of sustainability? A case study on Gedeo Land Use* (Southern Ethiopia). Treemail Publishers.
3 The Gedeo have the *baallee gada* system (Kanshie, 2002).
4 *Wadaad* was a pre-Islamic name for the traditional religious heads; the term is also used for Muslim Somali sheikhs since the conversion (Cerulli, 1957: 149).
5 *Dacawaaleh* or *Dawocaaleh* or just *da 'awaaleh* depending on transliteration and dialect is a word meaning hyena and the name of rock art site in Dhaymooleh, near Berbera.
6 TIYA – World Heritage Site. https://whc.unesco.org/en/list/12 [accessed: 30/08/2017].
7 In the Oromo language, the word *qoccumaan* (also *hoccumaan*) means navel, womb or ovary (Loo, 1991).
8 According to Loo (1991, glossary) *qallacca* is a phallic symbol worn on the forehead of the *Abba Gada*. The word *qallu* means 1. Muslim diviner-healer; and 2. A specialist in exorcism. However, *Qallu* also means 'spiritual chief of the Alabdu'. The word *qullu* (also *qulluicco*) means 1. pure, saintly; and 2. tenth *Gada* class. *Qalla* means to slaughter in many Eastern Cushitic speaking languages, including the Oromo, Somali and Konso. The *Qalllu* can also refer to the person who slaughters the ritual game during the ritual hunt as well as domestic sacrificial animals. *Kallacca* or *Qallacca* is therefore the regalia of the *Qallu* or *Abba Gada*.
9 In Joussaume's (2007) book, fig. 166: 2, p. 201.

Bibliography

Adamson, J. 1967. *The Peoples of Kenya*. London: Collins & Harvill Press.
Almeida, Manuel. 1954. *Some Records of Ethiopia, 1593–1646*. Edited and translated by C. F. Beckingham and G. W. B. Huntingford. London: Hakluyt Society.
Alvares, F. 1881. *Narrative of the Portuguese Embassy to Abyssinia, 1520–1526*. Translated and edited by Lord Stanley of Alderley. London: Hakluyt Society.
Anfray, F. 1982. Les stèles du Sud, Shoa et Sidamo. *Annales d'Ethiopie*, 12: 1–221.
Azaïs, M. and Chambard, R. 1931. *Cinq Années de Recherches Archéologique en Éthiopie*. Edited by P. Geuthner. Paris: Librario Instituto.

Bartels, L. 1983. *Oromo Religion: Myths and Rites of the Western Oromo of Ethiopia. An Attempt to Understand.* Berlin: Deitrich Reimer Verlag.

Baxter, P. 1990. Oromo Blessings and Greetings. In A. Jocobson-Widding and W. van Beek (eds.) *The Creative Communion. African Folk Models of Fertility and the Regeneration of Life.* Uppsala: Acta Universitatis Upsaliensis.

Bekele Testeye. 2000. *Plant Population Dynamics of Dodonaea angustifolia and Olea europaea ssp. cuspidata in Dry Afromontane Forests of Ethiopia.* Uppsala: Acta Universitatis Upsalensis.

Brandt, S. A. 1986. The Upper Pleistocene and Early Holocene Prehistory of the Horn of Africa. *The African Archaeological Review,* 4: 41–82.

Brandt, S. A. and Carder, N. 1987. Pastoral Rock Art in the Horn of Africa: Making Sense of Udder Chaos. *World Archaeology,* 19(2): 194–213.

Braukämper, U. 2004. *Islamic History and Culture in Southern Ethiopia: Collected Essays.* Gottinger Studien Zur Ethnologie. Munster: Lit Verlag Munster.

Burton, R. 1966 [1898]. *First Footsteps in East Africa.* Edited by G. Waterfield. Travellers and Explorers Series. New York: Praeger.

Cassen, S. 1995. Une Enquête Ethno-Archéologique sur la Production Céramique de Haro (Éthiopie). In R. Joussaume (ed.) *Tiya – L'Éthiopie des Mégalithes. Du biface à l'art rupestre dans la Corne de l'Afrique.* Mémorie XI. Minisère des Affaires Étrangères, Minitère de la Coopération, Ambassade de France en Èthiopie, UNESCO, UPR 311 du CNRS.

Cerulli, E. 1957. *Somalia. Scritti vari Editi ed Inediti.* Vol. I. Roma: Istituto Poligrafico dello Stato. P. V.

Chittick, H. N. 1974. Excavations at Aksum, 1973–74. A Preliminary Report. *Azania,* 9: 159–205.

Conti Rossini, C. 1905. Note sugli agau: 1. Appunti sulla lingua khamta dell' Averghellé. *Giornale della Società Asiatica Italiana,* 17: 109–122.

Ehret, C. 1976. Cushitic Prehistory. In M. L. Bender (ed.) *The Non-Semitic Languages of Ethiopia.* East Lansing: Michigan State University Press.

Ehret, C. 1995. The Eastern Horn of Africa, 1000 BC to 1400 AD: The Historical Roots. In A. J. Ahmed (ed.) *The Invention of Somalia.* Lawrenceville, NJ: Red Sea Press.

Ehret, C. 2002. *The Civilizations of Africa: A History to 1800.* Oxford: James Currey.

Evans-Pritchard, E. E. 1940. *The Nuer.* Oxford: Clarendon Press.

Evans-Pritchard, E. E. 1954. The Meaning of Sacrifice Among the Nuer. *Journal of Royal Anthropological Institute,* 84: 21–33.

Fattovich, R. 1987. Some Remarks on the Origins of the Aksumite Stelae. *Annales d'Ethiopie,* 14.

Fattovich, R., Bard, K. A., Petrassi, L. and Pisano, V. 2000. *The Aksum Archaeological Area: A Preliminary Assessment.* Napoli: Instituto Universitario Orientale, Centro Interdipartimentale de Servizi Per L'Archaeologia.

Fernández, V. M. 2011. Schematic Rock Art, Rain-Making, and Islam in the Ethio-Sudanese Borderlands. *African Archaeological Review,* 4(28):170–300.

Finneran, N. 2003. Evil Eye Belief in Ethiopia and the Magical Symbolism of Iron Working. *Folklore,* 114(3): 427–436.

Fortes, M. and Evans-Pritchard, E. E. 1940. *African Political Systems.* London: KPI/IAI.

Galaal, M. I. H. 1970. *Stars, Seasons and Weather in Somali Pastoral Traditions.* Mogadishu: Celho.

Godet, E. and Pierre, I. 1993. Les stèles sculptées du Soddo (Éthiopie); Recherches sur leur symbolism. In C. Berber, C. Clerc, and N. Grimal (eds.) *Hommage à Jean Leclant*. Vol. 2, pp. 151–168. Le Caire: IFAO.

Groom, N. 1981. *The Incense Trade*. London: Longman.

Grottanelli, V. L. 1947. Asiatic Influences on Somali Culture. *Ethnos*, 4: 153–181.

Hallpike, C. 1972. *The Konso of Ethiopia: A Study of the Values of an Eastern Cushitic People*. Oxford: Clarendon Press.

Hamilakis, Y. 2014. Archaeology and the Senses: Human Experience, Memory and Affect. Cambridge: CUP.

Hildebrand, E., Shea, J. J. and Grillo, K. M. 2011. Four Middle Holocene Pillar Sites in West Turkana, Kenya. *Journal of Field Archaeology*, 36(3): 181–200.

Hodder, I. 1982. *Symbols in Action*. Cambridge: Cambridge University Press.

Hodder, I. (ed.). 1989. *The Meaning of Things: Material Culture and Symbolic Expression*. 4th ed. Lexington: WIN.

Huntingford, G. W. B. 1955. *The Galla of Ethiopia: The Kingdoms of Kafa and Janjero*. London: International Africa Institute.

Jensen, A. E. 1936. *Im Lande des Gada. Wanderungen zwischen Volkstrümmern Süd-Abessiniens*. Stuttgart: Strecker und Schröder.

Joussaume, R. 1974. *Le Mégalithisme en Ethiopie. Monuments Funéraires Proto-historiques du Harar*. Laboratoire de Préhistoire CNRS Laboratoire Associe 184. Paris: Museum National d'Histoire Naturelle.

Joussaume, R. 1981. L'Art Rupestre de l'Ethiopie. In C. Roubet, H. J. Hugot and G. Souville (eds.) *Préhistoire Africaine: Mélanges offerts au Doyen Lionel Balout*. pp. 159–175. Paris: ADPF.

Joussaume, R. 1983. Les Steles graves de Tiya. *Archaeologia*, 185: 42–47.

Joussaume, R. (ed.). 1995. *Tiya – L'Éthiopie des Mégalithes. Du biface à l'Art Rupestre dans la Corne de l'Afrique*. Mémoire XI. Ministère des Affaires Étrangères, Ministère de la Coopération, Ambassade de France en Èthiopie, UNESCO, UPR 311 du CNRS.

Joussaume, R. (ed.). 2007. *Tuto Fela et les stèles du* sud de L'Ethiopie. Paris: Éditions Recherche surles Civilisations.

Joussaume, R. 2011. Amorigé and the Anthropomorphic Stelae with Compart-mented Faces of Southern Ethiopia. *Annales d'Ethiopie*, 26(1): 105–117.

Kanshie, K. T. 2002. *Five Thousand Years of Sustainability? A Case Study on Gedeo Land Use (Southern Ethiopia)*. Heelsum: Treemail Publishers.

Karlsson, L. M. and Dalbato, A. L. 2013. Early Growth and Development of Ensete ventricosum (Musaceae) Seedlings. *Journal of Plant Sciences*, 1(1): 11–17.

Kassam, A. and Megerssa, G. 1996. Sticks, Self, and Society in Booran Oromo: A Symbolic Interpretation. In M. J. Arnoldi and K. L. Hardin (eds.) *African Material Culture*. Bloomington and Indianapolis: Indiana University Press.

Kirk, J. W. C. 1905. The Yibirs and Midgans of Somaliland, Their Traditions and Dialects. *Journal of African Society*, 4: 91–108.

Kusow, A. M. 1995. The Somali Origin: Myth or Reality. In A. J. Ahmed (ed.) *The Invention of Somalia*. Lawrenceville, NJ: Red Sea Press.

Lane, P. J. and Read, A. 2016. Editorial. Azania at Fifty. *Azania*, 50(4): 425–436.

Layton, R. 1989. The Political Use of Australian Aboriginal Body Painting and Its Archaeological Implication. In I. Hodder (ed.) *The Meaning of Things: Material Culture and Symbolic Expression*. London: Unwin Hyman.

Legesse, A. 1973. *Gada. Three Approaches to the Study of an African Society*. London: Collier-Macmillan Limited.

Legesse, A. 2000. *Oromo Democracy: An African Indigenous Political System*. Lawrenceville, NJ: Red Sea Press.

Le-Quellec, J. L. 1987. Les Trois Fonctions dans le Soddo et Éthiopie. *Revue de l'Histoire Des Religions*, 231–238.

Levine, D. N. 2000. *Greater Ethiopia: The Evolution of a Multiethnic Society*. 2nd ed. Chicago and London: University of Chicago Press.

Lewis, I. (ed.). 1966. *Islam in Tropical Africa*. London: IAI and Indiana University Press.

Lewis, I. 1961. *A Pastoral Democracy*. London: Oxford University Press.

Lewis, I. 1994a. *Blood and Bone: The Call for Kinship in Somali Society*. Lawrenceville, NJ: Red Sea Press.

Lewis, I. 1994b. *People of the Horn of Africa: Somali, Afar and Saho*. London: IAI/ Haan.

Lewis, I. 1998. *Saints and Somalis: Popular Islam in a Clan-Based Society*. Lawrenceville, NJ and Asmara, Eritrea: Red Sea Press.

Loo, J. van de. 1991. *Guji Oromo Culture (with the Collaboration of Bilow Kolo)*. Berlin: Dietrich Reimer Verlag.

Luling, V. 1988. The Man in the Tree. A Note on a Somali Myth. In A. Puglieli (ed.) *Proceedings of the Third International Congress of Somali Studies*. Rome: II Pensario Scientifico.

Lynch, M. and Donahue, R. 1980. A Statistical Analysis of Rock-Art Sites in Northwest Kenya. *Journal of Field Archaeology*, 7: 75–85.

Lynch, M. and Robbins, L. H. 1978. Namoratunga: The First Archaeoastronomical Evidence in Sub-Saharan Africa. *Science*, 200: 766–768.

Mansur, A. O. 1995. The Nature of the Somali Clan-System. In A. J. Ahmed (ed.) *The Invention of Somalia*. Lawrenceville, NJ: Red Sea Press.

Marcus, J. and Flannery, K. 1994. Ancient Zapotec Ritual and Religion: An Application of the Direct Historical Approach. In C. Renfrew and E. W. Zubrow (eds.) *The Ancient Mind: Elements of Cognitive Archaeology*. Cambridge: Cambridge University Press.

Mire, S. 2007. Preserving Knowledge, Not Objects: A Somali Perspective for Heritage Management and Archaeological Research. *African Archaeological Review*, 24: 49–71.

Mire, S. 2008. The Discovery of Dhambalin Rock Art Site, Somaliland. *African Archaeological Review*, 25: 153–168.

Mire, S. 2010. Somaliland: Archaeology in a Breakaway State. *Current World Archaeology*, 43: pp. 26–33. (Report with original research).

Mire, S. 2015a. Mapping of the Archaeology of Somaliland: Religion, Art, Script, Time, Urbanism, Trade and Empire. *African Archaeological Review*, 32(1): 111–136.

Mire, S. 2015b. Wagar, Fertility and Phallic Stelae: Cushitic Sky-God Belief and the Site of Saint Aw-Barkhadle in Somaliland. *African Archaeological Review*, 32(1): 93–109.

Mire, S. 2017. The Role of Cultural Heritage in the Basic Needs of East African Pastoralists. *African Study Monographs, Supplementary Issue*, 53: 147–157.

Morin, D. 2004. *Dictionnaire historique afar (1288–1982)*. Paris: Kharthala.

Mukhtar, M. H. 1995. Islam in Somali History; Fact and Fiction. In A. J. Ahmed (ed.) *The Invention of Somalia*. Lawrenceville, NJ: Red Sea Press.

Munro-Hay, S. A. 1991. *Aksum – An African Civilization in Late Antiquity*. Edinburgh: Edinburgh University Press.

Munro-Hay, S. A. 2002. *Ethiopia- the Unknown Land: A Cultural and Historical Guide*. London and New York: I.B. Tauris.

Paulitschke, P. 1888. *Ethnographie Nordost Afrikas, I. Die materielle Cultur des Danâkil, Galla und Somâl II. Die geistige Cultur des Danâkil, Galla und Somâl*. Vol. 2. Berlin.

Phillipson, D. W. 1997. *Ancient Ethiopia. Aksum: Its Antecedents and Successors*. London: British Museum Press.

Phillipson, D. W. 2000. *Archaeology at Aksum, Ethiopia, 1993–7*. Vols. I–II. Memoirs of the British Institute in Eastern Africa: Number 17. Report 65, Research Committee of the Society of Antiquaries of London.

Phillipson, D. W. 2012. *Foundations of an African Civilization: Aksum and the Northern Horn 1000 BC to 1300 AD*. Oxford: James Currey; Addis Ababa: Addis Ababa University.

Posnansky, M. 2009. *Africa and Archaeology: Empowering an Expatriate Life*. London: Radcliffe Press.

Posnansky, M. 2017. Archaeology and the Local Community in Africa: A Retrospective. *Journal of Community Archaeology and Heritage*, 4(2): 77–84.

Prouty, C. and Rosenfeld, E. 1994. *Historical Dictionary of Ethiopia and Eritrea*. Metuchen, NJ and London: The Scarecrow Press, Inc.

Renfrew, C. 1994. Towards a Cognitive Archaeology. In C. Renfrew and E. W. Zubrow (eds.) *The Ancient Mind: Elements of Cognitive Archaeology*. Cambridge: Cambridge University Press.

Révoil, G. 1882. *La Vallée du Darror: Voyage aux Pays Çomalis Dis Mois à la Cote Orientale D'Afrique*. Paris: Challamel aîné.

Serjeant, R. B. 1976. *The South Arabian Hunt*. London: Luzac.

Shack, W. A. 1966. *The Gurage: A People of the Ensete Culture*. London, New York, and Nairobi: Oxford University Press.

Shinn, D. H. and. Ofcansky, T. P. 2004. *Historical Dictionary of Ethiopia*. Oxford: The Scarecrow Press, Inc.

Soper, R. 1982. Archaeo-Astronomical Cushites: Some Comments. *Azania*, 17: 145–162.

Thesiger, W. 1935. The Awash River and the Awsa Sultanate. *The Geographical Journal*, 85: 1–23.

Tilley, C. 1984. Ideology and the Legitimation of Power in the Middle Neolithic of Sweden. In D. Miller and C. Tilley (eds.) *Ideology, Power and Prehistory*. Cambridge: Cambridge University Press.

Tilley, C. 1989. Interpreting Material Culture. In I. Hodder (ed.) *The Meaning of Things: Material Culture and Symbolic Expression*. London: Unwin Hyman.

Tilley, C. 1991. *Material Culture and Text: The Art of Ambiguity*. London and New York: Routledge.

Tournemire, C. 2003. Découvertes de stèles monolithiques dans le pays Guragué. *Annales d'Éthiopie*, 19: 83–117.

Trimingham, J. S. 1965. *Islam in Ethiopia*. 2nd ed. Oxford: Oxford University Press.

Ucko, P. J. 1969. Ethnography and Archaeological Interpretation of Funerary Remains. *World Archaeology*, 1: 262–280.

Ucko, P. J. and Rosenfeld, A. 1967. *Grottkonst.* Stockholm: Bonniers.
Ullendorff, E. 1955. *The Semitic Languages of Ethiopia: A Comparative Phonology.* London: Taylor's.
Whitley, D. S. and Hays-Gilpin, K. 2008. Religion Beyond Icon, Burial and Monument: Introduction. In D. S. Whitley and K. Hays-Gilpin (eds.) *Belief in the Past: Theoretical Approaches to the Archaeology of Religion.* Walnut Creek, CA: Left Coast Press.
Zubrow, E. B. 1994. Cognitive Archaeology Reconsidered. In C. Renfrew and E. W. Zubrow (eds.) *The Ancient Mind: Elements of Cognitive Archaeology.* Cambridge: Cambridge University Press.

7   Conclusions

In my discussion of the Horn of Africa's common foundations, I have emphasised similarities in geography, linguistics, subsistence economies, environments, political systems, cultural practices and religious systems. In my consideration of the latter, I have tried to give a firm shape to the essential indigenous and continuing religious ideas that extend beyond the present Islamic or Christian official domain. I have done this by identifying the rituals, the religious materials and the regalia associated with indigenous traditions such as fertility and ritual hunt/sacrifice/*zar*, *gudniin*, *siti*, *wagar* and the belief of the Sky-God *Waaq*. I have outlined how gudniin/FGM is between humans and the divine rather than between men and women. I have shown it is a fertility sacrifice and about extending sacred righteous blood. I have also demonstrated that the zar (the spirit) is related to the Sky-God (tosa, zar, Waaq, etc.), a transformation caused by the adoption of Christianity and Islam. I have shown that the belief in the Sky-God is a religion mainly based on fertility ideology in a kinship/lineage society.

Moving from ideas to materials in the synthesis of my own ethnographic research, I also conclude that there is a set of materials and arrangements that are configured in similar rituals in a sacred ritual landscape. This Ritual Set may prove useful in making sense not only of the current complex material culture of the Horn but also of the archaeological data of the region. In Chapter Six, I used this theoretical framework to contextualise and (re)interpret some of the archaeology associated with apposite traditions such those revealed at the stelae cemeteries of Aw-Barkhadle and Tiya, which seem to date to about the same time. I have also shed light on how Aksum and Lalibela, for example, are linked with these indigenous traditions.

I use the discoveries of sites in Somaliland and a comparative analysis of the ethnography together with evidence from archaeological sites in Ethiopia to reveal a wider picture of the Horn. I recognise the fact that traditions and practices can change through time – as, it seems, can the languages that groups speak.

The Ritual Set I have constructed is based upon observation. This, for the first time, articulates the solid evidence and interconnections associated with the ideology of divine fertility. It reveals common and rather systematic affinities within the peoples of the Horn of Africa; its elements include the phallic symbolism and the sacred olive trees.

Geographical barriers are often nothing of the sort in real life. I have visited sites such as Sameeno Fuerte in Sanaag and the Aksum and Lalibela landscapes as well as the Somali region and the Soddo region of Ethiopia during the course of my analysis of the archaeology and practices presented in this book. I have come to realise that the idea of lowland and highland serving as a barrier for deeper interaction is merely a product of our imagination. In much the same way, I now understand that notions of Islam and Christianity may not always be as divisive as they are thought to be. A Muslim wedding can take place at a place like Aksum which is not only a major pre-Christian religious centre and the earliest centre of Christianity in the Horn of Africa but also the place of refuge for the earliest Muslim family members of the Prophet Mohammed. Then again, there is Aw-Barkhadle, which is arguably the holiest pilgrim centre for Muslims in the Horn of Africa. According to legend, it is the earliest seat of Islamic teaching in the Somali region and the possible site of the first and lost capital of the medieval Islamic Kingdom of Awdal. Yet even here can be found not only a fourth–seventh century type Christian cross burial but also a phallic symbol, the dolmens, the cairns and the rituals associated with an older religion. And at Lalibela, its Christian religious and political rulers officially linked their rule to their Aksumite predecessors through interweaving their Christianity with their own pre-Christian heritage. The old Somali sheikha, a *Muriid* of a tomb, has a cross tattooed on her forehead. And at Aw-Barkhdale, people not so long ago painted crosses on their foreheads using the sacred chalk from the mountain of Bu 'ur Ba 'ayr, a ruler strongly associated with non-Islamic, and even allegedly 'Jewish', activities.

The past cannot be judged through the lens of the present. Time, however, is cyclical. The people of the Horn of Africa believe that God is one and omnipresent. Put simply, there seems to be something about this region and its indigenous ideologies that challenges neither Islam nor Christianity. Instead, people are drawn to both Islam and Christianity, perhaps because a belief in a monotheistic religions(s) is embedded in their past through religions such as the Sky-God or through those found today in Nubia and Egypt. It appears that people have embraced and interpreted both Christianity and Islam in ways that have allowed them to continue to offer up sacrifices and worship God in the interests of peace, prosperity and fertility. They recognise God as an omnipresent being and the saints and sacred ancestors as his representatives on Earth. And kinship is the medium through which they seek to connect with God's prophets.

Bibliography

Abbink, J. 1998. An Historical-Anthropological Approach to Islam in Ethiopia: Issues of Identity and Politics. *Journal of African Cultural*, 11(2): 109–124.

Achebe, C. 1958. *Things Fall Apart*. London: William Heinemann Ltd.

Adamson, J. 1967. *The Peoples of Kenya*. London: Collins & Harvill Press.

Alexander, J. A. 1979. The Archaeological Recognition of Religion: The Examples of Islam in Africa and 'Urnfields' in Europe. In B. C. Burnham and J. Kingsbury (eds.) *Space, Hierarchy and Society*. Oxford: British Archaeological Reports. BAR International Series 59.

Almeida, M. 1954. *Some Records of Ethiopia, 1593–1646*. Edited and translated by C. F. Beckingham and G. W. B. Huntingford. London: Hakluyt Society.

Alvares, F. 1881. *Narrative of the Portuguese Embassy to Abyssinia, 1520–1526*. Translated and edited by Lord Stanley of Alderley. London: Hakluyt Society.

Amborn, H. 2009. The Phallsification of the Kallačča: Or, Why Sometimes a Cigar Is a Cigar. In S. Ege, H. Aspen, B. Teferra and S. Bekele (eds.) *Proceedings of the 16th International Conference of Ethiopian Studies*. Trondheim Norwegian University of Science and Technology.

Andah, B. W. 1995. Studying African Societies in Cultural Context. In P. R. Schmidt and T. C. Patterson (eds.) *Making Alternative Histories: The Practice of Archaeology and History in Non-Western Settings*. Santa Fe, NM: School of American Research Press.

Andrezejewski, B. W. 1974. The Veneration of Sufi Saints and Its Impact on Oral Literature of the Somali People and Their Literature in Arabic. *African Language Studies*, 15: 15–53.

Anfray, F. 1982. Les stèles du Sud, Shoa et Sidamo. *Annales d'Ethiopie*, 12: 1–221.

Anshan, L. 2012. *A History of Oversees Chinese in Africa to 1911*. New York: Diasporic Africa Press.

Arberry, A. J. 1953. *Sufism: An Account of the Mystics of Islam*. London: Allen and Unwin.

Arnold, T. W. 1929. *The Islamic Book*. Paris: The Pegasus Press.

Arnoldi, M. J. 1986. The Artistic Heritage of Somalia. In K. Loughran, J. Loughran, J. Johnson and S. Samatar (eds.) *Somalia in Word and Image*. Washington, DC: Foundation for Cross Cultural Understanding and Indiana University Press.

Asad, T. 1983. Anthropological Conceptions of Religion: Reflections on Geertz. *Man*, 18(2): 237–259.

Asad, T. 1993. *Genealogies of Religion: Discipline and Reason of Power in Christianity and Islam*. Baltimore: John Hopkins University Press.

Assaad, M. B. 1980. Female Circumcision in Egypt: Social Implications, Current Research and Prospects for Change. *Studies in Family Planning*, 11(1): 3–16.

Atalay, S. 2006. Indigenous Archaeology as a Decolonizing Practice. *American Indian Quarterly*, 30(3 & 4): 280–310.

Auffret, S. 1983. *Des Couteaux contre des Femmes – de l'Excision.* Paris: Des Femmes.

Azaïs, M. and Chambard, R. 1931. *Cinq Années de Recherches Archéologique en Éthiopie.* Edited by P. Geuthner. Paris: Librario Instituto.

Barclay, H. 1964. *Buuri al Lamaa: A Suburban Village in the Sudan.* Ithaca: Cornell University Press.

Bartels, L. 1983. *Oromo Religion: Myths and Rites of the Western Oromo of Ethiopia. An Attempt to Understand.* Berlin: Deitrich Reimer Verlag.

Baxter, P. 1990. Oromo Blessings and Greetings. In A. Jocobson-Widding and W. van Beek (eds.) *The Creative Communion. African Folk Models of Fertility and the Regeneration of Life.* Uppsala: Uppsala University.

Beach, D., Bourdillon, M. F. C., Denbow, J., Hall, M., Lane, P., Pikirayi, I. and Pwiti, G. 1997. Review Feature: Snakes and Crocodiles: Power and Symbolism in Ancient Zimbabwe by T. N. Huffman. *South African Archaeological Bulletin*, 52: 125–143.

Beachey, R. W. 1990. *The Warrior Mullah: The Horn Aflame. 1892–1920.* London: Bellew Publishing.

Beek, G. W. Van. 1960. Pre-Islamic South Arabian Shipping in the Indian Ocean – A Surrejoinder. *Journal of the American Oriental Society*, 80(2).

Bekele Testeye. 2000. *Plant Population Dynamics of Dodonaea angustifolia and Olea europaea ssp. cuspidata in Dry Afromontane Forests of Ethiopia.* Uppsala: Acta Universitatis Upsalensis.

Besteman, C. L. 1999. *Unrevalling Somalia: Race, Violence and the Legacy of Slavery.* Philadelphia, PA: University of Pennsylvania Press.

Boddy, J. 1982. Womb as Oasis: The Symbolic Context of Pharaonic Circumcision in Rural Northern Sudan. *American Ethnologist*, 9(4): 682–698.

Brandt, S. A. 1986. The Upper Pleistocene and Early Holocene Prehistory of the Horn of Africa. *The African Archaeological Review*, 4: 41–82.

Brandt, S. A. and Carder, N. 1987. Pastoral Rock Art in the Horn of Africa: Making Sense of Udder Chaos. *World Archaeology*, 19(2): 194–213.

Braukämper, U. 2004. *Islamic History and Culture in Southern Ethiopia: Collected Essays.* Gottinger Studien Zur Ethnologie. Munster: Lit Verlag Munster.

Brück, J. 1999. Ritual and Rationality: Some Problems of Interpretation in European Archaeology. *European Journal of Archaeology*, 2(3): 313–344.

Burton, R. 1966 [1898]. *First Footsteps in East Africa.* Edited by G. Waterfield. Travellers and Explorers Series. New York: Praeger.

Buxton, D. 1957. *Travels in Ethiopia.* London: E. Benn.

Cassanelli, L. 1982. *The Shaping of Somali Society: Reconstructing the History of a Pastoral People, 1600–1900.* Philadelphia, PA: University of Pennsylvania Press.

Cassen, S. 1995. Une Enquête Ethno-Archéologique sur la Production Céramique de Haro (Éthiopie). In R. Joussaume (ed.) *Tiya – L'Éthiopie des Mégalithes. Du biface à l'art rupestre dans la Corne de l'Afrique.* Mémorie XI. Minisère des Affaires Étrangères, Minitère de la Coopération, Ambassade de France en Èthiopie, UNESCO, UPR 311 du CNRS.

Casson, L. 1989. *The Periplus Maris Erythraei.* Text with Introduction, Translation and Commentary by L. Casson. Princeton: Princeton University Press.

Cerulli, E. 1957. *Somalia. Scritti vari Editi ed Inediti.* Vol. I. Roma: Istituto Poligrafico dello Stato. P. V.

Červiček, P. 1979. Some African Affinities of Arabian Rock Art. *Rassegna di studi ethiopici*, 27: 5–12.

Chakrabarti, K. D. 1998. The Indus Civilization and the Arabian Gulf: An Indian Point of View. In C. S. Phillips, D. T. Potts and S. Searight (eds.) *Arabia and Its Neighbours. Essays on Prehistorical and Historical Development*. Abiel II. New Research on the Arabian Peninsula. Turnhout: Brepols.

Chittick, H. N. 1969. An Archaeological Reconnaissance of the Southern Somali Coast. *Azania*, 4: 115–130.

Chittick, H. N. 1974. Excavations at Aksum, 1973–74. A Preliminary Report. *Azania*, 9: 159–205.

Chittick, H. N. 1975. An Archaeological Reconnaissance in the Horn: The British-Somali Expedition. *Azania*, 11: 117–133.

Colson, E. 1997. Places of Power and Shrines of the Land. *Paideuma*, 43: 47–57.

Conti Rossini, C. 1905. Note sugli agau: 1. Appunti sulla lingua khamta dell' Averghellé. *Giornale della Società Asiatica Italiana*, 17: 109–122.

Conti Rossini, C. 1928. *Storia d'Etiopia*. Milano: Officina d'arte grafica A. Lucini.

Curle, A. T. 1937. The Ruined Towns of Somaliland. *Antiquity*, 11: 315–327.

Davies, M. I. J. 2013. Stone Cairns Across Eastern Africa: A Critical Review. *Azania*, 48(2): 218–240.

Davis, W. 1989. Towards an Archaeology of Thought. In I. Hodder (ed.) *The Meaning of Things: Material Culture and Symbolic Expression*. London: Unwin Hyman.

Declich, F. 1996. Poesia Religiosa Femminile- Nabi-Ammaan: Nel Contesto Rurale Della Somalia. *Africa: Rivista trimestrale di studi e documentazione dell'Istituto italiano per l'Africa e l'Oriente Anno*, 51(1): 50–79.

Declich, F. 2000. Sufi Experience in Rural Somali: A Focus on Women. *Social Anthropology*, 8(3): 295–318.

Dunn, R. 1989 [1325–1354]. *The Adventures of Ibn Battúta. A Muslim Traveller of the Fourteenth Century*. Berkeley, CA: University of California Press.

Durkheim, É. 2001. *The Elementary Forms of the Religious Life*. Translated by C. Cosman. Oxford: Oxford University Press.

Edwards, D. N. 2005. The Archaeology of Religion. In M. Diaz-Andreu, S. Lucy, S. Babić and D. N. Edwards (eds.) *The Archaeology of Identity: Approaches to Gender, Age, Status, Ethnicity and Religion*. Oxon: Routledge.

Ehret, C. 1976. Cushitic Prehistory. In M. L. Bender (ed.) *The Non-Semitic Languages of Ethiopia*. East Lansing: Michigan State University Press.

Ehret, C. 1995. The Eastern Horn of Africa, 1000 BC to 1400 AD: The Historical Roots. In A. J. Ahmed (ed.) *The Invention of Somalia*. Lawrenceville, NJ: Red Sea Press.

Ehret, C. 2002. *The Civilizations of Africa: A History to 1800*. Charlottesville: University Press of Virginia.

Ehret, C. and Posnansky, M. (eds.). 1982. *The Archaeological and Linguistic Reconstruction of African History*. Berkeley and London: University of California Press.

el-Safi, A. 1970. *Native Medicine in the Sudan: Sources, Conception and Methods*. Khartoum: Khartoum University Press.

el-Zein, Abdul Hamid. 1972. *The Sacred Meadows: A Structural Analysis of Religious Symbolism in an East African Town*. Unpublished PhD thesis, University of Chicago.

Encyclopaedia of Islam Online. 2005. Brill.

Eno, M. A. and Kusow, A. M. 2014. Race and Caste Prejudice in Somalia. *Journal of Somali Studies*, 1(2): 91–118.

Evans-Pritchard, E. E. 1940. *The Nuer*. Oxford: Clarendon Press.

Evans-Pritchard, E. E. 1954. The Meaning of Sacrifice Among the Nuer. *Journal of Royal Anthropological Institute*, 84: 21–33.

Fattovich, R. 1987. Some Remarks on the Origins of the Aksumite Stelae. *Annales d'Ethiopie*, 14.

Fattovich, R., Bard, K. A., Petrassi, L. and Pisano, V. 2000. *The Aksum Archaeological Area: A Preliminary Assessment*. Napoli: Instituto Universitario Orientale, Centro Interdipartimentale de Servizi Per L'Archaeologia.

Fauvelle-Aymar, F.-X., & Hirsch, B. (2004). Muslim historical spaces in Ethiopia and the Horn of Africa: A reassessment. *Northeast African Studies, 2004–2010,* 11(1), 25–54.

Favali, L. 2001. What Is Missing? (Female Genital Surgeries – Gudniin, Excision, Cliterodectomy – in Eritrea). *Global Jurist Frontiers*, 1(2).

Fernández, V. M. 2011. Schematic Rock Art, Rain-Making, and Islam in the Ethio-Sudanese Borderlands. *African Archaeological Review*, 4(28): 170–300.

Finneran, N. 2002. *The Archaeology of Christianity in Africa*. Stroud: Tempus.

Finneran, N. 2003. Evil Eye Belief in Ethiopia and the Magical Symbolism of Iron Working. *Folklore*, 114(3): 427–436.

Finneran, N. 2007. *The Archaeology of Ethiopia*. London and New York: Routledge.

Fortes, M. and Evans-Pritchard, E. E. 1940. *African Political Systems*. London: KPI/IAI.

Forward, M. 1994. Islam. In J. Holm and J. Bowker (eds.) *Worship*. Themes in Religious Studies. London: Pinter Publishers Ltd.

Fullerton, A. and Adan, A. 1995. Handicraft of the Somali Woman. In L. Prussin (ed.) *African Nomadic Architecture; Space, Place and Gender*. Washington, DC: Smithsonian Institute.

Galaal, M. I. X. 1970. *Stars, Seasons and Weather in Somali Pastoral Traditions*. Mogadishu: Celho.

Geertz, C. 1993. *The Interpretation of Cultures*. London: Fontana Press.

Gibbon, G. 1984. *Anthropological Archaeology*. New York: Columbia University Press.

Godet, E. and Pierre, I. 1993. Les stèles sculptées du Soddo (Éthiopie); Recherches sur leur symbolism. In C. Berber, C. Clerc and N. Grimal (eds.) *Hommage à Jean Leclant*. Vol. 2, pp. 151–168. Le Caire: IFAO.

Gonzalez-Ruibal, A. 2014. An Archaeology of Resistance. Materiality and Time in an African Borderland. Maryland: Rowman and Littlefield.

González-Ruibal, A. and Torres, J. d. 2018. The Fair and the Sanctuary: Gathering Places in a Nomadic Landscape (Somaliland, 1000–1850 AD). *World Archaeology*, 50(1): 23–40.

Groom, N. 1981. *The Incense Trade*. London: Longman.

Grottanelli, V. L. 1947. Asiatic Influences on Somali Culture. *Ethnos*, 4: 153–181.

Gutherz, X., Cros, J.-P. and Lesur, J. 2003. The Discovery of New Rock Paintings in the Horn of Africa: The Rock Shelters of Las Geel, Republic of Somaliland. *Journal of African Archaeology*, 1(2): 227–236.

Haldane, D. 1983. *Islamic Bookbinding*. London: World of Islam Festival Trust in Association with the Victoria and Albert Museum.

Hall, M. and Ismail, B. A. 1981. *Sisters Under the Sun. The Story of Sudanese Women*. London: Longman.

Hall, R. L. 1997. *An Archaeology of Soul: North American Indian Belief and Ritual*. Urbana: University of Illinois Press.

Hall, S. 1992. The West and the Rest: Discourse and Power. In S. Hall and B. Gieben (eds.) *Formations of Modernity*. Trowbridge: Redwood Books.

Hallpike, C. 1972. *The Konso of Ethiopia: A Study of the Values of an Eastern Cushitic People*. Oxford: Clarendon Press.

Hamilakis, Y. 2014. *Archaeology and the Senses: Human Experience, Memory and Affect*. Cambridge: Cambridge University Press.

Hassan, F. A. 1985. Radiocarbon Chronology of Neolithic and Predynastic Sites in Upper Egypt and the Delta. *African Archaeological Review*, 3: 95–116.

Hassan, F. A. 1998a. Toward an Archaeology of Gender in Africa. In S. Kent (ed.) *Gender in African Prehistory*. Walnut Creek, CA: AltaMira Press.

Hassan, F. A. 1998b. The Earliest Goddess of Egypt. In L. Goodison and C. Morris (eds.) *Ancient Goddesses: The Myth and the Evidence*. London: British Museum Press.

Hay, M. J. 1981. Review: The Hosken Report: Genital and Sexual Mutilation of Females by Fran Hosken. *The International Journal of African Studies*, 14(3): 523–526.

Hayes, O. R. 1975. Female Genital Mutilation, Fertility Control, Women's Roles, and the Patrilineage in Modern Sudan: A Functional Analysis. *American Ethnologist*, 2(4): 617–633.

Hays-Gilpin, K. 2008. Archaeology and Women's Ritual Business. In D. S. Whitley and K. Hays-Gilpin (eds.) *Belief in the Past: Theoretical Approaches to the Archaeology of Religion*. Walnut Creek, CA: Left Coast Press.

Helander, B. 1986. Notions of Crop Fertility in Southern Somalia. *Working Papers in African Studies 4*, University of Uppsala. African Studies Program (SOAS).

Helander, B. 1996a. The Hubeer in the Land of Plenty: Land, Labour and Vulnerability Among a Southern Somali Clan. In C. Besteman and L. V. Cassanelli (eds.) *The Struggle for Land in Southern Somalia*. Boulder and London: Westview Press and Haan.

Helander, B. 1996b. Rahanweyn Sociability: A Model for Other Somalis? In R. J. Hayward and I. M. Lewis (eds.) *Voice and Power*. London: SOAS.

Hersi, A. 1979. *The Arab Factor in Somali History*. Unpublished PhD diss., University of California-Los Angeles.

Heusch, Luc de. 1985. *Sacrifice in Africa: A Structuralist Approach*. Translated by L. O'Brien and A. Morton. Bloomington: Indiana University Press.

Hildebrand, E., Shea, J. J. and Grillo, K. M. 2011. Four Middle Holocene Pillar Sites in West Turkana, Kenya. *Journal of Field Archaeology*, 36(3): 181–200.

Hobsbawm, E. J. 1979. An Historian's Comment. In B. C. Burnham and J. Kinsbury (eds.) *Space, Hierarchy and Society*. Oxford: British Archaeological Reports. BAR International Series 59.

Hodder, I. 1982. *Symbols in Action*. Cambridge: Cambridge University Press.

Hodder, I. (ed.). 1989. *The Meaning of Things: Material Culture and Symbolic Expression*. 4th ed. Lexington: WIN.

Hosken, F. P. 1993. *The Hosken Report: Genital and Sexual Mutilation of Females*. Lexington, MA: Women's International Net Work News.

Hourani, G. F. 1995. *Arab Seafaring*. Princeton, NJ: Princeton University Press.

Hubert, H. and Mauss, M. 1964. *Sacrifice: Its Nature and Function*. Translated by W. D. Halls. Chicago: Chicago University Press.

Hultin, J. 1994. The Land Is Crying: State Intervention and Cultural Resistance Among the Matcha Oromo. In D. Brokensha (ed.) *A River of Blessings: Essays in Honor of Paul Baxter*. New York: Syracuse University.

Huntingford, G. W. B. 1955. *The Galla of Ethiopia: The Kingdoms of Kafa and Janjero*. London: International Africa Institute.

Ingold, T. 2013. *Making: Anthropology, Archaeology, Art and Architecture*. London and New York: Routledge.

Ingrams, W. H. 1937. A Dance of the Ibex Hunters in the Hadramaut. *Man*, 37: 12–13. London.

Insoll, T. 2017. First Footsteps in the Archaeology of Harar, Ethopia. *Journal of Islamic Archaeology* 4(2): 189–215.

Insoll, T. 1999. *The Archaeology of Islam*. London: Blackwell.

Insoll, T. (ed.). 2001. *Archaeology and World Religion*. London: Routledge.

Insoll, T. 2003. *The Archaeology of Islam in Sub-Saharan Africa*. Cambridge: Cambridge University Press.

Insoll, T. (ed.). 2004. *Archaeology, Ritual and Religion*. London: Routledge.

Jama, A. D. 1996. *The Origins and Development of Mogadishu AD 1000 to 1850*. Uppsala: Uppsala University Press. Studies in African Archaeology 12.

James, W. R. 1988. *The Listening Ebony: Moral Knowledge, Religion and Power Among the Uduk of Sudan*. Oxford: Oxford University Press.

Jardine, D. 1923. *The Mad Mullah of Somaliland*. London: Herbert Jenkins Limited.

Jensen, A. E. 1936. *Im Lande des Gada. Wanderungen zwischen Volkstrümmern Süd-Abessiniens*. Stuttgart: Strecker und Schröder.

Joussaume, R. 1974. *Le Mégalithisme en Ethiopie. Monuments Funéraires Proto-historiques du Harar*. Laboratiore de Préhistoire CNRS Laboratoire Associe 184. Paris: Museum National d'Histoire Naturelle.

Joussaume, R. 1981. L'Art Rupestre de l'Ethiopie. In C. Roubet, H. J. Hugot and G. Souville (eds.) *Préhistoire Africaine: Mélanges offerts au Doyen Lionel Balout*. pp. 159–175. Paris: ADPF.

Joussaume, R. 1983. Les Steles graves de Tiya. *Archaeologia*, 185: 42–47.

Joussaume, R. (ed.). 1995. *Tiya – L'Éthiopie des Mégalithes. Du biface à l'Art Rupestre dans la Corne de l'Afrique*. Mémorie XI. Ministère des Affaires Étrangères, Minitère de la Coopération, Ambassade de France en Èthiopie, UNESCO, UPR 311 du CNRS.

Joussaume, R. (ed.). 2007. *Tuto Fela et les stèles du sud de L'Ethiopie*. Paris: Éditions Recherche surles Civilisations.

Joussaume, R. 2011. Amorigé and the Anthropomorphic Stelae with Compartmented Faces of Southern Ethiopia. *Annales d'Ethiopie*, 26(1): 105–117.

Kanshie, K. T. 2002. *Five Thousand Years of Sustainability? A Case Study on Gedeo Land Use (Southern Ethiopia)*. Heelsum: Treemail Publishers.

Kaplan, S. 1986. The Africanisation of Missionary Christianity: History and Typology. *Journal of Religion in Africa*, 16(3): 166–186.

Kaplan, S. 1992. *The Beta Israel (Falasha) in Ethiopia*. New York: New York University Press.

Kapteijns, L. 2004–2010. I. M. Lewis and Somali Clanship: A Critique. *Northeast African Studies*, 11(1): 1–23.

Kapteijns, L. and Omar, M. A. 1996. Sitaat: Somali Women's Songs for the "Mothers of the Believers". In K. W. Harrow (ed.) *The Marabout and the Muse: New Approaches to Islam in African Literature*. pp. 124–141. Portsmouth, NH: Heinemann.

336   *Bibliography*

Kapteijns, L. and Omar, M. A. 2007. Sittaat: Women's Religious Songs in Djibouti. Halabuur. *Journal of Somali Literature and Culture*, 2(1–2): 38–48.

Karlsson, L. M. and Dalbato, A. L. 2013. Early Growth and Development of Ensete ventricosum (Musaceae) Seedlings. *Journal of Plant Sciences*, 1(1): 11–17.

Kassam, A. and Megerssa, G. 1996. Sticks, Self, and Society in Booran Oromo: A Symbolic Interpretation. In M. J. Arnoldi and K. L. Hardin (eds.) *African Material Culture*. Bloomington and Indianapolis: Indiana University Press.

Kennedy, J. G. 1970. Circumcision and Excision in Egyptian Nubia. *Man*, New Series, 5(2): 175–191.

Kent, S. 1998. Gender and Prehistory in Africa. In S. Kent (ed.) *Gender in African Prehistory*. Walnut Creek, CA: AltaMira Press.

Khaldun, Ibn. 1989 [1406]. *Prolegomena (Al-Muqqadimma). Introduktion till världshistorien*. Translated by Ingvar Rydberg. Lund: Alhambra.

King, G. R. D. 2004. *The Codex. The Islamic Book*. Unpublished manuscript. The School of Oriental and African Studies, Department of Art and Archaeology, London.

Kirk, J. W. C. 1905. The Yibirs and Midgans of Somaliland, Their Traditions and Dialects. *Journal of African Society*, 4: 91–108.

Knight, M. 2001. Curing Cut or Ritual Mutilation? Some Remarks on the Practice of Female and Male Circumcision in Graeco-Roman Egypt. *Isis*, 92(2): 317–338.

Knutsson, K. E. 1967. *Authority and Change. A Study of the Kallu Institution Among the Macha Galla of Ethiopia*. Göteborg: Elanders.

Kobishchanov, Y. M. 1979. *Axum*. University Park and London: The Pennsylvania State University Press.

Kobyliński, Z. 1994. Ethno-Archaeological Cognition and Cognitive Ethno-Archaeology. In I. Hodder (ed.) *The Meaning of Things: Material Culture and Symbolic Expression*. London: Unwin Hyman.

Kouba, L. J. and Muasher, J. 1985. Female Circumcision in Africa: An Overview. *African Studies Review*, 28(1): 95–110.

Kusow, A. M. 1995. The Somali Origin: Myth or Reality. In A. J. Ahmed (ed.) *The Invention of Somalia*. Lawrenceville, NJ: Red Sea Press.

Lane, P. 1994. The Use and Abuse of Ethnography in the Study of Southern African Iron Age. *Azania*, 29: 51–64.

Lane, P. J. and Read, A. 2016. Editorial. Azania at Fifty. *Azania*, 50(4): 425–436.

Layton, R. 1989. The Political Use of Australian Aboriginal Body Painting and Its Archaeological Implication. In I. Hodder (ed.) *The Meaning of Things: Material Culture and Symbolic Expression*. London: Unwin Hyman.

Legesse, A. 1973. *Gada. Three Approaches to the Study of an African Society*. London: Collier-Macmillan Limited.

Legesse, A. 2000. *Oromo Democracy: An African Indigenous Political System*. Lawrenceville, NJ: Red Sea Press.

Le-Quellec, J. L. 1987. Les Trois Fonctions dans le Soddo et Éthiopie. *Revue de l'Histoire Des Religions*, 231–238.

Levine, D. N. 2000. *Greater Ethiopia: The Evolution of a Multiethnic Society*. 2nd ed. Chicago and London: University of Chicago Press.

Lévi-Strauss, C. 1963. *Structural Anthropology*. New York: Basic Books.

Lévi-Strauss, C. 1982. *The Way of the Masks*. Translated by S. Modelski. Seattle: University of Washington Press.

Lewis, I. 1960. The Somali Conquest of the Horn of Africa. *The Journal of African History*, 1(2): 213–230.

Lewis, I. 1961. *A Pastoral Democracy*. London: Oxford University Press.

Lewis, I. 1962. Historical Aspects of Genealogies in Northern Somali Social Structure. *The Journal of African History*, 3(1): 35–48.

Lewis, I. (ed.). 1966. *Islam in Tropical Africa*. London: IAI and Indiana University Press.

Lewis, I. 1991. Introduction. In I. M. Lewis, A. Al-Safi and S. Hurreiz (eds.) *Women's Medicine. The Zar-Bori Cult in Africa and Beyond*. Edinburgh: International African Institute.

Lewis, I. 1994a. *Blood and Bone: The Call for Kinship in Somali Society*. Lawrenceville, NJ: Red Sea Press.

Lewis, I. 1994b. *People of the Horn of Africa: Somali, Afar and Saho*. London: IAI/Haan.

Lewis, I. 1996. *Religion in Context: Cults and Charisma*. Cambridge: Cambridge University Press.

Lewis, I. 1998. *Saints and Somalis: Popular Islam in a Clan-Based Society*. Lawrenceville, NJ and Asmara, Eritrea: Red Sea Press.

Lewis, I. 2004. Visible and Invisible Differences: The Somali Paradox. *Africa*, 74(4): 489–515.

Loo, J. van de. 1991. *Guji Oromo Culture (with the Collaboration of Bilow Kolo)*. Berlin: Dietrich Reimer Verlag.

Loubser, J. H. N. 2008. Discontinuity Between Political Power and Religious Status: Mountains, Pools and Dry Ones Among Venda-Speaking Chiefdoms of Southern Africa. In D. S. Whitley and K. Hays-Gilpin (eds.) *Belief in the Past: Theoretical Approaches to the Archaeology of Religion*. Walnut Creek, CA: Left Coast Press.

Luling, V. 1988. The Man in the Tree. A Note on a Somali Myth. In A. Puglieli (ed.) *Proceedings of the Third International Congress of Somali Studies*. Rome: II Pensario Scientifico.

Luling, V. 1991. Some Possession Cults in Southern Somalia. In I. M. Lewis, A. Al-Safi and S. Hurreiz (eds.) *Women's Medicine. The Zar-Bori Cult in Africa and Beyond*. Edinburgh: International African Institute.

Luling, V. 2002. *Somali Sultanate: The Geledi City-State Over 150 Years*. London: Transaction Publishers.

Lynch, M. and Donahue, R. 1980. A Statistical Analysis of Rock-Art Sites in Northwest Kenya. *Journal of Field Archaeology*, 7: 75–85.

Lynch, M. and Robbins, L. H. 1978. Namoratunga: The First Archaeoastronomical Evidence in Sub-Saharan Africa. *Science*, 200: 766–768.

Makris, G. P. and Al-Safi, A. 1991. The Tumbura Spirit Possession Cult of the Sudan. In I. M. Lewis, A. AL-Safi and S. Hurreiz (eds.) *Women's Medicine. The Zar-Bori Cult in Africa and Beyond*. Edinburgh: International African Institute.

Mansur, A. O. 1995. The Nature of the Somali Clan-System. In A. J. Ahmed (ed.) *The Invention of Somalia*. Lawrenceville, NJ: Red Sea Press.

Marcus, J. and Flannery, K. 1994. Ancient Zapotec Ritual and Religion: An Application of the Direct Historical Approach. In C. Renfrew and E. W. Zubrow (eds.) *The Ancient Mind: Elements of Cognitive Archaeology*. Cambridge: Cambridge University Press.

Martin, B. G. 1974. Arab Migration to East Africa in Medieval Times. *The International Journal of African Historical Studies*, 7(3): 367–390.

Marx, K. 1930. *Capital*. London: J. M. Dent.

Mather, C. 2003. Shrines and the Domestication of Landscape. *Journal of Anthropological Research*, 59: 23–45.

Mazrui, A. A. 1984. The Semitic Impact on Black Africa: Arab and Jewish Cultural Influences. *A Journal of Opinion*, 13: 3–8.

Mazrui, A. A. 1985. Religion and Political Culture in Africa. *Journal of the American Academy of Religion*, 53(4): 817–839.

Miller, D. and Tilley, C. (eds.). 1984. *Ideology, Power and Prehistory*. Cambridge: Cambridge University Press.

Mire, S. 2006a. Gaashaan, Somali Shield. In K. Lagat and J. Hudson (eds.) *Hazina: Traditions, Trade and Transition in Eastern Africa*. Nairobi, Kenya: National Museums of Nairobi.

Mire, S. 2006b. *Sacred Materials and Associated Rituals of an Ideology of Fertility in Early Second Millennium AD Ethiopia: Contextualizing the Archaeology of the Horn of Africa*. Unpublished MA thesis, University College London.

Mire, S. 2007. Preserving Knowledge, Not Objects: A Somali Perspective for Heritage Management and Archaeological Research. *African Archaeological Review*, 24: 49–71.

Mire, S. 2008. The Discovery of Dhambalin Rock Art Site, Somaliland. *African Archaeological Review*, 25: 153–168.

Mire, S. 2009. *Divine Fertility: Sacrifice and Sacred Landscapes in the Horn of Africa and the Significance of the Site of Aw-Barkhadle, Somaliland*. Unpublished PhD diss., University College London.

Mire, S. 2010. Somaliland: Archaeology in a Breakaway State. *Current World Archaeology*, 43: 26–33. (Report with original research).

Mire, S. 2011. The Knowledge-Centred Approach to the Somali Cultural Emergency and Heritage Development Assistance in Somaliland. In F. Sulas ed. Africa's Fragile Heritages. *Special Issue African Archaeological Review*, 29(1): 71–91.

Mire, S. 2015a. Mapping of the Archaeology of Somaliland: Religion, Art, Script, Time, Urbanism, Trade and Empire. *African Archaeological Review*, 32(1): 111–136.

Mire, S. 2015b. Wagar, Fertility and Phallic Stelae: Cushitic Sky-God Belief and the Site of Saint Aw-Barkhadle in Somaliland. *African Archaeological Review*, 32(1): 93–109.

Mire, S. 2016a. Somalia: Studying the Past to Create a Future. In B. Rodrigue, L. Grinin and A. Korotayev (eds.) *From Big Bang to Galactic Civilizations: A Big History Anthology*. pp. 279–288. Delhi: Primus Books.

Mire, S. 2016b. "The Child That Tiire Doesn't Give You, God Won't Give You Either" – the Role of Rotheca myricoides in Somali Fertility Practices. *Anthropology and Medicine*, 23(3): 311–331.

Mire, S. 2017. The Role of Cultural Heritage in the Basic Needs of East African Pastoralists. *African Study Monographs, Supplementary Issue*, 53: 147–157.

Miskell, J. 2000. *An Ecological and Resource Utilisation Assessment of Gacan Libra, Somaliland*. IUCN Eastern Africa Programme. Somali Natural Resources Management Programme. IUCN the World Conservation Union.

Mohammed, M. A. 1991. *Histoire des Croyances en Somalie*. Paris: Annales Littéraires de l'Université de Besançon.

Moore, H. L. 1996. *Space, Text and Gender. An Anthropological Study of the Marakwet of Kenya*. 2nd ed. Cambridge and New York: Cambridge University Press.

Moorey, P. R. S. 1998. Did Easterners Sail Round Arabia to Egypt in the Fourth Millennium BC? In C. S. Phillips, D. T. Potts and S. Searight (eds.) *Arabia and Its*

Neighbours. Essays on Prehistorical and Historical Development. Abiel II. New Research on the Arabian Peninsula. Turnhout Brepols.

Morin, D. 2004. *Dictionnaire historique afar (1288–1982)*. Paris: Kharthala.

Mukhtar, M. H. 1987. Arabic Sources on Somalia. *History in Africa*, 14: 141–172.

Mukhtar, M. H. 1995. Islam in Somali History; Fact and Fiction. In A. J. Ahmed (ed.) *The Invention of Somalia*. Lawrenceville, NJ: Red Sea Press.

Munro-Hay, S. A. 1991. *Aksum – An African Civilization in Late Antiquity*. Edinburgh: Edinburgh University Press.

Munro-Hay, S. A. 2002. *Ethiopia- the Unknown Land: A Cultural and Historical Guide*. London and New York: I.B. Tauris.

Munro-Hay, S. A. 2011. Chinese Source for Aksumite History in the 6th and 7th Centuries AD. *Annales d'Ethiopie*, 26(1): 99–104.

Muriuki, G. 1975. *A History of Gikuyu; 1500–1900*. Oxford: Oxford University Press.

Muriuki, G. 2005. *The Sacred Mugumo Tree: Myth and Gender Construction in Gikuyu, Cosmology and Worship*. Lecture at School of Oriental and African Studies' Linguistics Department on 3rd of March 2005, London.

Nelson, S. M. and Rosen-Ayalon, M. (eds.). 2001. *In Pursuit of Gender: Worldwide Archaeological Perspectives*. Lanham, MD: AltaMira Press.

Paulitschke, P. 1888. *Ethnographie Nordost Afrikas, I. Die materielle Cultur des Danâkil, Galla und Somâl II. Die geistige Cultur des Danâkil, Galla und Somâl*. Vol. 2. Berlin.

Phillipson, D. W. 1997. *Ancient Ethiopia. Aksum: Its Antecedents and Successors*. London: British Museum Press.

Phillipson, D. W. 2000. *Archaeology at Aksum, Ethiopia, 1993–7*. Vols. I–II. Memoirs of the British Institute in Eastern Africa: Number 17. Report 65, Research Committee of the Society of Antiquaries of London.

Phillipson, D. W. 2007. From Yeha to Lalibela: An Essay in Cultural Continuity. *Journal of Ethiopian Studies*, 40(1–2): 1–19.

Phillipson, D. W. 2012. *Foundations of an African Civilization: Aksum and the Northern Horn 1000 BC to 1300 AD*. Oxford: James Currey; Addis Ababa: Addis Ababa University.

Phillipson, L. and Sulas, F. 2005. Cultural Continuity in Aksumite Lithic Tool Production: The Evidence from Mai Agam. *Azania*, 40: 1–18.

Posnansky, M. 2009. *Africa and Archaeology: Empowering an Expatriate Life*. London: Radcliffe Press.

Posnansky, M. 2013. Present: Past. *South Carolina Antiquities*, 45: 47–49.

Posnansky, M. 2017. Archaeology and the Local Community in Africa: A Retrospective. *Journal of Community Archaeology and Heritage*, 4(2): 77–84.

Potts, D. T. 1990. *The Arabian Gulf in Antiquity*. Vols. I–II. Oxford: Clarendon Press.

Potts, D. T. 2007. Revisiting the Snake Burials of the Late Dilmun Building Complex on Bahrain. *Arabian Archaeology and Epigraphy*, 18(1): pp. 55–74.

Prouty, C. and Rosenfeld, E. 1994. *Historical Dictionary of Ethiopia and Eritrea*. Metuchen, NJ and London: The Scarecrow Press, Inc.

Radcliffe-Brown, A. R. 1951. The Comparative Method in Social Anthropology. *Journal of Royal Anthropological Institute*, 51: 15–22.

Ratnagar, S. 1987. Pastoralists in the Prehistory of Baluchistan. *Studies in History*, 3: 137–154.

Renfrew, C. 1994. Towards a Cognitive Archaeology. In C. Renfrew and E. W. Zubrow (eds.) *The Ancient Mind: Elements of Cognitive Archaeology*. Cambridge: Cambridge University Press.

Révoil, G. 1882. *La Vallée du Darror: Voyage aux Pays Çomalis Dis Mois à la Cote Orientale D'Afrique*. Paris: Challamel aîné.

Rikitu, M. 2001. *The Oromo of the Horn: A Cultural History*. London: Biiftuu Diiramaa Association.

Robertson Smith, W. 1894. *The Religion of the Semites: The Fundamental Institutions*. London: A. and C. Black.

Ryckmans, J. 1988. The Old South Arabian Religion. In W. Daum (ed.) *Yemen. 3000 Years of Art and Civilisation in Arabia*. Felix: Penguin.

Said, E. W. 1978. *Orientalism*. London: Routledge & Paul Kegan.

Samatar, S. S. 1982. *Oral Poetry and Somali Nationalism: The Case of Sayid Mahamad 'Abdille Hasan*. Cambridge: Cambridge University Press.

Scarre, C. 2008. Shrines of the Land and Places of Power: Religion and the Transition of Farming in Western Europe. In D. S. Whitley and K. Hays-Gilpin (eds.) *Belief in the Past: Theoretical Approaches to the Archaeology of Religion*. Walnut Creek, CA: Left Coast Press.

Schmidt, P. R. 1983. An Alternative to a Strictly Material Perspective: A Review of Historical Archaeology, Ethnoarchaeology, and Symbolic Approaches in African Archaeology. *American Antiquity*, 48(1): 62–79.

Schmidt, P. R. and Patterson, T. C. (eds.) 1995. *Making Alternative Histories: The Practice of Archaeology and History in Non-Western Setting*. Santa Fe, NM: School of American Research Press.

Seligman, B. Z. 1914. On the Origin of the Egyptian Zar. *Folklore*, 25: 300–323.

Sellassie, S. H. 1972. *Ancient and Medieval Ethiopian History to 1270*. Addis Ababa: United Printers.

Serjeant, R. B. 1976. *The South Arabian Hunt*. London: Luzac.

Shack, W. A. 1966. *The Gurage: A People of the Ensete Culture*. London, New York, and Nairobi: Oxford University Press.

Shinn, D. H. and Ofcansky, T. P. 2004. *Historical Dictionary of Ethiopia*. Oxford: The Scarecrow Press, Inc.

Sihab ad-Din, Ahmed, b. Abd al-Qadir b. Salam b. Uthman. 2003. *Futuh al-Habasha*. (Written Between 1540–1560). History of Ethiopia 1490–1889. Translated by Paul Lester Stenhouse. Annotations by Richard Pankhurst. Hollywood, CA: Tsehai.

Smith, L. T. 1999. *Decolonizing Methodologies: Research and Indigenous Peoples*. London: Zed Books.

Smith, M. C. and Wright, H. T. 1988. The Ceramics from Ras Hafun in Somalia: Notes on a Classical Maritime Site. *Azania*, 25: 115–141.

Soper, R. 1982. Archaeo-Astronomical Cushites: Some Comments. *Azania*, 17: 145–162.

Spencer, H. 1882. *The Principles of Sociology*. Vol. I. New York: D. Appleton and Company.

Spivak, G. C. 1988. Can the Subaltern Speak. In C. Nelson and L. Grossberg (eds.) *Marxism and the Interpretation of Culture*. pp. 271–313. Urbana: University of Illinois.

Stewart, C. and Shaw, R. 1994. Introduction: Problematizing Syncretism. In C. Stewart and R. Shaw (eds.) *Syncretism/Anti-Syncretism: The Politics of Religious Synthesis*. London: Routledge.

Tamrat, T. 1972. *Church and State in Ethiopia 1270–1527*. Oxford: Clarendon Press.

Thesiger, W. 1935. The Awash River and the Awsa Sultanate. *The Geographical Journal*, 85: 1–23.

Tiilikainen, M. 2010. Sitaat as Part of Somali Women's Everyday Religion. In M. L. Keinänen (ed.) *Perspectives on Women's Everyday Religion*. Stockholm: Acta Universitatis Stockholmiensis.

Tilley, C. 1984. Ideology and the Legitimation of Power in the Middle Neolithic of Sweden. In D. Miller and C. Tilley (eds.) *Ideology, Power and Prehistory*. Cambridge: Cambridge University Press.

Tilley, C. 1989. Interpreting Material Culture. In I. Hodder (ed.) *The Meaning of Things: Material Culture and Symbolic Expression*. London: Unwin Hyman.

Tilley, C. 1991. *Material Culture and Text: The Art of Ambiguity*. London and New York: Routledge.

Tonkin, E. 1992. *Narrating Our Pasts. The Social Construction of Oral History*. Cambridge: Cambridge University Press.

Tonkin, E., McDonald, M. and Chapman, M. 1989. Introduction. In E. Tonkin, M. McDonald and M. Chapman (eds.) *History and Ethnicity*. London: Routledge.

Tournemire, C. 2003. Découvertes de stèles monolithiques dans le pays Guragué. *Annales d'Éthiopie*, 19: 83–117.

Trimingham, J. S. 1952. *Islam in Ethiopia*. 1st ed. Oxford: Oxford University Press.

Trimingham, J. S. 1965. *Islam in Ethiopia*. 2nd ed. Oxford: Oxford University Press.

Trimingham, J. S. 1971. *The Sufi Orders in Islam*. Oxford: Clarendon Press.

Ucko, P. J. 1969. Ethnography and Archaeological Interpretation of Funerary Remains. *World Archaeology*, 1: 262–280.

Ucko, P. J. 1994. Forward. In D. L. Carmichael, J. Hubert, B. Reeves and A. Schanche (eds.) *Sacred Sites, Sacred Places*. London: Routledge. One World Archaeology 23.

Ucko, P. J. and Rosenfeld, A. 1967. *Grottkonst*. Stockholm: Bonniers.

Ullendorff, E. 1955. *The Semitic Languages of Ethiopia: A Comparative Phonology*. London: Taylor's.

Ullendorff, E. 1960. *The Ethiopians. An Introduction to Country and People*. London and New York: Oxford University Press.

Vansina, J. 1973. *Oral Traditions: A Study in Historical Methodology*. Translated by H. M. Wright. Harmondsworth, Middlesex: Penguin University Books.

Veer, P. van der. 1994. Syncretism, Multiculturalism and the Discourse of Tolerance. In C. Stewart and R. Shaw (eds.) *Syncretism/Anti-Syncretism: The Politics of Religious* Synthesis. London: Routledge.

Wallis Budge, E. A. 1970 [1928]. *A History of Ethiopia: Nubia and Abyssinia*. Oosterhout: Anthropological Publications.

Whitley, D. S. and Hays-Gilpin, K. 2008. Religion Beyond Icon, Burial and Monument: Introduction. In D. S. Whitley and K. Hays-Gilpin (eds.) *Belief in the Past: Theoretical Approaches to the Archaeology of Religion*. Walnut Creek, CA: Left Coast Press.

Wiessner, S. 2011. The Cultural Rights of Indigenous Peoples: Achievements and Continuing Challenges. *The European Journal of International Law*, 22(1): 121–140.

Yount, K. M. and Carrera, J. S. 2006. Female Genital Cutting and Reproductive Experience in Minya, Egypt. *Medical Anthropology Quarterly*, 20(2): 182–211.

Zubrow, E. B. 1994. Cognitive Archaeology Reconsidered. In C. Renfrew and E. W. Zubrow (eds.) *The Ancient Mind: Elements of Cognitive Archaeology*. Cambridge: Cambridge University Press.

Internet sources

Al-Jazeera. 2017. *The Cut: Exploring FGM*. www.aljazeera.com/programmes/aljazeeracorrespondent/2017/10/cut-exploring-fgm-171002112108882.html [accessed: 06/10/2017].

Kairu, P. 2015. Today a Sheep Will Die in Dagoretti Because a Branch Fell Off This Fig Tree. *Daily Nation*. June 19. www.nation.co.ke/lifestyle/DN2/a-branch-fell-off-a-mugumo-fig-tree-dagoretti/957860-2756998-2wj48n/index.html [accessed: 15/07/2017].

Onyulo, T. 2016. Alternative to Genital Mutilation Emerges for Kenyan Maasai Girls. March 26. www.newsweek.com/female-genital-mutilation-kenya-female-circumcision-un-unicef-equality-now-439666 [accessed: 08/07/2017].

TIYA – World Heritage Site. https://whc.unesco.org/en/list/12 [accessed: 15/06/2017].

UNESCO. 2011. *Konso Cultural Landscape*. http://whc.unesco.org/en/list/1333 [accessed: 23/02/2016].

UNICEF. 2016. *Female Genital Mutilation/Cutting: A Global Concern*. New York: United Nations Children's Fund. February. www.unicef.org/media/files/FGMC_2016_brochure_final_UNICEF_SPREAD.pdf [accessed: 07/07/2017].

USDA National Resources Conservation Service. *Plants Profile*. https://plants.sc.egov.usda.gov/java/nameSearch [accessed: 22/01/2017].

Youth for Change. 2016. I Will Meet the Powerful King 'Aba Gada' to End FGM Among My Kenya's Borana Community. September 13. www.youthforchange.org/latest-posts/2016/8/31/tackling-social-norms-fgm-kenya [accessed: 08/07/2017].

Appendices

Appendices

Appendix 1

Saint Aw-Barkhadle's genealogy
(confirmed by Lewis, 1998)

Sharif Yusuf Barkhadle, b. Ahmed b. Mahammed b. 'Abdillahi b. Isma'il b. Musa b. Huseyn b. 'Ali b. Hamsa b. Qasim b. Yahya b. Huseyn b. Ahmad b. Quwayi b. Yahya b. 'Ise b. Mahammed b. Taqi al-Hadrama b. 'Abul b. Hadi b. Mahammed b. 'Ali b. Musa b. Ja'far b. Mahammed b. 'Ali b. Hasan 'Ali Talib.

Appendix 2

The list of sheikhs and sheikhas buried at Aw-Barkhadle

The Male list

1) Sh. Cabdillahi Geele
2) Sh. Muxumed Gaboobe
3) Sh. Moxamed Fadhiid
4) Sh. Faarax Liibaan
5) Sh. Maxamed Hindi
6) Sh. Muusa Igare
7) Sh. Muuse Ereg
8) Sh. Yuusuf Dheere
9) Macalin Food
10) Macalin Maxamuud
11) Aw-Jamal Maygaag
12) Sh. Cabdikariim Jigjigaawe
13) Sh. Cabdiraxmaan Sh. Macalin Cumar
14) Sh. Axmed
15) Sh. Maxamuud Samane
16) Sh. Rooble Sh. Mataan
17) Shariif Mursal
18) Shariif Haadi
19) Sh. Maxamed Isaaq Ceelaabe
20) Sh. Muxumed Seed

Female Sheikhas

1) Sh. Faadumo Axmed
2) Sh. Caasha Xasabale
3) Sh. Nuuriya
4) Sh. Faadumo Mahdiyo

Source of Lists: Two Sufis based at Aw-Barkhadle; the temporary keeper of the key to the tomb of Saint Aw-Barkhadle, Sh. Rooble and Sh. Aw-Sa'iid, the brother of the current *Muriid*

Appendix 3
Glossary

Ab kin, family
Abtirsiimo counting the kins, genealogical line
Abu hunt headman (Arabian Hunt, Arabic)
Afartanbah lit. forty-out, ceremony for fortieth-day after delivery of a child,
Allah God (Arabic)
Asli authentic, real
Awlad children, offspring
Awliyo religious ancestors
Amran sacred, blessed
Arish house/enclosure (Arabic), *Ariish* house/hut (Somali)
Aqal house
Aqal gal lit. entering a house, getting married
Ashaab (ashaab) friends (*asxaabta nabiga*, friends of the Prophet)
Aw Saint, the prefix *Aw* means saint
Baamboy military drumming
Baanashada nurturing, a fertility practice
Barkin, headrests
Bar/barro a spot or a drop (of rain or water)
Baqqar ibex, cattle
Bishaarada good news
Biito a game allegedly originates from Bucur Bacayr era
Bun coffee
Bun dahaadan unopened coffee beans
Buur a mountain or hill
'Amal 'alaa niya lit. the work of belief, 'it will be what you believe'
'Aw ('aw) palm leaves
'Awaan ignorant, popular term of pagan (see *Jâhilliya*)
'Ishai second evening prayer (the fifth prayer)
Alaqad zar healer
Calanqad or calaqad (healer)Da'arbah (dacarbax)
Dabiib heal, cure
Dawaafa a walk, a ritual walk
Dampi sacred stick of the Oromo

Dhagax /dhagah/ dhagaha/ dhagaxa stone
Dhalka delivery of a baby, giving birth
Dhaim fault, a contamination (see *sinah*)
Dhehe/ dhexe middle
Dhibic, a drop (of water, rain)
Dhikri a dervish religious chanting to a state of ecstasy
Dhirbaanta medicinal herbs
Diri' Somali (transparent) female dressing gown
Dihin fat
Dihda rain, wet pouring substance
Dibbi a bull
Dooha wadi
Dumarka the women
Fakhidh thigh (Arabic)
Fandhaal, spoon
Gadamoji the Oromo religious leadership
Gember (*gambadh*), wooden stools
Gambis netted conical basket that is turned upside down over incense burner
Geed tree
Godka jinka the hole of devil
Gub burn
Guur move,
Guursi being wedded, wedding
Guri a house
Haan container woven by women from grass or palm leaves
Habbash black stone (Arabic)
Habaasuud an indigenous medical plant
Habbaha a derogatory name for Ethiopians (black people)
Haram sacred enclosure (Arabic)
Hawtah sacred enclosure (Arabic)
Haydh (xaydh) animal fat
Hoosta lit. 'down there' the vagina, vulva
Herta (xerta) Sufi religious group, the religious authority of the *Siti* ceremony (women)
Hijr an area (Arabic)
Hildiid an indigenous medical plant
Hulbad an indigenous medical plant
Illbah modern/widening eyes
Iid Eid, celebration
Ilmo children
Ilmo adeer cousins on their father's side, they were the sons of two brothers
Ilhun evil eye
Ilku'da' occurrence of evil eye
Jâhilliya an Islamic concept of 'ignorance of divine guidance' or 'the state of ignorance of the guidance of God' (wipidea/dictionary.com reference)

Jin devil (Arabic and Somali)
Ka'ba the sacred black stone in Mecca
Kawnka the north and south pools of the globe
Khad ink
Khat/ evergreen shrub (*catha edulis*) whose leaves are chewed fresh for stimulating effects (Somali and Ethiopian)
Khala open country, pastures
Khamiis a male dressing gown
Kitaab a book (the Qur'an)
Kolay a box (a private box)
Maame allegedly Ethiopian zar spirit
Ma'rifa spiritual knowledge (Sufi term)
Mag compensation, capital or material
Mohoga (moxoga) abdominal part
Makanka uteri
Makiinad razor blade
Mansab hunt law head (Arabian hunt, Arabic)
Maraq soup
Marqaha piece of cloth or piece of bark of acacia tree
Meesha or jinka place of devil
Middi (mindi) knife
Miyi countryside, the pastoral landscape
Mugumo a sacred tree (*Ficus natalensis*) (Kenya)
Muqdums chest ribs (Arabic)
Muriid the custodian of a religious site (Arabic lit. disciple)
Musbaar screw
Muqumad sundried meat cut into small pieces
Nabi a prophet
Nabi amaan praising the Prophet
Nadaafadiisa ritual gifts
Ood fence of shrubs or staffs, enclosure
Rabb God (Arabic)
Rasuulka the Prophet
Roobdoon (rain searching), name of rain-making ritual, *roob* rain, *doon* search, rain-searcher
Roohaan spirits
Saan leather
Saaciiido good luck
Salool popcorn
Saqaf, or *shanlo* combs
Sayyid now Islamic religious title
Shaydaan devil (see *jin*)
Seefo swords
Sinah faulting (Arabic)
Siqe/siiqqee sacred staff, from a sacred

*Siti (sitaat)*or *xaawa (haawa) iyo faadumo (Fatima)*, ceremony

Qallu Oromo religious leader

Qasida religious poems

Qawanin laws

Qadhaadh bitter

Qayd a cloth women use to carry a child

Qibla the direction towards which Muslims turn to pray, Mecca

Qiswad (or kiswah) a decorative veil draped over the walls of the Ka'ba, now made of black brocade embroidered in gold with inscriptions from the Koran

Qoftaan ritual gifts

Qur'an the holy book of Islam

Qurbaan sacrificial offerings, ritual gifts

Taran growth, extension (lineage, family)

Tbrw wild cow (Arabic)

Tiire a bark of medical acacia tree

Timir dates

Tirsiimo counting, from *abtirsiimo*, counting the kins, genealogical line

Tooray dagger

Ubad offspring, children

Umadaha/ umada hoose underground beings (see *jins*)

Udub middle pillar of the hut, the house bearing pillar of a hut

Ureaus God (ancient Greek)

Uunsi prepared incense (mix of aromatic oils, roots and other aromatic herbs)

Wadi a channel, watercourse

Wagar a sacred tree (*Olea africana*)

Waaq the Sky-God

Waqlo/ Waqlaal naming of a child

Weli Saint

Yawm al-qiyaama the day of judgement

Zar spirit possession

Ziyarah pilgrimage

ziyaro pilgrimage

Index

European iii, xxi, 13–14, 42, 178, 253, 306

Evans-Pritchard, E. E. 251, 264

Eve and Fatima 4, 152–153, 185; *see also abaay siti*; *Haawa iyo Faadumo*; *siti* ceremony

evil: eye 93, 136, 152, **241–244**, 253, 265, 277, 280, 291, 295, 397, 348; spirit xxi, 93, 113, 148, 150, 153, 157, 159–160, 163, 168, **242**, 253, 263, 275, 277–278, 292; *see also* devil; *jin/jins*

excavation 4, 22, 53, 55, 68, 105, 108, 129, 270

falaadh 307; *see also* astronomy; healing by burning; scarification

Falasha 28, 30; *see also* Beta Israel

fall/fal falla 36; *see also* witchcraft

fandhaal 138, 348; *see also* spoon (Somali traditional wooden spoon) with vulva bowl and/or phallic handle; vulva

Fardowsa Islamic ruined town xv, 193–194, *197*, 199

Fatima (daughter of the Prophet) 152, 155–156, 185

Fattovich, R. 10–12, 38–39, 264, 266, 281, 312

female Muriid 143, 165; *see also* sheikhas

female rituals 4, 97, 128, 190

female saints 225

female sufi societies 154; *see also Eve and Fatima, Haawa iyo Faadumo*; *nabi amaan*; *siti*; *sagaalaysi*; *siti* ceremony; *xerta/hert*

feminine identity 136; *see also* fertile body

fertile atmosphere 136; purification; consecration; fertility bath; caleemo saar

fertile body 137 (*see also* feminine identity)

fertility xi (*see also* divine fertility; peace; rite of passage); fertility bath (*see also* purification bath; ritual bath; smoke)

fertility bath ix, xi, 4, 94, 133, 135–138

fertility ideology 2, 5, 40, 44, 114, 183, 229, 258, 281, 322, 328 (*see also* ideology of fertility)

fertility pools 318 (*see also* rivers; sacred springs; sacred water sources; sacred well)

fertility rites xii, 133, 138, 170, 260; *see also* divine kinship; fertility ideology; fertility rituals

fertility rituals xxii, 1, 3, 4–6, 21–51, 68, 85–97, 91–98, 100–114, 116, 122–123, 128–129, 133–135, 147, 156–162, 170, 175, 179–180, 185, 190–191, 200, 208, 214, 218, 220, 226, 231, 235, 240, 241–246, 253–255, 266–320 (*see also* blood shedding; FGM (female genital mutilation); istunka (Stick fight); killing and bearing; ritual walk (*dawaafa*); sacrifice; wagar; *waqlaal/waqlo*)

fertility stones xiv, 33, *34*, 67, 89, 100–104, 115, 126–128, 134, 191, 223, 263, 265, 272 (*see also daga dareemu*; Dhagaha (Dhagaxa) Dhalka (fertility stone); Goroyo Cawl fertility stone or rocks; phallic stones)

fertility symbolism 138, 246, 248, 277, 295

Finneran, N. 10, 14, 37, 93

FGM (female genital mutilation) iii, ix, xv, xxvi, xxviin1, 1, 133, 135, 168–171, 176, 184, 186, **241–244, 246**; *see also* circumcision; cliterodectomy; *gudniin*; infibulation

foetal body position 27; *see also* Tiya

folklore 15, 267

fool-dherer 142; *see also* FGM (female genital mutilation)

foreheads (ritual) 30, 79–85, 130n9, 253–254, 263, 312, 322n9, 329; *see also* smearing/soiling chalk

Fortes, M. 251

frankincense (*yagcar*) xiv, 74, *74–75*, **247**, 278, 321 (*see also* incense; myrrh); tree (*Boswelia sacra*) 75

Fullerton, A. 43, 137

funerary monoliths 11

Gabooye xxv, 32

Gadamoji 252, 348

Gada-system 166, 180–214, 235, **241–242**, 244, 252, 275, 285, 300; *see also* age-grade system

garaad 66, 134, 136